ROUTLEDGE LIBRARY EDITIONS: 18TH CENTURY PHILOSOPHY

Volume 2

BERKELEY: THE PHILOSOPHY OF IMMATERIALISM

BERKELEY: THE PHILOSOPHY OF IMMATERIALISM

I.C. TIPTON

LONDON AND NEW YORK

First published in 1974 by Methuen & Co Ltd

This edition first published in 2019
by Routledge
2 Park Square, Milton Park, Abingdon, Oxon OX14 4RN

and by Routledge
52 Vanderbilt Avenue, New York, NY 10017

Routledge is an imprint of the Taylor & Francis Group, an informa business

© 1974 I.C. Tipton

All rights reserved. No part of this book may be reprinted or reproduced or utilised in any form or by any electronic, mechanical, or other means, now known or hereafter invented, including photocopying and recording, or in any information storage or retrieval system, without permission in writing from the publishers.

Trademark notice: Product or corporate names may be trademarks or registered trademarks, and are used only for identification and explanation without intent to infringe.

British Library Cataloguing in Publication Data
A catalogue record for this book is available from the British Library

ISBN: 978-0-367-13518-8 (Set)
ISBN: 978-0-429-02691-1 (Set) (ebk)
ISBN: 978-0-367-13526-3 (Volume 2) (hbk)
ISBN: 978-0-367-13550-8 (Volume 2) (pbk)
ISBN: 978-0-429-02711-6 (Volume 2) (ebk)

Publisher's Note
The publisher has gone to great lengths to ensure the quality of this reprint but points out that some imperfections in the original copies may be apparent.

Disclaimer
The publisher has made every effort to trace copyright holders and would welcome correspondence from those they have been unable to trace.

I. C. TIPTON

BERKELEY

The Philosophy of
Immaterialism

Methuen & Co Ltd *London*

First published in 1974
by Methuen & Co Ltd, 11 New Fetter Lane, London EC4P 4EE
First published as a University Paperback in 1976
© 1974 I. C. Tipton
Printed in Great Britain
by T. and A. Constable Ltd

ISBN 0 416 08230 0 (hardback edition)
ISBN 0 416 70440 9 (paperback edition)

This title is available in both hardback and paperback editions. The paperback edition is sold subject to the condition that it shall not, by way of trade or otherwise, be lent, resold, hired out or otherwise circulated without the publisher's prior consent in any form of binding or cover other than that in which it is published and without a similar condition including this condition being imposed on the subsequent purchaser.

Distributed in the USA by
HARPER & ROW PUBLISHERS, INC.
BARNES & NOBLE IMPORT DIVISION

Contents

Preface page vii
1 Introduction *1*
2 Berkeley and Common Sense *15*
3 The Philosophical Approach *57*
4 The Approach from Ordinary Usage *96*
5 The Psychological Approach *131*
6 Perception *179*
7 The Perceiving Self *256*
8 God *297*
Notes 351
Bibliography 388
Index of Persons 393
Index of Subjects 396

Preface

For Berkeley's writings I have in the main relied on the excellent nine-volume edition edited by Luce and Jessop, henceforth referred to simply as *Works*. The abbreviations I use for particular titles are more or less standard. Most of Berkeley's works are divided into short sections, and the reader will be able to follow up references to the *Theory of Vision* and the *Principles* in any edition. The *Dialogues*, though, present more of a problem. Here we have three long dialogues, and these are not divided into sections. When I refer, for example, to *Dialogues*, iii, 324, I am giving the page number in *Works* II as well as the dialogue number. But I have sometimes myself found it difficult to trace a passage when the author refers to an edition I do not have to hand, so in the hope that this will help some readers I am supplying a concordance comparing the pagination in *Works* II with that in Armstrong's *Berkeley's Philosophical Writings* and Warnock's edition of the *Principles* and *Dialogues*.

The only other complication concerns Berkeley's *Philosophical Commentaries*: notebooks filled during the period *circa* June 1707 to August 1708 in preparation for the first major publications. There were originally two notebooks and these were bound together in the wrong order. They were discovered by Fraser and published by him, still in the wrong order, as the *Commonplace Book*. It is to Professor Luce that we owe the present title and the first, and only, adequate editions. I use the splendid *editio diplomatica* published in 1944, and when I refer to a note on an entry I am invariably referring to that edition. There are shorter notes accompanying the text in *Works* I.

References in the text to books and articles are usually dependent upon the bibliography. For example, 'Luce 1' refers to the first item listed under 'Luce' in the bibliography. And when I attribute a view to Austin and give simply a page number in brackets, the reference is to the one work listed under 'Austin'.

I am greatly indebted to Dr. David Berman, Dr. O. R. Jones and Mr. Peter Smith for reading the typescript and making many extremely helpful comments on it. And I must add a special word of thanks to Professor R. I. Aaron who encouraged me to write this book and who helped me with it at every stage.

Three Dialogues between Hylas and Philonous

	Works II	Armstrong	Warnock
i pp.	171-175	135-139	149-154
	176-180	139-144	154-161
	181-185	144-149	161-167
	186-190	149-154	167-173
	191-195	154-159	173-178
	196-200	159-164	178-184
	201-207	164-171	184-192
ii	208-212	171-175	193-198
	213-217	175-180	198-204
	218-222	180-186	204-211
	223-226	186-189	211-215
iii	227-231	189-194	216-221
	232-236	194-199	221-227
	237-241	199-204	227-233
	242-246	204-209	233-239
	247-251	209-214	239-245
	252-256	214-219	245-251
	257-263	219-225	251-259

CHAPTER ONE

Introduction

'So much understanding, so much knowledge, so much innocence, and such humility, I did not think had been the portion of any but angels till I saw this gentleman.' (Bishop Atterbury)

I

In March 1685, when Locke was in Holland with the *Essay Concerning Human Understanding* still unfinished, the man who was to become his most influential critic was born near Kilkenny, Ireland. Berkeley's grandfather was born in England, and it has recently been confirmed that his father was too, but George, who did not cross the water until 1713, appears to have had no doubt that he was Irish. George Berkeley 'was of gentle birth; his folk were well connected, but not ennobled, comfortably off, but not affluent (Luce 8, p. 24). He went to Kilkenny College and then to Trinity College Dublin, from which he graduated in 1704, the year of Locke's death. At Trinity the broadly based course combined with opportunities for wider reading did much to prepare the young man who was to reveal such a breadth of knowledge in his early publications. His most important works were published when he was still very young. The first of these was his *An Essay towards a New Theory of Vision* (1709), and this was followed by *A Treatise concerning the Principles of Human Knowledge* (1710) and *Three Dialogues between Hylas and Philonous* (1713). It is the doctrines propounded in the *Principles* and *Dialogues* that will concern us most in this volume.

In restricting our attention largely to Berkeley's case for immaterialism we run the risk of underestimating our man. When the bicentenary of his death was celebrated in Dublin in 1953 the papers included one entitled 'Berkeley's Critique of the Newtonian Analysis of Motion' by a mathematician, and another on Berkeley's influence as an economist. A professor of English paid tribute to his style, and the Dean of St. Paul's ranked Berkeley 'with Joseph Butler and William Law, as one of the saintliest figures in the Anglican communion during the eighteenth century'. More recently A. D. Ritchie has published a book in which Berkeley's philosophy is reappraised in the light of the view that *NTV* 'is the main, central, constructive, and most strictly scientific work' (p. 2), and a substantial volume (by Paul J. Olscamp) has been devoted to Berkeley's moral philosophy. In their different ways and for different reasons *De Motu* (1721), *Alciphron* (1732), the *Analyst* (1734) and *Siris* (1744) all merit attention. Indeed one could wish that *Alciphron* in particular were more widely read. As Professor Jessop says, 'as a work of art it stands supreme in the whole body of our English literature of philosophy, and perhaps supreme also in our literature of religious apologetics' (*Works* III, p. 2).

Berkeley's life can be conveniently treated as falling into three main periods. The first, from 1685-1712, finds him in Ireland. By the end of it he had developed his doctrine of immaterialism – the doctrine that there is no material reality but only spirits and their ideas or sensations – and had published both the *NTV* and the *Principles* and written the *Dialogues*. To this period too belong *Arithmetica*, *Miscellanea Mathematica* and *Passive Obedience*. Berkeley was elected Junior Fellow at Trinity in 1707 and ordained in 1709. In a brief account of his life we must necessarily be selective, and I can perhaps allow myself the indulgence of pointing out, with Luce, that Berkeley's first extant sermon 'is noteworthy for its very free use of the argument of "Pascal's Wager" ' (Luce 8, p. 43):

> Whatever effect brutal passion may have on some or thoughtlessness & stupidity on others yet I believe there are none amongst us that do not at least think it as probable the Gospel may be true as false. Sure I am no man can say he has two to one odds on the contrary side. But wn life & immortality are at stake we should play our part with fear & trembling tho 'twere an hundred to one but we are cheated in the end. Nay if there be any the least prospect of our winning so noble a prize. & that there is some: none, the beastliest libertine or most besotted Atheist, can deny. (*Works* VII, pp. 12-13)

Berkeley never had much patience with atheism, and we shall see that while throughout his life his interests ranged very widely, the one predominant concern was his opposition to those whose writings tended to undermine religious belief. It is, I suppose, a mark of his genius that his contributions in various specialist fields must be taken seriously by those who may have little interest in what Berkeley took to be the really basic issues at stake.

The period 1713-34 includes his travels. In January 1713 he went to London 'to benefit his health, to publish his book, to broaden his mind, and to meet "men of merit" ' (Luce 8, p. 56). The book referred to here is the *Dialogues*. The *Principles* had not been well received and Berkeley postponed (and later abandoned) a plan to publish further parts, and instead published the *Dialogues* 'to treat more clearly and fully of certain principles laid down in the First, and to place them in a new light' *(Preface)*. He travelled twice on the continent, first as chaplain to the Earl of Peterborough and then as tutor to the son of the Bishop of Clogher. He returned to London in 1721 and published *De Motu* in the same year. This short treatise brings us to the 'new field for inquiry' which Berkeley had mentioned in *NTV* 138. As Luce says, the title '*Motion without Matter*, would fitly describe its scope and content' *(Works* IV, p. 3). The work was entered for, but failed to win, a prize offered by the Royal Academy of Sciences at Paris for an essay on the cause of motion.

Soon after his return to London Berkeley conceived of a project for founding a college in Bermuda. In 1728, now Dean of Derry and with a wife, Anne, who was to bear him seven children, he sailed for America. The Bermuda Project was nothing if not ambitious. Berkeley resolved to devote the remainder of his life to a college in the West Indies in which 'the English youth of our plantations may be educated in such sort as to supply the churches with pastors of good morals and good learning' and where 'a number of young American savages may be also educated till they have taken their degree of Master of Arts' *(Works* VIII, p. 127). In the letter to Percival in which he announced the plan he gave seven reasons for choosing Bermuda. The case was more fully spelt out in his *A Proposal for the Better Supplying of Churches in our Foreign Plantations, and for converting the Savage Americans to Christianity* (1724). Shortly after this a charter was granted to St. Paul's College, and Berkeley was named as first president. Berkeley stayed for nearly three years in Newport, Rhode Island, during which time it became clear to him that Bermuda was perhaps not the best site for the college. It also came to seem likely and then definite that the treasury grant which had been promised, and on which he relied, would not be paid. Disillusioned, he returned to

England in 1731.¹ *Alciphron* was published in 1732 and *The Theory of Vision . . . Vindicated and Explained* a year later.

The remaining period of his life, 1734-53, was, but for a few months at the end, spent in Ireland, now as Bishop of Cloyne. The period was not an unfruitful one. Of the forty writings listed by Luce as published by Berkeley (*Works* IX, pp. 147-50) twenty-six were published during this time; and though some of them are very minor they include the *Analyst*, *A Defence of Free-thinking in Mathematics* (1735), the *Querist* (1735-7), and that puzzling work *Siris*. This last marked a new enthusiasm. Berkeley had become convinced that an infusion of tar offered the hope of being a panacea, and he devoted himself to perfecting a recipe and subjecting the medicine to trials. Sects. 1-119 in *Siris* make the case for tar-water.² But Berkeley believed that 'there is no chasm in nature, but a Chain or Scale of beings rising by gentle uninterrupted gradations from the lowest to the highest, each nature being informed and perfected by the participation of a higher' (sect. 274), and he allows a chain of reasoning to lead him, through a study of the role given to aether by the ancients as well as the moderns, to his doctrines concerning efficient causality and observations on God and the Trinity. The later sections may not have been appreciated by the majority of his readers, but *Siris* was an immediate success and it saw six editions in the one year.

In August 1752 Berkeley moved to Oxford, apparently to be with his son, George, who was at Christ Church. There, five months later, he died.

II

Judgements on Berkeley's character and on his doings have tended to polarize at extremes. Somehow typical is the account of his meeting with members of the Scriblerus Club at a time when he was keen to win support for his scheme for a college in Bermuda:

> The members of the Scriblerus Club met at Lord Bathurst's house for dinner. Berkeley was there. The members rallied him on his project. He listened patiently to their jests and arguments, and then asked to be heard in reply. He put the plan before them with such animation and eloquence that they were struck dumb and carried off their feet. After a pause they all rose up together, exclaiming, 'Let us set out with him immediately'. (Luce 8, pp. 97-8)

Fifteen years earlier Percival had told him of first reactions to the *Principles*:

> A physician of my acquaintance undertook to describe your person, and argued you must needs be mad, and that you ought to take remedies. A bishop pitied you that a desire and vanity of starting something new should put you on such an undertaking. (*Works* IX, p. 10)

But in reply Berkeley was able to say:

> As for the physician I assure him there are (besides several others) two ingenious men in his own profession in this town, who are not ashamed to own themselves every whit as mad as myself, if their subscribing to the notions contained in my book can make them so. I may add that the greatest Tory and greatest Whig of my acquaintance agree in an entire assent to them, though at this time our party men seem more enflamed and stand at a wider distance than ever. (*Works* VIII, p. 38)

Towards the end of his life there were plenty to pour scorn on him and his panacea. There were also prominent people prepared to believe in the supposed panacea and to count the Bishop of Cloyne a benefactor to mankind.

One story about Berkeley may be sufficient to give us some understanding of Atterbury's eulogy, and of Pope's too, for Pope attributed to him 'ev'ry virtue under heav'n'.[3] The winter of 1739-40 was a severe one and it was to be followed by sickness and plague. Berkeley's conduct was exemplary:

> On the first Sunday of the great frost the Bishop came down to breakfast without a grain of powder in his wig. Mrs. Berkeley, the chaplain, and some visitors all called out at once, asking what ailed his Lordship. He replied that a great deal ailed him; there would be a very long frost; the potatoes would perish, and the poor must depend on flour, or starve. 'So no powder will I, or shall any individual of my family wear until next harvest.' During the frost and until the summer he gave £20 in gold or a banknote every Monday morning to be distributed among the poor of Cloyne, 'besides what they receive daily, hourly, out of his kitchen and housekeeper's room'. (Luce 8, p. 199)

This very practical concern with what was happening in his own diocese was reflected on a grander scale in the *Querist* which was devoted to examining the economic causes of the poor situation in Ireland. In another direction, it was his apparent success with tar-water against the outbreak of dysentery that followed the hard winter which led him to experiment further with the liquid and eventually to the publication of *Siris*.

Berkeley's concern for the physical well-being of his fellow-men was matched by his concern for what he conceived of as their moral and spiritual well-being. His studies were, indeed, 'no barren speculations'. There is no mention of God in the first edition of *NTV* and the work was to be influential among those who had no interest in any religious implications, but, as we shall see, the ultimate aim was to bring the reader to a greater appreciation of his dependence on God. This aim becomes explicit in the *Principles* and *Dialogues*. *De Motu* aims to distinguish a scientific explanation of motion in terms of mechanical principles from the ultimate explanation in terms of 'the Mind which moves and contains this universal, bodily mass' (sect. 69). *Alciphron* is, as the sub-title says, 'An Apology for the Christian Religion, against those who are called Free-thinkers'. And *Siris* leads us, in the well-known phrase, 'from tar-water to the Trinity'. Even the *Analyst*, which is a difficult work aimed at mathematicians, has ultimately a practical purpose:

> The occasion [of the *Analyst*] was this: Mr. Addison had given the bishop an account of their common friend Dr. Garth's behaviour in his last illness, which was equally unpleasing to both those excellent advocates for revealed religion. For when Mr. Addison went to see the doctor, and began to discourse with him seriously about preparing for his approaching dissolution, the other made answer, 'Surely, Addison, I have good reason not to believe those trifles, since my friend Dr. Halley who has dealt so much in demonstration has assured me that the doctrines of Christianity are incomprehensible, and the religion itself an imposture.' The bishop therefore took arms against this redoubtable dealer in demonstration, and addressed the *Analyst* to him, with a view of shewing, that mysteries in faith were unjustly objected to by mathematicians, who admitted much greater mysteries, and even falsehoods, in science, of which he endeavoured to prove that the doctrine of

fluxions furnished an eminent example. (Quoted in *Works* IV, pp. 56-7)

'Truth', Berkeley says, 'is the cry of all, but the game of a few' (*Siris*, 368). And he believes that the search for truth must lead us ultimately to a deeper knowledge of God and our duty to the benefit of our immortal souls.

On the whole, then, Berkeley is a most attractive figure. Even when our first reaction to some event in his life is critical, closer examination of the circumstances will often lead us to change our attitude. For example, at first it does seem absurd that a bishop should champion a panacea for bodily ills. Many of his contemporaries found this both improper and ridiculous. But then we find that much of the contemporary opposition was motivated by professional jealousy, that there was no doctor resident in Cloyne when Berkeley began experimenting with the medicine, that his theoretical knowledge exceeded that of many professional physicians, and that his belief in tar-water was based on very careful trials as well as theory. Perhaps most significantly, we discover that it is parodying his position to suggest that he was obsessively committed to tar-water as a certain cure for any patient suffering from any disease. As he says in a letter:

> ... I must explain to you that by a panacea is not meant a medicine which cures all individuals (this consists not with mortality), but a medicine that cures or relieves all different species of distempers. (*Works* V, p. 175)

And in the same letter:

> It must be owned I have not had opportunities of trying it myself in all cases; neither will I undertake to demonstrate *a priori* that tar-water is a panacea. But yet methinks I am not quite destitute of probable reasons, which, joined to what facts I have observed, induced me to entertain such a suspicion.

In short, the more we read and the more we come to know about this episode, the more we find ourselves sympathizing with Berkeley. More generally, when we read his works we are impressed by his expertise in various very different fields, his brilliantly original mind, and the excellence of his style.[4] When we read about his life we are impressed by his near saintliness, his concern for his fellow-men whether in the plantations or in his diocese, his generosity, and the devotion he was able to inspire in others. Berkeley did have at least almost 'ev'ry virtue under heav'n'.

It is perhaps not surprising that those who study Berkeley in any depth tend to develop something approaching love for their man, and that sometimes we find even a little tetchiness in their responses to criticisms of him. Yet of course there are criticisms. The breadth of vision and generosity of spirit which made it possible for him to envisage setting up a college in Bermuda, or to go into print to champion a panacea, laid him open to the jibes of smaller men, and it is against these jibes that we want to defend him.[5] But there was also room for reasoned criticism. The Bermuda scheme was impracticable, and it seems that Berkeley himself may have come to see that this was so. And of course tar-water was not a panacea. Perhaps Berkeley should, with some of his contemporaries, have been just a little more sceptical about the prospect of finding a panacea and about the virtues of tar-water in particular. A similar thought may strike us when we turn to the younger Berkeley. We may feel not just that Berkeley was wrong in supposing that all sensible objects exist only in the mind, but that he must have lacked some praiseworthy quality shared by the majority of his readers who felt that there was definitely something wrong with immaterialism even if they could not put their fingers on what it was. But of course once we reach this area we realize that it has become difficult to distinguish faults from virtues. Only a man with Berkeley's virtues could have made Berkeley's mistakes, and his willingness to follow any line of thought or action through if he thought it the correct one explains in part why we recognize him as an important philosopher and a good man.

If there is a side to Berkeley that some may find less than attractive it was perhaps revealed in one relatively minor episode in his life. In 1726 his brother Thomas was sentenced to death for bigamy. We know little about the circumstances and it is not even clear whether the sentence was carried out. But Berkeley's one reference to the affair, which is contained in a letter written from London, is less than charitable:

> Ned Synge I understand is in the country, I must therefore desire you to pay out of the mony in your hands the charges you tell me Dr. Helsham hath been at in my brother's tryal. Give my service to him

and tell him I am obliged to him as he intended a service to me in advancing that mony, without my knowledge, but that if I had been aware of it I wou'd not have disbursed half the sum to have saved that villain from the gallows. (*Works* VIII, p. 166)

We are told too of another occasion when Berkeley dined for three days alone in his library to avoid meeting a brother. 'He is a genuine scoundrel. I trust God will forgive him upon his repentance; but I will never see him while I breathe.' As Luce says (8, p. 185n), this may again have been Thomas. So far as the letter is concerned, Luce tells us in his note (*Works* IX, p. 67) that 'Stock omits all but the last paragraph. Monck Berkeley and Fraser omit the letter altogether because, I suppose, of the reference to the trial of Berkeley's brother.'

Now if Berkeley's attitude on this one occasion does not reflect to his credit, it would be a mistake to make too much of it. No doubt there are things that could be said in mitigation. Thomas's character and actions may have been worse than we could expect even Berkeley to tolerate, and there is the point too that in 1726 Berkeley was campaigning for his college in Bermuda and would have felt any disgrace that reflected on the family particularly badly. Above all, we must remember with Luce that 'for all his breadth of mind, Berkeley was stern and uncompromising where morals were concerned'. To some this may seem a virtue, to others it will not. We have to recognize, though, that his charity and tolerance did have definite limits, and I do think that this sometimes affected his judgement. Witness here his treatment of the free-thinkers in *Alciphron*. As Dobrée says in an otherwise eulogistic piece:

> Berkeley is no more tender of the feelings of those he is arguing against than either Shaftesbury or Mandeville; it might indeed be argued that he is less so, not quite so candidly putting himself in their place as either of his two great targets are ready to do with their opponents. In actual tactics he seems to me, dare I say it? a little unjust. In the third *Alciphron* dialogue he never really gives his minute philosophers their due; and if in the second he may be defended as describing the kind of person a follower of Mandeville might become, he traduces Mandeville himself. Indeed it may be permitted to think that Mandeville's *Letter to Dion* is a dignified rebuke, written in noble language, and that there is something to be said for his riposte that the real merit of Crito and

Euphranor consists in their being able, for a whole week, to put up with 'two such insupportable, out of the way rascals' as Alciphron and Lysicles. (pp. 64-5)

Certainly, if Berkeley can be generous to those he feels deserving of generosity (and there are many instances of this) he can be very harsh to those whose behaviour or writings he takes to be inimical to things he holds dear.⁶

III

I shall have no more to say about Berkeley's character in this volume and, as I said, my main concern will be with the views he was concerned to propound in the *Principles* and *Dialogues*. Here the dominant view is, of course, that there is no such thing as matter and that for sensible objects '*esse* is *percipi* [to exist is to be perceived], nor is it possible they should have any existence, out of the minds or thinking things which perceive them' (*Pr*. 3). At first sight at any rate the view seems outrageous and as insupportable as his later claim that tar-water is a panacea. As Warnock says:

> Dean Swift is reported (perhaps apocryphally) to have left him standing on the door-step when he came to call, saying that if his philosophical views were correct he should be able to come in through a closed door as easily as through an open one. This tale is indeed typical of the common view of Berkeley's doctrines; it was said that he represented the whole of our experience as a dream, and the material world as a collection of 'ideas' in the mind, dependent for its very existence on being observed. After all, he explicitly denied the existence of Matter; he asserted that we perceive only 'our own ideas'; and what is this but to say that we are all in a dream? Why open the door if there is really no solid, impenetrable door to be opened? So far from being acclaimed as the rescuer and defender of Common Sense, Berkeley was charged with an absurd and almost frivolous indifference to the plain and fundamental convictions of all sensible men. (Warnock 1, p. 17)

Berkeley, then, came in for at least his fair share of ridicule.

We should not suppose, of course, that even if his views were odd, and indeed in direct conflict with the plain facts of experience, this would necessarily deny him a reputation as an important philosopher.

Introduction

In philosophy one can perform a real service by enthusiastically following a wrong track, so even if it were true that Berkeley had done no more than follow initially attractive principles through to a patently absurd conclusion he might deserve credit for thus revealing the inadequacy of the principles. We might value his contribution even if we accepted both that the conclusion was absurd and that Berkeley himself had never realized this. But to do justice to Berkeley we have to appreciate that, though he did recognize that he had *surprising* things to say, he also held that people ridiculed his claims only because they misunderstood them. He believed that anyone who did understand his position would see that the supposedly absurd consequences just do not follow. Berkeley *does* hold that the sensible world is composed of ideas which cannot exist unperceived, and he *does* deny the existence of matter, but the supposed consequence that we should, for example, be able to walk through a closed door, is not a consequence at all. In *Pr.* 34 he tells us that 'by the principles premised, we are not deprived of any one thing in Nature. Whatever we see, feel, hear, or any wise conceive or understand, remains as secure as ever, and is as real as ever. There is a *rerum natura*, and the distinction between realities and chimeras retains its full force.' As Warnock suggests, Berkeley liked to think of himself as on the side of common sense. Indeed in a certain mood he was capable of going so far as to say, 'I side in all things with the Mob' (*PC* 405). We shall see that some commentators take this claim very seriously indeed and even go so far as to suggest that by and large it is a justified one.

The student reading Berkeley for the first time is likely to find himself puzzled and confused, and this not just because the doctrines he finds in the *Principles* and *Dialogues* seem eccentric. Certainly he cannot complain about a turgid style, the occurrence of long and complex arguments, or the use of an involved technical vocabulary. Berkeley has a most attractive style, he does not waste words, and *superficially* he is the clearest of writers. If the reader is puzzled it is at least partly because Berkeley is perhaps *too* economical in his use of arguments, particularly in the *Principles*, so that things are taken to be simply evident where we feel the need of arguments in support of them and conclusions drawn where it seems that not enough has been said to establish them. It helps here to keep an eye on the *Dialogues*, which Berkeley wrote 'to introduce the notions I advance, into the mind, in the most easy and familiar manner' (*Preface*). It is also necessary to know something about the beliefs and assumptions of those Berkeley thought of as his philosophical opponents. For though Berkeley's idealism is opposed to what he calls *materialism*, he in fact accepts, and does not always feel it necessary to argue for, certain of the doctrines of his opponents. There is an instance of this in *Pr.* 1 where he takes it to be an *agreed* truth that in sense experience we are directly acquainted only with 'ideas actually imprinted on the senses'.

In order to understand Berkeley and to be in a position to evaluate his doctrines we need to be able to answer three questions and to see how the various answers are related. In the first place we need to see why he committed himself to the *negative* thesis that there is no material reality. In the second place we need to be clear as to his reasons for embracing the *positive* thesis that sensible objects are just mind-dependent sensations. And in the third place we need to be able to answer the question as to how someone holding the negative and positive theses could believe that he was defending common sense and that on his principles 'the distinction between realities and chimeras retains its full force'. We shall see that Berkeley committed himself to the negative thesis because he had in mind certain doctrines concerning the supposed material reality which made it seem to him that it was absurd to believe there could be any such thing. We shall see that he propounded the positive thesis because it seemed to him that once the negative thesis was accepted one had no choice but to embrace idealism. And we shall see that Berkeley thought of himself as defending common sense views basically because he saw these as being grossly affronted by the materialism which he was concerned to attack.

Perhaps the really important point to get hold of here is that for Berkeley there was the narrowest of gaps between opposition to 'matter' *as philosophers conceived of it*, and acceptance of the view that the sensible world is mind-dependent. It may be tempting to reserve the term 'immaterialism' for the negative doctrine and 'idealism' for the positive doctrine, but if the aim is to understand Berkeley we would do better to regard the two terms as referring to one basic claim which has a negative and a positive face. The claim, in the *Principles* at least, is that there is no 'matter' *so* there must be just ideas, and this is the immaterialist or idealist claim.[7] We can take this line if our aim is to *understand* Berkeley. If we want to *oppose* him, or to see why we can agree with him in his dislike of 'matter' without seeing him as a defender of ordinary views, we will want to do what he fails to do and clearly distinguish between the two doctrines. We will want to say that there is a huge gap between denying 'matter' (as conceived by philosophers) and affirming the sole existence of spirit and ideas, and one way of making this point would be to insist that immaterialism and idealism make very different claims, and to deny that acceptance of the one should lead to acceptance of the other. If there is no 'matter' it does *not* follow that there are just ideas.

In Ch. 2 I try to answer the questions as to how Berkeley could at once hold the odd views he does hold *and* see himself as siding with the mob or defending the common-sense outlook. As I point out there, he would not have felt it necessary to defend common sense unless he had supposed that others were mounting an attack. Berkeley thought that certain current philosophical doctrines constituted a direct affront to common sense, and only when we see what those views were and appreciate that he did argue against them can we understand how it was that he could see himself as representing the vulgar. He was defending common sense because he opposed *materialism*, and materialism he took to be inimical to beliefs which every right-thinking man knows to be true. Berkeley's idealism does *not*, though, accord with the ordinary man's thinking. We shall see that he over-states the case when he says that he sides *in all things* with the mob, and this because, while on one crucial point he is with the mob and against the materialist, on another he is opposed to both the mob and his philosophical opponents.

Berkeley holds that sensible objects exist only in the mind, and in Chs. 3-5 I look at three approaches to this position. In *Pr.* 1-2 the argument seems to be that things like apples, stones, trees and books are collections of *ideas*, that ideas cannot exist unperceived, and that therefore apples, stones, trees and books cannot exist unperceived. I describe this as *the philosophical approach* since it seems to depend on certain supposed truths agreed among philosophers. *The approach from ordinary usage* is one I take to be involved in *Pr.* 3. We are asked to 'attend to what is meant by the term *exist* when applied to sensible things'. Having done this we are expected to see that it is intuitively true that *esse* is *percipi*. In *Pr.* 5-6 it is claimed that the notion that things can exist unperceived depends upon illegitimate abstraction, and we are told that it is in fact impossible to think of an unperceived object. The approach here I call *the psychological approach*.

I think it desirable to distinguish these three approaches and to treat them in order. We should not assume at the outset, however, that Berkeley thought of them as involving independent arguments, each adequate on its own to demonstrate the truth of his central contention.

I shall argue that the approach from ordinary usage and the psychological approach both fail to prove what Berkeley would like to prove, and that if there is life in the philosophical approach this depends on certain supposedly agreed truths which are in fact highly dubious. Central here is the claim that in sense experience we are directly acquainted only with mind-dependent entities, which may or may not represent an external material reality. In the *Principles* Berkeley argues that *given* we are directly acquainted only with mind-dependent entities, it is nonsense to suppose that these represent an external reality, or that the real world is a material world. But in the *Dialogues* he appears to start a stage further back, providing arguments designed to show that in sense perception we are indeed aware only of sensations or appearances in the mind. I look at these arguments in Ch. 6. In Ch. 7 I say something about Berkeley's views on the self or perceiving subject, and in Ch. 8 we come to what Berkeley thought so important – the proof (or proofs) that the sensible world is dependent for its existence upon the infinite mind of God.

CHAPTER TWO

Berkeley and Common Sense

> 'I do not see how to refute it, though temperamentally I find it repulsive.'
> (Bertrand Russell on Berkeley's idealism.
> Russell 1, p. 194.)

I

Before getting down to a detailed examination of Berkeley's philosophy it may be useful if we step back and take a long view with a particular problem in mind. And the problem is that there seems at first sight to be a striking discrepancy between the judgement most of us want to make on his general position and the judgement he seems to have expected us to make on it. For whereas the man in the street would clearly regard it as nonsense to suggest that chairs, tables, grass and the planet Venus, indeed 'all the choir of heaven and furniture of the earth' (*Pr.* 6), exist only in the mind and for so long as they are perceived, Berkeley, whose metaphysic rests upon this proposition, regarded himself as a champion of common-sense views.

As a matter of fact, Berkeley was apprised of the reaction of some of his contemporaries within weeks of the publication of the *Principles*, for Sir John Percival was to write from London that its reputation was such that people preferred to ridicule it than read it. A French reviewer who presumably did read it, though not very carefully, summed up thus:

> Mr. Berkley (*sic*) ... a poussé sans ménagement les principes de sa secte fort au delà du sens commun, & il en a conclu, qu'il n'y a, ni corps, ni matiere, & que les esprits seuls existent. ... Tout ce que nous imaginons de corporel ne sont que des idées qu'un autre esprit nous imprime, & qui n'ont point d'existence hors de nous, & cessent d'être quand on cesse de les appercevoir.[1]

Berkeley felt he could say 'I side in all things with the Mob', but the mob then and now would probably think itself better represented by

Dr. Johnson, who expressed his conviction about the corporeality of a stone by kicking it to show that it had a real and independent existence, exclaiming, as he did so, 'I refute it *thus*.'² Johnson's judgement on immaterialism was thus the same as Swift's, and Swift's reaction was, as Warnock says, 'typical'.

Berkeley himself believed that the ridicule and the criticism rested on *ignoratio elenchi* resulting from a prejudiced approach to the work and careless reading, and in 1713, three years after the publication of the *Principles*, he published the *Dialogues* to put what had been said in the earlier work 'in a new light'. Hylas, who supposes himself the representative of sound common-sense views, starts by thinking of Philonous, the Berkeleian, as a purveyor of paradoxes and scepticism:

> You were represented in last night's conversation, as one who maintained the most extravagant opinion that ever entered into the mind of man, to wit, that there is no such thing as *material substance* in the world. (i, 172)

Indeed, even when he has been convinced that what the Berkeleian says is *true*, it still seems to him that he has been led into 'paradoxes' and argued into scepticism (ii, 211). He ends up, though, by agreeing that while the Berkeleian does hold the view attributed to him, the implications of this position are not what he thought. He sees, or thinks he sees, that immaterialism does justice to certain basic beliefs which he and other men hold, while these beliefs are affronted by philosophies which centre on the notion of material substance. In short, Berkeley's position is not extravagant.

If the French reviewer and Dr. Johnson represent one extreme response to Berkeley, simply asserting that he denies corporeality and affronts common sense, there are those who take the other extreme and basically reaffirm the judgement Hylas makes at the end of the *Dialogues*. Pre-eminent here is Professor Luce, who has combined the role of being the most important and influential Berkeley scholar of the century with that of chief apologist for the Berkeleian philosophy. Luce holds that Berkeley's doctrines are, by and large, right, but he also holds that they tie in very well with the plain man's views. Thus:

> As I write, I look back to the days before I took up with philosophy. I had never heard of Berkeley, and they hadn't told me about matter.

I trusted my senses and the sensible. I was a young man of common sense, or thought I was. I picked the yellow buttercup I saw, the very one. I ate the white bread I saw and touched, and drank the fragrant tea. I knew that other folk perceived by sense *as* I did, and *what* I did . . . In all these basic beliefs *sum qualis eram*. I am more aware of them than I was. I see more in them than I did; but philosophy has made no change in them. (Luce 9, p. 82)

He goes on to say: 'I, for one, am satisfied that Berkeley's account of the sensible, rightly understood, is common sense.' This is certainly a very sympathetic attitude to Berkeley's position, but it is one which in the end we shall not be able to confirm.

Now in this chapter I do want to take Berkeley's claim that he is on the side of common sense very seriously, but in fairness we must appreciate that he did not think of siding with common sense as necessarily involving agreeing with the man in the street on everything. He never believed in philosophy by referenda, and common sense was never for him simply common consensus. Further, there is a certain ambivalence in his attitude here. In one mood he will talk about siding in all things with the mob, and in another he will insist that the supposition that tangible objects exist without the mind is a 'vulgar error' (*Pr.* 44). He will at one stage point to 'those odd paradoxes, that the *fire* is *not hot*, nor *the wall white*, etc.' (*Pr.* 99, first edition) and count it as a merit in his system that it avoids such absurdities, and yet a little earlier he has given it as a consequence of his position that *really* fire does not heat nor water cool (*Pr.* 51). His suggestion here that 'in such things we ought to *think with the learned, and speak with the vulgar*' points to what C. J. Sullivan has nicely described as Berkeley's *Janus-faced* defence of common sense and ordinary language. That Berkeley does at least sometimes like to think of himself as defending ordinary views cannot, though, be doubted, and it cannot be doubted either that he felt the need to defend certain notions because he saw these as being threatened by doctrines promulgated by other philosophers.

When Berkeley is in a mood to talk of siding with the mob we can, I think, find at the root of his attitude the view that while the ordinary man can be fundamentally mistaken on important issues, the philosopher is especially prone to making a certain type of mistake; and that in particular a move in philosophy can lead to assertions which affront very basic beliefs about the world. In this sort of case further thought can show the move to be illegitimate. Like G. E. Moore, who also thought of himself as a defender of common sense, Berkeley believed that part of the function of philosophy was to clarify issues philosophers had distorted and to resolve paradoxes which were the creation of philosophy. Certainly it is by concentrating on Berkeley's attack on the position of other philosophers and on his defence of certain very basic beliefs of ordinary men that we can at least start to understand his claim that the tendency of *his* philosophy is to bring men back to common sense.

In this chapter, then, we will be primarily concerned with what Berkeley was writing *against*. This is not to suggest that the negative and positive aspects of his philosophy are neatly and nicely separable, that his own often odd ideas can be forgotten entirely, or that his Janus-faced attitude to common sense and ordinary language can be glossed over. Indeed the ordinary man might with some justification liken himself to the innocent gambler who was 'defended' against the charge that he had an Ace up his sleeve by someone who 'proved' that it was a King.[3] Berkeley attacks a position that is replete with paradoxes, and to this extent he defends common sense, but he does this from a supposedly adequate position which is perhaps just as paradoxical. All the same, the emphasis can be placed on the negative side, and this we shall now do. We shall see how a move in philosophy creates a problem, or how a fly gets into the fly-bottle. We shall also indicate the sort of way in which Berkeley thought the fly could get out.

II

From the beginning Berkeley had in mind one particular way of looking at the world, a way which he thought to be improper, to affront common sense, and, if properly understood, to lead inevitably to scepticism with regard to the very existence of the objects we normally take ourselves to be perceiving. He also believed, and he took this very seriously indeed, that it was potentially inimical to religion. Though it was certainly not exclusive to him, this way of looking at the world was inherent in the philosophy of John Locke, who, as well as being Berkeley's regular stalking-horse, was a major influence on him during the period in which he was formulating his own positive views.

Two entries from *PC* can be quoted to illustrate Berkeley's attitude to his great predecessor. The first:

> If in some things I differ from a Philosopher I profess to admire, 'tis for that very thing on account whereof I admire him namely the love of truth. (467)

And the second, exactly one hundred entries later:

> Wonderful in Locke that he could w^n advanc'd in years see at all thro a mist y^t had been so long a gathering & was consequently thick. This more to be admir'd than y^t he didn't see farther.

Berkeley believed that Locke had travelled on the right road but that he had not completed the journey, and it is interesting to contrast the French reviewer's assertion that Berkeley had pushed certain principles 'fort au delà du sens commun' with Berkeley's notion that 'the same principles which at first view lead to *scepticism*, pursued to a certain point, bring men back to common sense' (*Dialogues*, iii, 263). The principles are the same in each case, and they can be found in Locke.

It must be made abundantly clear that Locke did not set out to affront common sense and that he certainly did not see the tendency of his thought as sceptical. It is true that he was very conscious that there were areas in which finite human beings could not expect to have knowledge, but in general his concern was to emphasize how much we *can* be assured of and the extent to which our ordinary and scientific beliefs about the world *are* justifiable. It is a feature of the *Essay* that, where a line of thought seems to run counter to common sense, the author's tendency is to fail to follow the line of thought through or to write as if the difficulty has been, or at least quite certainly could be, solved. Berkeley, however, had no doubt at all that Locke's way of looking at the world was potentially disastrous, and he believed that the mistakes in it were rooted in the account of what it is to perceive a physical object.

There is a paradoxical position we can talk ourselves into in three easy stages, and it can be argued that Locke did just this. In the first place, Locke never seriously doubted that the things we observe in the world around us exist 'out there', located in space as public objects which, putting it crudely, wait to be seen. But, secondly, Locke did not doubt that the answer to the question as to *how* we perceive them was essentially a scientific one. The details of the scientific account Locke subscribes to need not concern us at this stage, but basic to it is the view that seeing a table, for example, is the end result of a process, and a process which starts with the object and ends with the percipient having sensations. Thus in *Essay* II i 3 he says:

> ... our Senses, conversant about particular sensible objects, do convey into the mind several distinct perceptions of things ... which when I say the senses convey into the mind, I mean, they from external objects convey into the mind what produces there those perceptions.

The third stage comes when we consider the implications of the fact that perception (by any sense) can be explained in terms of processes. For we can be led to suppose that science shows that we are not *really* acquainted with the remote causal objects at all, but only with the perceptions or sensations produced in us *as a result of* the processes. J. C. Eccles makes just this move in a passage quoted by Flew:

> ... physiological investigation reveals that all perception depends on very complex processes of detection by sense organs and of transmission of signals (nerve impulses) from them to the brain. ... Thus in the case of perception, the sequence of events is that of a stimulus to a sense organ causing the discharge of impulses along afferent nerve fibres which, after various synaptic relays, eventually evoke specific spatio-temporal patterns of impulses in the neuronal network of the cerebral cortex. ... Yet, as a consequence of these cerebral patterns of activity, I experience sensations (... percepts) which in my private perceptual world are 'projected' to somewhere outside the cortex. ... (See Flew 2, p. 299)

Locke calls the perceptions produced in the mind *by* sensible objects 'ideas', and we find him saying, in IV iv 3, that the mind 'perceives nothing but its own ideas'.

The paradox should be clear enough by now. We start from the common-sense viewpoint that in sensory experience we are aware of, or perceive, public objects in an external world. We accept that the explanation of how we perceive them must lie in a scientific account in terms of processes. But when we consider the implications of the scientific story we begin to suspect our earlier belief that we are, in a quite straightforward sense, acquainted with the things 'out there'. If the scientist is right we experience *sensations* in a 'private perceptual world'; we perceive *ideas*. The result of this is that, unless we surrender our common sense starting point altogether, we find ourselves wanting to say at once (a) that we are aware of public objects and (b) that *really* what we are aware of are private percepts. We may indeed 'project' these, but they remain *mental*.

The perhaps naive response of the man in the street when faced with this dilemma might be that we only started talking about sensations or ideas once we had been convinced that these terms played a useful role in explaining how we come to perceive external objects, so that if it turns out that a wedge can be driven between the sensations and the things in such a way as to cast doubt on the notion that we are acquainted with the things, he will go back to his starting point – the perception of external things – and leave it to the experts to decide whether the mistake was made by the scientist or the philosopher. His inclination, then, will be to insist on (a) and to allow that we are aware of sensations if and only if this can be shown to be reconcilable with it. And before complicating things further it is worth suggesting that this naive view ought not to be too easily despised. That the plain man is basically right here will be argued for later, but at this point we can at least agree with him that on the argument as so far presented sensations *were* introduced to perform an explanatory role. If it turns out that they do not help to explain how we perceive objects, and indeed make it difficult to maintain that in any straightforward way we do, then it may be that they should be dispensed with and that another way of describing what goes on when we perceive should be sought for. There is certainly no very clear case for accepting (b) and rejecting or questioning (a).

Many, though, have been tempted to suppose that if we accept scientific thinking we will have to deny that we are acquainted with external things in perception. Thus Russell for example tells us that when a physiologist studies a living brain 'what the physiologist sees is in his own brain' (Russell 3, p. 146).[4] And more recently, Grover Maxwell has outlined what he calls the *argument from neurophysiology and psychophysics* and the *argument from physics and neurophysiology* and concluded:

> In a real and important sense, then, all of the external world, including even our own bodies is unobserved and unobservable. (p. 152)

Berkeley certainly thought that Locke was committed to this sort of position and that it just would not do. He saw the doctrine that we are not in any straightforward sense acquainted with tables, chairs and other ordinary objects as representing a radical departure from common sense, and it also seemed to him that taking this position was tantamount to admitting that we have no experiential basis at all for making claims about the existence of external objects. Thus in *PC* 74 he says:

> Allowing there be extended solid etc substances without the mind tis impossible the mind should know or perceive them. the mind even according to ye materialists perceiving onely the impressions made upon its brain or rather the ideas attending those impressions.

Reading Maxwell, Berkeley would make two points. First, he would say that the view that 'all of the external world . . . is unobserved and unobservable' is an affront to the healthy realism of the plain man. But, second, he would insist that if we hold this view then we will in the end be driven inexorably to scepticism. The plain man believes in the existence of the table because he sees it and feels it. If it turns out to be the case that 'in a real and important sense' he neither sees it nor feels it, then the basis for his certainty about the existence of the table has gone.

It will be clear from *PC* 74 that when Berkeley attacks the 'materialist' he at least sometimes has in mind one who, whatever other objectionable doctrines he may hold, is a Causal Theorist and committed to what Jonathan Bennett has called the 'veil-of-perception doctrine'. The doctrine involves the view that the things our senses are conversant about are to be radically distinguished from the objects we are immediately aware of in experience, and it seems to leave us stranded, like the prisoners in Plato's Cave, looking at shadows.[5] The French philosopher Malebranche was not in fact a Causal Theorist, but he too made a fundamental distinction between the external objects which we *behold* (regarder) and mental entities which we *see* (voir). As Berkeley saw it, the difficulty facing Locke was the same as that facing Malebranche, viz. the problem as to how we can be justified in holding beliefs about external objects when it is admitted that the immediate objects of perception are only ideas in our own minds.

Before closing this section there are two questions we should look at, the first concerning the argument we allowed to draw us towards the conclusion that *really* we are aware only of sensations produced in our minds by external objects. For there *is* something very odd about the argument and the position known as *representative realism* which it is supposed to support. One point we can make here is that there is certainly no excuse for supposing that science shows us that we are aware only of sensations and thus that the existence of external objects must be open to doubt. For if there are no external objects then the scientific story in terms of processes originating with them must be false, and if the scientific story is false then there can be no question of appealing to it in order to show that we are aware only of sensations. Equally, there can be nothing in the theory that a consideration of the implications of the scientific story will show that we have and can have no knowledge of the supposed external objects. For, as Hospers says of this notion:

> The theory seems to assume that it itself is not true. It is self-contradictory. *In the very process of showing* that we can have no knowledge of an external world, but only of our own sensations ... *we have assumed that there is an external world and that we have knowledge of it*, at least enough knowledge to know that there are things in the world which stimulate sense-organs, which in turn stimulate nerves and send 'messages' to the brain. (p. 390)

But this brings us to a more fundamental point and this is that it must be wrong to hold that the scientific story does show that we are aware only of sensations. As we said earlier, the scientist sets out to explain *how* we perceive external objects, and when he has explained this in terms of causal processes he is certainly not entitled to suppose that his account shows that *really* we do not perceive external objects at all. If he seems to be driven to this conclusion we must suspect either that there is something radically wrong with his account or that his account has been misinterpreted.

The truth is, I think, that the three stage argument we are considering is incoherent if it is taken to lead to the conclusion that really we are aware only of private percepts, or of 'pictures' or sensations in our own minds. The way out of the difficulty is not to deny the propriety of scientific accounts of perception in terms of processes but rather to resist the temptation to reify sensations or to treat sensations as if they were themselves perceptual objects.[6] We must remind ourselves that the scientist's starting point is the same as the plain man's and that what he seeks to account for is our sensory awareness of a physical object. If we accept his account it will be because it succeeds in providing an explanation of this awareness. But if this is so it follows that the end result of the causal process cannot be awareness of a sensation, if awareness of a sensation is supposed to be incompatible with awareness of a physical object. Indeed, if we go along with the scientific account of the perception of a table, and if we believe that the scientist succeeds in answering the question he is set, then we must hold that the end result of the causal process is, not a perceptual object of a worrying sort, but rather the sensing of the table.[7]

This is not the place to look closely into the second question which is that of how deeply Locke was in fact committed to a representative theory of perception, but we should at least note that it would be a grave injustice *simply* to attribute to him the view Berkeley attributes to the materialist, viz. that the mind perceives 'onely the impressions made upon its brain or rather the ideas attending those impressions'. Certainly we do not have to look very hard to find passages in which he talks of us perceiving external objects. There is for example the following from II viii 12:

> ... since the extension, figure, number, and motion of bodies of an observable bigness, may be perceived at a distance by the sight, it is evident some singly imperceptible bodies must come from them to the eyes, and thereby convey to the brain some motion; which produces these ideas which we have of them in us.

Here, then, we have Locke supposing, not only that we perceive external objects, but also that it is *because* we see them at a distance that we have to give a scientific account of how they produce ideas in us which includes reference to particles travelling from them to the eye. Indeed for much of the time Locke talks as if sense perception was quite simply the awareness of things in the world.

On what is I suppose the standard interpretation of Locke[8] we should see him as reluctantly committed to representationalism because he saw no alternative, but we should also see him as totally committed to the view that there are external objects and that somehow sense perception does provide an adequate experiential basis for knowledge of them. The following from IV iv 3 is often quoted to show that Locke was aware that there was a problem here:

> It is evident the mind knows not things immediately, but only by the intervention of the ideas it has of them. Our knowledge, therefore, is real only so far as there is a *conformity* between our ideas and the reality of things. But what shall be here the criterion? How shall the mind, when it perceives nothing but its own ideas, know that they agree with things themselves?[9]

But though, as Fraser points out in his note, Reid saw in this the germ of modern scepticism, for Locke it was a problem but a problem he never doubted must have an answer. Thus, still in IV iv 3, he tells us that 'there be two sorts of ideas that we may be assured agree with things'. Again, while Locke writes he sees white and black, 'and that something really exists that causes that sensation in me' he cannot bring himself to doubt (IV xi 2). Indeed in the very next section he asserts, though he never satisfactorily shows, that in such circumstances we have 'an assurance that deserves the name of *knowledge*'. Of course given the standard interpretation Locke must be seen as letting his enthusiasm run away with him when he talks *as if* we were directly acquainted with external objects, and the standard account does not deny that he does often talk in this way. Consistency, though, has never been accounted one of Locke's virtues.

What I have referred to as the standard interpretation is not the only interpretation possible. Very recently it has been argued by Yolton that 'the way of ideas is misread as a representative theory of perception' (p. 14). Yolton says:

> I see no evidence in the *Essay* that Locke thought of ideas as entities. They were, I have been suggesting, his way of characterising the fact that perceptual awareness is mental. (p. 134)

And on this interpretation we would come nearer doing justice to Locke if we saw him as saying that the end result of the causal process originating with the external object is not (disastrously) an idea-thing which as it were *comes between* us and the real thing but rather (and better) the awareness of the external object itself.[10] Here, though, we shall adopt the standard interpretation, and this partly because it *is* still the one most generally accepted, partly because I still think he was a representationalist, though not an enthusiastic one, but also because it is against this background that we can best hope to understand how Berkeley came to formulate his own position. Berkeley certainly saw Locke as a representative realist.

On the standard interpretation, then, Locke's conception of external objects as the causes of sensations or ideas produced in the mind necessitated his holding a three-term theory of perception in which really the mind perceives the sensations in the mind rather than the external objects we normally take ourselves to be perceiving. And this of course does seem to represent a radical departure from common sense and to invite the sceptic's and Berkeley's challenge – How can you properly make claims about external objects if you say that you are only ever aware of ideas in the mind?

III

While remembering that we are not here concerned to consider Locke for his own sake, to look for the most favourable interpretation of what he says at any point, or indeed to take notice of anything in the *Essay* that is not immediately relevant to an understanding of Berkeley, we must all the same stay with him for a while and examine his views about qualities (here and in sect. IV) and substance (sect. V). In the course of this study we shall become aware of other factors adding to the temptation to make a radical distinction between external objects and ideas, but the basic issues may become somewhat obscured as well as more complicated. For, though Locke thought of himself as making something of a new start in philosophy, he was in fact influenced by and often insufficiently critical of the thinking of other philosophers, while at the same time there was the strong influence of contemporary scientific notions which have by now been modified or discarded altogether.

We start by considering Locke's thoughts on qualities, and the best way of introducing this topic may be to look back at what we said about the scientific account of perception and note that someone, perhaps the scientist, might want to point out that of course the scientist does not begin his story with the familiar, ordinary things the plain man takes himself to be perceiving. He starts, rather, with *unfamiliar* things such as molecules, atoms, electrons, particles and so on. If he does concern himself with a table, it might well be thought that the table is a strange one. This view is taken in a well-known passage from Sir Arthur Eddington:

> My scientific table is mostly emptiness. Sparsely scattered in that emptiness are numerous electric charges rushing about with great speed; but their combined bulk amounts to less than a billionth of the bulk of the table itself. (p. xii)

The scientific table Eddington contrasts with another which 'has been familiar to me from earliest years', and he tells us that the scientific table 'does not belong to . . . that world which spontaneously appears around me when I open my eyes'.

And the objection clearly does have some point. The scientist does describe the table in terms which seem strange to the layman, and it may indeed be tempting to think of him as describing a quite different entity. But if the objection has point, so too does the suggestion that the scientific story must concern the familiar table. There is not, as Eddington thinks, one scientific table dissolving 'quite naturally into scientific smoke' when it is set alight, and another (miraculously) undergoing 'a metamorphosis of its substantial nature'. There is rather one table which we see undergo its metamorphosis *because* it has dissolved into scientific smoke. If we took Eddington seriously we would have to deny that the scientist could ever give any explanation of the behaviour of familiar objects. And just as the scientist can explain why the familiar ball bounces off the familiar surface only by telling us things about *that* ball and *that* surface, so his explanation of how we come to see the familiar table as brown or feel it as solid will depend upon a special account of the very table which we do see as brown and feel as solid. Eddington's scientific table is in fact our familiar table described in perhaps unfamiliar terms.

It is this principle that lies behind the criticisms of Eddington's position made by Susan Stebbing in a chapter appropriately entitled with a phrase from Berkeley – 'Furniture of the Earth'. In it she objects to talk about two tables and the suggestion that there are two worlds, especially when the talk is allowed to carry the implication that the scientific world is somehow more real than the world we know in ordinary experience. To make the basic point again, the scientific table can play a role in explanation only if it is the table we are familiar with in experience; the table we see, touch and sit at. But in attacking Eddington's view, Miss Stebbing says:

> It seems to me that in his theory of the duplicate worlds Eddington has fallen into the error of which Berkeley accused the Newtonians. . . . It seemed to Berkeley that the metaphysics of Descartes and Newton resulted in the description of a 'real world' that had all the properties of the sensible world except the vital property of being seeable. (pp. 60-1)

And though there is room to quibble about the details of what is said here, Miss Stebbing is surely right, both in putting her finger on one weakness of the two world view, and in crediting Berkeley with having spotted it. We might note that the metaphysic being attacked is attributed to Descartes, whom we normally think of as being a philosopher, and to Locke's younger contemporary Newton, who was essentially a scientist. It is not here attributed to Locke, but Berkeley would certainly say it could have been.

The talk of two tables and of two worlds can, of course, be unexceptionable, and philosophers should not get excited and belligerent every time they meet a phrase such as 'the world of science'. The objection is only to taking such talk too seriously. Reference to two worlds (or to three or more, for we can also refer to the world of physics, the world of chemistry and so on) are quite acceptable as didactic devices, so long as we realize that all that is involved is different ways of looking at and talking about one world. If 'wives can also be lovers', as the song has it, Mr. Smith can have a wife and a lover without committing adultery, for both might be Mrs. Smith. And similarly we can talk of two worlds so long as we remember that in an important and fundamental sense the two worlds are one. Of course it might turn out that Smith's lover is Miss Jones and not Mrs. Smith so that the wife and lover really are two people, but the world of science *must* be the familiar world even if it is described in novel terms. On this see Ryle 1, pp. 68-81.

As traditionally interpreted Locke does make the mistake of duplicating worlds,[11] and as a result the world which lies on the dark side of the veil of perception turns out to be the world as it is described by the scientist, or rather as it was described by the scientist in the seventeenth century. Locke accepted the dominant view that objects in the external world are made up of very large numbers of atomic units or corpuscles which can be correctly described in various ways. But while they believed that certain predicates could be used to describe the corpuscles, Locke and his contemporaries saw that there were other predicates which were wholly inappropriate. The basic idea is not outmoded. Russell makes the point when he says:

> . . . molecules have no colour, atoms make no noise, electrons have no taste, and corpuscles do not even smell. (Russell 2, p. 145)

It is worth our noting in passing that immediately after making this point Russell goes on to draw attention to a problem which is in fact the one Berkeley highlights. Thus:

> If such objects are to be verified, it must be solely through their relation to sense-data: they must have some kind of correlation with sense-data, and must be verifiable through their correlation *alone*. But how is the correlation itself ascertained? A correlation can only be ascertained empirically by the correlated objects being constantly *found* together. But in our case, only one term of the correlation, namely, the sensible term, is ever *found*: the other term seems essentially incapable of being found. Therefore, it would seem, the correlation with objects of sense, by which physics was to be verified, is itself utterly and for ever unverifiable.

We shall return to this difficulty later. For the moment our concern is with the suggestion that there are certain qualities which we clearly can't predicate of atoms, electrons and corpuscles. It is in a similar spirit that Eddington takes himself to task for thinking of (or, presumably, visualizing) his electrons and protons as being coloured.

Going back to the sixteenth century we find in Galileo a nice statement of the view that influenced Locke:

> To excite in us tastes, odours, and sounds I believe that nothing is required in external bodies except shapes, numbers, and slow or rapid movements. I think that if ears, tongues, and noses were removed, shapes and numbers and motions would remain, but not odours or tastes or sounds. (See Popkin 3, p. 67)[12]

And, as he also says, colours would disappear together with eyes. It is to qualities such as these that Locke's friend Boyle is referring when he says in his *The Origin of Forms and Qualities*:

> ... we have been from our infancy apt to imagine, that these sensible qualities are real beings, in the objects they denominate ... whereas indeed ... there is in the body, to which these sensible qualities are attributed, nothing of real and physical, but the size, shape, and motion, or rest of its component particles, together with that texture of the whole, which results from their being so contrived as they are ... (pp. 40-1)

Qualities which are 'real and physical' Boyle calls *primary*.

It is abundantly clear from the *Essay* that Locke's view of what the external world is like in itself was essentially the same as Boyle's. He says for example:

> Concerning these qualities we may, I think, observe these primary ones in bodies that produce simple ideas in us, viz. *solidity, extension, motion* or *rest, number*, and *figure*. (II viii 9 – first three editions)

His thinking seems to have been that *any* object, whether it be atom or apple, *must* have these qualities. Thus:

> These, which I call *original* or *primary* qualities of body, are wholly inseparable from it, and such as in all the alterations and changes it suffers, all the force can be used upon it, it constantly keeps; and such as sense constantly finds in every particle of matter which has bulk enough to be perceived; and the mind finds inseparable from every particle of matter, though less than to make itself singly be perceived by our senses: v.g. Take a grain of wheat, divide it into two parts; each part has still solidity, extension, figure, and mobility: divide it again, and it retains still the same qualities; and so divide it on, till the parts become insensible; they must retain still each of them all those qualities. (II viii 10 – first three editions. The bulk of this passage occurs in sect. 9 in the fourth edition.)[13]

For Locke there is an important sense in which these primary or original qualities are the only qualities of things in themselves.

It might be wondered at that Boyle and Locke were prepared to refer to the colour, taste and other non-original qualities of objects as *qualities* of them, even if these qualities are clearly distinguished from the primary, for the whole point of the doctrine as contained in the quotation from Boyle and accepted by Locke is that they are not actual attributes at all. That they did so is a tribute to their desire not to affront ordinary usage unnecessarily, and perhaps also to their innate common sense. Locke was in fact following Boyle, who was prepared to describe colours, tastes, odours and sounds as *qualities* both 'for shortness of speech . . . since it is already so generally received' (p. 57) and also for a more substantial reason. As against Galileo who said that in the absence of sentient beings redness, for example, would be just a name with nothing existent corresponding to it, Boyle decided that we should recognize the fact that there would remain something intrinsic to the object corresponding to the colour word we use to describe it. Thus:

> I do not deny, but that bodies may be said, in a very favourable sense, to have those qualities we call sensible, though there were no animals in the world: for a body in that case may differ from those bodies, which now are quite devoid of quality, in its having such a disposition of its constituent corpuscles, that in case it were duly applied to the sensory of an animal, it would produce such a sensible quality, which a body of another texture would not . . .
> (p. 47)

It is this sort of thinking that lies behind Locke's claim that the *secondary* qualities of objects 'are nothing in the objects themselves but powers to produce various sensations in us by their primary qualities' (II viii 10). Not that too much should be made of the difference between Galileo and Locke. Locke agrees that when the sensory organs are not functioning 'colours, tastes, odours, and sounds, *as they are such particular ideas*, vanish and cease, and are reduced to their causes, i.e. bulk, figure, and motion of parts' (II viii 17).

IV

The situation is complicated by the fact that Locke's terminology is notoriously confused and confusing, and in particular by the fact that he tends to slip from the language appropriate to a Causal Theorist – e.g. '*original* or *primary qualities* . . . produce simple ideas in us' (II viii 9), to more ordinary ways of speaking – e.g. 'we perceive these *original*

B*

qualities' (II viii 12). Again, sometimes he talks of ideas as if they were qualities of objects, while often he talks of them as things produced in our minds *by* objects and as a result of their having the qualities they do. It is when he thinks of ideas as sensations produced in us by things that he finds it natural to ask whether the sensations *resemble* the qualities of the things, and his answer is that there are two sorts of idea produced in us by external objects and that, while the ideas of primary qualities do resemble the primary qualities, the ideas of secondary qualities have no likeness to anything in the object. Thus:

> ... the ideas of primary qualities of bodies are resemblances of them, and their patterns do really exist in the bodies themselves, but the ideas produced in us by these secondary qualities have no resemblance of them at all. There is nothing like our ideas, existing in the bodies themselves. They are, in the bodies we dominate from them, only a power to produce those sensations in us: and what is sweet, blue, or warm in idea, is but the certain bulk, figure, and motion of the insensible parts, in the bodies themselves, which we call so. (II viii 15)

The notion seems to be that colour, for example, *as we experience it* is not in the object itself, though as a power it is, while shape, for example, is a quality of the object which is mirrored by the idea.

Berkeley was quite convinced that this doctrine just would not do, firstly because it involved another radical departure from common sense, and secondly because there were insuperable arguments against it. In *PC* 392 he says:

> There are men who say there are insensible extensions, there are others who say the Wall is not white, the fire is not hot &c We Irish men cannot attain to these truths.

One basic objection to the doctrine was that, as Berkeley saw it, we could never know whether it was true or not. As he says in *PC* 51:

> A man cannot compare 2 things together without perceiving them each, ergo he cannot say any thing wch is not an idea is like or unlike an idea.

And again in *PC* 47:

> Qu: Did ever any man see any other things besides his own ideas, that he should compare them to these & make these like unto them?

The point is of course that if we perceive only ideas imprinted on the senses then we would seem to have no experiential basis for saying anything about the unperceived qualities of things in themselves. Not only do we apparently have no evidence for denying that the wall is really white (for we have never perceived it as it is in itself), we also have no basis for any claim as to its shape. Indeed Berkeley raises the question as to whether it even *makes sense* to suppose that things of which we are aware (ideas) are like or unlike things of which we are not aware (qualities of things in themselves), and his claim is that 'nothing can be like an idea but an idea' (*PC* 484).

In trying to understand what is going on in the relevant chapter in Locke's *Essay* we have to *start*, I think, from the viewpoint of seventeenth-century science. And to find one more sample of the sort of thinking which influenced Locke we can look, though the work was not published until 1704, at a passage from Newton's *Opticks* in which the author takes himself to be speaking 'philosophically and properly' in saying of colours:

> . . . colours in the object are nothing but a disposition to reflect this or that sort of rays more copiously than the rest. In the rays they are nothing but their dispositions to propagate this or that motion into the sensorium, and in the sensorium they are sensations of those motions under the form of colours. (Quoted in Flew 2, p. 89)

What is noteworthy here is that Newton is not so much denying that objects are really coloured as telling us what it is for an object to be coloured. His view is that colour in the object is a disposition to reflect rays so as to produce, ultimately, 'sensations . . . under the form of colours'. Similarly we have found Boyle affirming that 'bodies may be said, in a very favourable sense, to have those qualities we call sensible', and we have seen how Locke allowed that there are secondary qualities in objects corresponding to (but not resembling) colours as we see them. It was easy to slip from saying that colours-as-we-experience-them are not in the objects as they are in themselves to saying that colours are quite simply not in the objects, and Locke does sometimes say the latter, thus appearing to accept what Berkeley saw as 'odd paradoxes'. The claim that Locke has it that objects are not really coloured does, though, involve a measure of distortion. Indeed even if he and Boyle had been prepared to talk of colours as qualities *just* 'for shortness of speech . . . since it is already so generally received', it is not at all clear that they would have been any worse off *vis-à-vis* common sense than is Berkeley when he tells us that though fire does not *really* heat it is desirable that we speak with the vulgar and *as if* it did.

Clearly, though, the scientists thought of themselves not as affronting common sense but as advancing knowledge and understanding. A tempting analogy was that with the discovery that the earth moves round the sun. The astronomer recognized that for normal purposes we should continue to talk as if the sun moved round the earth, for we see it rising and setting, but he held, at the same time, that it was *really* the earth that was moving. The notion became not so much that our ordinary ways of talking are straightforwardly false (though this may sometimes be suggested) as that they reflect what must from a scientific point of view seem an essentially parochial standpoint. The scientist has a fuller picture of what is going on, and of course given this picture he can explain many things including why from where we are it *looks* as if the sun is moving. Similarly the scientist could recognize that from our standpoint, and given the nature of our sensory apparatus, objects will look to us as if they have their familiar colours, he could allow that it is useful for us to continue to speak as if things were as they characteristically appear, and he could do this while supposing that science revealed what things are like in themselves. This was the age of the microscope, and at the level of observation the scientist could feel that he was coming nearer to discovering the true nature of the things he studied and that he was, in a sense, undermining the opinions of the layman. He noted that objects lose the colouring we normally associate with them when they are examined under a microscope, and he sometimes went further and suggested that under a sufficiently powerful microscope all colouring will disappear. Certainly for ordinary purposes he would be prepared to talk of blood as if it were uniformly red, but his discoveries led him to suggest that it is not really red at all but just *looks* or *seems* red to the naked eye. Again, when he entered the realm of physical *theory* the scientist found it natural to suppose not only that he was theorizing about the nature of objects as they are in themselves but that his theories were such as to suggest that our ordinary beliefs were, if not downright false, at least less than ultimately true. Even if it is the familiar table that Eddington has discovered to be 'mostly emptiness' he can feel that what he says is in some sort of conflict with the belief of the uneducated that it is solid, for, surely, what is solid cannot be mostly emptiness. If we do think in this way we find ourselves saying that science can explain how things come to feel to us as if they were solid while showing that they are not, and, similarly, that it explains how we come to see things as if they had their familiar colouring while attributing to them only powers to absorb and reflect light. If for day to day purposes we are allowed to carry on speaking as we have always spoken, so that the table can be talked of as solid and brown, we may well regard the extension of our knowledge as more than compensating for our 'naive' pre-scientific belief that it looks as it really is.

Now this way of thinking about things, whether it will do or not, probably does justice in some measure to what Locke and his contemporaries were after. And here it is important to appreciate that the picture does not depend for its attractiveness on our holding a three-term theory of perception, or our supposing that we never (really) perceive external objects. In sect. II we suggested that instead of saying we perceive only sensations or ideas produced in us by external objects we should insist that the end result of the causal process involved in, say, seeing a table is simply the perception of the table. But having got this far we certainly have to recognize that the way it appears to us when we perceive it by a given sense depends in part on the way in which we are constituted. Now *if* we were to decide that the table is not *really* brown, and indeed not *really* coloured at all, a natural way of stating our position would be to say that though the table is not really coloured in itself we see *it* (the table 'out there' in the external world) as brown because our sensory apparatus is as it is. There is no need for us to say, and we should not say, that we see something – an idea-thing – which is brown and which is not the surface of the table. If we do say this it will be because we happen to hold a three-term theory of perception. Berkeley is largely responsible for the notion that the primary/secondary quality distinction must fall together with representationalism.

What is not clear is the extent to which Locke thinks that in II viii he is *proving* that the distinction between qualities must be made as it was made by the scientist in the seventeenth century. Though in sect. 18 he does talk of having 'proved' that a body can operate only 'by the size, motion, and figure of its insensible parts', it seems more natural to interpret him as in general *assuming* that the scientific account is the right one but adopting temporarily the role of public relations officer for the scientist and trying to persuade the reader that thinking of the things in themselves in scientific terms is at least much more plausible than he might at first suppose. What is certainly true is that Locke derived the corpuscular hypothesis from the scientist – it is with reason that in sect. 22 he asks to be excused 'this little excursion into natural philosophy' – and never looks like providing a convincing demonstration that either it or the primary/secondary quality distinction must be correct. I find myself in sympathy with Yolton when he argues that the corpuscular hypothesis 'was one of a number of ingredients in Locke's metaphysic of nature' and that he was more concerned to *use* it than to ask 'the usual justificatory questions philosophers put to existential claims' (p. 11). Yolton believes that such questions 'are, for the most part, irrelevant to Locke'.

Be this as it may, Berkeley was intensely concerned with justificatory questions and he thought (perhaps not without excuse) that he detected 'arguments, which are thought manifestly to prove that colours and tastes exist only in the mind' (*Pr.* 15). If these arguments are to be found in Locke it is in the 'examples' he offers in sects. 19-21. In sect. 19, for example, Locke says:

> Let us consider the red and white colours in porphyry. Hinder light from striking on it, and its colours vanish; it no longer produces any such ideas in us: upon the return of light it produces these appearances on us again. Can any one think any real alterations are made in the porphyry by the presence or absence of light; and that those ideas of whiteness and redness are really in porphyry in the light, when it is plain *it has no colour in the dark*? It has, indeed, such a configuration of particles, both night and day, as are apt, by the rays of light rebounding from some parts of that hard stone, to produce in us the idea of redness, and from others the idea of whiteness; but whiteness or redness are not in it at any time, but such a texture that hath the power to produce such a sensation in us.

Similarly in sect. 20:

> Pound an almond, and the clear white colour will be altered into a dirty one, and the sweet taste into an oily one. What real alteration can the beating of the pestle make in any body, but an alteration of the texture of it?

As Berkeley saw it, the basic argument involved drawing our attention to situations where the appearance of an object with respect to some supposed quality changes, this because something is done to the object itself (the almond is pulped), or because of some modification of the medium through which it is observed (the light dims), or because of some modification of or peculiarity in the perceiver's condition. And in such cases we are supposed to conclude that the apparent quality is not really a quality at all.

The scientists themselves were clearly influenced by the fact of perceptual relativity. Boyle, like Locke, uses the case of the same water feeling warm to one hand and cool to the other and suggests that we can explain this by treating the warmth and coolness felt as sensations produced in us by the water, rather than as attributes of the water itself. But philosophers too have always found the relativity of perception challenging. Turning to the introduction to a volume of readings on perception we find a useful list of sample cases where changed circumstances alter the appearance of an object with respect to some supposed quality. Thus:

> . . . a round plate may look elliptical when seen from an angle or a square table look diamond-shaped; the same water may feel cool to one person and warm to another; the same wine may taste sweet or dry according to what one has just been eating; hills may look blue at a distance and green close to; a red cloth may look black to a colour-blind man. (Hirst, p. 4)

Certainly such common phenomena have to be taken into account in any philosophical theory concerning perception, and they point to the fact that a distinction has to be made between on the one hand how things *look* or *seem* and on the other how they *are*. Or, to put it another way, we have to recognize that there is a distinction to be made between the logic of 'being P' and the logic of 'appearing to be P'. But this is minimal, and some philosophers have thought the distinction radical enough to justify an epistemological dualism according to which we are never directly acquainted with the qualities of external things but only with discrete *appearances*.

Bearing in mind Locke's immediate concern, the trouble with the argument from the relativity of perception is that it 'proves' at once too much and too little. To take the first point first, the very fact that Hirst's examples include reference to apparent shape as well as to changes in apparent colour suggests that the argument is not going to be able to separate colours from shapes and to show that the former are not properly attributable to objects while the latter are. As the light dims the apparent colour of the plate changes, but, as Hirst points out, when we look at it from different angles the apparent shape changes. If, then, we want to say that because the apparent colour changes according to circumstances no colour is properly attributable to it, why should we not say the same about shape? Or as Berkeley concludes in *PC* 20:

> Primary ideas prov'd not to exist in matter, after the same manner y^t secondary ones are prov^d not to exist therein.

And again in *Pr.* 15:

> In short, let anyone consider those arguments, which are thought manifestly to prove that colours and tastes exist only in the mind, and he shall find they may with equal force, be brought to prove the same thing of extension, figure, and motion.

Thus if the argument proves that the plate is not really white because it does not always *look* white, then it must prove too that the plate is not really round because it does not always *look* round. Equally, if the argument proves that the colour we see is just an idea in the mind, then so too does it prove that the shape we see is just an idea.

In making this point Berkeley was not being particularly original. Malebranche devoted several chapters of the *Recherche* to showing how the senses deceive us with regard to the qualities Locke thinks of as original, and in articles in Bayle's *Dictionary* the moral is drawn and the case made for detaching these qualities too from the supposed external objects. Thus for example in Remark G in the article on Zeno:

> The 'new' philosophers, although they are not sceptics, have so well understood the bases of suspension of judgement with regard to sounds, smells, heat, cold, hardness, softness, heaviness and lightness, tastes, colours, and the like, that they teach that all these qualities are perceptions of our soul and that they do not exist at all in the objects of our senses. Why should we not say the same thing about extension? . . . Would you dare to reason in this way today, 'Since certain bodies appear sweet to one man, sour to another,

bitter to a third, and so on, I ought to affirm that in general they are savoury, though I do not know what savour belongs to them absolutely and in themselves'? All the 'new' philosophers would hoot at you. Why then would you dare to say, 'Since certain bodies appear large to one animal, medium to another, and very small to a third, I ought to affirm that in general they are extended, though I do not know their absolute extension'? (See Popkin 3, p. 348)

Almost certainly Berkeley read and was influenced by Bayle's powerful articles on Zeno and Pyrrho, in which the tendency towards scepticism implicit in the new science was enthusiastically emphasized and developed. And, again almost certainly, it was from Bayle that Berkeley got a number of the arguments he was to use against the materialist.

At an early stage Berkeley was prepared to put great stress on the sort of argument he hints at in *PC* 20. It seemed to him that if philosophers could appeal to perceptual relativity to pull colours, smells, tastes and sounds into the mind, then he was justified in making the same appeal to pull the supposed original qualities into the mind. Later, however, he came to feel that, though he could certainly use the argument from the relativity of perception, it did not in fact prove that *any* quality, whether it be roundness or whiteness, did not exist in the supposed external object. Thus in *PC* 265:

> ffrom Malbranch, Locke & my first arguings it cant be prov'd that extension is not in matter ffrom Lockes arguings it can't be prov'd that Colours, are not in Bodies.

And immediately following the claim quoted earlier from *Pr.* 15:

> ... it must be confessed this method of arguing doth not so much prove that there is no extension or colour in an outward object, as that we do not know by sense which is the true extension or colour of the object.

In short, the argument proves too little.

As Berkeley does find a use for the argument from the relativity of perception we can leave further examination of it for a later chapter. There is one problem though that we can mention here. It has been thought puzzling that Berkeley makes considerable use of the argument in the *Dialogues* when in the *Principles* he had seemed to explicitly recognise its limitations and to regard it as having mainly *ad hominem* value. I think there is a solution to this problem and I shall go into it in some detail later. Here I just want to suggest that we cannot even begin to see our way round the difficulty unless we appreciate that the weaknesses the argument has were not necessarily the weaknesses Berkeley spotted. I believe that he did see that the argument proved less than he would have liked, but that he still thought it proved more than it does. In a way he was hoist with his own petard. Because he insisted on seeing the primary/secondary qualities doctrine as being inextricably entangled with the doctrine of representative realism he was encouraged to see the argument from the relativity of perception as showing that all perceived qualities are in the mind, but as unfortunately failing to show that there are not unperceived qualities really in external objects. The *real* weakness of the argument, and the weakness I take it Berkeley did not spot, is that it does not in fact show that all perceived qualities are in the mind.

We can conclude, then, by looking at the situation as I believe Berkeley saw it. The materialists argued that there were external objects which *had* qualities and which *produced* ideas in our minds, and Berkeley took it to be an essential ingredient of this position that we never perceive the external objects but only the ideas in our minds. When I am aware of colour what I am aware of is in my mind and similarly when I am aware of shape what I am aware of is in my mind, and this is true for the materialist even though he believes that the idea in the mind resembles the external object in respect of shape but not in respect of colour. Now Berkeley certainly thought it an objection to materialism that the materialist could never have any reason for believing that his claims about the outside world were true. He never perceives external objects and so has no experiential backing for the claim that they exist, and even if we allow that they exist he never perceives them and thus cannot know what qualities they have. If there is an external orange it may be square and blue. Of course if all this is right the materialist's position begins to look rather unattractive, but Berkeley wanted to be able to prove that materialism was false. It was from this standpoint that Berkeley saw the argument from the relativity of perception as proving too little. For it seemed to him that as Locke has used it to show that the colours, smells, tastes and sounds we perceive are (as perceived) only ideas in the mind, he could legitimately extend its use to show that all qualities *as perceived* are in the mind. Unfortunately, though, the argument did not show that there were not unperceived and unperceivable qualities in external objects or behind the veil of perception. But by the time he came to publish the *Principles* it seemed to Berkeley that he had powerful arguments which showed just this. The notion of an unperceived object with qualities we never perceive is, he will say, a contradictory one.

V

It is as well to consider what Locke says about qualities as one issue and to separate it as far as possible from what he says about corporeal substance or the something-we-know-not-what that he supposes must exit to provide support for the qualities. Interpreting Locke backwards, as it were, through Berkeley, the two issues tend to get blurred in that Berkeley concentrates his attack on an overall view according to which the independent reality on the dark side of the veil of perception is made up of substance-supported sets of original qualities. In fact, though, the reasoning which lies behind the substance doctrine is essentially distinct from that which lies behind the primary/secondary qualities doctrine. The scorn that Berkeley is able to pour on the former should not reflect on the latter.

It would certainly be a mistake to suppose that Locke was an enthusiastic proponent of the view that the qualities of objects require the support of a substratum, the nature of which is unknown and unknowable. The truth is, rather, that since Aristotle philosophers and the theologians had been keen and confident advocates of doctrines about substance-in-general and that Locke, though he did not feel able to dispense with the concept altogether, was an influential critic of some of the received notions. Thus O'Connor points out that Locke gave the substratum theory 'a blow from which it never recovered' and as a result of which 'it has not been taken seriously by philosophers for many years' (p. 83). And Bennett has gone so far as to suggest that 'Locke's treatment of "substance in general" was mainly sceptical in content and ironical in form' (p. 61). So far as Berkeley was concerned this was perhaps a case where Locke had seen some way through the mist and might be excused for not seeing farther.

We can conveniently start our brief consideration of Locke's position by looking at what he says about particular sorts of substances. And in summary his views seem to be that for the ordinary man a substance of a particular sort is thought of as being made up of certain qualities which experience teaches us to associate together. Thus he says:

> It is the ordinary qualities observable in iron, or a diamond, put together, that make the true complex idea of those substances, which a smith or a jeweller commonly knows better than a philosopher . . . (II xxiii 3)

The 'ordinary qualities' here would seem to be those a man takes to be attributable to a substance of a particular sort, so that for the laymen the yellowness of gold as perceived will form part of the complex idea of gold though the scientist knows that in the object the yellowness is but a power.

Our feeling that the story cannot end here is reflected, Locke thinks, in our conviction that the qualities we associate together in fact belong together, in the inconceivability of their subsisting by themselves, in the philosophical tradition according to which qualities are accidents, but fundamentally in our ordinary ways of talking. Thus:

> . . . when we speak of any sort of substance, we say it is a thing having such or such qualities; as body is a thing that it extended, figured, and capable of motion . . . and so hardness, friability, and power to draw iron, we say, are qualities to be found in a loadstone. These, and the like fashions of speaking, intimate that the substance is supposed always *something besides* the extension, figure, solidity, motion . . . or other observable ideas, though we know not what it is. (II xxiii 3)[14]

We speak of the qualities as existing *in* something and of gold, say, as being a *thing which has* certain qualities, and we do this '*because we cannot conceive how they should subsist alone, nor in one another*' and have to suppose them 'supported by some common subject' (II xxiii 4).[15]

As it is, having made this point and having added that volitions and acts require a support in spiritual substance, Locke can do little more than to emphasize his and our ignorance of the nature of substance. He says:

> . . . here, as in all other cases where we use words without having clear and distinct ideas, we talk like children: who, being questioned what such a thing is, which they know not, readily give this

satisfactory answer, that it is *something*: which in truth signifies no more, when so used, either by children or men, but that they know not what; and that the thing they pretend to know, and talk of, is what they have no distinct idea of at all, and so are perfectly ignorant of it, and in the dark. The idea then we have, to which we give the *general* name substance, being nothing but the supposed, but unknown, support of those qualities we find existing, which we imagine cannot subsist *sine re substante*, without something to support them, we call that support *substantia*; which, according to the true import of the word, is, in plain English, standing under or upholding. (II xxiii 2)

In the same section Locke likens our position with respect to substance to that of the Indian who was asked to explain what supported the world and who, after having asserted that it rested on a great elephant which in turn rested on a great tortoise, was reduced when asked what the tortoise rested on to saying just *something* 'he knew not what'. This is the second time Locke has told this little story, and Berkeley is citing the first occurrence when he says:

Material substance banter'd by Locke b.2 c.13 S.19 (*PC* 89)

And of course Locke did in a way prepare the ground for Berkeley's outright attack on the notion of a material substratum of qualities. After summarizing Berkeley's objections Warnock says:

Curiously enough, in urging all these points Berkeley is hardly saying more than Locke had himself already admitted. Locke had confessed with complete candour that neither he nor anyone else could explain what matter was, or what the expression 'material substance' meant. But at the same time he seemed to find a 'necessity of thought' obliging him to assert the existence of this unknowable, 'bare' support of qualities. (Warnock 1, p. 103)

Presumably Warnock finds it *curious* that Berkeley's objections to matter are based so squarely on an endorsement of Locke's admissions about it because he thinks of Berkeley as being primarily concerned to argue with Locke. But this I think distorts the picture slightly, for we have to remember that both Berkeley *and Locke* are concerned to argue against a tradition. Locke does believe that a necessity of thought requires us to posit a support of qualities, but his main point is that we are and will remain ignorant as to its nature and that all the disputes about it and doctrines giving it prominence are in fact a waste of effort. It is Locke's firm conviction that we can advance our knowledge only by examining the qualities of particular things and discovering truths about sorts of things, though we might note in passing that while he regarded debates about substance-in-general as arid he thought of the corpuscular hypothesis as providing an intelligible and exciting account of the real essence of particular substances. Indeed Yolton has it that Locke 'tried to replace the talk of substratum and subject by the notion of an internal, insensible configuration of particles' (p. 43).[16] Berkeley was, in effect, able to develop Locke's case against taking substance too seriously into a case against the existence of substance. If Berkeley's case involves an attack on Locke it is because Locke reveals that there is so little to be said for or about substance and yet still insists on recognizing its existence.

To a degree, then, Locke hands Berkeley the case against corporeal substance on a plate. Locke had admitted that the idea of substance is one 'which we neither have nor can have by sensation or reflection' (I iii 19), and it seemed as clear as day to Berkeley that if this is so then talk of substance must be meaningless. Nor will it do to say that though we have no clear idea of what substance *is* we at least know what it *does*. For as Berkeley says:

> ... though you have no positive, yet if you have any meaning at all, you must at least have a relative idea of matter; though you know not what it is, yet you must be supposed to know what relation it bears to accidents, and what is meant by its supporting them. It is evident *support* cannot here be taken in its usual or literal sense, as when we say that pillars support a building: in what sense therefore must it be taken? (*Pr.* 16)

Berkeley does not expect that the materialist will be able to answer. Of course there *is* an attack on Locke here. The passage just quoted can be seen as a direct criticism of what Locke says in II xxiii 2 for example. Berkeley *is* concerned to reveal that Locke's something-we-know-not-what is a non-entity. The one point I want to stress, though, is that if we can see Berkeley as striking a blow at Locke and the substratum theory we can also quite properly see him as completing an attack on a theory which Locke himself had done much to undermine. If Berkeley could insist that given his admission Locke should have allowed no place for substance in his system, the orthodox Stillingfleet had been shocked at Locke's wholly unenthusiastic acceptance of it, accusing him of having 'almost discarded substance out of the reasonable part of the world' (see Fraser's note on II xxiii 37). Berkeley could easily have echoed Stillingfleet's words here, but whereas with Stillingfleet the words ring with reproach, Berkeley should have been congratulating Locke on getting as far as he had.

On the positive side, with the notion of a material substratum debunked the way is clear for Berkeley to see a particular substance such as an apple as *just* a collection of qualities. In *PC* 512 he asks:

> Qu: whether the substance of Body or any thing else, be any more than the Collection of Ideas included in that thing. Thus the substance of any particular Body is extension solidity figure. of General Body no idea.

And five entries later he says:

> I take not away substances. I ought not to be accus'd of discarding Substance out of the reasonable World. I onely reject the Philosophic sense (wch in effect is no sense) of the word substance. Ask a man never tainted with their jargon w^t he means by corporeal substance, or the substance of Body, He shall answer Bulk, Solidity & such like sensible qualitys. These I retain. the Philosophic nec quid nec quantum nec quale whereof I have no idea I discard. if a man may be said to discard that wch never had any being was never so much as imagin'd or conceiv'd.

Again Berkeley feels he can represent the vulgar here, for, as he repeats in *Pr.* 37, he takes it that so far as the vulgar are concerned the word 'substance' does just stand for a collection or group of associated sensible qualities. What he takes away *from the philosophers* is substance as that unknown and unknowable support of qualities – 'if one may be said to take away that which never had any existence, not even in the imagination'.[17]

Of course it turns out that for Berkeley sensible *qualities* are in fact *ideas* or mind-dependent entities, and this has three interesting consequences which we can outline just briefly here. In the first place it means that Berkeley has an additional and specialist argument against the notion of a material substratum. For if qualities *are* ideas and these can have no existence outside a mind it follows that there are no external accidents for the supposed material substratum without the mind to support. As he says in *Pr.* 17:

> But why should we trouble ourselves any farther, in discussing this material *substratum* or support of figure and motion, and other sensible qualities? Does it not suppose they have an existence without the mind? And is not this a direct repugnancy, and altogether inconceivable?

If matter is posited as the support of *external* qualities and all qualities are *internal* in the sense of being mind-dependent it follows (absurdly) that the unknown support has nothing to support. The second consequence is that Berkeley has to be able to give an account of what makes an apple, say, a thing, without supposing, as the plain man does perhaps suppose, that the apple is, as it were, one chunky item composed of qualities. In fact Berkeley is not very forthcoming here, but it appears that the things of which ultimately the sensible world is composed are not apples and pears, chairs and tables as the plain man might believe, nor sub-microscopic particles as the scientist would have claimed, but rather discrete mental items which *are* colours, tangibilia, sounds, smells and tastes, and which Berkeley variously terms *sensations, qualities, appearances*, and, of course, *ideas*. These are produced in us in a systematic fashion so that we *come to think of them as* belonging together or making up chunky items, though in fact they remain discrete. We shall have more to say on this later. Finally, because Berkeley holds that qualities are ideas and that ideas can exist only in a mind, he is able and unfortunately eager to make some sense of the notion of a substratum of qualities. Ideas (and thus qualities) do require the support of a substance, and this substance is not something external to the mind but rather the mind itself. Thus it turns out that philosophers are not wrong when they suppose that qualities must inhere in something. Where they go wrong is in supposing that qualities are external to the mind and that they must therefore inhere in a mysterious *something* external to the mind.

At this level, then, we must see Berkeley not as rejecting all talk about substratum-substance but rather as insisting that to be meaningful such talk must be cashed in terms of spiritual and not corporeal substance. In *Pr.* 91 for example he says:

> It were a mistake to think, that what is here said derogates in the least from the reality of things. It is acknowledged on the received

principles, that extension, motion, and in a word all sensible qualities, have need of a support, as not being able to subsist by themselves. But the objects perceived by sense, are allowed to be nothing but combinations of those qualities, and consequently cannot subsist by themselves. Thus far it is agreed on all hands. So that in denying the things perceived by sense, an existence independent of a substance, or support wherein they may exist, we detract nothing from the received opinion of their *reality*, and are guilty of no innovation in that respect. All the difference is, that according to us the unthinking beings perceived by sense, have no existence distinct from being perceived, and cannot therefore exist in any other substance, than those unextended, indivisible substances, or *spirits*, which act, and think, and perceive them. . . .

The extent to which this is opportunist and reflective of a desire to win the approval even of the Stillingfleetians if possible (cf. *PC* 700) is perhaps debatable,[18] but it remains the case that Berkeley takes very seriously the notion that many questions that are difficult and indeed unanswerable when asked about matter turn out to be unproblematic when asked about spirit. Spirit, Berkeley claims, is something we are aware of in experience, so we do have an experiential basis for our talk about it. Further, given Berkeley's doctrines we can make some sense of the notion that qualities require support. The mind, we are told, supports ideas in the sense that it *perceives* them, and of course each of us is aware of himself as a perceiving being. In this way the notion that qualities require the support of a material substratum is replaced by the central Berkeleian contention that sensible qualities (i.e. sensed ideas) cannot exist or be supposed to exist without a mind. But the story does not end here. For the feeling that qualities must somehow and in some totally mysterious way be bound together by a substratum if they are to be qualities of things can be rendered meaningful in terms of the synthesizing activity of mind whereby discrete mental items are associated together and thought of as constituting one thing.

VI

In *PC* 266 Berkeley at first wrote that he 'was sceptical at 8 years old', but either immediately or sometime after he looked at what he had written, decided that the word 'sceptical' would not do, and substituted 'distrustful'. When he made the change is unimportant, but I think it quite likely that he made it at once, for in entry 79 he had written:

> Mem. that I take notice that I do not fall in wth Sceptics Fardella etc, in y^t I make bodies to exist certainly, wch they doubt of.

The word 'sceptical' was certainly not one Berkeley wanted to apply to himself, it being associated in his mind with a particular type of doubt – in fact Pyrrhonism – which he wanted nothing to do with. His determined opposition to scepticism is enshrined in the full titles of both the *Principles* and *Dialogues* and it is reiterated throughout these works and *PC*. We shall see that his opposition to scepticism and his supposed support of the common sense outlook are in fact closely related.

Just as Bayle was aware that the ' "new" philosophers' were not sceptics, Berkeley was aware that Locke was not actually a sceptic, at least so far as the existence of bodies was concerned. It seemed to Berkeley, though, that what we have in the *Essay* is an attempt to marry certain empiricist principles with certain ontological assumptions in such a way that the tendency is bound to be towards scepticism. In a nutshell, the problem is that if the range of our knowledge is bounded by the limits of our experience and at the same time real and substantial objects are supposed to lie beyond the limits of experience, then a sceptical position is ultimately inescapable. Locke's refusal to take this problem sufficiently seriously, whether it is put down to temperament or to a laudable refusal to reject the common-sense assumption that perception does somehow inform us of real things, in no way lessens the dangers inherent in his position.

One place where Locke does seem to face up to the challenge of scepticism is in IV xi where he says:

> The notice we have by our senses of the existing of things without us, though it be not altogether so certain as our intuitive knowledge, or the deductions of our reason employed about the clear abstract ideas of our own minds; yet it is an assurance that deserves the name of *knowledge*. If we persuade ourselves that our faculties act and inform us right concerning the existence of those objects that affect them, it cannot pass for an ill-grounded confidence: for I think nobody can, in earnest, be so sceptical as to be uncertain of the existence of those things which he sees and feels. (sect. 3)

Clearly the 'things without us' are the objects which cause us to have sensations or produce ideas in our minds, so this passage amounts to a claim that the apparently unbridgeable gap between ideas and the external things can be and is bridged by the percipient. Here, and in IV ii 14 where he claims that we have 'an evidence that puts us past doubting' for the existence of things without us, Locke reveals that he has little patience with the sceptic. Whether he succeeds in answering the sceptic is of course another matter.

Now if we have in mind the problem that Berkeley sees as facing Locke the summing up on his attempts to convince us that the gap between ideas and things can be bridged must be that he fails completely. And this is so even though Locke's aims are not particularly ambitious in that, firstly, he wants to claim only that I can know the things I am confronted with now exist (and not that other things exist), and, secondly, he allows that the knowledge I have even in this restricted field falls short of other types of knowledge. The certainty I have is such that 'going beyond bare probability . . . [it] passes under the name of *knowledge*' (IV ii 14). The knowledge I have that there is something external to me now is said to fall short of the (intuitive) knowledge I have that I am affected with ideas, the (intuitive) knowledge I have that I exist as a person, and the (demonstrative) knowledge I *can* have that God exists. Basically, though, Locke fails because he never comes to grips with the special problems the Causal Theorist has to face. He is of course right to insist that the sceptic's doubts concerning the existence of objects must be in a sense unreal and that the writer, for example, cannot bring himself to feel genuine doubt about the existence of the paper he writes on. But to say this is not enough and it in no way absolves him from answering the theoretical case for scepticism, especially and particularly because that case seems to be implicit in his own position. It is because he tells us that 'the mind knows not things immediately, but only by the intervention of the ideas it has of them', and because he thinks of ideas as having a representative function, that *he* has a case to answer.

It is in a way paradoxical, then, that when Locke does face up to scepticism he almost certainly has it in mind to answer Descartes. For while Descartes, unlike Locke, did play the sceptic, and clearly worried Locke by claiming that if we relied on the senses there could be no escape from philosophical doubt, his overall position was no more sceptical than was Locke's. It is a commonplace observation, and one Berkeley found in Malebranche, that Descartes' programme of systematic doubt is more challenging than his retreat from doubt is convincing. But the case is similar with Locke to the extent that while his analysis of perception does seem to invite sceptical questions, his rejection of scepticism rests on little more than the proposition that it would be pointless for the sceptic to argue with anyone and an appeal to the fact that we all can, surely, tell the difference between, say, putting our finger in real fire and dreaming or imagining that we do the same. What Locke says here is doubtless true, but the problem Berkeley poses in *PC* 74 (above p. 22) certainly remains.

Up till now we have done little more than mention Malebranche, but his influence on the young Berkeley was considerable. Luce describes the way in which the influence worked thus:

> Many reflective scholars can remember some schoolmaster of theirs to whom they are indebted for years of solid grounding. But they remember too a personality who crossed their path perhaps after school and even after college days, and who was to them an intellectual stimulus of a higher order. Contact may have been brief, but the influence deep and strong. It was so with Berkeley, I submit. Locke taught him, but Malebranche inspired him. (Luce 2, pp. 6-7)

Possibly the case is overstated here, and we might want to say that Malebranche alarmed Berkeley rather than inspired him. Certainly while Berkeley admired Locke he was alienated by the 'fine spun metaphysics' (*Works* VIII, p. 41) of the Frenchman, and he found the central doctrine – that we do not see material things directly but only through ideas in the mind of God – 'incomprehensible' (*Pr.* 148). But in Malebranche he found the case for scepticism more nearly explicit than it was in Locke, and he could see that scepticism was as much implicit in the Cartesian tradition as it was in the science of Boyle and the philosophy of Locke.

Malebranche taught that the escape from doubt could not be accomplished as easily as Descartes had supposed. For him, as for Descartes, the senses are deceivers, and he asserts that their range is limited to what we see (the *visible* or *intelligible*) as distinct from what we behold (the *material*). The material things are said to be 'invisible'. But, against Descartes, Malebranche did not believe that the exercise of reason could enable us to escape from the scepticism implicit in this situation and to reach certainty about the existence of the material. Thus:

> ... though M. *des Cartes* has given the strongest arguments, that bare reason could furnish out, for the existence of bodies: though it be evident, that God is no deceiver, and it may be said he would really deceive us, did we deceive our selves, whilst we made a due use of our mind, and the other faculties whereof he is the author: yet it may be affirmed that the existence of matter is not yet perfectly demonstrated. For, in fine, in point of philosophy, we are to believe nothing till the evidence of it obliges us; but to make use of our liberty as much as we can; giving no greater extent to our judgments than our perceptions. Wherefore when we see bodies, we should judge only that we see them [i.e. not that we are beholding anything], and that these *visible* or *intelligible bodies* actually exist: but why must we judge positively there is a *material world*, without us like the *intelligible world* we perceive? (Tome II, p. 122)

We might compare the later part of this with what Locke says in IV iv 3 and Berkeley's note in *PC* 74. Had Malebranche left the matter here he would have been a sceptic with regard to the existence of the material world. But he in fact draws back from the brink and asserts that if we are to transcend the sceptical position it must be on the basis of that liberty to believe which is the essence of faith.

We can probably sum up on Berkeley's attitude to all this by saying that he was appalled by the extent to which scepticism was allowed its head, unconvinced by the half-hearted pulling on the reins at the end, and disturbed by the cool disregard for what he thought of as common sense. But stressing the features of Malebranche's position which Berkeley found distasteful and absurd – and he held that 'upon the whole there are no principles more fundamentally opposite than his and mine' (*Dialogues*, ii, 214) – does not mean that we have to deny that he was influenced by Malebranche in a positive way. There was indeed enough in common between the doctrines of the *Principles* and those of the *Recherche* to encourage early critics to see Berkeley as a disciple of Malebranche.[19] The really fundamental point here, though, is that it seemed to Berkeley that the role Malebranche gave to the material was such that there remained no good reason for wanting to believe in it. For not only were material things said to be invisible, they were allowed no causal role in the production of ideas in our minds. The problem of *how* changes in the external world could bring about events in the mind had been 'solved' by a denial that they did, and these changes were said to be merely the *occasions* of God's introducing ideas into our minds. In brief, then, by minimizing the role of the material and at the same time stressing the role of God, Malebranche suggested to Berkeley how he might give an account of perception and what we perceive which gave due prominence to God and dispensed with material things altogether.

On Bayle we do not need to say much more. In the two articles already referred to he made it clear that scepticism was implicit in what the philosophers were saying, and if Berkeley was not aware of the dangers before reading Bayle he certainly would have been afterwards. Bayle sees the new philosophers as late and potentially very radical representatives of the ancient Pyrrhonian tradition, who escape from scepticism only by failing to follow their arguments through to the logical conclusion. That Bayle makes reference to Fardella, coupling his name with that of Malebranche, may be enough to account for Berkeley's one mention of that philosopher in *PC* 79.[20]

VII

Thus Berkeley was fully aware of the sceptical tendency implicit in the Cartesian as in the empiricist approach to philosophy, as well as in the thinking of the scientists. And he located the root cause exactly. The point is nowhere better made than in *PC* 606 where he says:

> The supposition that things are distinct from Ideas takes away all real Truth, & consequently brings in a Universal Scepticism, since all our knowledge & contemplation is confin'd barely to our own Ideas.

The point can be made in various ways. To tie it in with our discussion of the Causal Theory: if the external objects are causes and we are aware only of effects, scepticism about the existence of the external objects is bound to follow. To tie it in with our discussion of qualities: if it is allowed that there are external objects and that these have qualities, then if we are aware only of ideas we can never know which qualities should be attributed to a given object. And to tie it in with Malebranche: if sense experience informs us only of the visible or intelligible then scepticism concerning the existence of the material is again unavoidable. As Berkeley says in *Pr.* 20:

> ... if there were external bodies, it is impossible we should ever come to know it; and if there were not, we might have the very same reasons to think there were that we have now.

His basic point is thus that if we adhere to a three-term theory of perception and allow for the perceiver, his ideas *and* external objects we will not be able to answer the sceptic's challenge.

Berkeley's solution to the problem is in essence staggeringly simple. He holds that if the root cause of scepticism is to be found in the supposition that real things are distinct from ideas, opposition to scepticism must rest on the contrary supposition, viz. that ideas and things are to be identified. The tactic involves pushing the sceptic's case to the limit and denying that there is a material world lying behind what we actually experience when we perceive. But having done this Berkeley can turn the tables on the sceptic by claiming that there is no longer any case for scepticism. The truth as he sees it is that there is only one world, a world which our senses inform us of and which is made up of ideas, and that this world is the real world. It has been thought unreal only by those who have made the mistake of supposing that there is *another* world beyond the limit of experience and of which the world as we know it in immediate experience can be only a shadow. In *Pr.* 40 he says:

> That what I see, hear and feel doth exist, that is to say, is perceived by me, I no more doubt than I do of my own being. But I do not see how the testimony of sense can be alleged, as a proof for the existence of any thing, which is not perceived by sense. We are not for having any man turn *sceptic*, and disbelieve his senses; on the contrary we give them all the stress and assurance imaginable; nor are there any principles more opposite to scepticism, than those we have laid down. ...

Perhaps the neatest way of illustrating what Berkeley does is to see him making two amendments to a simple chart which refers to the situation philosophy was reaching:

	Perceivable	*Existent*	*Real*
Sensible world	✓	✓	✗
Material world	✗	?	✓

And here we have on the one hand all those things we are aware of in sense experience, which in an obvious sense exist, but which are supposed to represent, rather than to be, things in a real world. On the other hand, ontological priority is given to a world of material objects which is supposed to lie on the dark side of a veil of perception so that the sceptic can very easily make a case for doubting its existence. Berkeley's case against this analysis involves essentially two changes. Thus:

	Perceivable	*Existent*	*Real*
Sensible world	✓	✓	✓
Material world	✗	✗	✗

Making the first change Berkeley goes further than the sceptic, and rather than doubting the existence of the material world he positively denies its existence. But making the second change he claims that it is the sensible world, a world composed of ideas, that is real. Berkeley believed that it was very important indeed to see that he was making the two points, and that many of his critics misunderstood his position simply because they saw him as making only the first. Taking this line they could represent him as denying the existence of real things.

The examination of Berkeley's case for this analysis will take up much of this book. At this stage, though, we can return to the problem outlined at the beginning of this chapter and clarify the issue as to how it was that Berkeley was able to think of himself as the champion of common-sense views. We can also indicate that his critics were quite right to be suspicious of this claim.

In summary, then, we have seen that there was a tendency for philosophers to distinguish between the-world-as-it-appears-to-us on the one hand and the-world-as-it-is on the other, and to make this distinction in such a radical form that they appeared to be thinking not of one world but of two. We have also seen how the first of these worlds can be thought of as being made up of mind-dependent ideas, while the second can be thought of as being made up of things having original qualities, these perhaps inhering in a material substratum. Now it seemed to Berkeley that in positing two worlds the philosophers were not only inviting scepticism, they were departing from the common sense convictions of ordinary men. The ordinary man believes that, when he opens his eyes and look or sniffs and smells, what he is aware of is quite simply characteristics of the real world. He does not believe that what he is aware of are shadowy representations of the real. In *PC* 740 Berkeley says:

> We must wth the Mob place certainty in the senses.

And his claim to represent the vulgar is based firmly in his recommendation of a two-term theory of perception according to which there is just the perceiver and the real, sensible world he perceives, and no material world which is unfortunately placed so that it is forever beyond our perceptual grasp.

It is in just these terms that Berkeley wants us to evaluate his dispute with the materialist. In the *Dialogues* Philonous asks Hylas to open his eyes to the beauties of nature:

> Look! are not the fields covered with a delightful verdure? Is there not something in the woods and groves, in the rivers and clear springs that soothes, that delights, that transports the soul? At the prospect of the wide and deep ocean, or some huge mountain whose top is lost in the clouds, or of an old gloomy forest, are not our minds filled with a pleasing horror? Even in rocks and deserts, is there not an agreeable wildness? How sincere a pleasure is it to behold the natural beauties of the earth! (ii, 210)

And he concludes:

> What treatment then do those philosophers deserve, who would deprive these noble and delightful scenes of all reality? How should those principles be entertained, that lead us to think all the visible beauty of the creation a false imaginary glare? (ii, 211)

It is in a similar spirit that Luce examines the buttercup he holds in his hand. He looks back to the days before he studied philosophy and before he had heard of matter as an inaccessible reality, and he sees Berkeley as doing justice to his common sense conviction that perception affords him direct acquaintance with the buttercup, the real thing. We might add that as Berkeley saw it the denial that colours as we see them are genuine qualities of the real things, that smells, tastes and sounds form part of the reality of nature, was closely linked with the absurd doctrine that perception is never acquaintance with the real.

He felt that his attack on materialism should be supported by the masses and that his immaterialism amounted to a defence of common sense.

Clearly, though, this is only half the story, and Berkeley is going too far when he says that he sides *in all things* with the mob. We could easily bring this out by adding a column to each of the charts. For the mob does not believe, as Berkeley did believe, that the real world is mind-dependent and that sensible objects can exist only so long as they are perceived. Indeed on this point the materialists seem to come off rather better than Berkeley *vis-à-vis* common sense, for their real world does exist when it is not perceived and it has an existence quite independent of the perceiving mind. In asserting that the fields covered with a delightful verdure are made up of ideas which can exist only in a mind Berkeley seems to be departing very radically at least from the common consensus.

The truth is that Berkeleian immaterialism has two sides to it. It involves a denial that the real world is forever hidden from us and an assertion that what we perceive is the real world. But it also involves the claim that the real world is made up of mind-dependent ideas. Looking at the first side we can see Berkeley as representing the vulgar. Looking at the other side this becomes more difficult. And of course really he knows all along that his notions are going to bring him into conflict with ordinary views and that he cannot disassociate himself altogether from other philosophers and the learned. Thus in a key passage towards the end of the *Dialogues* he has Philonous say:

> I do not pretend to be a setter-up of *new notions*. My endeavours tend only to unite and place in a clearer light that truth, which was before shared between the vulgar and the philosophers: the former being of opinion, that *those things they immediately perceive are the real things*; and the latter, that *the things immediately perceived, are ideas which exist only in the mind*. Which two notions put together, do in effect constitute the substance of what I advance. (iii, 262)

There are two supposed truths here. By putting the emphasis on his acceptance of the first proposition Berkeley can present himself as the champion of common sense. But by putting the emphasis on the latter the critics can, without *ignoratio elenchi*, see him as the most outrageous affronter of it.

CHAPTER THREE

The Philosophical Approach

'But, say you, it sounds very harsh to say we eat
and drink ideas, and are clothed with ideas.'
(*Pr.* 38)

I

Accepting Dr. Luce's first canon of Berkeleian exegesis, which is that 'the *Principles* is the primary source' (Luce 9, p. 76), we turn now to that work. The work divides naturally into three main parts: the first (sects. 1-33) arguing for Berkeley's theistic immaterialism, the second (34-84) envisaging and dealing with a numbered series of possible objections, and the third (85-end) taking, as Berkeley says, 'a view of our tenets in their consequences'. Clearly, then, the first thirty-three sections are crucial, and just fourteen pages of the standard edition provide not only the purported justification for the basic claim that bodies are mind-dependent, but also observations about causality, the mind, and God. In this chapter and the three following we shall not be concerned with all these matters, and initially at any rate we shall give in to the temptation to concentrate on the argumentation of the first six sections leading up to the conclusion in the last of them that:

> Some truths there are so near and obvious to the mind, that a man need only open his eyes to see them. Such I take this important one to be, to wit, that all the choir of heaven and furniture of the earth, in a word all those bodies which compose the mighty frame of the world, have not any subsistence without a mind, that their being is to be perceived or known . . .

It is with something approaching a state of shock that the reader finds it suggested that the basic case for immaterialism has been made before a thousand words have been got through.

From a tactical point of view this effect probably works to Berkeley's advantage. By the time he has reached sect. 6 the reader will almost certainly be quivering with objections, but the attack on cherished notions is completed so quickly and confidently that he is likely to feel at the very least discomforted so that his response is made in a spirit tinged with desperation and even defeatism. Berkeley would state the case by saying that, though the reader might want to think of himself as having been unfairly attacked before his defences were prepared, what has actually happened is that he has been exposed to 'the obvious tho' amazing truth' (*PC* 279), which truth is essentially simple and, to the unprejudiced mind, undeniable. The dealing with objections is, then, in Berkeley's view, largely the dispelling of the prejudices and misapprehensions which prevent people from seeing the obvious.

In fact, however, the first six sections are not at all easy, and the argumentation in them is far from straightforward. The difficulty arises partly from Berkeley's terminology, and especially from his use of the term 'idea', partly because he seems to expect us to find certain supposed but somehow unlikely truths inescapable (the word 'evident' occurs twice, 'manifest' once, and 'obvious' once in these sections) without sufficient argument for their truth,[1] and partly because, instead of just one argument clearly designed to make his central contention seem well founded to the reader, there appear to be three approaches to immaterialism none of which does quite the job expected of it. For convenience we can refer to these approaches as, first, *the philosophical approach*, second, *the approach from ordinary usage*, and third, *the psychological approach*. As a rough guide, the first dominates the first two sections, the second is contained in sect. 3, and the third is proposed in sect. 5 and again in sect. 6. It is not at all obvious either what the relationship between these three approaches is or what Berkeley took it to be.

A good starting point, though, is an argument which is contained in sect. 4 and which can be set out as follows:

(1) Sensible objects are the things we perceive by sense,
(2) the things we perceive by sense are ideas,
(3) ideas cannot exist unperceived,
∴(4) sensible objects cannot exist unperceived.

And this argument, if accepted, would provide justification for the claim made for sensible objects at the end of the preceding section, viz. that 'their *esse* is *percipi*, nor is it possible they should have any existence, out of the minds or thinking things which perceive them'. We will stop with this argument for a while.

The first point we can make about it is that, as so often with Berkeley's arguments, it is, by virtue of its formal structure, patently valid. But clearly the conclusion goes against what ordinary men and most philosophers believe and have believed and thus against common consensus if not common sense. And of course really Berkeley was under no illusion about this. As we have noted, the truth which he took to be 'obvious' he recognized to be also 'amazing', and to reinforce the point we can note that in the Preface to the *Principles* he affirms that his truth runs 'contrary to the prejudices of mankind', and that here in sect. 4 he refers to 'an opinion strangely prevailing amongst men' which is in fact the contrary of his own conclusion. Men hold, he admits, that 'sensible objects have an existence natural or real, distinct from their being perceived'. His tendency to exaggerate the extent to which he agrees with the vulgar has always to be seen against this background.[2]

Objecting to the conclusion, then, it is incumbent upon the plain man or the philosopher to find fault with one or more of the premisses which lead up to it. And it will not take much detective work to determine where suspicion is likely to fall first. A convenient way of approaching this is to refer to the key passage already quoted from the end of the *Dialogues* where the Berkeleian sees the truth he has to convey as resulting from a synthesis of two elements, one appreciated by the vulgar, viz. 'that *those things they immediately perceive are the real things*', and one appreciated by the philosophers, viz. 'that *the things immediately perceived, are ideas which exist only in the mind*'. The clear implication is that philosophers have failed to appreciate the first, which is surely intended as a formulation of premiss (1) in the argument we are considering, while the plain man has failed to appreciate the second, which can be seen as combining premisses (2) and (3). And if this is so we should expect the philosophers Berkeley has in mind to counter the argument by objecting to premiss (1), while the layman should object to one or both of premisses (2) and (3).

If we allow Hospam (the non-philosopher holder of the 'opinion strangely prevailing amongst men') to represent the plain man here, we can agree that it is indeed the premisses indicated that will strike him as being suspicious. For Berkeley has already made it clear that by 'sensible objects' he means both things, such as houses, mountains and rivers, and the qualities of things. And this being so Hospam will regard premiss (1) as being completely obvious, while the conclusion drawable from premisses (2) and (3) alone – viz. that the things we perceive by sense cannot exist unperceived – will strike him as being quite as odd as the conclusion from the argument as a whole. Going further, he may well observe that what seems to him particularly odd is the use of the term 'idea', which functions as the middle term in the argument from premisses (2) and (3). He may note that, in sect. 4 anyway, Berkeley seems to be using 'idea' as a synonym for 'sensation', and given this he may well think that the root of the trouble lies with premiss (2). For combining this with the first premiss we get the odd conclusion that sensible objects (e.g. houses) are ideas (i.e. sensations). And Hospam will not want to allow this, being quite clear in his own mind that while houses, mountains and rivers can all be perceived they are certainly *not* sensations. You can *have* sensations, but you can't *see*, *smell* or *taste* them, and you can't build them, climb them or swim in them either. Finally, having pointed the finger at premiss (2), he may well observe that premiss (3) comes near to asserting the truism that there cannot be sensations without a sentient being actually having them, though it cannot be cleared of suspicion entirely in that it does suggest, rather oddly, that we *perceive* sensations rather than *have* them.

This I think is the sort of response the articulate man in the street is likely to make to the argument of sect. 4 and it is the sort of response Berkeley must have expected from him, but from the philosophers he had reason to expect a different response. There is, however, a difficulty here concerning terminology. As Berkeley saw the position, the materialists were committed to the view that there are real objects (including houses, mountains and rivers) which lie on the dark side of the veil of perception and which we don't directly perceive. But they were also committed to the view that there are ideas which we do perceive. It will be remembered that in *PC* 74 he attributes to them the notion that the mind perceives 'onely the impressions made upon its brain or rather the ideas attending those impressions'. So far as premiss (1) of the argument of sect. 4 is concerned the problem is whether it is the real objects or the ideas that are to be termed *sensible*. We must look at the two possibilities from the materialist's point of view. First, then, we saw earlier that in *Essay* II i 3 at any rate, sensible objects for Locke were those objects our senses are conversant about which produce ideas in our minds, and if it is allowed that we perceive only the ideas then this must mean that we do not perceive sensible objects. So given *this* usage, the materialist will reject premiss (1). The other possibility is that the materialist will say that because we don't perceive the real objects directly, these are not to be thought of as *sensible*. On this view ideas will be the only sensible objects. Now given *this* interpretation the materialist *could* accept the premiss and indeed let the argument go through, for the conclusion will be only that sensible objects (i.e. ideas) cannot exist unperceived, and of course the materialist never thought they could. But he must be careful here. For Berkeley has made it clear that he does not regard his conclusion as being an uncontroversial one concerning just ideas or sensations, but rather a contentious one concerning houses, mountains and rivers. So the materialist should interpret premiss (1) as making a claim about his external objects, and this being so he must regard it as false.

Given that the materialist is going to reject premiss (1) *in the sense that Berkeley intends it* anyway, this terminological problem may seem completely trivial. But we should be alert for ambiguities. Certainly Berkeley's materialist when he faces up to the argument of sect. 4 should get quite clear in his own mind how he is going to use the term 'sensible'. Very simply, if he overlooks the fact that premiss (1) refers to things like houses, mountains and rivers and decides to accept it on the ground that the sensible objects here must be ideas, he should not forget this when he comes to the conclusion and assume that he has been forced to admit that sensible objects including external things such as houses, mountains and rivers cannot exist unperceived. This is a warning Berkeley's materialist should take very seriously. It has been argued, by David Givner, that the key to Berkeley's strategy will be found in an ambiguous use of the term 'sensible'.

The important point to grasp now, though, is that just as the materialist and the plain man will have different reasons for regarding the argument of sect. 4 as unsatisfactory, so Berkeley has to fight on two fronts if he is to persuade the layman and the philosopher to accept his doctrine that the real table cannot exist unperceived. He has to convince the materialists that *'those things they immediately perceive are the real things'*, and he has to convince the rest of his readers of what the materialists are supposed already to accept, viz. that *'the things immediately perceived, are ideas which exist only in the mind'*.

The fact that there are two quite different positions opposed to Berkeley's is extremely important, but it can be obscured by the fact that the two positions can be stated in verbally identical terms. Thus we can attribute to the plain man *and* the philosopher the view that houses, mountains and rivers 'have an existence distinct from their being perceived', but if we take this step we must make it clear that the two camps interpret this claim differently. Basically, the plain man does believe that he perceives things like tables (and this is why he accepts premiss (1)), but he also believes, contrary to Berkeley, that these real and substantial things are such that they can continue to exist when they are not perceived by him or anyone else. But against this, and as Berkeley saw, there was a tendency for philosophers to think we *never* perceive the real objects, but only mind-dependent representations of them in sensation. Thus the plain man certainly accepts that the real book or table is perceivable, though he holds that it exists when it is not perceived and so to that extent has an existence distinct from being perceived, and only the philosopher would be tempted to the view that the real and substantial book and the real and substantial table are not perceivable at all. It is the philosopher who adheres to what Berkeley thinks of as the *reverse* of the *Esse-percipi* principle (*PC* 304 and 311), which Luce takes to be that *esse est non-percipi* (Luce 6, p. 9). When I refer to *the philosophical standpoint* I shall have in mind the view that real things are neither perceived nor perceivable, and when I refer to *the plain man's standpoint* the view will be that things like tables are sometimes perceived (and always in principle perceivable) although they are not always actually perceived.

II

That it is important to keep the two standpoints opposed to Berkeley's in mind throughout is, I suppose, obvious. But it is especially important because of the idealist's tendency to talk as if either he or the representative realist must be in the right about the status of chairs, tables and the like. Consider for example the following passage in which Hospers makes the case for idealism:

> ... if an idealist were asked, 'Are there physical objects or aren't there?' he would reply, 'That depends on the sense you mean. If you mean in the realist's sense, as something unknown and un-

knowable, no. Even to assert that they do is, in my opinion, to contradict yourself.[3] But if you mean in the ordinary sense, in which chairs and tables are *experienced* entities, then by all means yes: they exist *as* sensations.' (p. 394)

Hospers is here concerned only to put up a case for examination, but he certainly does justice to the tactics of the idealist. Note how one of the options facing us is given a sentence all to itself – physical objects may be 'unknown and unknowable'. In the final sentence, though, the idealist blurs the distinction between the plain man's view and his own by suggesting that in pressing the claim that physical objects are sensations which can exist only when actually perceived he is supporting and espousing the *ordinary* view, viz. that 'chairs and tables are *experienced* entities'.

Another passage reads:

But do only sensations exist? Don't *things* exist? It is indeed a peculiarity of language, the idealist replies; but it only *sounds* strange. Actually idealism comes far nearer to common sense than does the representative realist's position. Whatever common sense means by words like 'table' and 'chair', it does *not* mean something unknown and unknowable; it means something *experienced*. Now, only sensations are experienced. Thus chairs and tables are sensations; it's as simple as that. True, common sense would say we know things, not sensations; in fact, most people wouldn't even know what the word 'sensation' (in this sense) means. People do not realize, however, what the difficulties in realism are; once they are made aware that *things* are unknowable in realism, they would become idealists; for people are sure of one thing: that they *are* acquainted with tables and trees, woods and fields. If to be knowable they must be sensations, then very well, they are sensations.

What is interesting is the tactics deployed in this passage. It is true that it is claimed (twice) that we are aware only of sensations, but we have been given no *reason* why we should accept this, and indeed no reason has been given before this in the relevant section except that the idealist does not wish to quarrel with the representative realist on *this* issue. All the stress is on 'the difficulties in realism'. Now when the idealist talks of 'the difficulties in realism' he means to refer (as is clear from the context) to the difficulties involved in *representative* realism. But if the ordinary man is a *direct* realist – believing that sense perception affords direct acquaintance with objects that can exist unperceived – he will certainly not be persuaded to become an idealist merely by being shown that insuperable difficulties are involved in a view he does not hold. He is, after all, opposed to both the idealist *and* the representative realist. The point is, of course, that the idealist may be able to provide the most admirable arguments to show that it is absurd to suppose that physical objects are unknowable, but that these arguments need not disturb the plain man at all. What the plain man needs to be convinced of is that there are insuperable difficulties in *direct* realism. What would disturb him is the revelation that nothing other than sensations is ever known.

The very next paragraph again illustrates the tendency to take only two standpoints seriously:

> Tables and trees, then, in the sense of complexes of sensations, do exist and are experienced. For them to exist *is* for them to be experienced. *Esse est percipi* (to be is to be perceived). Apart from experience, they have no existence; in fact, as we have seen, to assert that they exist but are never experienced, as realists must say, is to assert something self-contradictory . . .

Once again the supposed absurdity of *representative* realism is appealed to to buttress the case for idealism. The alleged fact that it is contradictory to suppose that physical objects are never perceived is brought in to support the claim that they exist only when perceived. Apparently we should not take seriously the popular view that physical objects can be, but need not be, perceived.

To account for this tendency to ignore the plain man's standpoint we need to note that idealism was developed in reaction to representative realism when this theory was found wanting. Thus to understand Berkeley's position we have to see him as examining a theory which contained two components – (a) the claim that physical objects are not directly perceivable, and (b) the claim that we perceive only mind-dependent ideas. He became convinced that (a) was absurd and was thus left with (b). If, then, we see Berkeley as debating within a philosophical tradition we can say that he feels he can take for granted the accepted view that perception acquaints us only with ideas, and thus assumes that if he can show that there are no unknown and unknowable external objects his opponents (the representative realists) will have to accept that after all only ideas exist. Of course the materialist will at first be inclined to suppose that he is being forced to the view that there are no real things (cf. *Pr.* 34), but Berkeley believes that this is too hasty. The proper view is that real things are complexes of sensations or ideas.

The representative realist's position is reflected in the following diagram where we have a dot for the mind, a broken circle for the ideas perceived by the mind, and an outer circle for the external objects which the mind does not perceive:

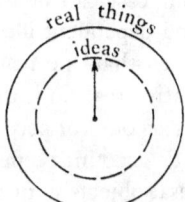

Perhaps most students who have sat through a course on the Empiricists will be familiar with this. Berkeley is seen as in effect erasing the outer circle and then claiming that there is no reason why the mind-dependent ideas we are left with should not be thought of as making up real objects.[4]

There is a lot to be said for interpreting Berkeley in this way, but if we do there are two points we need to make. Firstly, it does seem that the plain man has some excuse for thinking that his position is totally untouched by what is going on. If the representative realist is committed to (a) and (b) and Berkeley can show that (a) is absurd, then it may be that the representative realist will remain committed to (b). But as the plain man takes (a) and (b) to be equally false a demonstration from Berkeley that (a) is indeed false will not incline the plain man to believe that he must commit himself to (b). As we said earlier, it is premiss (2) of the argument of sect. 4 that he will need to be convinced of. It may of course be that Berkeley does have arguments which should convince the plain man that (b) is true.

The second point is that it is not obvious that once the representative realist has spotted that his theory is defective he should regard himself as still committed to the view that we perceive only ideas. The principle operative here is that if I hold two beliefs (A) and (B), and I hold (B) partly because I am convinced of (A), then if (A) is shown to be incoherent I shall have some excuse for wanting to reconsider (B). Even if I have supposed myself to have some independent arguments for (B) I may want to reconsider these in the light of the changed circumstances. If, then, the representative realist is convinced of (b) – the claim that we perceive only ideas – partly *because* he is committed to (a) – the claim that physical objects are not directly perceivable – proof that (a) won't do gives him a reason for having a fresh look at (b). His position now will be similar to that of the plain man. He will want to satisfy himself that given there are no unknown and unknowable external objects a strong case can be made for supposing that the things we perceive are mind-dependent ideas.

Now we have already seen that one reason why philosophers have been attracted to representative realism is that they have supposed that acceptance of the scientist's account of perception in terms of processes requires this. The scientist's account seemed to suggest *both* that we cannot be aware of the causal objects with which the processes originate *and* that we perceive only what is produced in our minds as a result of the processes. So it might well be thought that given the notion of unperceived causal objects turns out to be an incoherent one then we have a good reason for taking a close look at the rest of the story. If there are no unperceived causal objects then there are no processes originating with such objects and there are no effects for us to perceive. We need to make a fresh start.

To repeat, it may well be (though it may well not be) that there are strong independent arguments to justify the claim that we perceive only mind-dependent entities. But to the extent that Berkeley can be seen as reaching his standpoint by deleting one item in the Causal Theorist's catalogue there would seem to be some case for saying that he reaches his position only because he fails to spot the really fundamental weakness in his opponent's theory. As we noted in the last chapter, the basic mistake made by the Causal Theorist is that of supposing that the end result of the process described by the scientist must be the perception of an entity quite distinct from the causal object. In fact, we said, the scientist must be seen as purporting to explain not how we perceive things produced in our minds by objects but, rather, how we perceive the causal objects. From the scientist's point of view, and as we found Don Locke saying, 'what we perceive is the thing, whatever it is, that comes at the beginning'.

What happens is that misunderstanding of what the scientist is doing leads the Causal Theorist to make two related mistakes – first the mistake of supposing that we cannot be acquainted with the external objects, and second that of supposing that we are acquainted only with effects in the mind.

Of course it may well be that Berkeley is right when he says that it is absurd to suppose there are unknown and unknowable external objects and that he thus makes a valid point against the Causal Theorist. But it also seems to be the case that the really fundamental weakness is the one we have indicated. Now if we make the mistake of supposing with Berkeley that the really important issue is that concerning the claim about unperceivable objects, and fail to spot the more basic error, it may indeed seem that criticism of the Causal Theory leaves us just with perceivers and sensations existing in their minds. But if we concentrate on what is fundamentally wrong with the theory and remember that it rests on 'a gross, and implausible, misrepresentation' of the scientific enterprise, we will come to a quite different conclusion. Very simply, we will find ourselves left with the common sense assumption that perception is two-term, involving the perceiver and what he perceives, but with no reason for supposing that what the perceiver perceives is mind-dependent. Hospers says:

> Idealism builds on the basis of the theory of representative realism and is most easily made plausible with reference to it. Assuming the main contentions of representative realism, idealism modifies it in one important respect: it denies that there are external physical objects to cause our sensations. (p. 391)

The point we are making is that the really radical criticism of the Causal Theory does not leave us with just sensations, and that the idealist needs to show that there are quite independent grounds for believing that what we perceive exists only in the mind.

III

Consideration of what I have called *the approach from ordinary usage* and *the psychological approach*, both of which are concerned with the meaning of 'exist', must wait for later chapters, and in this chapter we will look at the tricky first two sections of the *Principles* which suggest what I have called *the philosophical approach* to immaterialism. First we will have a general look at the argumentation in these sections and then we will say something about particular problems of interpretation.

The ground for seeing these sections as containing a philosophical approach to immaterialism is that, instead of arguing for the premiss we have supposed the philosophers (but not the vulgar) would accept, Berkeley takes it as 'evident' in a passage which was without doubt designed to win immediate acceptance from the Lockian. Thus:

> It is evident to any one who takes a survey of the objects of human knowledge, that they are either ideas actually imprinted on the senses, or else such as are perceived by attending to the passions and operations of the mind, or lastly ideas formed by help of memory and imagination, either compounding, dividing, or barely representing those originally perceived in the aforesaid ways.

Clearly this is a philosopher writing for philosophers, or at least for those apprised of and sympathetic to as much as was generally agreed amongst philosophers committed to the new way of ideas. While our plain man will presumably feel rather lost at this stage we can usefully compare this opening with the following from Locke's *Essay*:

> The understanding seems to me not to have the least glimmering of any ideas which it doth not receive from one of these two [sensation or reflection]. *External objects* furnish the mind with the ideas of sensible qualities, which are all those different perceptions they produce in us; and *the mind* furnishes the understanding with ideas of its own operations. These, when we have taken a full survey of them, and their several modes, combinations, and relations, we shall find to contain all our whole stock of ideas; and that we have nothing in our minds which did not come in one of these two ways. (II i 5)

Quite deliberately, as I believe, Berkeley echoes this, seeking for a statement he believes can win assent from the representative realist and proposing what is basically the Lockian starting point in very nearly the Lockian way.

This sort of opening was probably planned at quite an early stage, and if this is so we can make good sense of *PC* 571, an entry which can very tentatively be dated as having been written around March 1708. Here Berkeley writes:

> Mem: To begin the 1st Book not with mention of Sensation & Reflection but instead of those to use perception or thought in general.

The word Luce takes to be 'those' he admits is quite illegible and he suggests it could even be 'reflection'. This is tempting, but in any case we can certainly see Berkeley as at one stage intending to start the *Principles* with the Lockian distinction between sensation and reflection, and even as having drafted a suitable opening, and then as deciding on a subtle change so that in the published version there is no use of the term 'reflection', but instead the reference to objects *perceived* 'by attending to the passions and operations of the mind'. Earlier still, in entry 378, he had set down the bare bones of arguments which, he says, 'must be proposd shorter & more separate in the Treatise', and here he starts with two axioms derived from Locke, claiming that (1) all significant words stand for ideas and (2) all knowledge is about our ideas. Ideas are then divided into those coming 'from within' and the sensations coming 'from without'. Here too it is plain that Berkeley intends starting from Lockian principles.

Of course there is one important difference between the first sentence of the *Principles* and the passage we have quoted from the *Essay*, and this is that while the passage from Locke refers to 'external objects', Berkeley makes no mention of these. The omission is crucial and entirely deliberate. Berkeley does not *say* at this stage that there are no outward objects in the Lockian sense, his approach is more subtle than that. Rather he neglects to mention them and proceeds without reference to them, leaving it until later and (supposedly) after he has established his own position to consider and dispose of the suggestion that as well as ideas there might be material objects hidden behind them. The fact is that the first sentence of sect. 1 can be seen as embodying Locke's starting point but without Locke's presupposition of the existence of outward objects, and Berkeley is in effect preparing us both for his own development of this starting point and for his negative thesis that if the objects of the understanding are what Locke says they are then there can be no room for claims about external things.

We have seen how the opening of sect. 1 introduces three classes of objects of knowledge, but at this stage it is the 'ideas actually imprinted on the senses' that concern Berkeley. He continues by considering the sorts of objects that are imprinted on the various senses:

> By sight I have the ideas of light and colours with their several degrees and variations. By touch I perceive, for example, hard and soft, heat and cold, motion and resistance, and of all these more and less either as to quantity or degree. Smelling furnishes me with odours; the palate with tastes, and hearing conveys sounds to the mind in all their variety of tone and composition.

The continuation becomes more explicitly Berkeleian. Things, he tells us, are *collections* of such ideas:

> And as several of these are observed to accompany each other, they come to be marked by one name, and so to be reputed as one thing. Thus, for example, a certain colour, taste, smell, figure and consistence having been observed to go together, are accounted one distinct thing, signified by the name *apple*. Other collections of ideas constitute a stone, a tree, a book, and the like sensible things . . .

In sect. 2 he tells us that ideas cannot exist without a mind or unperceived (and this is premiss (3) of the argument of sect. 4), so it seems we have to conclude that the apple, stone, tree and book exist only in the mind or when perceived. As Flew notes, 'at the very beginning of *The Principles of Human Knowledge* Berkeley lays down a Lockean principle; from which even before the end of the first paragraph he has already drawn a peculiarly Berkeleyan conclusion' (Flew 2, p. 339).

Obviously there is a lot in the first two paragraphs that needs explaining, but it strikes one immediately that as they stand they are not going to convince anybody, and that the Lockian *and* the vulgar are going to have objections to the claim that things like apples are simply collections of mind-dependent ideas. The Lockian objection will be the one Berkeley envisages at the beginning of sect. 8:

> But say you, though the ideas themselves do not exist without the mind, yet there may be things like them whereof they are copies or resemblances, which things exist without the mind, in an unthinking substance.[5]

Anticipating this objection Berkeley must expect the Lockian to insist that things like apples are without the mind and that they are certainly not collections of ideas. Ideas and collections of ideas do exist only in the mind or when perceived, but external objects, or real things, do not. The plain man's objection will be that if, as he suspects, admitting that something is an *idea* involves recognizing it as mind-dependent, then it is certainly not obvious to him that sense perception acquaints us with ideas, or that things like apples are collections of ideas. In short, the materialist has so far been given no reason for accepting premiss (1) of the argument of sect. 4, and the plain man has been given no reason for accepting premisses (2) and (3). The materialists can still deny that '*those things they immediately perceive are the real things*' and the vulgar have been given no ground at all for supposing that '*the things immediately perceived, are ideas which exist only in the mind*'.

IV

Although our main concern at present is with the objects of sense perception we should perhaps digress at this point to look at two questions which have been raised concerning the objects Berkeley says we perceive 'by attending to the passions and operations of the mind'. We will return to our main theme in section V. The two questions are these. In the first place we want to know just what objects it is supposed we do perceive when we attend to the passions and operations of the mind. And in the second place, it is necessary to ask whether these objects are supposed to be *ideas*.

The answer to the first of these questions I would have thought obvious, but as an incorrect answer has been given it may be as well to come to the right solution by way of criticism of the wrong one. Luce gives the answer I take to be incorrect when he says:

> It is clear to me that the objects we perceive 'by attending to the passions and operations of the mind' are ourselves, other finite spirits, and God. These objects, together with ideas, make up the full tale of objects studied in the *Principles*, and Berkeley could not possibly omit any of them from his opening 'survey'. It is a roundabout way of saying, what is said clearly later, that there are two main types of knowable objects, and only two – spirits and ideas. (Luce 5, p. 39)

But this will not do for the simple reason that the objects we are concerned with here, whatever we may decide Berkeley means to refer to, are covered by the survey of the objects of human knowledge in sect. 1, while spirit is introduced in sect. 2 as something existing 'besides all that endless variety of ideas or objects of knowledge'. Minds or spirits are supposed to be entities additional to the objects dealt with in sect. 1, so it cannot be supposed that they are covered by the survey.

Nor is it difficult to decide what objects Berkeley does want to place in the second of the three classes. For the objects here are, rather obviously, just the passions and operations of the mind. Though his terminology has changed in the interim, Berkeley is following the line of approach he had planned when he penned PC 378. After the two propositions already mentioned he continues:

3 All ideas come from without or from within.
4 If from without it must be by the senses & they are call'd sensations.
5 If from within they are the operations of the mind & are called thoughts.

Basically the occupants of the first class of objects of knowledge referred to in sect. 1 are *sensations*, while the occupants of the second class are *thoughts*. When Berkeley refers to *passions* he has in mind things like love, hatred, joy and grief (the list he gives at the end of sect. 1), while when he refers to *operations* he has in mind such things as willing, imagining and remembering (the list he gives in sect. 2). It is quite true that the mind for Berkeley is something we know in and through its activities, but it remains the case that it is the passions and operations of the mind he wants to include in the second class of objects of knowledge.

Luce himself gives the clue as to how he came temporarily to overlook the obvious answer and to make the mistake he did when he says that Berkeley 'could not possibly omit' any of the objects he regarded as knowable from the opening survey, for I take it that Luce has moved from the arguable claim that Berkeley *should* not have omitted the reference to the false claim that he *could* not and *did* not. So perhaps it behoves us to consider why Berkeley did not do what there is some case for saying he should have done. And to make the difficulty quite clear we can put it by saying that at the opening of sect. 1 Berkeley gives what very much looks as if it is intended to be a complete survey which does not include mind, and then in sect. 2 introduces mind, thus forcing us to say either that the original survey was not after all complete or that when he does bring in mind he is introducing something which on his stated principles he has no ground for introducing.

The objection Berkeley was in fact prepared to meet was that on his principles he had no excuse for including mind in his system at all, but wider issues are involved here and we can leave consideration of them until we come to Ch. 7. The right way out of the present difficulty is to accept the first alternative and to say that the opening survey is not as it stands complete but that it is completed as soon as mind is introduced in sect. 2. If Berkeley had been criticized for omitting mind from the list of objects of knowledge in sect. 1 I suspect he would have answered, and with some justification, that the objection was merely a quibble, since mind is given sufficient prominence in sect. 2.

If it is insisted that the omission does still need to be explained we can, I think, make two points. The first is that Berkeley formulated his 'mature' thoughts about spirit rather late in the day, and that at a very late stage he was still uncertain as to whether he should say that we *know* spirit. Two entries towards the end of *PC* suggest that not very long before he published he would have regarded his survey of the objects of knowledge as complete even though it did not mention mind. Thus:

> The Will is purus actus or rather pure Spirit not imaginable, not sensible, not intelligible, in no wise the object of ye Understanding, no wise perceivable. (828)
>
> Substance of a Spirit is that it acts, causes, wills, operates, or if you please (to avoid the quibble y^t may be made on ye word it) to act, cause, will, operate its' substance is not knowable not being an Idea. (829).

I would say that there is no problem in explaining how Berkeley could have *drafted* the opening as he did. For if we allow that he could not possibly omit any of the objects he regarded as knowable from his opening survey, we can easily understand him omitting to include mind in that survey at a stage when he held that its substance was 'not knowable not being an Idea'.

The second point is suggested by the fact that the opening sentence was intended to echo the Lockian survey. For Locke points out that '*the mind* furnishes the understanding with ideas of its own operations' and Berkeley parallels this in *PC* 378 by drawing attention to 'the operations of the mind' (the ideas 'from within') and in *Pr.* 1 by including 'the passions and operations of the mind'. Locke does not include the mind itself in his survey though, as we shall see, he believed the person was intuitively known. The tactical advantages of following Locke's lead here are obvious, and Berkeley might well have thought that they outweighed the minor disadvantage of having to leave mention of mind for sect. 2.

The second issue to be looked at is one Luce deals with in the paragraph immediately following that in which he suggests that Berkeley has minds in view as the second class of objects of knowledge in sect. 1. The fact is that most readers approaching the first section will assume that in it Berkeley means to point to three classes of *ideas*, and thus that he holds that we have ideas of the passions and operations of the mind (or, if Luce was taken to be right on the first issue, of mind itself). Yet it was certainly Berkeley's view at this time that we do *not* have ideas of the mind and its operations, though both are known in experience. Berkeley had in fact *redefined* the term so that it covered only 'any sensible or imaginable thing' (*PC* 775), and a consequence of this was that the mind and its acts, which are not sensible or imaginable, were not ideas nor known by way of idea. In *PC* 663 he says:

> I have no Idea of a Volition or act of the mind neither has any other Intelligence for that were a contradiction.

It might be argued that if Locke says we do have ideas of the operations of the mind and Berkeley says we do not then the disagreement is a purely verbal one, and to some extent this would be right. Locke uses 'idea' in what we might think of as a wide sense to cover whatever the mind can be employed about in thinking, while Berkeley deliberately restricts its use to cover the sensible or imaginable only. But Berkeley would want to stress that there are genuine reasons for preferring his definition. As he says with reference to spirit in sect. 139:

> . . . all the unthinking objects of the mind agree, in that they are entirely passive, and their existence consists only in being perceived:

whereas a soul or spirit is an active being, whose existence consists not in being perceived, but in perceiving ideas and thinking. It is therefore necessary, in order to prevent equivocation and confounding natures perfectly disagreeing and unlike, that we distinguish between *spirit* and *idea*.

Berkeley does not want to deny that we have awareness of the self and its acts, but he does want to insist that the knowledge here is different in kind from our knowledge of things which are *essentially* objects.

This is Berkeley's firmly held view and we will have to consider it in more detail later, but while looking at *Pr.* 1 we should certainly say something about the fact that he seems here to go against his own view by suggesting that we do have ideas of the operations of the mind. For Luce, though he offers a confident solution, the difficulty is even more pronounced. For us the difficulty is one about mental operations, and we can note that mind is left to sect. 2 where nothing is said about how we know it and it is indeed introduced as something 'besides all that endless variety of ideas or objects of knowledge'. But for Luce the objects covered in the second class *are* minds, and whereas Berkeley in fact has nothing more to say about mental operations in succeeding sections in the first edition, he repeats a number of times, and very forcefully, that we have no idea of the mind.

When he published his *The Development of Berkeley's Philosophy* in 1923 G. A. Johnston felt able to claim that it was 'generally accepted' that Berkeley did mean to list three classes of ideas in sect. 2, and he was probably justified in this, though the tendency was, following Fraser, to assume that Berkeley deliberately used the term in two senses, a broad sense in which, as in sect. 1, it was allowable that we have ideas of the mind and its operations, and a narrow sense in which, as in sect. 139, this was not allowable. Certainly in a note to *Pr.* 27 in his edition of Berkeley's works published in 1901 Fraser suggests that he is actually quoting from *Pr.* 1 when he refers to '*ideas* perceived by attending to the "operations" of the mind', and if it had been pointed out to him that Berkeley did not use these exact words he would surely have claimed that they did justice to what was obviously *meant*. Johnston, however, felt he could show the generally accepted interpretation of the first sentence in sect. 1 to be mistaken. Thus:

> It has always been assumed that this is the meaning of the first sentence in the *Principles*. But a careful examination of the sentence

will show, I think, that it does not mean what it is commonly taken to mean . . . It is assumed by commentators on Berkeley that the second class of objects of knowledge is a class of ideas, *i.e. ideas* perceived by attending to the passions and operations of the mind. Now, this interpretation can be shown to be erroneous both grammatically and philosophically. (pp. 143-4)

The grammatical point is, or so Johnston says, that properly construed the word 'such' in the phrase 'such as are perceived' must be seen as referring to 'objects of knowledge' and not to 'ideas', so that the standard interpretation must depend either on a misunderstanding of the grammar or on commentators approaching the sentence with the quite definitely false notion that for Berkeley all objects of knowledge are ideas. Johnston concludes:

What Berkeley really says is that the objects of human knowledge include, in addition to the *two* classes of *ideas* . . . a class of *objects of knowledge* perceived by attending to the passions and operations of the mind. He does *not* say that these objects of knowledge are ideas . . .

This is the answer adopted by Luce.

What might appear as an objection here is that even if Johnston were right about the syntax from a strict grammarians point of view, the structure of the sentence is surely such as to *suggest* to the reader that three classes of ideas are being enumerated. Thus Hedenius, disagreeing with Johnston's conclusion, sees it as very strange and hardly credible that Berkeley 'should have formulated a proposition of fundamental importance in such a way as to be misunderstood by all his readers before Johnston' (p. 77). Yet this objection had been foreseen and allowed for by Johnston:

. . . he [Berkeley] seems, indeed, to use an awkward construction deliberately, in order to avoid committing himself to the statement that these objects of knowledge are ideas. (pp. 144-5)

And Luce, who regards it as 'unpardonable' to have Berkeley 'disrupt his whole philosophy in his opening sentence', has to make the same move:

He had considered the wording of the opening sentence and the apparent vagueness is probably not due to carelessness, but to design. The passage is reminiscent of Locke, and Lockian readers

> would naturally take these words to mean 'ideas of reflection'. Berkeley was a diplomatic writer, and may well have been content that they should so take the words *at first*. . . . he would have found it awkward to explain at the outset his technical reasons against ideas of the mind and its operations. (Luce 5, p. 40)

I think there is a lot in this. The point is that Berkeley's primary concern in the early sections was with the status of the ideas imprinted on the senses, and he wanted to tackle the Lockian on this. It would have been quite unnecessary for him to alienate the Lockian at the outset by challenging him on an issue which was not of immediate concern, or to bring into prominence differences in their terminology where the aim was to stress what was agreed on.

Unfortunately, though, Johnston's analysis of the troublesome sentence will not do. Here we are indebted to Furlong for an impressive paper (Furlong 1) in which he first shows that syntactical considerations point in the opposite direction from that which Johnston and Luce suppose, and then gives his own tentative explanation of how Berkeley came to say what he did not really believe. On the syntactical question Furlong's claims are, first, that the words Johnston concentrates on are ambiguous so that as they stand they allow us to suppose that 'such' refers to 'objects of human knowledge' *or* to 'ideas', and, second, that the continuation of Berkeley's sentence shows that we should understand 'ideas'. For after the words Johnston focuses on we find Berkeley referring to 'ideas formed by help of memory and imagination, either compounding, dividing, or barely representing those originally perceived in the aforesaid ways'. Now syntactically it is perhaps just *possible* that 'those' might again refer to 'objects of knowledge', but philosophically this reading is insupportable. As Furlong says:

> . . . there is no trouble here about the things perceived in the first of the two aforesaid ways, namely, the 'ideas actually imprinted on the senses'. By, for example, 'barely representing' a colour we get the mental image of a colour; this is an idea 'formed by help of memory and imagination'. But now consider the things perceived in the second of the aforesaid ways. By 'combining, dividing or barely representing' these things we are able to form ideas. But if so, these things, the things of the second class, must be themselves ideas. We could hardly form ideas out of anything but ideas.

This argument, which was anticipated by Hedenius, Furlong takes to be 'apparently unanswerable', but it is supported by another 'persuasive' one in that at the opening of sect. 2 Berkeley does seem to be equating 'ideas' and 'objects of knowledge'.

It now looks as if Johnston was wrong in criticizing commentators who supposed that the second class of objects of knowledge is presented as a class of ideas, but the problem of explaining how Berkeley came to 'disrupt his whole philosophy in the opening sentence' demands a solution. Of course the solution given by Fraser and others *might* do. We could argue that Berkeley deliberately used 'idea' in two senses. But this supposed solution must in the end be rejected. The only argument for it is that Berkeley does indeed on occasion allow that, as he has it in *Pr.* 142 (second edition), 'if in the modern way the word *idea* is extended to spirits, and relations and acts; this is after all an affair of verbal concern'. But not too much should be read into this, and we should certainly not read into the concession any implication that Berkeley was himself willing to use the term in the extended sense. For the allowance is always made against the background of the specific objection that if (as Berkeley says) we have no idea of spirit then we cannot know it, and Berkeley saw that this objection seems unanswerable to the objector only because he supposes that 'idea' is being used by Berkeley in the modern or Lockian way. His answer is to explain why he uses the term in the way he does but to concede that *if* the term is used in the Lockian sense, which usage he consistently deprecates, then we can be said to have ideas of spirit and acts. It is *only* in *Pr.* 1 that he seems to commit himself to talking of ideas of acts of mind.

Furlong's way out of the difficulty involves, as he admits, a certain amount of guesswork, but he makes an entirely plausible case for supposing that sect. 1 as it appears in the *Principles* as published resulted from successive revisions of a draft written at a time when Berkeley *did* hold the view that awareness of the operations of the mind was awareness of ideas. We have seen that in *PC* 378 when he made notes for his 'Treatise' he accepted that we have ideas of mental operations, and the draft opening could have been prepared at about this time. The view is not questioned until entry 490 when he asks:

> Qu: whether it were not better not to call the operations of the mind ideas, confining this term to things sensible?

Soon after, he decides to answer this question in the affirmative, and he quickly becomes very enthusiastic about his decision, affirming in entry 663 that (because an idea is 'any sensible or imaginable thing') the notion of an idea of an act of mind must involve a contradiction. Clearly if a draft opening was in existence at the earlier stage the decision would have necessitated revision of it, and Furlong envisages Berkeley crossing out the word 'idea', which he had originally included when introducing the second class of objects of knowledge, and leaving the word 'such' so as to allow the reader to suppose *at first* that we do have ideas here but without actually committing himself to affirming or denying this. 'In doing this', Furlong supposes, 'he fails to notice the trouble created by the phrase "aforesaid ways".' So the conclusion is that Berkeley does commit himself to ideas of mental operations in sect. 1, but that he does this *by accident*.

Furlong's case involves 'imaginative reconstruction', but the answer he comes up with is probably just about right. It provides a solution to a problem that has exercised commentators for quite some time and it rests upon a point which I think deserves emphasis. This is that Berkeley must have been thinking very hard about the opening of his great work at a time when his terminology was much closer to Locke's than it was when he published. For this suggests that his decision to start from the area of maximum agreement was made against the background of more actual agreement, so far at least as terminology was concerned, than obtained when the time came for final drafting. At an early stage the idea of starting with the philosophical approach and a near paraphrase of Locke which could be presented as 'evident' must have seemed very attractive. As his thought developed, however, the plan may have continued to seem too attractive to discard while at the same time appearing as something of an embarrassment.

V

If the things we perceive by sense are ideas and the things we eat, drink and wear are perceived by sense, the odd sounding conclusion will follow that 'we eat and drink ideas, and are clothed with ideas'. But we have already seen that Berkeley's use of the key term differs from Locke's, and the possibility has to be faced that given this the conclusion may just be odd *sounding*. The fact that it seems harsh may, as Berkeley suggests at the beginning of his answer to the objection of *Pr.* 38, result partly or largely from the fact that he 'varies from the familiar use of language'. Things *may* remain as real as ever.

To understand Berkeley's claim here we have to remind ourselves of the *two* basic moves he makes in reacting from materialism and reaching his own position. Concentrating on the first of these moves, then, we can see him as looking at the Lockian picture according to which in addition to minds the universe is populated with (Lockian) external objects and (Lockian) ideas, and as denying that (Lockian) external objects exist while retaining (Lockian) ideas. When Austin says that 'in Locke's view there are "ideas" and also "external objects" . . . in Berkeley's doctrine there are *only* ideas' (p. 61) he has in mind the first of Berkeley's basic moves and the one in which something is *subtracted from* Locke's universe.[6]

Now if we concentrate on this move we are going to suppose that 'all that is real and substantial in Nature is banished out of the world' (*Pr.* 34). In the words of the French reviewer, 'Tout ce que nous imaginons de corporel ne sont que des idées'. At one time Berkeley seems himself to have thought that his principles detracted from the reality of sensible things. Very quickly, though, he came to the view that to say that the things we perceive by sense are *ideas* need not mean that we have to regard them as somehow deficient in reality. When Hylas accuses the Berkeleian of 'changing all things into ideas' Philonous replies:

> You mistake me. I am not for changing things into ideas, but rather ideas into things; since those immediate objects of perception, which according to you, are only appearances of things, I take to be the real things themselves. (Dialogues, iii, 244)

The changing of Lockian ideas into things is the second basic move.

Perhaps two simple insights encouraged Berkeley in his conviction that ideas could be turned into things. Very simply, the first of these was that those who thought of ideas as shadowy and unreal did so because they thought of the unperceived objects on the dark side of the veil of perception as being real things. It was by contrast with these non-existent entities that ideas were made to seem somehow ethereal. For Locke the ideas of sense were merely representational entities which provided clues as to the nature of an external reality, but Berkeley came to see that his own ideas of sense need not be thought of as mere proxies for the real. Berkeley's ideas of sense do not suffer by comparison with a material world for his main negative point is that there is no material world of the sort philosophers suppose. Similarly they need not be thought of as shadowy, for the claim is that there is nothing they shadow, and they cannot be thought of as merely representational since Berkeley has shown that there is nothing for them to represent. It is as if the Lockian external object had withdrawn from the contest for the title of *real thing*, leaving the prize for the only other contender.

Appreciating the other insight involves approaching the question from another angle and forgetting for the moment Berkeley's own acceptance of the view that we perceive only mind-dependent entities. Now Berkeley was a keen and appreciative observer of the wonders of nature, and he felt very strongly that the materialist was saying something distasteful as well as absurd when he claimed that what we are actually or immediately aware of when we look around us are representations of the real. He was himself convinced that as he looked around he saw the fields, woods, groves, rivers and springs, the things themselves. Certainly he could tell the difference between a real tree and an imagined tree, between a climbable thing and a dream image, but the crucial point was that the real tree, like the mental image, was something he was aware of and not something perpetually outside his perceptual range. Criticizing the Lockian, then, Berkeley can take the line that it is absurd to suppose that the real world is made up of remote causal objects, and looking to the plain man he can find support for his view which is that the real tree is the thing he knows in experience as he looks at it, and sits on a branch. In short, rather than denying that there is a real world Berkeley just wants to insist that the real world is, in a quite straightforward sense, *sensible*. The sting here comes in the tail, for having asked us to look about us, feel, taste, hear and smell to locate the real world and distinguish it from the imaginary, Berkeley informs us that this real world is made up of mind-dependent ideas. He will ask us to note, though, that in making this move he is certainly not undermining our belief in the reality of the sensible world. We can all locate the real world without difficulty. What Berkeley is doing is to give us perhaps surprising information *about* that real world.

Both these insights are, I think, reflected in the following passage from Luce in which he explains Berkeley's use of the key term:

> The technical term *idea* is a piece of short-hand notation, like *Ranunculus* in botany. When Berkeley names the Three Rock mountain an idea, and proceeds to argue about that idea, he is not speaking or arguing about anything other than the Three Rock itself which he could see from his college rooms. He is not speaking about a photograph or copy of it, mental or somatic; he is speaking of the mountain itself, or some part of it; he is speaking of an idea that *is* the mountain, out there *in rerum natura*. He is speaking of an idea-thing, a sensible idea, an idea that can be seen or touched, or otherwise perceived by sense, an idea covered with heather where the grouse may nest. (Luce 9, p. 76)

So commonsensical, so one-of-us does Berkeley begin to seem that we are inclined to forget that not everything Berkeley believes about his idea-thing is coincident with what most of us believe about the Three Rock mountain. We need to be reminded, as Luce does eventually remind us, that by calling the mountain an idea Berkeley meant to convey the supposed truth that 'it cannot exist otherwise than in a mind perceiving it'. Its *esse* is *percipi*. Apparently, though, we should not be too worried by the mind-dependence of idea-things. As Jessop says, by calling corporeal things *ideas* Berkeley does not mean to 'subtilize, etherealize, or mentalize the corporeal. The corporeal is exactly what it is experienced to be – the extended, coloured, hard, and so forth, qualities that cannot be assimilated to mind' (*Works* II, p. 10).

Now I take it that this line has some plausibility so long as we keep our eyes fixed on the undoubtedly unsatisfactory position Berkeley is concerned to attack. With this in mind we can see him as denying that there is a material reality which we can never perceive and as affirming that the corporeal reality is, without question, a *sensible* reality. As Jessop puts it in the introduction to his *Berkeley: Philosophical Writings*:

> The sensed is itself the real corporeal world, perception interposing no screen, whether opaque or diaphanous, of mental entities between us and it. (p. xiii)

Certainly at this point the plain man is going to be sympathetic, for what is said here is totally in the spirit of premiss (1) of the argument of *Pr. 4*, and it accords with the belief of the vulgar that '*those things they immediately perceive are the real things*'. We can, with Luce and Jessop, wax lyrical about Berkeley's fidelity to common sense insights so long as we concentrate on his opposition to the notion that the external reality is not perceivable. But again it needs emphasizing that Berkeley's standpoint is not the only standpoint compatible with the belief that the corporeal is sensible and that if the average reader finds his thinking outrageous it is because he insists that '*the things immediately perceived, are ideas which exist only in the mind*'. Berkeley's position seems odd precisely because he holds, not just that it is nonsense to talk of a wholly occult corporeal reality, but also that physical things are collections of ideas. The plain man will feel that though he can be quite happy about the debunking of the notion of a realm of *unperceivable* physical objects, yet the mind-dependent ideas Berkeley leaves us with do seem somehow inadequate to constitute what is normally thought of as a sensible *reality*. For the plain man a real knife can be seen and touched, but for Berkeley (strictly) no idea can be seen and touched. For the plain man the real knife can cause us pain, but for Berkeley (strictly) no idea can *do* anything. And the story may not end here. For the plain man the real knife can be perceived by anyone, but, though the issue is not so clear-cut here, it isn't *obvious* that any Berkeleian idea is public. Indeed it isn't *obvious* that for Berkeley the particular idea I perceive now can exist when *I* cease to perceive it.[7]

To understand Berkeley and the line taken by those most sympathetic to his doctrines it is I think quite essential to disentangle the claim about what there is not, i.e. an external reality as the philosophers conceive of it, from the claim about what there is, i.e. minds and their ideas. We have already noted the general tendency to suppose that disposing of the unperceivable reality of the philosophers is tantamount to showing that things must be actually perceived, and we can now give some examples to show how the width of the gulf between the negative point and the positive doctrine can be obscured.

We can consider first what Luce says about Berkeley's use of the phrase 'in the mind'. What does it mean to say that sensible objects exist 'only in the mind'? Luce says:

> Berkeley's term *in the mind* is flexible, at times indefinite, but it is not intentionally ambiguous; if it is ambiguous to us, we must not

blame Berkeley.... *Mind*, in the *Principles*, is a very flexible term. It may mean the divine mind or the human mind, or it may be the negation *not-matter*. When Berkeley is merely the controversialist, attacking materialism, his *in the mind* means *not in matter*. Matter, *ex hypothesi*, is outside the mind and beyond its range.... But of course he does not long remain at the stage of denial; *mind* soon becomes to him positive and a substance. (Luce 4, p. 286-7)

Now it might well be thought that here we *do* have a paradigm of ambiguity. Apparently when Berkeley says that sensible things exist only in the mind he may be making the positive point that they can exist only in a spiritual substance, or he may simply be making the negative point that they do not exist in something which lies outside our perceptual range. But whether ambiguity or flexibility is involved here the ambivalence is clearly unfortunate. We can accept the claim that the notion of matter as something 'outside the mind and beyond its range' must be rejected *without* agreeing with Berkeley's positive doctrine, but the elastic phrase will facilitate a slide from the perhaps acceptable negative point to the highly debatable view that sensible things require a spiritual substrate. At the very least it is surely undesirable to state the negative point in terms more obviously appropriate to the quite different positive point.

Closely associated with this is a tendency to slip from the claim that corporeal things must be *sensible*, i.e. such that they can be sensed, to the claim that they are *sensible objects*, meaning now that they are mind-dependent entities which exist only when sensed. We shall be looking carefully at this later, but here we can just note Marc-Wogau's location of 'a wholly unwarranted transition from the definition of "sensible things" as those objects, "which *can* be perceived immediately by sense" to the definition: "sensible things are those only which *are* immediately perceived by sense" ' (Marc-Wogau 2, p. 322). The definitions will be found in *Dialogues*, i, 174, and the italics are (of course) supplied by Marc-Wogau. The danger here is that we will focus on the first definition and accept that corporeal things are sensible (i.e. that there is no veil of perception) and then slide to the conclusion that they are sensible in the sense indicated by the second definition (i.e. that they are mind-dependent ideas). Clearly too the slide can work in the opposite direction. The doctrine that corporeal things are sensible, i.e. mind-dependent entities, can be made to appear a pure statement of common sense if attention is shifted back to the first definition and the claim construed as a claim that corporeal things *can* be sensed.

The final example brings us again to Berkeley's use of the term 'idea', for it seems to me that far from being a 'term of precision' as Luce holds (Luce 9, p. 76), it has a role to play in facilitating the slide from a denial of a wholly occult material reality to the affirmation of a mind-dependent corporeal reality. As I read him, the claim that we perceive only ideas is one that sometimes seems quite obvious to Berkeley because he takes it as asserting that the physical world is something we are acquainted with in sense experience. Additionally, though, he is always ready to interpret the claim in the light of his positive belief that the things we immediately perceive can exist only when perceived. If this is right there is a possibility of sliding from the proposition that we perceive only ideas, meaning that the corporeal reality lies within our perceptual grasp, to the proposition that we perceive only ideas, meaning now that we perceive only mind-dependent entities. On this view the term 'idea' will be elastic in just the way that Luce says the expression 'in the mind' is elastic.

To illustrate how this elasticity works we can start by looking at the ideas of sense Berkeley introduces in *Pr.* 1. And what I want to suggest here is that, though Luce often warns of the *danger* of confusing the Berkeleian idea with the Lockian idea, there really is good reason for insisting that the ideas Berkeley has us start with *are* Lockian ideas. Admittedly Berkeley does not think of ideas of sense as *representing* objects in an external physical world (and he is going to maintain that they are adequate to constitute a corporeal reality) but it does seem quite natural to think of them as what the materialist is left with once it has been shown that there is no external reality of the sort he posits. It will seem quite *obvious* to Berkeley that these ideas are mind-dependent, and this because he is working within the Lockian framework and denying only that there is an external material reality in addition to ideas in the mind. If Locke's universe contains external objects and mind-dependent ideas and we subtract the external objects then we are left, *of course*, with mind-dependent ideas. Nor is mind-dependence all Berkeley is concerned with when he accepts the Lockian ideas and rejects his external reality. Another thing about the ideas Berkeley introduces in *Pr.* 1 is that they are thought of as being *conveyed to* and *produced in* the mind. For Berkeley, as for Locke, the ideas of sense are essentially *effects*, and the dispute is solely one about the nature of the causal agent. For Locke the ideas are produced in our minds by external objects, while for Berkeley (as it will turn out) the cause is God. Indeed, at the end of the day it appears that the ideas we perceive may after all be representational entities, for Berkeley certainly has some sympathy with the notion that they represent archetypal ideas in the mind of God.

Unfortunately, as we have already suggested, it does seem implausible to suggest that these *Lockian* ideas can make up solid and permanent objects such as the plain man takes physical objects to be. One point here is that we normally think of physical objects and their qualities as public, but if we think of ideas as entities produced in us (whether through the agency of external objects or of God) it will be natural for us to suppose that the idea produced in my mind must be numerically distinct from the idea produced in yours and thus that ideas are private. When we talk of a *real* rose we normally have in mind one item which we can all admire, but if Berkeley's claim is that I perceive only Lockian ideas and the particular Lockian idea I perceive exists only in *my* mind, then the public rose seems to be lost. That Berkeley does sometimes think of ideas as private in the sense indicated is suggested by, for example, the following passage in which his primary concern is with our knowledge of other minds:

> . . . as we conceive the ideas that are in the minds of other spirits by means of our own, which we suppose to be resemblances of them: so we know other spirits by means of our own soul, which in that sense is the image or idea of them, it having a like respect to other spirits, that blueness or heat by me perceived hath to those ideas perceived by another. (*Pr.* 140)

Here it is quite clear that Berkeley regards the idea I perceive when I perceive blueness as numerically distinct from, though probably qualitatively similar to, the idea you have when you perceive blueness. For a comparison with Locke see II xxxii 15.

But if Berkeley often thinks of his ideas as Lockian ideas, as we have suggested he does, it is also true that he sometimes thinks of them in a quite different way and as what we can term, following Luce, *idea-things*. The point about idea-things is that these are conceived of much as the plain man conceives of physical objects. We can illustrate this by looking again at the question as to whether two agents can perceive one and the same idea. For often Berkeley does talk as if ideas were public in this sense. Thus we have the following in *Pr.* 48:

> ... though we hold indeed the objects of sense to be nothing else but ideas which cannot exist unperceived; yet we may not hence conclude they have no existence except only while they are perceived by us, since there may be some other spirit that perceives them, though we do not. Wherever bodies are said to have no existence without the mind, I would not be understood to mean this or that particular mind, but all minds whatsoever.

Berkeley makes this point in answering the challenge that on his principles 'things are every moment annihilated and created anew' and he clearly assumes that the thing I now perceive – and this must be an idea – may continue to exist though I cease to perceive it, this given that some other spirit perceives the same idea. Now it is true that Berkeley does suppose here that there can be no object without *some* mind perceiving it, and in this sense ideas remain mind-dependent, but we can neglect this point for the moment. The point we must seize on is that here he does seem to allow for the possibility that one and the same idea might exist in (i.e. be perceived by) more than one mind. The line he takes here seems to be quite incompatible with the one he takes in *Pr.* 140, and Grave is surely right when he says:

> The positions seem to me quite irreconcilable, and I think Berkeley was driven into them by two conflicting desires: one, to oblige men to see that if there were no minds there would be nothing at all; the other, to meet the demands of common sense. (p. 298)

Clearly it does seem very odd to suggest that I eat, drink and wear objects composed of Lockian ideas each of which can exist only in some one particular mind, but it seems at least less odd to claim that these objects are idea-things which can be perceived by various agents.[8]

VI

In trying to make sense of Berkeley one line we can take is always to interpret what he says about idea-things in the light of his doctrines about Lockian ideas. Thus in answering the question as to whether Berkeley *really* thinks of ideas as public Grave makes a persuasive case for supposing that *Pr.* 48 does not reflect his fundamental commitment, and that basically his belief is that if A and B do perceive the same thing it must be in the special sense that the two ectypal ideas resemble each other and one divine archetype. The general line taken by Grave is that 'the illusion of two conflicting sets of opinions is generated by the expression of paradoxical opinions in unparadoxical language' (p. 300). On this interpretation we must see God as producing (Lockian) ideas in the minds of his creatures in such a way that the idea I now perceive will be numerically distinct from the idea produced in your mind, though my idea may be qualitatively similar to yours and both will resemble some numerically distinct idea in God's mind. The idea that continues to exist when I cease to perceive it will thus be not the same item but a *similar* item.

It is perhaps worth noting that the Berkeley who emerges here is not just a paradoxical Berkeley, but one who is faced with very real difficulties. Commentators have often pointed out that if he does indeed believe in an archetypal reality of ideas in God's mind to which our ideas (supposedly) correspond then he is in effect offering his own particular brand of representationalism which will be open to at least some of the objections he himself puts to Locke's representationalism. Clearly too solipsism threatens. If I am aware only of ideas *in my own mind*, Berkeley is going to have to show that I can somehow break out of the circle of my own ideas and be justified in asserting that anything exists besides my own mind and its ideas. Hence Russell's judgement that Berkeley's idealism 'ought, of course, in any case to be solipsism' (Russell 1, p. 194).

If we are going to look for a consistent Berkeley, Grave's interpretation is probably the one we should accept. On this interpretation Berkeley's ideas of sense will be Lockian ideas or 'sensa', each of them will be dependent on the particular mind perceiving it, and Berkeley's thinking will not be nearly as close to ordinary thinking as is sometimes supposed. The alternative would be to follow Luce and to put all the emphasis on idea-things. Idea-things can be thought of as *qualities* of things and things as collections of qualities, and we can suppose that the idea I perceive now might be perceived by others. Obviously now Berkeley's thinking has come much closer to our ordinary thinking. The problem is that it has become difficult to see why Berkeley should think that for an idea to exist it must be perceived by anyone at all. Rather than committing myself to either of these interpretations, though, I prefer at this stage to stay with the inconsistent Berkeley, the Berkeley who can look both ways and maintain at once that we perceive only our own Lockian ideas *and* that we perceive idea-things which are quite adequate to constitute a *rerum natura*.[9] Certainly it seems to me that we miss something important if we suppose that the real Berkeley believed in Lockian ideas and that all talk about idea-things is *just* propaganda, for the essential thing about the Berkeley who wrote the *Principles* and *Dialogues* is that he is quite capable of believing his own propaganda, and that this accounts both for his feeling that he is faithful to common sense and for his conviction that the truth he has to convey is at once obvious and amazing. Very simply, he took it to be obvious that corporeal things are ideas (i.e. *sensible* things or things that can be perceived) and he is quite happy to identify these with qualities or collections of qualities. But he combines this insight with the questionable Lockian principle that we perceive only Lockian ideas in such a way as to reach the Berkeleian conclusion that it should be obvious to all that the things we perceive (i.e. qualities and collections of qualities) can exist only when perceived. So, as Berkeley sees the position, it is that if we deny that things such as tables are ideas (i.e. idea-things which can be sensed) then we are absurdly denying both the obvious truth that sensible things are *sensible* and the common-sense proposition that we eat our dinner off a sensible thing, while if we agree that they are ideas we must accept that these things are mind-dependent because of course, and as the materialists acknowledge, ideas exist only in the mind. In *Pr.* 1-2 it isn't *shown* that the things we immediately perceive are Lockian ideas, for this is taken to be 'evident', and it isn't *shown* that real things are idea-things or things that can be sensed, though Berkeley thinks this obvious. But more importantly from our point of view, it isn't *shown* that if now, when I take myself to be perceiving a book, I am perceiving a Lockian idea, I can properly think of myself as perceiving a book which remains as real as ever. A real book is, after all, commonly supposed to have some features not shared by Lockian ideas.[10]

Commentators have often been puzzled by Berkeley's double use of 'idea', and Marc-Wogau has raised the question whether it is supposed to be analytic that the *esse* of ideas is *percipi*, or whether we can accept that we perceive only ideas without thereby committing ourselves to the view that the things we perceive exist only when perceived.

Here sects. 1-2 in the *Principles* seem to point one way and sect. 3 the other. In summarizing sect. 1 we assumed that Berkeley was introducing ideas which *of course* cannot be unless they are actually perceived, and we said that given apples and the like are collections of ideas it would *follow* that apples and the like exist only in the mind. This reading would seem to be supported by sect. 38, for there he says that qualities and corporeal things 'exist only in the mind that perceives them' and adds that 'this is all that is meant by calling them *ideas*'. We could not, we might think, have a clearer statement than this. By calling something an *idea* we mean that the thing is mind-dependent, and indeed, more than this, we mean that it exists only in the particular mind that perceives it. But sect. 3 does seem to point the other way, for here Berkeley sets out to *show* that ideas imprinted on the senses cannot exist unperceived, thus implying that we could after all have accepted the claims made in sect. 1 without admitting that things or collections of ideas exist only in the mind.

Marc-Wogau associates the ambivalence here with difficulties concerning the interpretation of *'esse'*. If it is the *essentia* of ideas that is *percipi* then it will be necessarily true that all ideas are actually perceived, but if it is the *existentia* of ideas that is *percipi* then this may not be the case:

> According to the latter interpretation of *'esse'* the principle may be non-analytic. It only states that there is, in respect to ideas, an intimate relation between their property to exist and their property to be perceived, a relation which does not necessarily follow from the meaning of the word 'idea'. Berkeley considered his *esse est percipi*-principle as a demonstrable principle. . . . It could then be concluded that the principle is not meant as an analytic statement in the given sense. There seems to be stronger evidence for the interpretation of the principle as a statement the truth of which does not follow from the definition of the term 'idea'. (Marc-Wogau 2, pp. 321-2)

As the wording here suggests Marc-Wogau recognizes that we can find evidence pointing either way, and I am sure that what he goes on to suggest *may* have been the case was the case and that Berkeley 'gave his principle different senses in different contexts'.

The truth is, surely, that when Berkeley thinks of ideas as what we are left with when we subtract the external reality from Locke's universe he does talk as if it were analytic that ideas are actually perceived, and in this case what he feels he needs to demonstrate is that nothing *like* an idea can exist without a mind. Against this, though, when he thinks of the ideal world as the sensible reality of the plain man as opposed to the material and insensible reality of the philosophers his language reveals some recognition of the necessity to show the ideal to be mind-dependent. It is *obvious* that the apples, stones, trees, books and their qualities are ideas (i.e. idea-things) because these are perceived, but familiar things have to be shown to be mind-dependent. It is *evident* that the things we immediately perceive are ideas (i.e. Lockian ideas), and we don't have to show these ideas to be mind-dependent because (a) this is universally acknowledged by philosophers and (b) saying that things are ideas is a way of saying that they exist only in the mind.

It should be obvious that Berkeley's problem of convincing the plain man, who believes that corporeal things are sensible, that these things are mind-dependent is very closely connected with the problem of showing that Lockian ideas can constitute a sensible reality. But this can be further illustrated. We shall see that early on in the *Dialogues* the Berkeleian tries to show that an intense heat (something we normally take to be a sensible *quality* of the object) can exist only when perceived. And what he does is to suggest that an intense heat is simply a great pain (that is, a bodily sensation). It follows, of course, that if we think of bodily sensations as mind-dependent we must concede intense degrees of heat to be mind-dependent. Now we are not concerned here with the question whether it is at all plausible to suggest that a great heat is just a great pain. The point is that in 'proving' heat to have no existence without the mind Philonous seems to have presented us with a very good reason for ceasing to think of it as a characteristic of the hot object. The dilemma is that if we think of heat as a sensible *quality* we are going to resist the suggestion that it is a bodily sensation, while if we agree that it is a bodily *sensation* it is no longer clear that we should think of it (any more than we do of pain) as a quality.

In more general terms, Pitcher claims in an important paper that Berkeley works with propositions which make an inconsistent triad, these being:

(A) The mind perceives ideas.
(B) The mind is wholly distinct from its ideas.

> (C) The alleged distinction between (i) the perceiving of an idea and (ii) the idea perceived, is a bogus one; there is no such distinction. (p. 198)

That Berkeley is, when it suits him, prepared to commit himself to each of these three is, I think, undeniable. He stresses (C) in order to support the claim that we cannot isolate the perception of the object from the object perceived so as to suppose that the perceiving, but not the object, is mind-dependent. He focuses on (B) when he wants to oppose the notion that ideas are mental and expects us to think of them as objects *for* mind. And of course he holds (A) because it is his view that 'besides all that endless variety of ideas or objects of knowledge, there is likewise something which knows or perceives them' (*Pr.* 2). Now it is natural to assume that (B) holds the mind to be *strongly* distinct from its ideas, as we would normally take Bill to be wholly distinct from the tree he kicks, rather than as *weakly* distinct from its ideas, as Bill might be said to be weakly distinct from his kicking of the tree. But:

> If it is indeed in this way that (B) is to be understood, then (A), (B), and (C) form an inconsistent trio of doctrines. One of the things the mind does is perceive ideas (proposition (A)); so the perceiving of an idea is either an act or a state of mind. Therefore the mind is not strongly, but only weakly, distinct from the perceiving of the idea. However, since the perceiving of an idea cannot be distinguished from the idea perceived (in virtue of (C)), the idea, like the perceiving, is only weakly distinct from the mind. And this contradicts (B), which says that an idea is strongly distinct from the mind. (p. 199)

Either (B) or (C) has to go, and Pitcher suggests that (C) is essential to Berkeley's case for mind-dependence and that (B) must be sacrificed. What is lost by the sacrifice is the possibility of an act-object account of perception, and with this go objects which can be thought of as public in an ordinary sense. But if we retain (B) and sacrifice (C) to get public objects there would seem to be no reason why we should not suppose that *these* objects might exist unperceived. We might put the same sort of point rather less rigorously by suggesting that if (as Luce thinks) I can *touch* a Berkeleian idea and others can touch it too, then we cannot rule out the possibility that the idea can exist untouched.

If, on the other hand, I can only feel it, *as I feel a bodily sensation*, then it is far from clear that I can properly think of myself or anyone else as touching it. Pitcher's analysis thus gives substance to the impression that Berkeley cannot bring off the coup of at once pulling the sensible object towards the individual's mind so as to make manifest its dependence on a perceiving mind while pushing the object away so as to preserve its objectivity.

Throughout the *Principles* Berkeley's terminology is such as to camouflage the considerable gap between his very odd views and our ordinary thinking. Here we can consider again and make a fresh point about his use of the expression 'in the mind'. To say that the things we perceive – 'all the choir of heaven and furniture of the earth' – exist only in the mind certainly sounds odd, but Luce assures us that the notion is indeed only odd sounding. It is 'official doctrine, explicit, decisive, and often repeated' (Luce 4, p. 285) that for an idea to exist in the mind is for it to be perceived *by* the mind and yet to be entirely distinct from the mind. Further:

> The *in* is the equivalent of *in relation to*; but the full phrase is too awkward for general use. In our idiom 'I have it in mind' is a neat expression for the cognitive relation in general, and Berkeley is correct linguistically in using 'in the mind' as an abbreviation for 'in direct cognitive relation to the mind'. . . . The preposition implies, not situation in, not forming part of, but apprehension by. Thus the British Museum is in my mind when I am in the British Museum, provided I am perceiving it or thinking about it. Things are not in my mind as the brain is *in* the head or as Monday is *in* the week or as the act of synthesis is *in* conception. (p. 286)

It would appear that if we are worried by the thought that perceived things are in the mind we need only remind ourselves that this comes down to the notion that the things we perceive are (tautologously) perceived by or apprehended by the mind.

Now in a way Luce is right here, for Berkeley is indeed explicit that claiming that perceived things are *in* the perceiving mind is the same thing as claiming that they are perceived *by* the perceiving mind. So the point needs making. All the same, Luce is telling just part of the story. If A = B then B = A, and if it is true that Berkeley regards existence in the mind as amounting to perception by the mind it is also true that he thinks of perception by the mind as coming down to the existence of an idea in the mind. It is certainly significant that Luce goes on to stress Berkeley's opposition to a three-term theory of perception, for it is in just this context that it does come naturally to Berkeley to insist that corporeal objects are the things we *perceive*. It will be remembered that it is on this point that he is at one with the vulgar, for the vulgar belief is that the things they perceive are the real things. Against this, though, when he is concerned to press his unorthodox claim that corporeal things exist *only* when perceived he is happy to switch to the other side of the equation and to stress, with the philosophers, that perceived things are ideas *in the mind*. We should not take it that if we are worried by the expression 'in the mind' we can just forget all about it and substitute the expression 'perceived by the mind' on each occurrence, for the claim that perception by the mind comes down to existence in the mind is itself a substantial one resting on the supposition that the philosophers' 'truth' is true. Assuming that it is true, and at the same time helping himself to the vulgar belief, Berkeley has two ways of speaking which he can *treat* as equivalent with the result that he can maintain both that it should be uncontroversial that sensible objects are in the mind (i.e. perceived by the mind) and that of course things perceived by the mind (i.e. things in the mind) are mind-dependent ideas.

If we look again at Berkeley's answer to the objection contained in the quotation which heads this chapter we find him juggling happily with the notions of perception by the mind and existence in the mind. He has envisaged his reader worrying about the oddity of saying that 'we eat and drink ideas, and are clothed with ideas', and in replying he begins:

> ... it is certain that any expression which varies from the familiar use of language, will seem harsh and ridiculous. But this doth not concern the truth of the proposition, which in other words is no more than to say, we are fed and clothed with those things which we perceive immediately by our senses.

This does indeed sound acceptable. In the preceding section (sect. 37) Berkeley has emphasized that he opposes only the philosophical notion of an unperceivable material reality, and we might well take it that his claim now is that in calling corporeal things *ideas* he merely wants to stress that they are the things we apprehend by sense – *the things which the vulgar recognize as real things*. We could agree that 'we are fed and clothed with those things which we perceive immediately by our senses' without supposing that these things are mind-dependent. Berkeley is at one with common sense. But the switch follows immediately, for Berkeley reminds us that he has *shown* that sensible qualities 'exist only in the mind that perceives them' and indeed claims that 'this is all that is meant by calling them *ideas*'. In the following section (sect. 39) he confirms this, telling us that it is because 'the objects of sense exist only in the mind, and are withal thoughtless and inactive' that he 'chose to mark them by the word *idea*, which implies those properties'. Further confirmation for the view that 'existence *in* the mind' is not for Berkeley simply a harmless variant for 'perception by the mind' is found in sects. 42-3. There he tells us that as things *seen* are in the mind it cannot be strictly true (as is popularly supposed) that things seen are at a distance from us.[11]

In *Pr.* 1, of course, the equivalence of perception *by* the mind to existence *in* the mind is assumed, and in general Berkeley blends language appropriate to the realist with language appropriate to his belief that perceiving qualities comes down to having ideas. For example, note that I *perceive* tangible qualities such as hard and soft but am *furnished with* odours while tastes and sounds are *conveyed to* the mind. Of course Berkeley thinks of *all* ideas of sense as being *produced in* our minds, and if we follow him here it will be natural for us to think of them on the model of bodily sensations. But these ideas are also things we perceive, and now the language prepares us to think of them as qualities and even as making up things like apples stones, trees and books. Normally we would not talk of being *furnished with* qualities or of *perceiving* (i.e. seeing, feeling, smelling, tasting or hearing) sensations, but we soon find ourselves encouraged to think of ideas as at once qualities *and* mind-dependent sensations and to talk of perceiving them *and* having them. In sect. 2 the assumption behind this is made explicit, but sects. 1-2 no more contain an argument for it than they do for the supposedly evident truth that we perceive only mind-dependent ideas.

CHAPTER FOUR

The Approach from Ordinary Usage

'I am content, Hylas, to appeal to the common sense of the world for the truth of my notion.'
(*Dialogues*, iii, 234)

I

What we have called the argument from ordinary usage is introduced in a way which makes it quite clear that, at this point at any rate, Berkeley wants us to accept that things and their qualities are *ideas* without thereby, and as a result of the very acceptance of the term, committing ourselves to the view that they can exist only when perceived. Thus in sect. 3 Berkeley refers to the three sorts of objects of knowledge introduced at the beginning of sect. 1 and says:

> That neither our thoughts, nor passions, nor ideas formed by the imagination, exist without the mind, is what every body will allow. And it seems no less evident that the various sensations or ideas imprinted on the sense, however blended or combined together (that is, whatever objects they compose) cannot exist otherwise than in a mind perceiving them. I think an intuitive knowledge may be obtained of this, by any one that shall attend to what is meant by the term *exist* when applied to sensible things.

Just as the classification of the objects of knowledge was said to be 'evident', so here the same is claimed for the view that sensible objects are mind-dependent. But – as Benson Mates very properly emphasizes (p. 170) – the obviousness of this is supposed to depend, not on the triviality of the truth that ideas are (by definition) 'in the mind', but rather on the meaning of 'to exist' and, as we shall see, of 'to be perceived'.

My eyes are open and I see something. We can speak, as Berkeley would say, *strictly* and say that I see light and colours patterned in a certain way, or we can say in a more normal sort of fashion that I see a typewriter. Of course the overall situation is more complicated than this, for I am touching the typewriter and using it, but we can cover the situation by saying that I perceive the typewriter and that because I perceive it now I know it exists now. And whether we call what I perceive now an idea, a collection of ideas, or a typewriter, the question remains the same for Berkeley: does it make sense to talk of what I now perceive as existing unperceived? Berkeley thinks it does not.

We should be clear, then, that Berkeley is making a very strong claim. Steinkraus interprets him wrongly when he says:

> Though reality 'without the mind' is always a logical possibility, it is not, on Berkeley's view, a reasonable probability. 'Though we should allow it possible, [it] must yet be a very unaccountable and extravagant supposition' (*Pr.* 53). Or as a friend, F. G. Ensley, once said: 'The fact that all the books we have ever known have had authors could hardly be adduced as evidence that there are authorless books.' (Steinkraus 1, p. 155)

What goes wrong here is that the quotation from *Pr.* 53 is taken out of context and misinterpreted. At this point Berkeley is considering a view, attributable to Malebranche and others, according to which matter exists but is devoid of causal power. As a result they have 'an innumerable multitude of created beings, which they acknowledge are not capable of producing any one effect in Nature'. It is a misreading of Berkeley to see him as saying that we should at least allow this improbable conjecture to be possible. What he is saying is that if *for the sake of argument* we do allow it to be possible '[it] must yet be a very unaccountable and extravagant supposition'. Berkeley's own position has been made quite clear: the very notion that things may exist without the mind involves 'a manifest repugnancy' (*Pr.* 23). We must emphasize, then, that whatever the merits or demerits of Ensley's argument, Berkeley is not primarily concerned to make a point about evidence but a point about meaning. He is not asking the question whether I can provide evidence that the typewriter exists when I do not perceive it, and he is not asking whether I can produce evidence to support my belief that it exists when not perceived by anybody. What he is doing is asking whether the supposition that it exists unperceived is a coherent one.[1]

It is clear that Berkeley thought of what he had to say about existence as being both original and momentous. Thus in *PC* 491 he says:

> ... 'tis on the Discovering of the nature & meaning & import of Existence that I chiefly insist. This puts a wide difference betwixt the Sceptics & me. This I think wholly new. I am sure 'tis new to me

And in entry 604:

> I am persuaded would Men but examine w^t they mean by the Word Existence they wou'd agree with me.

The argument of sect. 3 in which we 'attend to what is meant by the term *exist*' goes as follows:

> The table I write on, I say, exists, that is, I see and feel it; and if I were out of my study I should say it existed, meaning thereby that if I was in my study I might perceive it, or that some other spirit actually does perceive it. There was an odour, that is, it was smelled; there was a sound, that is to say, it was heard; a colour or figure, and it was perceived by sight or touch. This is all that I can understand by these and the like expressions.

There is no use of the term 'idea' here or in the two sentences which follow and complete the section, and in examining the argument we can progress for some way without referring to the term. Berkeley is writing about sensible things — tables, odours, sounds, colours and shapes — and the claim is that if we consider what we mean when we say these *exist* we will see that it makes nonsense to talk of them existing unperceived.

II

Objection might reasonably be made to our referring to what Berkeley says in sect. 3 as an *argument*. Thus Ardley insists that 'the principle is not something to be proved' (p. 14) and Mates tells us that:

> Berkeley's contention that ideas cannot exist unperceived is not, as many have supposed, based upon a definition of the word 'idea'. The words whose meanings are essentially involved are rather the verbs 'to exist' and 'to be perceived'. Berkeley does not *define* either of these in terms of the other; upon reflection he *discovers*

that for him they have the same meaning when applied to ideas, and he expects that the reader will make the same discovery about his own usage. In my case his expectation is correct, and I even share his confidence, to some extent, that with a little attention everyone will agree. (pp. 170-1)

Berkeley's use of the word 'intuitive' in this context certainly suggests that to an extent at least Ardley and Mates are right, for as Berkeley used that term what is known intuitively neither can be demonstrated nor stands in need of demonstration. What we know intuitively, that we just see to be so. What we have referred to as an argument can, then, be seen rather as a suggestion as to how we should direct our thoughts to grasp the obvious (though amazing) truth. To see whether Berkeley is right in his claim we have to reflect on the roles the two key terms play in our thought and discourse.

As it stands the argument or approach looks highly implausible. Indeed, if it does depend upon ordinary usage, as Mates suggests and I have supposed, it is hard to see how Berkeley could expect it to succeed. For it is clearly the case that according to ordinary usage it is quite proper to talk of something as existing or having existed while at the same time claiming that it is not and has not been perceived. For example, I have no doubt that there are weeds in odd corners of my garden that have so far escaped the notice of me or anyone else and which may well wither and die without being perceived by anybody. And, similarly, when we say 'there was an odour' we do not mean, nor do we necessarily imply, 'it was smelled'. There may have been nobody about to smell it. Hylas has the basic point when he says:

> Ask the first man you meet, and he shall tell you, *to be perceived* is one thing, and *to exist* is another. (*Dialogues*, iii, 234)

Clearly common speech does not confirm Berkeley's doctrine. Indeed we might have expected that Berkeley would have been the first to concede this. In recognizing it as the prevalent opinion (as he does in *Pr.* 4) that sensible objects do exist when not actually perceived, Berkeley is surely acknowledging that in ordinary usage *esse* is not *percipi*.

Given this it is tempting to take the short way and to say that when Berkeley appeals to 'what is meant by the term *exist*' he cannot, after all, be taking ordinary usage as the criterion.[2] And this would bring us to the interesting and important question as to what exactly he did mean by 'meaning'. This question we shall have to look at later, but there are two reasons for not giving up too quickly the notion that there is an approach from ordinary usage. The first point is that in the next section we will find Philonous responding to Hylas's claim that *esse* is not *percipi* by appealing to 'the common sense of the world' and to what the plain man actually says in a certain situation. And the second point is that here in *Pr.* 3 Berkeley does allow for what we ordinarily think and say to a greater extent than we have been supposing. He is trying to show that *to exist* is *to be perceived*, and this is what he concludes, but when examining what we mean by 'exist' he does seem to find room for our talk of things existing unperceived.

Looking closer at the passage, then, we find that Berkeley allows that we can refer to something as existing both when we are actually perceiving it and when we are not actually perceiving it. First we have the case where a man is actually perceiving something, where he is looking at it or touching, hearing, smelling or tasting it. And to cover this sort of situation Berkeley says:

> The table I write on, I say, exists, that is, I see and feel it . . .

But then there is the case when one wants to refer to something as existing even though one is not actually perceiving it. And here it appears that one of two things can be meant:

> . . . and if I were out of my study I should say it existed, meaning thereby that if I was in my study I might perceive it, or that some other spirit actually does perceive it.

Thus when I say a certain sensible thing exists, as an alternative to meaning (A) *it is perceived by me*, I can mean (B) *it could under certain circumstances be perceived by me*, or (C) *it is perceived by someone else*. It is usually supposed that (C) is very important to Berkeley and that he thinks of God's continued perception as providing for the existence of sensible things when no created spirit happens to be perceiving them. Here, though, it is (B) that will interest us. The reason for this is that while (A) and (C) can be run together as cases where what exists is actually perceived (by me or by someone else), (B) seems to allow for the notion that we can quite properly say that something exists even if we suppose it is not being perceived at all. And this concession is of the first importance in that it is inconsistent with the conclusion of the argument which is that *esse* is just *percipi*. Apparently when we say 'there was an odour' we need not mean 'it was smelled', for we might only mean that under certain circumstances it would have been smelled. And when I say there are weeds in my garden which have not been perceived, this is quite all right so long as I have it in mind that they could be perceived if someone went to the right spot and looked.

Of course there is something very odd about the suggestion that 'exist' can mean three different things when applied to sensible objects. For if anything seems intuitively clear it is that I am not using the word in different senses when I atttribute existence to, say, the book in my hand, the cooker in the empty room next door, and the magazine my wife is reading in the lounge. But what seems most unsatisfactory about the argument is the fact that Berkeley appears to proceed by appealing to the plain man's view and use of language, according to which it makes perfectly good sense to talk of things existing when not actually perceived, to justify his own quite different view, which is that sensible things can exist only when perceived. There is, then, a substantial gap between what is supposedly being justified and what is offered in justification. Berkeley's own view is well summed up in sect. 6 where he takes it that he has shown it to be true of sensible things that 'so long as they are not actually perceived by me, or do not exist in my mind or that of any other created spirit, they must either have no existence at all, or else subsist in the mind of some eternal spirit'. And here he holds that if a sensible thing exists it must be the case either (A) that it is perceived by me, or (C1) it is perceived by some created spirit, or (C2) it is perceived by an eternal spirit. There is no mention of (B), no allowance that a sensible thing, so long as it is perceivable, can exist unperceived.

My own view is that we just have to accept that the argument of sect. 3 does not prove what it is supposed to prove, but Luce has an interpretation of Berkeley's position which, if it were acceptable, would provide a way out of the difficulty. Briefly, Luce maintains that when Berkeley takes *esse* to be *percipi* he has in mind primarily the situation where one wants to say something one actually perceives exists. For example, I look at what is in front of me – a typewriter – and I ask myself what I mean when I say now that it exists. And here, according to Luce, I can only mean that it is perceived, that I perceive it. But if Luce is right Berkeley was prepared to *expand* his principle to cover the situation where I look away or go out of the room and still want to say the typewriter exists. The expansion suggested by Luce makes *esse* mean *percipi aut posse percipi*. Thus:

> The Berkeleian idea of sense is not a momentary existent, like a dream or the imagined dagger-in-the-mind; it is not something that ceases to be when it is no longer dreamed or imagined. On the contrary, the Berkeleian idea of sense is a continuing existent, still perceivable, still in relation to perception, even when it is not actually perceived. Accordingly, Berkeley's New Principle, if it is sound, must expand so as to cover the perceivable as well as the actually perceived. And so it does. (Luce 6, p. 6)

As Luce sees it, the short formula is important and true when we are considering the meaning of 'exist' in certain contexts, while the expanded formula contains the first but has a wider application.

The advantages of this interpretation must be obvious, for if we could accept it we would see Berkeley as holding a position very close to the common sense one, and we would have to see the approach of sect. 3 as involving an analysis of ordinary language leading to a statement of ordinary views. The obvious bar to accepting the interpretation is that it lacks all plausibility. Berkeley is quite definite about what he is going to show in sect. 3 – that the things we perceive by sense 'cannot exist otherwise than in a mind perceiving them.' His conclusion is equally positive – 'Their *esse* is *percipi*, nor is it possible they should have any existence, out of the minds or thinking things which perceive them.' And of course if there is any doubt at all as to how this should be interpreted we have only to look to sect. 6 to find Berkeley saying quite categorically that sensible things not actually perceived by any spirit 'have no existence at all'. We shall see later that Luce is unable to adhere consistently to his own reading.

III

At this point we will leave consideration of *Pr.* 3 for a while to look at what Philonous says in the *Dialogues* in answer to Hylas's challenge that the man in the street will confirm that '*to be perceived* is one thing, and *to exist* is another'. Our discussion here should certainly be relevant to the argument we have been looking at, and we shall in fact conclude that in the argument in the *Dialogues*, as in that in the *Principles*, there is a substantial gap between what is proved and what has to be proved.

We must be clear on the context at the outset. In challenging the view that 'the real existence of sensible things consists in their being actually perceived' Hylas appeals to what the man in the street will say. In response to this challenge Philonous himself appeals to the vulgar. Thus:

> I am content, Hylas, to appeal to the common sense of the world for the truth of my notion. Ask the gardener, why he thinks yonder cherry-tree exists in the garden, and he shall tell you, because he sees and feels it; in a word, because he perceives it by his senses. Ask him, why he thinks an orange-tree not to be there, and he shall tell you, because he does not perceive it. What he perceives by sense, that he terms a real being, and saith it *is*, or *exists*; but that which is not perceivable, the same, he saith, hath no being.

It will turn out that there is one very good reason for not taking this argument at its face value and for supposing indeed that Berkeley himself saw (or came to see) that it didn't prove quite as much as he would have liked. For the time being, though, I am going to take it very seriously and assume that the Berkeleian really does think that *his own* doctrine will be confirmed if we attend to the sort of thing we ordinarily say in situations like the one he has chosen. We can first outline very briefly what Berkeley might *like* to prove by means of this argument, and then consider at length whether the argument works.

We start with the gardener standing in the garden looking at a cherry-tree; just as in *Pr.* 3 we start with Berkeley sitting in his study, writing at his desk. And as he stands in the garden the gardener is prepared to assert both (i) what he perceives (the cherry-tree) exists, and (ii) what he does not perceive (an orange-tree) does not exist. And clearly if this is to be seen as indicating acceptance of the notion that 'the real existence of sensible things consists in their being actually perceived' it must be assumed that (i) betrays a recognition that (I) quite generally, whatever is perceived exists, while (ii) indicates acceptance of the truth that (II) quite generally, what is not perceived does not exist, or, for this comes to the same thing, that whatever exists is perceived. It would seem that Berkeley would like to have it that though the gardener may assert, as Hylas has insisted he will, that *esse* and *percipi* are distinct, a little attention to what he says in concrete situations will show that he does not really regard them as being distinct at all.

So much, then, for what Berkeley, through Philonous, would seem to be after. The next question is whether the common sense of the world really does support his notion. Now in evaluating the argument one's first inclination is just to accept (i) and (I) without further ado, but to press the gardener on just what he means when he asserts (ii) and to consider whether he would want to or should commit himself to (II). And the reason for taking this line would be that both (i) and (I) can be seen as logical truths, while it is doubtful whether the gardener is asserting (ii) as a logical truth or that (II) is a logical truth or indeed true at all. And if so, the conclusion would have to be that it does follow from the meaning of 'perceive' that what is perceived (by the gardener or anyone else) exists, but that it does not follow from the meaning of 'exist' that what exists must be perceived. This would of course tie in with our earlier thinking, for our conviction that there are weeds in the garden that have not been perceived is quite compatible with a recognition that any weeds we do perceive must exist. We will, though, spend a little more time on (i) and (I).

The reason for supposing that we might be dealing with logical truths here is that ordinary language does allow us to use 'see', 'feel' etc., and hence 'perceive', in such a way that it is necessarily false that X is perceived if X does not exist. Of course it is possible for A to say that he perceives X and for B to deny that X exists, but the logic of the situation requires A to agree that if B is right about the non-existence of X then he (A) is wrong in saying that he perceives it. On this view, just as we can only *know* what is in fact true – though fallible as we are, we often think we know something which turns out to be false – so we can only *perceive* what exists to be perceived.

One objection to treating (i) and (I) as logical truths might be that we sometimes do allow that people see non-existent things. For example we say that the subject *sees* things under hypnosis and that the drunk *sees* pink elephants, though we may not suppose for a moment that the things seen here really exist. An obvious answer to this is to say that in such contexts the verb is used in a weak, extended or scare-quotes sense, and we might support this by pointing out that when we talk of the drunk having *seen* pink elephants we are also ready to say that of course he didn't *really* see them but only thought he did. This is an area under dispute. Using the well-worn example of Macbeth's dagger Don Locke says:

> Obviously Macbeth didn't see *a dagger*, at any rate not a real dagger, but he did see something, something which he described as a dagger. Macbeth did see something, and that something did not exist. (p. 16)

Locke takes this to be obvious, but the issue is a tricky one. If we took Macbeth to be genuinely unsure as to whether there was a dagger before him it would at least be quite natural to tell him, not just that there was no dagger, but that he was suffering an hallucination, and consequently not really seeing anything at all. It remains true, though, that once it is accepted that Macbeth was suffering an hallucination it does seem quite proper to talk of him not only as having *seen* a dagger but also as having seen *a dagger*. The situation here is paralleled in our reports on dreams. In the first instance it is essential that I make it clear that I only *dreamt* I saw certain things (i.e. that I didn't really see them), but once it has been established that I am reporting on a dream I can quite happily go on talking about what I *saw* in that dream.

It is perhaps worth asking whether when in a dream I see something there must be something which I see and whether, if there must, this something should be supposed to *exist*. And it seems to me that when we are prepared to talk of having seen things in dreams we are also prepared to talk of there having been things which we dreamt about. Indeed, if Pharoah dreamt about fat kine then fat kine existed in his dream. We should be careful here, though. If it is proper for me to say *when reporting on a dream* that there was a rhinoceros, or that a rhinoceros existed in my dream, I must have made it clear that I *am* reporting on a dream, that there was no rhinoceros, and that I only dreamt there was. The truth seems to be that when reporting on a dream (and perhaps on an hallucination) I find it appropriate to use the language I would use for reporting on my sense experiences, but that when making it clear that I am reporting on a dream (or an hallucination) I must be as ready to qualify the claim that there *were* things as I am the claim that I *saw* them. I didn't really see anything (I only dreamt I did) and there was nothing I saw (I only dreamt there was).

It is interesting that though (Don) Locke starts off by insisting that we use the word 'in the ordinary sense' when we say Macbeth saw a dagger, that he *really* saw something, and that the statement that someone perceives something does not entail that what he sees exists, he does very quickly modify his position. For within a few pages he is telling us that what is perceived (whether veridically or in an hallucination) must after all exist *in some sense of that word*. 'Naturally', he tells us, 'it follows from the fact that something is perceived that it exists in some sense, but in this sense even hallucinations exist' (p. 20). Here he introduces a distinction between *real existence* and *perceived existence*, so in place of our supposed logical truth that what is seen, felt, tasted, smelt or heard must really exist we have the logical truth that what is seen, for example, must have real existence or perceived existence. I find the notion of *perceived existence* obscure, but it does at least seem clear that ultimately Locke is not after all wanting to deny that there is an entailment between 'X is perceived' and 'X exists', but rather to assert that if 'perceived' is used in what he takes to be the 'ordinary' sense then 'exists' does not mean 'has real existence'.[3]

Now I do not want to dwell here on the question of the desirability or undesirability of saying that Macbeth saw a dagger in the sense of 'see' that we use when we say he saw Duncan, but if we give Locke his head for a moment we can note that he does allow that philosophers are at liberty to restrict artificially the use of the word so that a thing will be said to be seen (or, more generally, perceived) only if the thing seen or perceived really exists. Indeed he says:

> The remark that he [Macbeth] didn't really see a dagger, that he only 'saw' one, would no doubt gain the acceptance of the man in the street, but that doesn't show that Macbeth didn't see something in the ordinary sense of 'see'. All that it shows is that *if* we draw a distinction between 'see' and 'really see', or between 'see' in a scare-quotes and 'see' in an ordinary sense, and say that Macbeth didn't really see, only 'saw' a dagger, *then* the point of this distinction will be obvious and the usage readily understandable. It does not show that ordinary language makes any such distinction, and does not show that people ordinarily object to saying that Macbeth saw something. (p. 16)

So if we decide to use the word in this stipulated sense (whether or not it is the ordinary sense) we can say that a thing can be perceived only if it has real existence. This will of course be a definitional truth. Contrasted with this we have Locke's usage according to which a thing can be perceived (in Locke's sense) only if it has real existence or perceived existence. And this is suggestive, for those who know their Berkeley will appreciate that Berkeley himself uses 'perceive' in such a way that whether I dream, suffer an hallucination, form a mental image or see a table, I am said to *perceive* an object. This object will exist, but it will not necessarily exist *in rerum natura*. Indeed in *PC* 473 he admits that 'I use the word Existence in a larger sense than ordinary' and that 'existence is vulgarly restrain'd to actuall perception'. And of course Berkeley holds not just that what is perceived (in the generous sense) must exist (in the large sense) but that whatever exists (in the large sense) must be perceived (in the generous sense). Thus for a thing to exist it must either be actually perceived or perceived as an object of the imagination etc.

It seems quite clear, though, that Berkeley saw his problem as being that of convincing his readers that the book they read, the house and its furniture and the scene outside were all such that they could not exist when not actually perceived. He introduces *Pr.* 3 by saying that 'every body will allow' ideas formed by the imagination to be mind-dependent. The object of the exercise is to convince everybody that the 'ideas imprinted on the sense' are in a similar position. So in dealing with Berkeley we do have some excuse for concentrating on perception as the perception of those objects which the plain man takes to exist independently of his mind, and on the question whether *their* existence is to be perceived.

Certainly our gardener will be a fairly tough-minded fellow, and his claim is that whatever he perceives *by sense* is a real being. He will be using words in what he takes to be their standard senses and I think we can take it that if he were persuaded that the cherry-tree enjoyed only the same status as the pink elephants he saw when drunk he would withdraw the claim that it existed and probably too the claim that he had seen it. Indeed, as against Locke I am strongly inclined to think that the man in the street will see the point of a distinction between ' "see" in a scare-quotes and "see" in an ordinary sense' primarily *because* it reflects his readiness in certain contexts to withdraw or qualify the claim that he has *seen* something and to substitute the claim that he *thought* he saw, *dreamt* he saw, or *imagined* he saw the thing. But be that as it may, apparently nobody wants to deny that what is perceived (in some sense of that word) must exist (in some sense of that word) and perhaps this admission is all Philonous and Berkeley need and we should give them (I).

Before going on to the converse, we should certainly stress the obvious point that the implausibility of *esse* is *percipi* does not arise from any implausibility in the suggestion that what is perceived must exist. Rather, it arises from the implausibility of the converse. When the man in the street says that '*to be perceived* is one thing, and *to exist* is another', it is because he believes that things can exist when not perceived, and not because he believes that he can see or feel things that aren't there. Similarly, if the claim is a claim about *meaning* and it is supposed that what is perceived must (logically) exist and what exists must (logically) be perceived, then the really substantial doubts will be about the second of these propositions.

Luce in particular tends to put too much weight on the non-controversial relationship, as when, discussing Berkeley's claim that 'exists' means 'is perceived', he says:

> *Prima facie* he has a good case. In ordinary conversation it would sound rather silly to say, 'I see the car, and it exists'. 'I see the car' is a sufficient statement, and the addition 'and it exists' is a redundancy, which adds nothing and may mislead folk into thinking the car could be seen and *not* exist. (Luce 6, p. 4)

Later in the paper he does concern himself with the converse, but here as he often does, Luce puts undue emphasis on what we have agreed may be a logical truth and clearly thinks that this gets us a goodly part of the way. In fact of course it does not. The plain man will certainly agree that if he sees his neighbour's car then his neighbour's car must exist, but recognition of this truth will do nothing to persuade him that if his neighbour's car exists then someone must be seeing it. Initially at any rate Berkeley's principle will seem just as silly to the ordinary man as would the claim that 'to be true' means 'to be known', and just as the fact that it is logically true that what is known must be true does not make the latter look any less silly, so the fact that what is perceived must exist does not make the former look plausible.[4]

Another attempt to make the principle look plausible is contained in the following passage. Luce asks:

> What do we mean when we assert or deny existence in ordinary life? The giraffe exists; the sea serpent does not exist. The giraffe exists.

The Approach from Ordinary Usage

> How do you know? Why, I have seen one in the Zoo. The sea serpent does not exist. How do you know? Well, I have never seen one, nor met anybody who has seen one. But if a credible witness came along and said he had seen one, we should say then, 'Of course it exists.' It would seem, so far, that Berkeley is right, and that when we say a thing exists we mean that it is perceived by sense. (Luce 5, p. 59)

But obviously this won't do. In the first place, though I may well justify my claim that giraffes exist by saying that I have seen one in the zoo, clearly the fact that I *have* seen one does not entail that any exist now. Of course given the fact that I did see one it follows that at least one giraffe existed then, but my judgement is that giraffes exist *now* even though it may be the case that nobody is perceiving them. Far from suggesting that *esse* is *percipi*, appeals to what people have seen to justify claims as to present existence rest upon the implicit assumption that things *can* exist unperceived. Nor can we accept the interpretation Luce puts upon what is said about the sea serpent. Of course it is in part because no reliable witness has ever come across one that we suppose there is no such creature, but it certainly doesn't *follow* from the fact that nobody has seen a sea serpent that there is no sea serpent to be seen. No witness has ever seen vegetation on Saturn, but it certainly *makes sense* to suppose that there is vegetation there. Further, consider what we would say if, as Luce suggests might happen, a reliable witness did come along and report that he had seen a sea-serpent. In this situation we might well conclude that of course it existed, but the suggestion would not be that it existed only when the witness saw it. We would suppose that it had existed all along and that in all probability it still existed somewhere near where the explorer saw it. There is nothing in all this to suggest that 'when we say a thing exists we mean that it is perceived by sense'.

There is one further point we can make about (I) and this is that the truth is that *if* something is perceived then that thing must exist to be perceived. In the particular case of (i) the truth is that *if* the gardener does indeed perceive a cherry-tree in the garden then there is a cherry-tree in the garden which he perceives. Now it is at least conceivable that the gardener may be mistaken both in thinking that he sees a cherry-tree and in supposing that the cherry-tree exists. If he is a very ignorant gardener (or rather drunk) or if the light is bad, it may be that he has mistaken an almond-tree for a cherry-tree. In this case he will be expected to withdraw the claim that he saw *a cherry-tree* and to substitute the claim that he saw a tree which he took to be a cherry-tree. More exceptionally (and perhaps when he is very drunk) there may be nothing in the garden which he sees and takes to be a cherry-tree. In this case he might be prepared (when sober) to withdraw the claim that he *saw* anything and to substitute the confession that it just seemed to him that he saw something.

Now it is sometimes argued that even in what may seem quite normal circumstances it is always *conceivable* that what I am perceiving is not what I take it to be and even that I am not perceiving anything at all. And this gives rise to the sceptic's challenge: how can you ever *know* that you are perceiving (say) a cup, or indeed that there is any real object that you now perceive, if it is always *conceivable* that your experience is hallucinatory or that you are dreaming? But I don't raise this problem in order to solve it here. Rather I want to stress that if it is a logical truth that what is perceived must exist, this truth is not relevant to a solution. The truth is that *if* I see a cup then that cup must exist and *if* I see something real then there is something real that I see, and acceptance of this truth does not help me if my worry is as to whether I am really seeing a cup or whether I am really seeing anything at all.

It is as well to be clear on this if only to avoid a mistake made by Luce who tends to confuse the logical truth with an answer to the sceptic's challenge. Thus in the following passage (from Luce 7, p. 120) he begins and ends by making claims about meaning, but in between devotes himself to what looks like an assertion that we can be sure that our experiences are veridical and that we are genuinely perceiving real things. He begins with a point about meaning:

> Berkeley's first concern was with the actually perceived; he could not say everything all at once; but he took things in order due, and he set himself to determine the status and nature of what we actually perceive when we are perceiving it. It exists, he says; it is; and its being or existence is *to be perceived*; for that is what the terms *being* and *existence* mean.

But he goes on:

> We smell a smell and take in its existence with the sniff. We see a book and see that it is. In touching a table we touch an existing

table. We taste strawberries, and can no more doubt their existence than we can doubt our own. We hear the sound of the horn and the cry of the hounds and then the View Halloo; and these sounds self-evidently exist; they are perceived. These are intuitive truths; one sees them *par simple vue*.

And here he seems to be claiming, not that *if* I smell, see, touch, taste or hear something that thing must exist (because of the meanings of the terms), but rather that I can know for certain both that I am genuinely perceiving something and what that something is. But it is to the logically based certainty that Luce returns in the sequel:

> On the other hand to add 'and it exists' to 'I see the table' is a gratuitous, misleading addition to a complete self-explanatory statement. The table could not be seen, if it did not exist . . .

Obviously there is something wrong with this passage and the trouble seems to be that Luce is confusing two kinds of certainty. Of course it may be that a case can be made for claiming that I can have certainty, even intuitive certainty, that I do, say, see a table. But the case needs making, and we need to be quite clear that if we have certainty in this area then the certainty is quite different from that attaching to the proposition that *if* I see a table then the table exists. This last proposition is one the sceptic will accept. His claim is that I can never be absolutely sure either that I am seeing a table *or* that the table exists. He will challenge Dr. Luce to tell him how he can be sure that he is indeed tasting strawberries and not just dreaming that he does.

What is happening in the quoted passage is that Luce is compounding a mistake made by Berkeley himself. As we have seen, Berkeley did use the term 'perceive' in a wide sense, and he would hold that even when I am drunk and see pink elephants there is some object that I see. More generally, whether I dream, suffer an hallucination, frame a mental image, or see a table, there is *something*, an idea or immediate object of perception, I am acquainted with. This thing will *exist*, though of course Berkeley admits that he uses the term 'in a larger sense than ordinary'. What he means by this concession is that not every case of perception is a case of 'actuall' perception or *sense* perception, and that not every perceptual object is a constituent of that sensible realm which he says remains 'as real as ever'. Now at one level Berkeley believes that I *can* have intuitive certainty concerning the perceptual object. Very simply, I can *know* both that I perceive an idea and what the idea is like. But so long as Berkeley wants (as he does) to preserve a distinction between realities and chimeras, between, say, suffering an hallucination and perceiving a genuine table, then even if we allow him his intuitive certainty that he perceives an idea this does not give him any intuitive certainty that he is perceiving a real and respectable table. One way of making this point is to say with Bracken that if for Berkeley the real table is a collection of ideas then 'the only way we can tell whether a given sense-datum is a constituent in a "collection of ideas" that goes to make up a "real" or an "illusory" object, is by waiting to see. The datum itself doesn't tell us' (Bracken 1, p. 47).

Now Berkeley is certainly capable of confusing his doctrine that we can have intuitive certainty concerning the existence of the idea we immediately perceive with the stronger claim (which he is not entitled to make on his principles) that we can have intuitive certainty that what we perceive exists *in rerum natura*. We find him doing this in *Pr* 88 when he says:

> I can as well doubt of my own being, as of the being of those things which I actually perceive by sense: it being a manifest contradiction, that any sensible object should be immediately perceived by sight or touch, and at the same time have no existence in Nature, since the very existence of an unthinking being consists in *being perceived*.

One truth Berkeley has in mind here is that if I actually perceive something *by sense* then that thing must exist *in Nature*. The other claim is that when I perceive something (though not necessarily by sense) I can be sure that it exists (though not necessarily in Nature). It is quite obvious that these cannot be combined to yield the conclusion that on occasion when I take myself to be perceiving by sense I have intuitive certainty that I perceive something in Nature. I may be dreaming.[5]

IV

We turn, then, to (ii) – the gardener's assertion that what he fails to see in the garden does not exist – and the crucial (II) – the quite general claim that what is not perceived does not exist. And, as we said earlier, our starting point will be that (ii), in the context in which it is asserted, does not look at all like a logical truth, while, even if it is in fact true, it does not suggest a recognition on the gardener's part that (II) is true.

Starting with (ii), we note that the gardener says what he does in a specific context. He is in a garden, which we can assume he works in and knows well, and he asserts, quite reasonably and doubtless rightly, that he perceives no orange-tree so there is no orange-tree to be seen. But even if we allow that the gardener's assertion is true, and well-founded given the circumstances, it certainly does not follow that it involves a logical truth. This point becomes clear if we suppose that the garden is a very big one employing perhaps many gardeners; if we suppose the gardener does not know the garden very well, is short-sighted or even blind; if we suppose that instead of making the claim about an orange-tree the gardener makes it about a very small object such as a buttercup, or even if we suppose he makes it about an object it would take a microscope to see. For in all these cases it is clearly possible that there might be something perceivable which the gardener fails to perceive. Of course we can so describe the circumstances that it will seem very unlikely or even *for practical purposes* inconceivable that the gardener should fail to perceive what is there to be perceived, but this inconceivability will never amount to *logical* inconceivability. When the gardener says that he does not perceive an orange-tree *and* that there is no orange-tree to be seen, the second half of the assertion is not a gratuitous, misleading addition to a completely self-explanatory statement. Given the situation the fact that the gardener does not perceive a tree provides an excellent reason for supposing there is no tree, but it is certainly *possible* that the first part of the claim should be true and the second false.

But we do not need to labour this point further, for whatever we might want to say about (ii) we are hardly likely to want to see (II) as a logical truth or indeed true at all. If I ask the first man I meet, and it may be the gardener, whether anything exists which is not being perceived he will certainly tell me that there are many such things, and indeed some which he has every reason to suppose have never been perceived at all. It is at this point that Berkeley seems to part company with common sense, for he says it is *meaningless* to talk of a sensible object existing unperceived. *Pr.* 3 contains only the unsupported claim that if we attend to the meaning of 'exist' we should find this unlikely claim intuitively obvious.

The key to understanding much that Luce says in interpretation and support of Berkeley lies in understanding that he wants to see the New Principle as amounting to a logical or conceptual truth but appreciates that, given the form in which Berkeley usually proposes it, it does not look like one. He is, as we have seen, impressed by the fact that what is perceived must exist, but at the same time unhappy that the converse does not seem to enjoy the same logical status. And this brings us once more to his suggested expansion of the principle which makes the *esse* of sensible things *percipi aut posse percipi*. In more detail, the claim is that the expanded formula is of quite general application if we are considering sensible things, while the short formula is intuitively true within a more limited context. We will start by considering whether the short formula can be saved by limiting its field of application.

What Luce suggests here is that we should concentrate for the moment not on the things we suppose we might perceive, but on those things we happen to be actually perceiving now. The reader should forget all about the things in other parts of his house and the things outside and concentrate on what he is perceiving *now*. Thus:

> Sooner or later the reader will have to deal with the question, What happens, on Berkeleian principles, to the object we are no longer perceiving? Let it be 'later', rather than 'sooner'. Put it off as long as you can. Berkeley expects the question to be raised, and answers it in outline on this his first mention of the New Principle [i.e. in *Pr.* 3]; but the main issue for him and everybody lies in the factors of *actual* perception. Take care of the percept, and the perceivable will take care of itself. Berkeley's business, first and foremost, is to explain the *esse* of things when they are being actually perceived. (Luce 5, p. 60)

The notion is that if we focus our attention on 'the factors of *actual* perception' we will find a suitable conceptual truth. And Luce tells us at once what he thinks the truth was that Berkeley found. Thus:

> He tells us that actual existence is to be actually perceived. If he is wrong, let someone tell us where he is wrong; let someone tell us what is the existence of this sight I see, this sound I hear, over and above my seeing the sight and hearing the sound.

The Approach from Ordinary Usage

The supposed truth contained in the unexpanded principle is, then, that 'actual existence is to be actually perceived'.

It hardly needs saying that this will not do. For Luce said he was going to reveal something about actual *perception* – and one suspects he had in mind the logical truth that what is actually perceived must actually exist – but instead he makes a wholly dogmatic assertion about actual *existence*, which assertion amounts to the implausible claim that the converse of the logical truth is itself a logical truth. All along we have been supposing that it makes perfectly good sense to talk of things existing unperceived, and we have been given *no* reason for changing our opinion. Certainly, talking of 'actual' existence at this point does not alter the picture, for surely we have been talking about actual existence all the time.

Clearly, though, we have not got to the root of the trouble yet. For Luce announces his conclusion, that to actually exist is to be actually perceived, in a passage in which he has asked us to 'put off' the question as to the existence or non-existence of things we don't happen to be perceiving. We are supposed to be concentrating *exclusively* on the existence of objects when we actually perceive them, but saying that actual existence is to be actually perceived seems to presuppose an answer to the question we are not supposed even to ask yet, namely the question whether the objects we are not actually perceiving can be said to have actual existence and whether *their* actual existence consists in being actually perceived. If Luce does mean to keep to his decision to restrict himself to questions about the existence of things we are actually perceiving when we are actually perceiving them, his conclusion must be interpreted as saying only that, if we are actually perceiving an existent object then necessarily that object is being actually perceived. But this is a trivial truth – just as it is a trivial truth that if an object is red and round then necessarily it is red – and the truth has nothing to do with the logic of 'exist'. The fact is, then, that Luce's conclusion is either a contentious proposition which can be asserted only if he exceeds his self-imposed brief, or a triviality.

It is clear, then, that this move does not get us anywhere, but it is rather surprising that Luce wants to make it at all for, if it did succeed and if it really did show that 'actual existence is to be actually perceived', there would seem to be no reason for expanding the principle in the way he thinks necessary. *Esse* would simply be *percipi*. There is some confusion here that needs explaining, and as the supposed necessity for the expansion springs from consideration of what we are to say about the existence of things we are not actually perceiving we can go on to look at this question.

Now it is easy to see why Luce finds it tempting to expand the principle. If you ask me whether there are weeds in my garden that are not being actually perceived I will affirm that I believe there are, and I will not find it a manifest truth that if they exist then they must be being perceived by someone. But I won't dissent for a moment from the proposition that if weeds exist in my garden they must at least be *perceivable*. Thus we may be inclined to agree with Luce when he says:

> The table could not be seen, if it did not exist; the notion of an invisible, intangible, insensible table *existing* is a contradiction, like a hot snowball or a round square. (Luce 7, p. 120)

On the one side here we have the familiar logical truth that if a thing is perceived it must exist, but on the other we have the supposed logical truth not that things like tables must be perceived but that they must be *perceivable*. Luce begins the next sentence by asserting that *esse* is *percipi*, but he warns that 'the Principle must expand and grow', and clearly what he has said supports only the expanded version of the principle. For the time being I am going to accept that it *is* absurd to talk of an insensible but existent table and I shall postpone consideration of where the absurdity lies.

The effect of the expansion is, I think, to make Berkeley's principle into something like an assertion of what we like to think of as the common sense view. The principle becomes, in Ardley's words, 'Berkeley's way of expressing our "at homeness" in the world, our sociability with everything' (p. 14), and the only people who need be offended by it are those philosophers who are so foolish as to deny that real things are perceivable. The question is, though, whether Berkeley would have accepted the suggested expansion and whether indeed Luce is really prepared to hold consistently to the view that this *was* Berkeley's principle. Berkeley's position on this seems pretty clear. It will be remembered that he holds it to be true of sensible things that 'so long as they are not actually perceived by me, or do not exist in my mind or that of any other created spirit, they must either have no existence at all, or else subsist in the mind of some eternal spirit'. It is impossible to escape the conclusion that Berkeley intended to commit himself to the view that sensible things must be actually perceived, either by us or by some eternal spirit, and thus that he held *esse* to be straightforwardly equivalent to *percipi*.[6]

That Luce is not very sure of his ground when he attributes the expanded principle to Berkeley is suggested by the following odd passage. He says:

> In point of fact the *esse est percipi* is an elastic principle, meant to stretch; it can cover the thought-form or existence-form under examination. Berkeley himself extends it to cover active existence, saying, 'existence is percipi or percipere, or velle i:e. agere'. In section 23 he argues that imagined existence is imagined perception . . . When, therefore, we are dealing with the perceivable, not actually being perceived by you or me, we are fully entitled to explain possible existence as possible perception. Berkeley does so, in effect, and his formula for passive existence thus expands naturally into *esse est percipi aut posse percipi*. (Luce 5, p. 61)

Some anonymous scribe has pencilled exclamation marks by 'possible existence' in my library copy. We shall see that Berkeley does find a use for a notion of 'hypothetical' existence, but nowhere else, I think, does Luce suggest that the expansion of the principle is meant to cover not the existence pure and simple of sensible objects but rather their 'possible existence'. We are faced with the problem of deciding what the phrase can possibly mean. Presumably the suggestion can only be that things having *possible* existence are things which don't *actually* exist but which might come to exist. But what is the principle as it concerns these things? It would seem that it must be either (a) that if a possible existent came into actual existence it would be actually perceived, or (b) that if it came into actual existence it would be perceivable. Of these possibilities it must be (a) Luce wants, for (b) has it that it is actual existents that are perceivable while he has just told us that it is the possible existents that are held to be perceivable. If we are asked to accept (a), though, we are in effect being pushed back to the unexpanded formula and informed that if a sensible object really exists (as distinct from being something that might at some stage exist) then it must be actually perceived. Further, if we do accept this interpretation of the expanded principle we now have something that may be more Berkeleian, but it is not something we can take to be consistent with or derivable from ordinary notions. The common view is that tables and the like exist in a quite full-blooded sense even when they are not actually perceived. In what follows, when I refer to existence I shall always mean existence, and not 'possible' existence.

The passage last quoted contains one other oddity suggesting that Luce's expanded formula is not quite the reflection of ordinary opinion we might like to think it. On the most natural reading the expanded principle would be interpreted as saying that sensible existents can be divided into two classes, the first containing sensible existents which are being actually perceived, and the second containing sensible existents which are not (as it so happens) being perceived. The *esse* of things in this second class is *posse percipi*. Now the oddity we are concerned with is that in introducing the perceivable Luce refers to 'the perceivable, not actually being perceived *by you or me*' (my italics). It is not to be supposed that by 'you or me' he means just Tipton or Luce, and of course what he is really suggesting is that there is a special problem concerning the existence of sensible things when they are not being perceived by any finite or created being. Here, though, he is running too fast. There is a problem concerning the existence of sensible things when they are not being perceived *at all*.

It is as well to be quite clear on what the plain man's position is here. Rightly or wrongly he believes that the table continues to exist when he leaves the room in exactly the same way as it existed when he was looking at it. Further, he holds that it makes perfectly good sense to suppose the table is not being perceived by anyone at all. It is because he believes this that he recoils from the notion that it is contradictory to suppose the table might exist unperceived but welcomes the claim that it must of course be perceivable. For him, then, the expanded principle is acceptable if it holds that sensible things may be supposed to exist both when they are actually perceived and when they are not perceived by anyone but none the less perceivable.

Given this it seems to follow that one problem which worries Berkeley is not going to worry the plain man at all. That is, the plain man need not be worried about the possibility that sensible objects pop in and out of existence as finite spirits perceive and cease to perceive them. For the plain man it is quite in order to talk of these as existing when unperceived by us and indeed when unperceived by *any* spirit because his notion is that when we say a sensible thing exists we are not committed to the view that it is perceived, but only to the claim that it could be. Only if we believe a sensible existent must be actually

The Approach from Ordinary Usage

perceived will we feel the need for God to preserve the existence of things by himself continuing to perceive them.

The position is, then, that if we take the *unexpanded* formula seriously (as I believe Berkeley did) we will find ourselves saying that either God is an omnipresent perceiver or things which no finite spirit is perceiving do not exist. But if we take the *expanded* formula seriously, interpreting it as genuinely reflecting the common view that things can be supposed to exist when not perceived at all, we will say that whether or not there is an omnipresent perceiver things not perceived by us can still be supposed to exist. When, though, Luce identifies the perceivable with the perceivable not actually being perceived *by you or me* it rather looks as if he is going to restrict himself to the perceivable *in this sense* and dodge altogether the question concerning the perceivable conceived of as that which exists but which is not perceived at all. In fact the position is worse than this, for Luce slips into supposing that though the perceivable not perceived by you or me does exist, because perceived by God, it remains nonsense to talk of the perceivable not perceived at all. This shows, of course, that it is the *unexpanded* formula that Luce takes seriously.

Thus we find Luce raising a question which shouldn't even be a question if he held that Berkeley really was committed only to the expanded formula. He says:

> *Esse est percipi.* But how, we naturally ask, can that apply to what I am not perceiving, the flower, the pudding, the page after next, etc.? At first sight it would seem that Berkeley's very definition of existence puts the perceivable off his map. (Luce 3, p. 4)

Now we might expect that Luce's answer to this question would be to point out that for Berkeley *to exist* is not simply *to be perceived* (let alone *to be perceived by me*). *Esse* is *percipi aut posse percipi*, and if this is so the perceivable is brought right back on the map. Instead he pulls God into the picture to save the day:

> Here comes in the distinction, all-important for Berkeley, between divine perception and human. There are many things which I am not perceiving, many things which no other man is perceiving, yet they exist, because they are perceived by God....

It must be stressed that the criticism of this passage is not that Luce approves the view that all sensible objects not perceived by man are in fact perceived by God. Before we could reasonably take exception to this we would have to dispose of the 'proof', which Luce takes to be valid, that there is indeed an omnipresent perceiver. There may be a God and it may be that he perceives all things. No, the objection to this passage is that it is assumed, contrary to what the expanded principle suggests, that unless there is an omnipresent perceiver things not perceived by creatures cannot be supposed to exist.

I have spent some time on Luce's case partly because it has been influential but also because, while each move he makes receives some support from Berkeley's text, Luce presents as a supposedly coherent and acceptable doctrine something which is clearly neither coherent nor acceptable. In the last chapter we found Luce accepting that ideas could be thought of both as chunky idea-things perceived by the mind and as clearly mind-dependent entities, and we suggested that neither he nor Berkeley could have it both ways. Here the situation is somewhat similar. Neither Luce nor Berkeley can have it both that the *esse* is *percipi* principle can be derived from an examination of the plain man's use of 'exist' *and* that the principle rules out the possibility of sensible objects existing unperceived. It certainly won't do to put forward the expanded principle as something quite compatible with ordinary views and then to interpret it in such a way that it denies there can be unsensed sensibles.

V

Suppose, though, we interpret the expanded formula in the way we at first found it natural to interpret it. We have agreed that there is something very odd indeed about the notion of an insensible table, but can we agree with Luce that 'the notion of an invisible, intangible, insensible table *existing* is a contradiction, like a hot snowball or a round square'?[7] If we could, we might be tempted to the view that an examination of ordinary usage shows, not that *esse* means *percipi*, but that it does mean *percipi aut posse percipi*. We might accept this if it could be shown that (1) if something exists it must (logically) be perceived or perceivable, and (2) if something is perceived or perceivable then it must (logically) exist. (2) invites sub-division into (2a) if something is perceived it must exist and (2b) if something is perceivable it must exist. We have already looked sympathetically at the case for accepting (2a) but (1) and (2b) require attention.

The Approach from Ordinary Usage

Of these, (2b) may at first seem obviously acceptable. If I talk about the table in the next room, the page after next, or the Empire State Building as being *perceivable* then surely I am committing myself to the view that these things *exist*. How could the Empire State Building be perceivable if it didn't exist? But the situation is not as simple as it might at first appear, and we need to consider how this commitment arises. Luce defines the word 'perceivable' in the following way:

> I use the term *perceivable* in its strict sense for that which we are not perceiving, but might perceive if we took the necessary steps. (Luce 3, p. 3)

But this definition will not serve the purpose. There is no need for us to dwell on the fact that the definition is no more strict than a definition allowing that what I am actually perceiving now is perceivable. I am inclined to say that the typewriter I am perceiving now is perceivable and that if it were not I could not be perceiving it. And if I do say this it is not clear that I am using the term loosely. We will let this pass though. There is no reason why Luce should not artificially restrict the term so that it covers only those unperceived objects we might perceive if we were suitably placed. The real objection to the definition is that if we accept it (2b) turns out to be false.

The first point here rests on the obvious fact that taking steps takes time. This being so it might be true at time t_1 that if I took the necessary steps I should perceive X at time t_2 without it having been the case that X existed at t_1. I am not perceiving an egg now and it may be that there is no egg in the hen-house now, but if I took the necessary steps and went to the hen-house I might well find an egg which had been laid while I was on my way. According to the definition this egg would have been perceivable even before I started walking, so if (2b) is true the non-existent egg must have existed then. It might be thought that this criticism is unfair. What Luce *means* is that the perceivable is what we are not in fact perceiving but would now perceive if we were suitably placed. This, though, brings us to the second point. For there are things which *don't* exist now that I would now perceive were I suitably placed. It is true for every sighted human being on the planet that if he were looking in my bathroom mirror he could perceive his own reflection there. But according to (2b) and the definition of perceivable as we are now construing it each of these in fact non-existent images must now exist. Clearly what we need is a sense of 'perceivable' which allows us to express the idea that had we taken the necessary steps (which we haven't) we would now be perceiving X without our taking the steps having been instrumental in bringing X into existence. The trouble is that it will be difficult if not impossible to find a definition which serves the purpose and which does not *rely on* the notion of existence. If we do presuppose the notion of existence it will be true that all perceivables exist, but only because the definition of a perceivable object involves a reference to its existence. I suspect indeed that the truth behind (2b) is the truism that if there *is* a perceivable object such as a table (i.e. if the perceivable table *exists*) then necessarily it must exist.

When we move on to (1) it is convenient to use 'perceivable' in the wider and perfectly proper sense according to which the actually perceived counts as perceivable. So (1) becomes simply, if something exists it must (logically) be perceivable. It must be stressed that this is only a matter of convenience. All of what follows could be rewritten using the word in Luce's allegedly strict sense. What I want to suggest is that if (1) is a logical truth its truth does not depend on the logic of 'exist'.

We must begin by noting that Berkeley would certainly agree that *as it stands* (1) is not a logical truth but a false statement. It is not necessary to prolong the discussion by considering whether such insensibles as numbers, laws and marriages can properly be said to exist, for Berkeley himself holds that the existent and the perceivable are not coextensive. The *esse* of the human mind is not for Berkeley *percipi*, nor is it *percipi aut posse percipi*: it is *percipere*. But this at once suggests that it is not because certain objects *exist* that they must be supposed to be perceivable but rather because they are objects *of a certain sort*. Now Berkeley makes it quite clear in *Pr.* 3 that his concern there is solely with the term *exist* 'when applied to sensible things'. But of course once we consider the significance of the fact that Berkeley is concerned only with *sensible* existents at this point it becomes immediately clear how he could see (1) as being logically true. For the claim must be that if something sensible exists it must (logically) be perceivable. Here we have found our logical truth. Unfortunately, though, this truth is one depending not on the logic of 'exist' but on the fact that 'sensible' and 'perceivable' as ordinarily used are synonyms.

Now when we come to the particular cases of the table, the odour, the sound, colour and figure, the situation is a little more complicated. If we are to begin to make headway with it we will do well to remind ourselves of the position Berkeley was most concerned to attack. Very briefly, then, the materialist was one who Berkeley took to be committed to the view that corporeal objects like tables were, with their original qualities, not perceivable. The table exists but it can never be perceived, and this because the mind perceives 'onely the impressions made upon its brain or rather the ideas attending those impressions'. It would doubtless be very nice if we could show this decidedly queer notion to be contradictory, but here unfortunately we can't hope to get anywhere by appealing to (1). The point is, of course, that given 'sensible' and 'perceivable' are to be used as synonyms the materialist is going to be as quick to deny that tables are sensible as he is to deny that they are perceivable. He will agree that *if* tables were sensible they would necessarily be perceivable, but however odd we may think the notion, his claim is that the real table is neither sensible nor perceivable. Equally, we should not get too excited if we find our opponent occasionally referring to the real table as *sensible* or as an *object of sense*. If we do find this we have a choice. We can suppose that our opponent really means what he says, in which case we will have to say that he does not really espouse the position Berkeley is concerned to attack. Or we can say that really he *is* a representative realist, in which case we must take it that he is either misusing the word 'sensible' or using it in an unusual and special sense. In either case the claim that the real table lies beyond the bounds of sense remains to be attacked.

I would suggest that three features of *Pr.* 3 contribute to obscuring from us what Berkeley's real case against the existence of an unperceivable table was. The first point is that here as elsewhere in the *Principles* he does not clearly separate the case *against* the existence of an insensible table from the case *for* supposing a table can exist only when perceived. Thus we often get the impression that Berkeley's case against representative realism hangs on and stands or falls with his own suspect case for mind-dependence. This is a complaint that is not relevant just to sect. 3 and we will not dwell on it here. The second point is that superficially at any rate the section seems to rely on a question-begging appeal to what the plain man means when he says an object such as a table exists. Taking the superficial view it is open to the materialist to answer that an appeal to ordinary usage no more shows that the real table is perceivable than it does that the real table is always perceived. Of course it may be salutary to remind the materialist that his notions contradict commonly held views and ways of talking which he will himself incline to in his non-philosophical moments. Indeed it may even be that the average materialist will submit once the extent of the discrepancy between his views and ordinary notions is brought home to him. The fact remains, however, that an enthusiastic materialist would be the first to emphasize that if his views are true then common notions are false, and he would certainly not accept that showing materialism to be in contradiction with more ordinary thinking amounts to showing materialism to be contradictory. Admittedly there is the suggestion that the materialist will not be able to answer the challenge to show that he attaches meaning to the words he uses, but it isn't clearly *shown* that he will not be able to answer or that it is indeed nonsense to suppose a table existing outside our perceptual range.

Now clearly Berkeley does have something to say here, though in practice the case gets entangled with the case for saying that references to corporeal objects must be references to mind-dependent ideas. We will not spell the case out in any detail here, but putting it very simply we can say that as Berkeley saw the position the materialist was open to the charge that when he talked of an insensible table he quite literally did not know what he was talking about. When the plain man talks about a table he is talking about something he can sit down at, eat his dinner off, admire the colour of, and even carve his initials on. When he refers to a table he is talking about the sort of thing he meets in experience. Nor is the concept of an *invisible* table an empty one. I can make good sense of this notion when I read about invisible objects in a fantasy. Berkeley would say, though, that I can have no conception of a wholly *insensible* table. It is because we cannot conceive of an insensible table that we can mean nothing if we say such a thing exists. Similarly with qualities. I can talk meaningfully about colours, smells, sounds, tastes, shapes and textures because I have come across all these things in experience, but if I talk of a smell that cannot be smelled or a shape that cannot be seen or felt, my words will be vacuous.

Of course the case here does need spelling out in more detail, and I will be taking note of how Berkeley would spell it out later. But the important thing for us to notice now is that any case based on this line of thought would have very little to do with the logic of 'exist'. And this brings us to the third suspect feature of *Pr.* 3. For the fact is that by putting the stress on the notion of *existence* Berkeley manages to obscure what I take to be his main point. The case for saying this has to be made with some care for, as we shall see, Berkeley had devoted some thought to the meaning of 'exist'. If, though, we ignore for the time being an argument which emerges later, we can say that there is some plausibility in the suggestion that it is not when the materialist says that insensible tables and unperceivable shapes *exist* that he goes wrong but when he claims to be able to conceive an insensible table and an unperceivable shape. Indirectly, of course, there is a point to be made about existence. If the claim is that an insensible table exists, and it can be shown that the notion of an insensible table is incoherent or empty, then obviously the claim will have been shown to be incoherent or empty. But this is a by-product. On the basis of what has been said so far it would appear that the weakness in the materialist's case lies with the concept he says is instantiated, and not in the claim that it is instantiated.

A similar criticism might be made of what Luce says in the quotation with which we opened this section. It will be remembered that Luce holds that 'the notion of an invisible, intangible, insensible table *existing* is a contradiction, like a hot snowball or a round square'. When we first met this claim we were inclined to be sympathetic to it. Now we need to ask what makes it seem promising. Of course it *may* be that there is some point to be made about the meaning of 'exist'. If I am right, though, the italicizing of the one word distracts us from the *obvious* point which does not directly concern existence at all. The fact is, surely, that when we read the sentence we are struck by the oddity of the expression 'insensible table', and we might well feel sympathetic to the claim that *this* expression is contradictory. But of course if a watertight case could be made out for supposing that it was indeed contradictory then we would have to see the contradictory notion of a round square as inviting comparison not with that of an *existent* insensible table but rather simply with that of an insensible table. Again, existence would come into the picture only indirectly. It is a contradiction to suppose that a *round* square [exists], not that a round square *exists*, and the claim would be that to talk of an *insensible* table [existing] is just as absurd.

VI

We must now return to the gap between what Berkeley purports to establish by an appeal to ordinary usage and what is actually suggested by such an appeal. In *Pr.* 3 the gap is just *there*, as something unacknowledged but something to be explained. Berkeley claims that when we say a sensible object exists we mean that it is perceived or might be, and from this he straightway concludes that it is absurd to talk of sensible objects existing when not actually perceived. Quite obviously the appeal neither suggests nor justifies such a conclusion. We should note now that in the corresponding passage in the *Dialogues* the existence of a gap is at least acknowledged. Clearly Philonous would *like* the gardener to say that whatever is not actually perceived does not exist. But the gardener does not say this. What he does say is, first, that the fact that he cannot see an orange-tree in the garden satisfies him that there is no orange-tree there, and, second, that in general 'that which is not perceivable . . . hath no being'. Thus from what the plain man says we can derive the principle that corporeal objects must be *perceivable*, but not the Berkelelan principle that they must be perceived.

Not surprisingly, Hylas seizes on this point. He says:

> Yes, Philonous, I grant the existence of a sensible thing consists in being perceivable, but not in being actually perceived.

But Philonous's reply is surprising. He asks:

> And what is perceivable but an idea? And can an idea exist without being actually perceived? These are points long since agreed between us.

We have left this rather puzzling development until now because with it the approach from ordinary usage fizzles out. Philonous is in effect admitting that he has not established what he promised to establish by appealing to the gardener. We should be quite clear about this. Hylas had asked:

> . . . do you in earnest think, the real existence of sensible things consists in their being actually perceived?

Philonous had confirmed that he did indeed think this and claimed that an appeal to 'the common sense of the world' would confirm the

The Approach from Ordinary Usage

truth of *his* notion. In the conclusion, however, he admits that his opinion is not in fact established by an appeal to the way we ordinarily talk, but that he needs the support of the principle that we perceive only mind-dependent ideas. So there *is* a gap between what the appeal was supposed to show and what it in fact suggests, and this gap has to be filled by independent argumentation for the claim that the things we perceive by sense are mind-dependent.

Given the admission Philonous makes, it is natural to suppose that the argument in *Pr.* 3 requires supplementation in a similar sort of way. This is in fact what Givner suggests. He quotes from sect. 3 and says:

> From this account of the meaning of the statement, 'A sensible thing exists', Berkeley concludes, 'Their *esse* is *percipi*, nor is it possible they should have any existence out of the minds or thinking things that perceive them.' But granting that any sensible thing is or can be perceived, it does not follow that it cannot exist apart from the mind. The argument needs another premise. The required proposition has not been omitted; it is stated at the very outset of Part I of the *Principles*. (p. 650)

The relevant claim made at the outset is, of course, that we perceive only *ideas*. Givner concludes:

> Hence Berkeley's argument against matter, in effect, is this: To say a sensible thing exists, is to say it is or can be perceived; all perceivable or sensible things are sensations.

We have two propositions here, and *only the first* is established by the appeal to the meaning of 'exist' in sect. 3.

Now this may be all right so far as it goes, but the analysis does not resolve all the problems. We are likely to remain dissatisfied with Berkeley's progress up to the end of sect. 3, and this for more than one reason. In the first place it will have to be admitted that Berkeley's presentation of the argument is extraordinarily confused and confusing. Note that if the argument of sect. 3 requires supplementation by a premiss the premiss must be not that we perceive only ideas which may or may not be mind-dependent, but that we perceive mind-dependent ideas. Thus it must be *assumed* in sect. 1 that when we talk about ideas we are talking about things which we recognize to be only

E*

in the mind. In sect. 3, though, Berkeley purports to be showing that *attention to the meaning of 'exist'* will reveal that 'ideas imprinted on the sense' are mind-dependent. Thus in sect. 1 'idea' must be being used in one sense, and in sect. 2 it must be being used in quite another.[8]

A second reason for dissatisfaction is that, though the argument of sect. 3 apparently requires supplementation by independent argumentation for the premiss that perceivable things are (mind-dependent) sensations, there has in fact been no such argumentation. We have seen that sect. 1 opens not with an *argument* for the claim that we perceive only ideas but with the brute assertion that this is 'evident to any one who takes a survey of the objects of human knowledge'. If we take it that the plain man will be reluctant to accept, and has so far been given *no* reason to accept, that we perceive only mind-dependent sensations, we must conclude that by the end of sect. 3 he has been given *no* reason for believing that *esse* is *percipi*. Finally, we have another reason for believing that the stress on the word 'exist' is misleading. It is suggested that attention to 'the nature & meaning & import of Existence' should convince us that sensible things cannot exist unperceived. But, given Givner's analysis, it seems that Berkeley looks to the meaning of 'exist' only to get the point that corporeal things must be perceivable. It is because perceivable things are mind-dependent ideas that they cannot exist unperceived.

Perhaps we cannot finally justify Berkeley's tolerance of, and apparent indifference to, the gap between what is indicated by and what he suggests is indicated by an appeal to the way we ordinarily talk. We can indeed see him as in effect appealing first to the philosophers, in sects. 1-2, for the principle that *'the things immediately perceived, are ideas which exist only in the mind'*, and then, in sect. 3, to the non-philosophers for the view that *'those things they immediately perceive are the real things'*. And of course given these elements Berkeley can achieve his synthesis. If we do interpret him in this way, though, we can fault him on the grounds already indicated. His *presentation* of the argument must be judged misleading, and the argument itself can hardly be thought satisfactory as it stands. There is indeed *no* argument for the first of the premisses, and though in sect. 3 the materialist is challenged to attach any meaning to his words when he talks of corporeal things and their qualities as being essentially unperceivable it isn't *shown* either that he won't be able to answer or that if an answer is in fact impossible this is because of the meaning of 'exist'.

If we want to *understand* Berkeley's tolerance of the gap we can perhaps make two points. The first point is that the gap as it appears in both the *Principles* and *Dialogues* is symptomatic of Berkeley's tendency to disregard the fact that his standpoint and the philosophical standpoint are not the only possible standpoints. It is because he fails to take the plain man's standpoint seriously as a viable alternative that he feels we have to choose between the materialist's claim that real things are *never* perceived and his own claim that their *esse* is *percipi*. Ardley sees Berkeley's principle as amounting to his 'rejecting as absurd the systematic disjunction of appearance and reality' (p. 124), but this is exactly half the story. The principle also reflects and states the view that sensible things *are* mind-dependent appearances. Too easily, though, Berkeley switches from the claim that the systematic disjunction is absurd to the claim that the sensible reality is and must be as he conceives it to be. *Pr.* 3 provides an illustration of this. Berkeley is prepared to appeal to the plain man for support for his view that there is something very wrong with the belief that real things are never perceived, but his unquestioning acceptance of the line that *of course* the things we perceive are mind-dependent ideas leads him to see this support as support for the claim that real things are always perceived. The fact is, then, that the notion that the things immediately perceived are (Lockian) ideas *dominates* these early sections, and in such a way that it leads to distortion in the argument.[9] The claim *might* be that attention to the meaning of *exist* 'when applied to sensible things' reveals the absurdity of supposing things like tables and their qualities to be *unperceivable*. But because Berkeley takes it for granted that perceivable things are (Lockian) ideas he suggests (misleadingly) that attention to the meaning of 'exist' will show that *to exist* means *to be perceived*. Obviously a similar analysis could be given of his claim in the *Dialogues* that 'the common sense of the world' supports *his* notion.

The second point has special reference to *Pr.* 3. For it seems to me that if Berkeley is at this point looking backward and relying on what was said in sect. 1, he is also looking forward to an argument which has not yet emerged. Looking backward he could say that of course corporeal objects must be actually perceived for they are perceivable things and perceivable things are mind-dependent ideas. But looking forward he could anticipate a quite independent line of argument which he thought did show that it must be nonsense to talk of things *existing* unperceived. The argument here concerns not what our casual employment of the term might suggest 'exist' means to us, but rather what Berkeley thought on reflection it *must* mean. But this argument is a specialist one and to get at it we have to switch our attention right away from ordinary usage.

CHAPTER FIVE

The Psychological Approach

' "Exist", of course, is itself extremely tricky.
The word is a verb, but it does not describe
something that things do all the time, like
breathing, only quieter – ticking over, as it were,
in a metaphysical sort of way. It is only too
easy to start wondering what, then, existing *is*.'
(J. L. Austin, p. 68n)

I

We said earlier that to see if Berkeley is right about the relationship between *esse* and *percipi* we should have to look at the roles the two key terms play in thought and discourse. In the last chapter the emphasis was on discourse – on what the plain man is prepared to *say*. Now our attention must switch to what can be *thought*. To suggest that this is a further task we must undertake may seem odd, for what a man says is in general a fair guide to what he thinks, and we might well be inclined to suppose that the plain man says that '*to be perceived* is one thing, and *to exist* is another' because this is what he thinks. But it was Berkeley's belief that as language users we are prone to using words in such a way as to suggest we are thinking the unthinkable. Anything can be said but not everything can be thought, and sometimes we string words together in such a way that what we say may seem acceptable, and even profound, although what we have said was meaningless. Ultimately the solution, in Berkeley's words, is to 'draw the curtain of words' (*Pr. Intr.*, 24) and to consider what it is we are talking about. To take one simple example, we can suppose we find someone claiming that a particular geometry textbook does not deal with the round square. And in response we might suggest that the critic should consider what the words 'round' and 'square' mean, what they signify or stand for, and we should expect him to see that though we can talk of the round square (for, to repeat, anything is sayable) we can have no concept of it. Berkeley makes this point in his *Defence of Free-thinking in Mathematics*:

> Nothing is easier than to define in terms or words that which is incomprehensible in idea; forasmuch as any words can be either separated or joined as you please, but ideas always cannot. It is as easy to say a round square as an oblong square, though the former be inconceivable. (sect. 48)

The example is uncontroversial in that most of us will be able to make something of the claim that the round square is unthinkable. To suggest that we cannot think of or conceive an unperceived existent is, of course, much more controversial. Berkeley supposes that we speak the unthinkable much more often than plausible examples could suggest.

As is so often the case, the key to understanding Berkeley's position here lies in Locke's *Essay*. Locke had had something to teach Berkeley in this area. As Berkeley says in *PC* 492:

> We have learn'd from Mr. Locke. that there may be and that there are several glib, coherent, methodical Discourses wch nevertheless amount to just nothing. this by him intimated with relation to the Scholemen.

The relevant section in the *Essay* is IV viii 9. It seemed to Berkeley, though, that Locke allowed *himself* to say meaningless things and that he did this because of mistakes in his thinking about what it is for words to be meaningful. In particular, Locke's account of *general* words had presupposed our ability to think in a way in which it was quite impossible we should think. And Berkeley was convinced that it was the attribution to the mind of a power it did not and could not have – 'a power of framing *abstract ideas* or notions of things' – that accounted for the formulation of certain erroneous philosophical views, and ultimately for mistakes made by the vulgar as well as the learned. He did not devote the bulk of his twenty-five section introduction to attacking the notion that there are abstract ideas just because he believed a certain theory of signification was wrong. The attack is given the prominence it is because the notion 'has brought forth innumerable errors and difficulties in all parts of philosophy and in all the sciences' (*NTV* 125) and because Berkeley believed that materialism was rooted in the doctrine.

In this chapter we shall look first at Locke's views on the signification of words, then at Berkeley's attack on those views, and finally, at the appeals Berkeley makes to the absurdity of abstraction when he comes to attack materialism. Should anyone think it would have been more natural to deal with the introduction before spending any time on the main body of the work as we have in the last two chapters, it must be said that the plan we have adopted should help keep us mindful of the fact that what Berkeley has to say about meaning is essentially subservient to his main purpose which, in the *Principles*, is to show that certain claims made by the materialist are straightforwardly meaningless. We shall not get bogged down in, though we can hardly avoid looking at, peripheral questions. We shall not be particularly interested in the positive theory of meaning reflected in the introduction for its own sake; we will gloss over the problem of universals, and we shall have less to say than those with a special interest in Locke might think desirable on the question whether or not Berkeley is fair to their man and whether he interprets him aright. And further to keeping in mind the subservience of the introduction to the main pre-occupations of the *Principles* it will be as well to have what Berkeley says in *Pr.* 5 in mind from the beginning. He is referring to the prevalent opinion that sensible things can exist unperceived, and he says:

> If we throughly examine this tenet, it will, perhaps, be found at bottom to depend on the doctrine of *abstract ideas*. For can there be a nicer strain of abstraction than to distinguish the existence of sensible objects from their being perceived, so as to conceive them existing unperceived? Light and colours, heat and cold, extension and figures, in a word the things we see and feel, what are they but so many sensations, notions, ideas or impressions on the sense; and is it possible to separate, even in thought, any of these from perception?

In sect. 6 he challenges the reader to 'reflect and try to separate in his own thoughts the being of a sensible thing from its being perceived'. The inability of the reader to do this will, he suggests in sect. 23, 'make it unnecessary to insist on any other proofs against the existence of material substance'.

II

At the beginning of the *Philosophical Investigations* Wittgenstein castigates a certain view of language which results from paying too much attention to certain sorts of words, the view being that the meaning of a word is the object for which it stands. In a little more detail, the notion is this:

> ... the individual words in language name objects – sentences are combinations of such names. – In this picture of language we find the roots of the following idea: Every word has a meaning. This meaning is correlated with the word. It is the object for which the word stands.

And Wittgenstein goes on to say that this notion, which he introduces with an account from St. Augustine of how we first learn to use words, has an initial plausibility only if we are 'thinking primarily of nouns like "table", "chair", "bread", and of peoples' names'. In Wittgenstein's opinion if we do concentrate on such words we are likely to end up with an inadequate theory of meaning, not just because it can at best be a theory covering the meanings of certain words, but because by neglecting other words and the function of language as a whole we will end up with a theory that fails to do justice even to those sorts of words we concentrated on.

Now when we turn to Locke we find that he does make the mistake Wittgenstein points to. Indeed he makes the classical mistake of concentrating *first* on proper names and *then* on general terms such as 'man', 'horse' and 'lead'. The danger here is that we will think of proper names as just *standing for* the individual things they name, and then be misled into taking the correlation of a proper name with that one thing which it names as providing a paradigm of what it is for a word to have meaning. If we do this we will find ourselves looking for one individual thing, though now not an ordinary thing in the world around us, for each general word to name. To embark on this programme, which for Plato ended up with the postulation of *Forms* is to commit what Ryle 2 has taught us to think of as the 'Fido'/Fido fallacy, and it does seem that Locke commits it. The opening of III iii sets the tone:

> All things that exist being particulars, it may perhaps be thought reasonable that words, which ought to be conformed to things, should be so too, – I mean in their signification: but yet we find quite the contrary.

Why Locke thinks that all words ought to denote uniquely is far from clear, for he goes on to point out that 'reason and necessity' demand that most words should be general, that a language of proper names would be impossible, and that if it were possible it would be useless. Still, there is the clear suggestion that proper names are behaving properly, predictably, and, let us say, *monogamously*, while other words are behaving eccentrically, surprisingly or *promiscuously*. And so it becomes a problem for Locke as to how words, which we feel ought to conform to things in their particularity, yet manage to be general in their signification.

Now the issue is complicated by the fact that for Locke words (*including* proper names) do not straightforwardly stand for *things* at all, for in his view they stand rather for *ideas*. As he says:

> ... words, in their primary or immediate signification, stand for nothing but *the ideas in the mind of him that uses them*, how imperfectly soever or carelessly those ideas are collected from the things which they are supposed to represent. When a man speaks to another, it is that he may be understood: and the end of speech is, that those sounds, as marks, may make known his ideas to the hearer. That then which words are the marks of are the ideas of the speaker: nor can any one apply them as marks, immediately, to anything else but the ideas that he himself hath ... (III ii 2)

We are, Locke admits, tempted to suppose that the words we use have a reference beyond our own ideas, both because for communication to be completely successful the idea I use a given word to stand for must correspond to the idea the hearer associates with that word, and because 'men would not be thought to talk barely of their own imagination, but of things as really they are'. But though Locke acknowledges that there is some real point in recognizing such indirect and secondary references (cf. II xxxii 8), he takes it that to suggest that these are the immediate or primary references 'is a perverting the use of words, and brings unavoidable obscurity and confusion into their signification'. This because, firstly, when I use a word, say 'gold', it may be, but it may well not be that my idea and yours exactly correspond or that we mean exactly the same thing by the word, and, secondly, it is quite possible for us to use a word meaningfully when it is not the case that there is anything real for it to signify. And in making this point we are not restricted to words like 'chimera' and 'mermaid'. Words like 'sacrilege' and 'adultery' have meaning quite independently of the contingent fact that there have been cases of sacrilege and adultery, as the word 'resurrection' *had* meaning before the resurrection and *has* meaning even for one who believes that no resurrection has ever taken place. Words, Locke seems to want to say, can have senses independently of any direct reference to things in the world, though for a word to have a sense when used by any one person is for it to refer to, mark out or stand for some idea he has in his mind.[1]

Given this, it would appear that for Locke 'Fido' will stand immediately not for Fido but for the idea the speaker has of Fido. And it turns out to be the case that in Locke's view the relationship between the idea of Fido and Fido himself is likely to be the simple one of resemblance, so that the agent is able to refer to the dog as 'Fido' because ultimately the word marks out an idea which pictures the dog. Locke himself takes the case of the words 'nurse' and 'mamma' as used by a small child, not as general terms, but to refer exclusively to *his* nurse and *his* mother. Thus:

> There is nothing more evident, than that the ideas of the persons children converse with . . . are, like the persons themselves, only particular. The ideas of the nurse and the mother are well framed in their minds; and, like pictures of them there, represent only those individuals. The names they first gave to them are confined to these individuals; and the names of *nurse* and *mamma*, the child uses, determine themselves to those persons. (III iii 7)

It is perhaps worth emphasizing the words 'like pictures' here. Locke does seem to think of the idea as a reproduction of the person in the form of an image, so that the simple relationship one might suppose must obtain between the person and the name by which we refer to him is closely paralleled by what Locke takes to be the more basic relationship between the idea of the person and the name. We have a new dualism here. If when he talks about perception Locke is a representative realist, we have to attribute to him the view that when I observe the table the *immediate* object is an idea representing some feature of the table. Now we find that when we use a proper name to refer to a person, the *immediate* reference is not the person named but rather the idea I have framed of that person.[2]

The most significant effect of shifting attention from the relationship between words and things to that between words and ideas is that the problem of how a word like 'man' can be used to refer to many things becomes the problem of how the word can stand for one idea when that idea cannot in any straightforward way picture any particular man in the world of real men. And Locke's answer is that as well as ideas that serve to mirror individual particular things in the world we have abstract general ideas which serve somehow to represent many particulars. Thus (still in III iii 7) we are invited to consider how the child, who already has the ideas of his nurse and his mother, comes to frame the general idea to which the word 'man' refers:

> Afterwards, when time and a larger acquaintance have made them observe that there are a great many other things in the world, that in some common agreements of shape, and several other qualities, resemble their father and mother, and those persons they have been used to, they frame an idea, which they find those many particulars do partake in; and to that they give, with others, the name *man*, for example. And thus they come to have a general name, and a general idea. Wherein they make nothing new; but only leave out of the complex idea they had of Peter and James, Mary and Jane, that which is peculiar to each, and retain only what is common to them all.

Basically the view seems to be that when I have framed the idea corresponding to the word 'man' I can (a) use that word significantly to refer to a *sort* of things, (b) mean something whenever I use the term, and (c) recognize instances as being *of* the sort so as to be able to describe each as a man. I frame the general idea by considering the ideas I have of particulars of the sort and 'by separating from them the circumstances of time and place, and any other ideas that may determine them to this or that particular existence' (III iii 6).

I take it, then, that for Locke general words, which appear to be behaving promiscuously in that each can be used to refer to a great many particular things, are in fact behaving monogamously and more like proper names than we might suppose, in that each marks out, or has as its primary or immediate signification, one abstract general idea. Warnock has this point in mind when he says:

> The word 'red', which clearly is not the proper name of any particular red object, is in effect regarded by Locke as the proper name of the abstract idea. (He speaks as if we first frame the abstract idea, and then we name it.) The 'immediate signification' of the word is thus an idea in our own minds, something that we have framed by abstraction. (Warnock 1, p. 64)

This seems to me right enough. But, right or wrong, it may be that some clarification of the interpretation is needed in the light of a criticism made by Bennett. Bennett has the last quoted passage in mind when he says:

> According to Warnock's Berkeley, Locke thought of general words as proper names, each referring to some one entity; and he postulated abstract ideas because they were needed to play the role of such entities – so that 'green', for instance, is the proper name of the abstract idea of green. Now, someone *might* arrive at the theory of abstract ideas by this route, but is there any evidence that Locke *did*? I have no reason to think that Locke regarded general words as proper names . . . (p. 23)

The point I want to make here may be a minor one, but I think we ought to be clear on it. It is that Warnock (and it is really Warnock rather than Warnock's Berkeley who is making the claim) does *not* hold that 'Locke thought of general words as proper names'. He holds that for Locke the word 'red' is *not* the name of any particular red object (i.e. it is *not* a proper name), but he also holds that the term 'is *in effect* regarded by Locke as the proper name of the abstract idea' [my italics].

Any interpretation which had it that Locke thought that general terms *were* proper names would be totally indefensible. We have to look no further than sects. 2-5 in III iii for the clearest evidence that he was very much alive to the difference between, say, 'horse' and 'Bucephalus'. There are sensitive observations on the reasons we have for giving proper names to some objects and for not giving them to others, and a case is made for supposing that general terms are essential for communication and the advancement of knowledge. We have every reason for supposing that Locke did *not* think of general words as proper names. Warnock is quite aware of this. Yet Warnock does have a point to make when he says that a general term 'is *in effect* regarded by Locke as the proper name of the abstract idea'. As Locke sees the situation there is a problem about general terms simply because they do not function as we might think words ought to function, that is as names of particular objects. And Warnock has been struck by the fact that Locke solves this 'problem' by finding *something* (though an idea and not an object in the world) for each general term to name. Rather similarly, Plato was quite aware that there was a difference between proper names and general terms, but his account of general words involves his seeing them as 'in effect' the proper names of Forms, and then explaining the promiscuous behaviour of a word like 'man' by seeing men as partaking in the Form. So far as Locke is concerned, the problem is solved by drawing attention to the *immediate* signification of the words we use and claiming that when a speaker uses any word (whether proper name or general term) the *primary* signification will be some idea he has framed in his mind. At the primary level 'Bucephalus' is the name of the idea I have framed of Bucephalus and 'horse' is the name of my idea of horse. The difference in function between proper names and general terms is to be explained by looking at the *secondary* level and noting that the idea I have of Bucephalus represents only Bucephalus while that of horse represents all particulars of the sort.

The interpretation given above is I think reconcilable with, and indeed demanded by, the following passage in which Locke affirms that general terms differ from proper names in that the latter, but not the former, signify each one particular thing, but then goes on to tell us what one thing it is that a general term stands for or is the sign of. He says:

> The next thing therefore to be considered is, What kind of signification it is that general words have. For, as it is evident that they do not signify barely one particular thing; for then they would not be general terms, but proper names, so, on the other side, it is as evident they do not signify a plurality; for *man* and *men* would then signify the same; and the distinction of numbers (as the grammarians call them) would be superfluous and useless. That then which general words signify is a *sort* of things; and each of them does that, by being a sign of an abstract idea in the mind . . . (III iii 12)

What the mind does with the abstract idea is to 'lay it up in its storehouse, the memory, as containing the essence of a sort of things, of which that name is always to be the mark' (II xxxii 7), and it is because we have laid the idea up that we are thenceforth able to attach a meaning to the term. It is interesting that when Bennett wants to support his claim that Locke did not think of general terms as proper names the one passage he cites is that in III iii 12. And of course Locke's observation that 'they do not signify barely one particular thing' is relevant here. But the passage also supports Warnock's claim, for the claim is that though Locke does deny that words conform to things in their particularity, he all the same looks for *and finds* one item (the abstract idea) for each general term to name. In this sense the meaning of the term 'man' is 'the object for which the word stands', and the object for which the word is 'in effect' the proper name.

III

It would be absurdly partisan to suggest that Berkeley solves (or even tackles) all the problems Locke was grappling with, but there are useful hints and suggestions in the introduction to the *Principles*. Thus he does seem to be on the right lines when he suggests that it is a mistake to look for one item for each general word to signify. He says:

> ... 'tis thought that every name hath, or ought to have, one only precise and settled signification, which inclines men to think there are certain *abstract, determinate ideas*, which constitute the true and only immediate signification of each general name. And that it is by the mediation of these abstract ideas, that a general name comes to signify any particular thing. Whereas, in truth, there is no such thing as one precise and definite signification annexed to any general name, they all signifying indifferently a great number of particular ideas.... 'Tis one thing for to keep a name constantly to the same definition, and another to make it stand every where for the same idea: the one is necessary, the other useless and impracticable. (sect. 18)

There also seems to be some merit in his suggestion that the role of signification can be overemphasized and that as well as using words to communicate or mark our ideas we also use them for other ends, 'as the raising of some passion, the exciting to, or deterring from an action, the putting the mind in some particular disposition' (sect. 20). Berkeley develops his 'doctrine of signs', with special reference to the scientist's concept of *force* and the theologian's concept of *grace*, in the seventh dialogue of *Alciphron*, and in such a way that it sometimes seems as if he may be working his way *towards* his own distinctive theory of meaning, and a theory which anticipates 'several notions which it was left to our own century to develop; in particular the suggestion, usually credited exclusively to the later Wittgenstein, that the meaning of a word may be identified with its use' (Flew 2, pp. 417-18).

There is currently some dispute as to just how Wittgensteinian Berkeley's most Wittgensteinian remarks are.[3] The issue is not one I will dwell on at this point. A general observation on Berkeley's attitude to questions concerning language and meaning may, though, be in order. The point I want to make is that whereas Locke has a very genuine interest in language, Berkeley's concern with language, though in its way no less genuine, is always subservient to his interest in problems which are not *essentially* problems about the nature and use of words. Thus in *PC* 378 he is happy to appeal to the principle that 'All significant words stand for Ideas' because he thinks that given this principle talk about external objects can be shown to be meaningless. In the introduction to the *Principles* he opposes the view that each word stands for one idea because he thinks that this will prepare the ground for his attack on several notions of the materialists. And in *Alciphron* he presses the point that a word need not stand for ideas to be meaningful because he needs to answer the charge that the term 'grace' must be meaningless because we have no idea in our minds when we use it. When he does have cause to make points about language there are important insights and promising suggestions as well as mistakes and muddles. But what we do not find is any full and sustained account of the nature of language to set alongside Locke's pioneering account in book III of the *Essay*. Nor is it clear that the various points he does make suggest one clear, coherent and consistent story about what it is for a word to have meaning.

So far as the introduction to the *Principles* is concerned Berkeley's main negative point is, of course, that using a general term meaningfully cannot depend upon the occurrence of an abstract general idea in the mind, and this for the simple reason that there can be no such idea. He proceeds by looking at the two stages he takes it Locke supposes are involved in framing one. First, it seems that we must be able to take an object which has certain qualities including, say, a particular shape and a particular colour, and then 'to consider each quality singly, or abstracted from those other qualities with which it is united' (sect. 7). There is scope for argument about exactly what view he has it in mind to attack here, but it seems fairest to represent him as denying that when we observe an object we can form by abstraction a mental image of, for example, its colour, without that image involving *some* shape, though not necessarily the shape of the original object. In the second edition he clarifies his position somewhat by saying:

> ... I own my self able to abstract in one sense, as when I consider some particular parts or qualities separated from others, with which though they are united in some object, yet, it is possible they may really exist without them. (sect. 10)

An example here might be that I can frame an idea of the colour of the rose in front of me without framing an idea of the smell or any smell, for colour can exist without fragrance. And, still in the second edition, he allows, as an example, that one may consider a figure as triangular without paying attention to the exact disposition of its sides or angles, as one could, presumably, think about the colour of a given object without noting its shape. But what he vehemently denies is 'that I can abstract one from another, or conceive separately, those qualities which it is impossible should exist so separated'. The denial here, it should be noted, is of abstract ideas of particular determinate qualities that cannot exist in isolation from other qualities of a certain sort, and these abstract ideas are not abstract *general* ideas.

Generality, in Berkeley's view, comes in at the second level of abstraction when, it is supposed, the mind can take, for example, various abstract ideas of particular colours and abstract from these to frame an abstract idea of colour in general. Thus:

> ... the mind by leaving out of the particular colours perceived by sense, that which distinguishes them one from another, and retaining that only which is common to all, makes an idea of colour in abstract which is neither red, nor blue, nor white, nor any other determinate colour. (sect. 8)

And Berkeley's objection to this seems to be, first, that abstraction at this level must be dependent on abstraction at the first level, which has been shown to be impossible, and second, that if when we think about colour we do frame an idea (or form an image) this idea must always be an idea of some particular colour. Introspection, he thinks, should convince us that we cannot frame an idea of colour in general. Similarly with the term 'man'. Referring to Locke's idea framed by abstraction, Berkeley says:

> ... the idea of man that I frame to my self, must be either of a white, or a black, or a tawny, a straight, or a crooked, a tall, or a

low, or a middle-sized man. I cannot by any effort of thought conceive the abstract idea above described. (sect. 10)

The idea 'above described' is, of course, the idea Locke describes in III iii 7, an idea framed by leaving out of the ideas we have of particular men that which is peculiar to each and retaining only what is common to all.

It will be apparent from the above summary that Berkeley's attack depends upon the assumption that framing an abstract idea must come down to forming some queer sort of *image*. Berkeley takes it to be obvious that we cannot frame an idea of man in general because he takes it to be evident that we cannot form a mental picture when we think about man without that picture being of *a* man with determinate characteristics. One objection that has been made here is that Locke certainly didn't think of the abstract idea as a sort of mental picture, and thus that Berkeley's polemic misses its mark. In a note to III iii 8 Fraser says:

> Our inability to *imagine* what we are able ... to have an *abstract notion* of, was afterwards shown conclusively by Berkeley, who did not thereby prove that we cannot form what Locke means by an abstract idea. He only proves that abstract ideas are not sensuous imaginations, and that our power of forming them implies possession of higher faculties than the one of sense.

Similarly, Aaron has it that Locke's 'definition of "idea" permits him to include the image within it, but it is also wider', so that 'there is nothing in the term as he used it to compel him to think of the universal as a particular image' (Aaron 1, p. 199). It is necessary, then, that we should at least note that there is scope for doubt as to what Locke's position actually was, and that those most sympathetic to Locke have often questioned Berkeley's interpretation. I myself, though, have some sympathy with Warnock's summing up on this issue. He says:

> ... it has often been objected that the view which Berkeley attributes to Locke and demolishes is not, in fact, a view which Locke ever held. It can perhaps be argued that this is so; but Locke is protected, if at all, only by the extreme vagueness and obscurity of his language. If Locke did not mean what Berkeley says that he meant, it is an extremely difficult problem to decide what he did mean. For the fact is that Locke neither stated nor held any one

clear theory at all; and Berkeley attributes to him one fairly precise doctrine which conforms with much, at least, that he actually said. (Warnock 1, p. 63)

We shall see that at one point Berkeley *does* misinterpret Locke, but we will not question his assumption that for Locke abstract ideas are sorts of images.

Even if we allow that Berkeley does not go wrong *here*, there is one quite powerful objection that can be brought against what Berkeley says. For he assumes that if any actual man must have some determinate colouring then any image we frame when we think of a man must have some determinate colouring, and in general that images must have determinate characteristics in just the same way that sensible things must have determinate characteristics. This is false. Bennett undermines the claim when he says:

> I am prepared to say confidently that something like a Lockean abstract idea can occur, on the grounds that someone can close his eyes and picture a woman's face, neither 'seeing' her as smiling nor 'seeing' her as unsmiling — which I take to imply that he has a somewhat abstract idea or image of her. Having a poor visual imagination, I prefer an example like this: I play a tune in my head, and I 'hear' it as orchestrated, which is different from 'hearing' it as played on a tin whistle; yet I do not 'hear' it as orchestrated in any completely specific fashion, neither as involving at least three oboes nor as involving fewer than three oboes; and so my auditory idea or image is abstract. (p. 22)

And Warnock makes this point and another when he says:

> It has often been pointed out that visual images may as a matter of fact be vague and schematic, wavering and incomplete, shifting and indefinite. When we imagine, say, a well-known face, how often can we claim to find in it every detail, exact and definite, of feature or of expression? But there is also a more serious point than this. Suppose I am trying to imagine, to visualize, an aeroplane flying through a cloud. Clearly, it would be absurd for someone to question me about the aeoplane's wing-span, or its weight, or its speed. I might perhaps say that I was imagining a large aeroplane travelling very fast; but it would be entirely inappropriate to insist that it must have a definite size and speed; it would be ridiculous to ask for the

figures. I could, of course, invent answers to such questions or give answers at random; but there is no way in which, having visualized my aeroplane, I could then set about *discovering* the answers. Imagined aeroplanes cannot be measured, weighed, and timed – though they can, of course, be assigned imaginary sizes, weights, and speeds. (Warnock 1, pp. 68-9)

It is clear that Berkeley's assumption will not do. This does not mean of course that there is nothing in the point he makes. Bennett notes that Locke's theory of meaning 'subjects the theory of abstractness to some strenuous demands' and demands which, by implication, it cannot meet. And Warnock considers words such as 'red' and 'motion' and (perhaps forgetting 'smell') affirms that Berkeley is right in supposing it to be 'wholly impossible to "frame" an *image* instantiating one and only one property'.

IV

Berkeley does not rest his case against Locke on the claim that it is impossible to frame a general idea by omitting all characteristics peculiar to some individuals of the sort. He had what he thought of as a 'killing blow' to deliver, and he had resolved to bring this in 'at the last' (*PC* 687). I want to consider this killing blow at some length, and one point we can make at the outset is that it relies not so much on anything Locke says in book III of the *Essay* as on a passing remark in book IV. In IV vii 9 Locke says:

> ... abstract ideas are not so obvious or easy to children, or the yet unexercised mind, as particular ones. If they seem so to grown men, it is only because by constant and familiar use they are made so. For, when we nicely reflect upon them, we shall find that *general ideas* are fictions and contrivances of the mind, that carry difficulty with them, and do not so easily offer themselves as we are apt to imagine. For example, does it not require some pains and skill to form the general idea of a triangle, (which is yet none of the most abstract, comprehensive, and difficult,) for it must be neither oblique nor rectangle, neither equilateral, equicrural, nor scalenon; but all and none of these at once. In effect, it is something imperfect, that cannot exist; an idea wherein some parts of several different and inconsistent ideas are put together.

Berkeley seized on this passage with enthusiasm, quoting part of it in *NTV* 125, where he questions Locke's ability 'to form the above-mentioned idea . . . which is made up of manifest, staring contradictions', and the whole of it in the introduction to the *Principles* (sect. 13), here italicizing the words 'all and none' and 'inconsistent'. Locke's absurd triangle turns up again in *Alciphron* (*Works* III, p. 332) and in the *Defence of Free-thinking in Mathematics* (sects. 45-8).

So far as the introduction to the *Principles* is concerned there are two points Berkeley wants to take up with Locke here, though to Berkeley they seem intimately related. And the first point is that Locke takes generalizing to be an extremely difficult exercise. Surely, Berkeley wants to say, it is not difficult. It is, quite literally, child's play. But for Berkeley this criticism is closely connected with another, for he takes it that Locke is going to think of generalizing as difficult *because* he supposes that anyone who frames an abstract general idea must have 'tacked together numberless inconsistencies'. Berkeley holds here, of course, that if generalizing did involve completing this sort of exercise it would be, not difficult, but *impossible*. As generalizing *is* possible it cannot involve framing an idea 'made up of manifest, staring contradictions', and therefore it cannot involve framing a Lockian abstract general idea. This is the killing blow.

I treat these two points as separate criticisms because obviously even if we decided that Berkeley was here misrepresenting Locke's view of the mechanics of abstraction we might still feel that Locke was open to the charge that Aaron brings against him. Aaron says:

> Fabricating universals is never for Locke – to use Berkeley's colourful language – the 'tacking together of numberless inconsistencies'. Yet he does depict it as difficult work, and the question remains whether it can be as difficult as Locke supposes it to be since children appear to frame general ideas with such ease. (Aaron 2, p. 31)

Children who 'prate together, of their sugar-plumbs and rattles and the rest of their little trinkets' (*Pr. Intr.*, 14) must have the appropriate general notions, and it is surely absurd to suppose that in acquiring them they have done anything at all tortuous. In fact any moderately observant parent knows that children tend at a very early stage to spot similarities between things and to use words 'promiscuously'. It may be tempting to suppose that using proper names correctly is a simple matter and that it *must* precede the first tentative steps towards using general terms, but we find that for a very small child learning to use a name appropriately to refer to just one person or thing is often very much a process of learning to *restrict* the use of a word he has at one stage used too generously. Often a slightly disgruntled father discovers that to an infant every man is *Daddy*.

For all this, I suspect that Locke is not too wrong about the difficulty involved in framing abstract concepts, for, firstly, he is not so much concerned in the passage in question with concepts such as those of *rattle* and *sugar-plumb* – and he does say that from ideas of particulars the mind proceeds relatively easily 'to some few general ones... taken from the ordinary and familiar objects of sense' – as with more difficult concepts such as that of *triangle* – 'which is yet none of the most abstract, comprehensive, and difficult' – and that of *whole*. And, secondly, he is not so much concerned at this point with the use of a general word to refer to any one of a number of things of a given sort as he is with general thought about sorts of things. I will expand on this second point.

It is desirable, I think, to distinguish between various functions abstract general ideas serve for Locke. And we can best do this by distinguishing between three questions he might hope to answer by reference to them. The first is the question as to what is going on in my mind when I use a general term. One can certainly understand how Locke could think that there must be *something* going on in my mind if I am using any term meaningfully rather than parroting, and that when the term is a general one the idea cannot be one representing just one particular of the sort. Thus in *Alciphron* the Berkeleian and his opponent consider the words, 'If a man thinketh himself to be something when he is nothing, he deceiveth himself'. It is agreed that when I use the word 'man' here 'I do not frame to myself the particular distinct idea of a man'. But the opponent, taking a Lockian line, insists:

> It is very true you do not form in your mind the particular idea of Peter, James or John, of a fair or a black, a tall or a low, a fat or a lean, a straight or a crooked, a wise or a foolish, a sleeping or waking man, but the abstract general idea of man, prescinding from and exclusive of all particular shape, size, complexion, passions, faculties, and every individual circumstance. (*Works* III, pp. 331-2)

It emerges very clearly in the ensuing discussion that Alciphron does not believe in this idea because he finds by introspection that he has it when he uses the term 'man', but rather because he cannot see how he can be communicating anything if he does not have it. Locke believes that we use words to convey the ideas in our minds for which they stand. When we use the general term 'man' the idea we have in our minds cannot be the idea of some particular: it must be an idea of a special sort.

The second question concerns how I can recognize a thing of a certain sort as being a thing *of that sort*. And here one can see how Locke could have convinced himself that I must possess some mental exemplar, stored in the memory, against which to check candidate instances. The mistake here is the one Wittgenstein exposes in the following passage from the *Blue Book*:

> If I give someone the order 'fetch me a red flower from that meadow', how is he to know what sort of flower to bring, as I have only given him a *word*? (Wittgenstein 1, p. 3)

Of course here we have the special case of obeying an order, but the basic problem is the problem of *recognition*. I must be able to recognize, to pick out the *red* flower, if I am to pick it and obey the order. Wittgenstein continues:

> Now the answer one might suggest first is that he went to look for a red flower carrying a red image in his mind, and comparing it with the flowers to see which of them had the colour of the image. Now there is such a way of searching, and it is not at all essential that the image we use should be a mental one. In fact the process may be this: I carry a chart co-ordinating names and coloured squares. When I hear the order 'fetch me etc.' I draw my finger across the chart from the word 'red' to a certain square, and I go and look for a flower which has the same colour as the square. But this is not the only way of searching and it isn't the usual way. We go, look about us, walk up to a flower and pick it, without comparing it to anything. To see that the process of obeying the order can be of this kind, consider the order '*imagine* a red patch'. You are not tempted in this case to think that *before* obeying you must have imagined a red patch to serve you as a pattern for the red patch which you were ordered to imagine.

Similarly, it is obvious that we don't (normally) recognize a flower as a flower, the flower as a primrose, or the primrose as yellow, by checking against exemplars, mental or otherwise, with the names attached. The mistake Wittgenstein exposes is, though, an easy one to make, and we can have some sympathy with Locke when he supposes both that we must possess patterns which enable us to classify things and that the pattern corresponding to a general term such as 'man' cannot be simply an image or likeness of one particular of the sort. And this brings us to the third question which Locke might hope to answer by introducing abstract general ideas. For there is the problem as to what I am talking *about* when I refer to, say, gold in general or man as such. Here the difficulty as he sees it is that I am certainly referring to *something* when I say that gold is malleable or man mortal, yet I am clearly not referring to any one item in the world. That which I am talking about, Locke says, is the *sort* or essence of the sort, and this essence is an abstract idea.

I would not suggest that Locke clearly distinguishes between these three questions. Indeed the fact that there are three quite different questions at issue is obscured in the *Essay* itself and in many later discussions of Locke's views. I think, though, that there is something to be said for the view that while the third question looms very large for Locke, Berkeley, in the introduction to the *Principles*, tends to put the emphasis on the first. As Aaron says:

> ... the charge can be made against Berkeley that in the *Introduction* he turned his back upon the main problem, that of the status and nature of what he called the 'sorts'. In the *Commonplace Book* [*PC*] and *Draft* he had touched on the problem but found it too difficult. Yet the argument of the *Introduction* is incomplete without a discussion of this matter and lacks a foundation. (Aaron 2, p. 65)

What is certainly true is that in IV vii Locke is wholly concerned with the formulation of general truths about sorts of things and with building on his answer to the third question. If we think in terms of his answer to the second question and take it that the child who refers to his train-set as a toy reveals that he has the general idea of toy, we may well be puzzled by the suggestion that he has done anything very difficult at this stage. But if we switch our attention to Locke's dominant concern we can quite see how he could feel that the child has attained to a new level of thought when he formulates general truths even about toys and other familiar sorts of things.

The chapter in which the passage about the triangle occurs is the one entitled 'Of Maxims' and we can look briefly at two points he wants to make in it. First, then, he had argued in book I of the *Essay* that there are no innate general truths and that the experience of particular things precedes the formulation of general maxims. With this in mind we can see why he should be concerned to stress that 'abstract ideas are not so obvious or easy to children, or the yet unexercised mind, as particular ones'. But in the second place he wants to emphasize that the most general maxims are 'not of much use to the discovery of unknown truths, or to help the mind forwards in its search after knowledge' (sect. 11). In particular, 'they cannot discover or prove to us the least knowledge of the nature of substances . . . any further than grounded on experience' (sect. 15). With the spirit of all this Berkeley should have been the first to agree. Clearly Locke does think that forming any general notion is a relatively sophisticated matter – and he regards the ability to frame abstract ideas as something that distinguishes men from the animals – but he is surely right in thinking that to attain to, and relate, the concepts necessary to an understanding of the proposition that the whole is equal to all its parts is no easy matter, and certainly well beyond the ability of children who can prate quite happily of their sugar-plums and rattles. Locke is making a fair point here even if he is wrong about the mechanics of abstraction.

Now when we turn to Berkeley's second criticism and the 'killing blow' the interesting fact that emerges is that the view he attributes to Locke on the basis of what is said in book IV is quite different from the view he attributed to him on the basis of what was said in book III. Indeed it seems that, whether or not Berkeley interprets the book IV passage correctly, the 'killing blow' has its effect, not against the line he initially attributed to Locke, but against a totally different one. That the account now being attributed to Locke is different from the one we located earlier should be obvious. For that view was that in framing the abstract general idea we take only those qualities that are common to all things of the same sort, *totally excluding* any qualities possessed only by some particulars of the sort. Thus in framing the general idea of a triangle we would include three-sidedness because this is an essential property of all triangles, but we would exclude, say, the property of being scalenon, this property not being essential to triangularity as such. On the view now being attributed to Locke, though, characteristics which cannot properly be jointly attributed to any one triangle are somehow *included* in the general idea, and it is on this view that Locke can be accused of asking us to tack together numberless inconsistencies. On the earlier view there can be no question of our having to tack together inconsistent properties, for all the properties included in the general idea will be properties jointly instantiated in all particulars of the sort.

That there are two views here has been well brought out by E. J. Craig, who shows both that Berkeley does mistakenly think that his criticism of the passage in book IV amounts to further criticism of the view he has already attacked, and that commentators have sometimes assumed that Berkeley is right here. Thus, for example, he draws attention to a passage in which Copleston, beginning with a quotation from sect. 9 of the introduction, writes:

> 'The idea of a man that I frame to my self, must be either of a white, or a black, or a tawny, a straight, or a crooked, a tall, or a low, or a middle-sized man. I cannot by any effort of thought conceive the abstract idea above described.' I cannot, that is to say, frame an image of a man which *both omits and includes* all the particular characteristics of real individual men. [Craig's italics]

But Craig is quite right in saying that this will not do. For in sect. 9 Berkeley is attributing to Locke the view that when framing the idea of *man* 'the mind . . . leaves out of the complex or compounded idea it has of Peter, James, and any other particular man, that which is peculiar to each, retaining only what is common to all'. There is no question here of our including 'all the particular characteristics of real individual men'. Indeed it is only when he comes to the book IV passage that Berkeley finds and seizes on the suggestion that peculiarities are somehow included in the general idea. It is an objection to the book III view that we cannot frame an image corresponding to the word 'man' without including qualities possessed only by some men, and it may be an objection to the book IV view that we cannot frame an image which instantiates inconsistent properties, but it is not an objection to the book III view that it requires us to include in the image properties that could not be jointly instantiated in any particular of the sort.

F

The question remains, though, whether Berkeley is right in his interpretation of what Locke says in the passage from book IV and whether Locke ever held the decidedly odd view that forming a general concept involves tacking inconsistencies together. And here I am inclined to say that Berkeley is wrong and that at this point he does misinterpret Locke. Locke does say that the general idea is 'something imperfect, that cannot exist', but we need not suppose with Berkeley that his reason for holding this is that he believes that the idea must somehow instantiate inconsistent properties. The point is that even if he adhered to the view that the general idea is framed simply by omitting characteristics peculiar to some individuals of the sort, he might still want to stress the essential difference between, say, any existent triangle and the abstract idea, this difference resulting from the fact that any existent triangle must have some of the peculiarities omitted from the abstract idea. Locke's passage lacks clarity, but it can well be argued, as it has been argued by some of Locke's commentators, that in it he does not mean to depart from what he said earlier. Aaron, for example, points out how differently we read the passage in book IV if we italicize not the word 'inconsistent', as Berkeley does, but rather the words 'some parts of'. And in a similar spirit Fraser claims in a footnote to IV vii 9:

> What Locke intends is surely that the idea (nominal essence) is applicable to all these [i.e. all particulars of the same sort], while it excludes the peculiarities of each; it contains them under its *extent*, while it excludes them from its *content*.

On this highly defensible interpretation Locke's view remains that which Berkeley supposed it to be and argued against *before* he came to deliver his final blow, that is that the general idea stands for, or has reference to, all the particulars of a sort, but is framed by leaving out all peculiarities rather than by our somehow managing to include these in its content.

V

Berkeley is being a little misleading when he suggests that the notion that sensible things can exist unperceived 'will, perhaps, be found at bottom to depend on the doctrine of *abstract ideas*'. The belief in unperceived existence is, after all, prevalent, but the sophisticated if erroneous thinking Berkeley attacks in his introduction hardly reflects a widespread view. Indeed, even if we forget the plain man and other philosophers, and concentrate exclusively on Locke, it seems quite clear that Locke did not believe in a three-term theory of perception, primary and secondary qualities and corporeal substance *because* his thinking about the nature of language and the signification of general terms was what it was. What may be widespread is a tendency to indulge in what Berkeley would think of as illegitimate abstraction, and abstraction which receives explicit sanction in what Locke says about general terms. And from this point of view Berkeley's claim must be that in exposing the *doctrine* to be found in Locke we become aware of a much more general tendency to abstraction, and a tendency which results in our missing important truths and saying meaningless things.

As has already been admitted, we cannot claim that Berkeley provides us with a full and coherent account of what it is to use language meaningfully. He notes, though, that I can use words significantly without having appropriate ideas in my mind – 'names being for the most part used as letters are in *algebra*, in which though a particular quantity be marked by each letter, yet to proceed right it is not requisite that in every step each letter suggest to your thoughts, that particular quantity it was appointed to stand for' (*Pr. Intr.* 19).[4] More importantly, he holds that not all words do stand for ideas. In a chapter which is for some unaccountable reason usually cut from abridged editions of the *Essay* Locke had conceded that particles (words such as 'if', 'but' and 'not') do not stand for ideas, and Berkeley seizes on this in *PC* 661 and 667. Unfortunately, Berkeley follows Locke in supposing that if such words do not stand for ideas then they must stand for *something*, and he agrees with Locke that they stand for operations of the mind. At an early stage the word 'spirit', personal pronouns, and words such as 'love' and 'memory' are added to the list of words that are used meaningfully though they do not stand for ideas, and the words we use to signify the relations between things are added in the second edition of the *Principles*. Finally, in *Alciphron* language is seen as an *instrument*, and 'the true end of speech' as 'not merely, or principally, or always, the imparting or acquiring of ideas, but rather something of an active operative nature, tending to a conceived good: which may sometimes be obtained, not only although the ideas marked are not offered to the mind, but even although there should be no possibility of offering or exhibiting any such idea to the mind' (VII 14). Even in *Alciphron*, however, Berkeley's opposition to abstraction remains as strong as ever. At the beginning of VII 15 he warns against the confusions which follow 'whensoever men quit particulars for generalities, things concrete for abstractions, when they forsake practical views, and the useful purposes of knowledge for barren speculation, considering means and instruments as ultimate ends, and labouring to obtain precise ideas which they suppose indiscriminately annexed to all terms'.

Just as Berkeley supposes the acceptance of abstract ideas 'has brought forth innumerable errors and difficulties in all parts of philosophy and in all the sciences', so he believes that his demonstration of the absurdity of positing such ideas provides him with a powerful tool to be used in the clarification of a large number of issues and the disentangling of various knots which he sees as impeding progress in many fields of inquiry. It is worth noting that the introduction to the *Principles* is not intended just as an introduction to the one part he actually published but to the projected four-part work as a whole. As it is he appeals to the supposed absurdity of abstraction in a variety of contexts. In *NTV*, for example, when he is arguing for the heterogeneity of the objects of sight and touch, we find him claiming that the extension men suppose themselves to both see and feel is an abstract idea. In *Pr.* 116-7 he tells us that the notion of absolute space is an abstract idea and claims that once we see this 'we are freed from that dangerous *dilemma*, to which several who have employed their thoughts on this subject, imagine themselves reduced, to wit, of thinking either that real space is God, or else that there is something beside God which is eternal, uncreated, infinite, indivisible, immutable'. Further, it is part of his case against the distinction between primary and secondary qualities that the doctrine presupposes that the so-called primary qualities can be abstracted from, and conceived as existing separated from, the so-called secondary.[5] We will return to this point in a moment. First, though, we should say just something about what Berkeley thinks is going on when we think in general terms about sensible things.

The key point here is that in Berkeley's view all reasoning is ultimately about particulars. For example, general truths about man or about the triangle or about motion are at root about each, every and any particular man, all triangles, or all bodies in motion. In my thinking about the triangle I may rely on linguistic signs (words and definitions) or I may pay attention to some particular drawn or imagined triangle which I take as representing all other figures of the same sort. The truths I formulate will not, though, be truths about some odd item (whether conceived as a Platonic Form, an Aristotelian real essence, or a Lockian abstract idea), but rather truths about any particular three-sided plane figure which can be drawn or imagined. When a geometer draws a line in making a demonstration this line functions as a sign which 'owes its generality, not to its being the sign of an abstract or general line, but of all particular right lines that may possibly exist', and similarly the *name* 'line' 'must be thought to derive its generality from the same cause, namely, the various particular lines which it indifferently denotes' (*Pr. Intr.* 12). In the same way, Berkeley would say, when I formulate a truth about man in general this truth must in fact be a truth about all men, though in my formulation of it I may use a linguistic sign, which in itself is a particular, and picture some individual man as representative of the sort.[6] The mistake we make is to suppose that a general name 'hath, or ought to have, one only precise and settled signification' and that as the term 'line', say, quite obviously doesn't signify any one particular line that can be drawn or imagined it must signify some special type of item or an abstract idea. Difficulties and absurdities arise when we allow ourselves to lose sight of the relationship between a legitimate generalization and the particular actual or possible states of affairs it covers, and in particular when this leads us to reify the universal. In Berkeley's view the physicist's absolute space and absolute time are such reifications. And Newton's absolute as opposed to relative motion is another abstraction.

Berkeley is very keen that in our speculative reasoning we should keep returning to the concrete case, both so as to check that we are not quitting legitimate generalization for illegitimate abstraction, and so as to ensure that we can conceive or envisage states of affairs which will be covered by any claims we make. This determination that we should keep our eyes firmly fixed on the particular case is reflected in many passages, as for example in what he says about time in *Pr.* 97. But it is also reflected in his thinking about primary and secondary qualities, and we must now return to this issue. In *Pr.* 10 he says:

> They who assert that figure, motion, and the rest of the primary or original qualities do exist without the mind, in unthinking substances, do at the same time acknowledge that colours, sounds, heat, cold, and

such like secondary qualities, do not, which they tell us are sensations existing in the mind alone, that depend on and are occasioned by the different size, texture and motion of the minute particles of matter. This they take for an undoubted truth, which they can demonstrate beyond all exception. Now if it be certain, that those original qualities are inseparably united with the other sensible qualities, and not, even in thought, capable of being abstracted from them, it plainly follows that they exist only in the mind. But I desire any one to reflect and try, whether he can by any abstraction of thought, conceive the extension and motion of a body, without all other sensible qualities. For my own part, I see evidently that it is not in my power to frame an idea of a body extended and moved, but I must withal give it some colour or other sensible quality which is acknowledged to exist only in the mind. In short, extension, figure, and motion, abstracted from all other qualities, are inconceivable.

I confess I cannot agree with Bennett (pp. 90-1) in seeing any real difficulty of interpretation here. Berkeley *is* making the strong point Bennett says he is sometimes thought to be making, that is 'that secondary qualities are essential to the concept of body'. And in making this claim he challenges us to conceive (or frame an idea of) any body which is, say, extended but not coloured. Our inability to do this should, he thinks, convince us that we are talking nonsense when we speak of the one quality as being original to body and the other not.

Of course Bennett is quite right when he says that if Berkeley is indeed making this strong point he must be faulted on it. Thus:

> What he says, on that reading of it, is certainly relevant to Locke's thesis; but it is also a manifest falsehood which could be believed, I think, only by someone who had lapsed into thinking of perception too exclusively in terms of sight. Granted that we could not see things to have sizes and shapes without seeing them to have (not necessarily chromatic) colours, the crucial point is that we could perceive objects to have sizes and shapes without ever seeing them — and, it can be added, without ever hearing or tasting or smelling them either.

We can in fact reject the argument of *Pr.* 10 without even looking at the assumption that colours are only in the mind, and without criticizing Berkeley's thinking about language and meaning at any main point. Framing an idea of colour may come down to visualizing an extended coloured patch, and our inability to picture an object which is coloured but not extended may convince us that talk of such an object would be nonsense. But the argument does not work the other way round. A blind man would certainly be amused at the suggestion that he could not frame an idea of an extended object without visualizing it or 'seeing' it as a coloured thing.

Berkeley himself seems to appreciate that he is dealing with something of a special case when he claims that we are indulging in illegitimate abstraction when we separate *esse* from *percipi*. The colour and shape of any object are after all distinguishable characteristics, and we go wrong, in Berkeley's view, when we suppose that there can be shape without colour. On his own terms the case is clearly supposed to be different with *esse* and *percipi*. For, leaving aside the fact that *esse* and *percipi* are not qualities or characteristics of things, Berkeley's main contention is that no distinction can properly be made between them. To exist *is* to be perceived. Significantly we find Berkeley claiming (in *Pr.* 5) that there can be no 'nicer strain of abstraction than to distinguish the existence of sensible objects from their being perceived'. 'I might', he says, 'as easily divide a thing from it self' as abstract the one from the other. It is clear, then, that there is good excuse for those commentators who have failed to see any real link between the attack on abstraction in the introduction to the *Principles* and the attack on the notion that sensible things can exist unperceived. And this is one puzzle about *Pr.* 5. The other puzzle is that though Berkeley *asserts* that it is 'impossible for me to conceive in my thoughts any sensible thing or object distinct from the sensation or perception of it', there is really nothing said to convince the doubter that this is true. Here again we feel the need for some argument.

One thing is clear and this is that Berkeley *thought* there was a link between his attack on abstractionism and his case for mind-dependence. It is also clear that he thought this link was crucial. The link may indeed have been more tenuous than he thought, but certainly the language he uses when elaborating on the absurdity of abstracting *esse* from *percipi* is remarkably similar to that he uses in the introduction to the *Principles* and again in *Pr.* 10. Thus to see the absurdity of the distinction between primary and secondary qualities the reader has only 'to reflect and try, whether he can by any abstraction of thought, conceive the extension and motion of a body, without all other sensible qualities'. And it is in a similar spirit that the reader is challenged in *Pr.* 6 to 'reflect and try to separate in his own thoughts the being of a sensible thing from its being perceived'. Berkeley believed that this little experiment should prove decisive. Thus:

> I am afraid I have given cause to think me needlessly prolix in handling this subject. For to what purpose is it to dilate on that which may be demonstrated with the utmost evidence in a line or two, to anyone that is capable of the least reflexion? It is but looking into your own thoughts, and so trying whether you can conceive it possible for a sound, or figure, or motion, or colour, to exist without the mind, or unperceived. This easy trial may make you see, that what you contend for, is a downright contradiction. (sect. 22)

We have already noted that he believes that the inability of his reader to do the required trick will 'make it unnecessary to insist on any other proofs against the existence of material substance'. In the parallel passage in the *Dialogues* (i, 200) he repeats that he is 'content to put the whole upon this issue'.[7]

VI

In the *Dialogues* Hylas has the knack of putting forward the right objections and then of accepting very puzzling and unsatisfactory answers with equanimity, and on this issue he certainly says what most of us would feel like saying on meeting the challenge of *Pr.* 6 and 22. Thus:

> If it comes to that, the point will soon be decided. What more easy than to conceive a tree or house existing by itself, independent of, and unperceived by any mind whatsoever? I do at this present time conceive them existing after that manner.

And of course Hylas is right. The reader has been challenged to do a certain trick and he does it without any difficulty at all. The reader will find himself able to think of the cooker in his kitchen or the carpet in his hall as existing with nobody there to see, of *a* kitchen or *a* hall (unspecified) existing unperceived, and in general of sensible things existing with nobody near. What more easy? The same is true of qualities. It is just because I take the iron to be hot though I do not feel its heat that I take steps to avoid feeling what I might feel, and to prevent children and others from getting too close. Our first reaction, then, is to say that there is no life in Berkeley's challenge.

To see why Berkeley thought his challenge to be so powerful we can look at Philonous's reply to Hylas's protest. The exchange continues:

> *Philonous* How say you, Hylas, can you see a thing which is at the same time unseen?
> *Hylas* No, that were a contradiction.
> *Philonous* Is it not as great a contradiction to talk of *conceiving* a thing which is *unconceived*?
> *Hylas* It is.
> *Philonous* The tree or house therefore which you think of, is conceived by you.
> *Hylas* How should it be otherwise?
> *Philonous* And what is conceived, is surely in the mind.
> *Hylas* Without question, that which is conceived is in the mind.
> *Philonous* How then came you to say, you conceived a house or tree existing independent and out of all minds whatsoever?

And Hylas admits his 'pleasant mistake', which was to suppose that he could conceive an unperceived tree, or one existing independently of the mind, 'not considering that I myself conceived it all the while'. The same line of argument occurs in *Pr.* 23:

> But say you, surely there is nothing easier than to imagine trees, for instance, in a park, or books existing in a closet, and no body by to perceive them. I answer, you may so, there is no difficulty in it: but what is all this, I beseech you, more than framing in your mind certain ideas which you call *books* and *trees*, and at the same time omitting to frame the idea of any one that may perceive them? But do not you your self perceive or think of them all the while? This therefore is nothing to the purpose: it only shows you have the power of imagining or forming ideas in your mind; but it doth not shew that you can conceive it possible, the objects of your thought may exist without the mind: to make out this, it is necessary that you conceive them existing unconceived or unthought of, which is a manifest repugnancy. When we do our utmost to conceive the existence of external bodies, we are all the while only contemplating

our own ideas. But the mind taking no notice of itself, is deluded to think it can and doth conceive bodies existing unthought of or without the mind; though at the same time they are apprehended by or exist in it self.

With reason commentators have tended to treat this argument with scant respect. J. F. Thomson describes it as 'contemptible' (p. 431), Wisdom says that it is 'entirely specious and not worth a moment's academic discussion' (p. 8), and Benson Mates in his 'Berkeley was Right' has to admit that 'this is a tricky argument and one which I cannot accept' (p. 171). As Thomson points out, Warnock just ignores it. Berkeley, though, set great store by it.[8]

A number of odd things are said during the exchange between Hylas and Philonous and in the parallel passage in the *Principles*, and in a moment we shall have to look critically at the way in which it seems to be just assumed that what most of us would want to accept as figuratively true is literally true – viz. that 'that which is conceived is in the mind'. And in connection with this we will want to look at the way in which conceiving a tree is supposed to amount to imagining a tree and this in turn to perceiving it. But first we can prepare the ground by making some points which do at least indicate that there are deficiencies in the argument. And in the first place we can note that some unacceptable consequences follow from the assumption that whatever I conceive must exist, and exist (as do *all* the things I perceive) in my mind. For if Berkeley does believe this, he would seem (absurdly) to be committed to denying that I can conceive things, for example mermaids and chimeras, which I suppose or know *not* to exist. Equally, there is a problem about things I suppose to exist which do not in fact exist. It is quite possible, for example, that I should think of the house I was born in as existing now, but later discover that it was demolished many years ago. And in this case it would seem that, as Berkeleians, we must say both that the house existed when I conceived it (my conceiving it being a sufficient condition for its existence) and that it did not exist (it having been demolished). And *here*, surely, is a manifest repugnancy.

In the second place, we can consider the case where I suppose, not that a particular book in my closet exists *now* (though I do believe this), but that it existed yesterday and at a time when nobody was perceiving it or thinking about it. No question of fact arises here. I may indeed be wrong in supposing that nobody was thinking about it. The issue concerns only the coherence of my assumption (true or false) that it was unperceived. Now if my belief *is* coherent, as we would normally suppose it was, then it would seem that I can conceive something as having existed without a mind, and thus of existence without perception. But if the supposition is *not* coherent, clearly Berkeley has to *show* that this is so. And the line of argument he pursues in *Pr.* 23 does not help him here. For we could accept that whatever we suppose to exist or to have existed must be in our minds at the moment we make the supposition, without accepting that we cannot conceive it as having existed unthought of. So it may be, that to defeat Philonous, Hylas has only to refuse to think of the tree or house he believes exists unperceived now, and instead to wait a second and then claim that it existed a second previously. As Marc-Wogau suggests, Berkeley's argument locates 'no contradiction in the supposition of an idea existing unperceived at all other times except the time, when the supposition is made' (Marc-Wogau 2, pp. 338-9).

For the third point we turn again to the present tense and note that Berkeley here seems to go against a principle which he elsewhere accepts, viz. that I can suppose things to exist when unperceived *by me* provided I suppose that they are perceived by some other spirit. For if Berkeley's argument is sound it will follow that I cannot suppose anything to exist when unperceived by me. Certainly on the assumption that thinking of X as existing involves perceiving X, Hylas will find it just as difficult to think of something as existing but unperceived by Hylas as he will to think of it as existing altogether unperceived. If he tries to conceive an object existing in Philonous's mind, but not his own, he will discover that the object is conceived by him and thus in *his* mind. Of course if we *reject* the assumption that conceiving X involves perceiving X then there would seem to be no reason why Hylas should not claim that he can, after all, think of something existing in Philonous's mind when not perceived by him. But in this case there would seem to be no reason why he should not renew his claim to be able to think of something as existing when not perceived at all.[9]

The exposure of these difficulties does not get to the root of what is wrong with the basic argument, but it should confirm us in the view that, as it stands, the argument will not do. To the second and third points, which correspond to points Marc-Wogau makes to show that if the argument proves anything it proves at once less than Berkeley needs and more than he would want, it is difficult to see that he could have made any plausible response at all. I think he would have had something to say in reply to the first point, but his answer here would, I believe, simply have exposed more difficulties.

In answer to the first point Berkeley *might* suggest that he is not committed by this particular argument to saying that what is conceived by me must exist, but only to saying that it is a necessary condition for my thinking of X as existing that I conceive or perceive X. That is, what I conceive may not exist, as in the case of mermaids or the house that has been demolished, but this does not alter the fact that I cannot conceive X or think of X as existing without perceiving X. But Berkeley would probably not want to make this move in this form, basically because it involves the supposition that *esse* and *percipi* are not the same, and that though *esse* implies *percipi*, *percipi* does not imply *esse*. What he is more likely to say is that the repugnancy we supposed we had found does not obtain, for though there is *a* sense in which the house does exist when I think about it, there is *another* sense in which he is quite happy to admit that it does not exist. Rather similarly perhaps, there is a sense in which Mary and Jane are men (and included in the judgement that all men are mortal) and a more usual sense in which, being female, they are *not* men.

This is the line he takes in *PC* 472-3. First, we have an entry which has an added interest in that it shows that at one stage Berkeley was prepared to use an argument very similar to that of *Pr*. 23 to deal with the problem of what happens to things when we are not perceiving them. In the *Principles*, of course, he makes sense of the supposition that the table exists when I stop perceiving it by claiming that when I say it exists I mean 'that if I was in my study I might perceive it, or that some other spirit actually does perceive it', though ultimately he seems to pin his faith on that other spirit. But in *PC* 472 he tries a different move. What he suggests is that when I talk of the books in the empty study they *are* perceived because *I* conceive them, and that as they are perceived they must exist. Thus:

Whenever they are mention'd or discours'd of they are imagin'd & thought on therefore you can at no time ask me whether they exist or no, but by reason of y^t very question they must necessarily exist.

The notion is an odd one and various objections spring to mind. One wants to ask for example about past and future tense claims. If I talk about something I suppose to have existed or about something I believe will exist in the future, it would seem that the very fact of my mentioning these things must bring them into existence *now*. But in more general terms the problem is that it would seem to follow from what Berkeley says not only that it is necessarily true that the books in my study exist if I suppose they do, but that 'mermaids exist' is a necessary truth while 'griffins do not exist' involves some sort of contradiction. In short, any positive existential claim about a supposed sensible object must be true, and any negative claim false.

Now Berkeley was quite aware that there was a difficulty here, and in the very next entry he tries to deal with it. The entry reads:

> But say you then a Chimaera does exist. I answer it doth in one sense. i.e it is imagin'd. but it must be well noted that existence is vulgarly restrain'd to actuall perception. & that I use the word Existence in a larger sense than ordinary.

We met this generous sense of 'exist' in the last chapter. Using it, Berkeley is in a position to claim that though the demolished house does not exist in the ordinary or vulgar sense of that word (and we can refer to this by 'exist$_a$'), it *does* exist in Berkeley's larger sense ('exist$_b$'). The house I think of does not exist$_a$ because it has been demolished, but it does exist$_b$ because I have it in mind. The belief that there is a contradiction here arises only if we fail to distinguish the two senses of 'exist'.

As we have two senses of 'exist' here, it is tempting to distinguish two senses of 'perceive'. For Berkeley does refer to 'actuall perception', and clearly what he has in mind here is the perception *by sense* of an existent$_a$ object. When we have 'actuall perception' in mind we can use 'perceive$_a$'. But clearly Berkeley does not think that when I frame an idea of the mermaid or of the demolished house I perceive$_a$ either object. This isn't *sense* perception. What I do is to perceive$_b$ the mermaid or house—I conceive or imagine it. So given this convention, and recognizing that in the published works Berkeley does not take pains to make it unmistakeably clear that his sense of 'exist' is not the common one, we can summarize his position by saying that neither Hylas nor the reader of the *Principles* can conceive X as existing$_a$ without perceiving$_b$ it and thereby having it in mind. In supposing that we can conceive something as 'existing independent and out of all minds whatsoever' we are misled by the fact that when we frame the idea we can easily refrain from visualizing any person perceiving$_a$ the object. What we forget is that we ourselves are perceiving$_b$ it; that we have it in *our* minds.

The claim that I cannot conceive a sensible object as existing$_a$ without perceiving$_b$ it is trivially true if it means only that I cannot propose to myself that a certain thing exists$_a$ without thinking about that thing. The claim does not entail, though, that I cannot conceive a sensible object as having existence$_a$ at times when neither I nor anybody else is perceiving$_b$ it. If I must perceive$_b$ what I talk about when I talk about it, this does not mean that what I talk about depends for its existence on my (or anybody else's) perception$_b$ of it. Past and future tense claims are relevant here. If my proposition is that my pen will exist unthought of in ten minutes time, that proposition is clearly not falsified by the fact that to make the proposition I must be thinking about it now. Similarly with the past. The tree in my garden may have existed unthought of during the night, and I can at least suppose that this was so. But this supposition is clearly not rendered incoherent by the fact that to make it I have to perceive$_b$ that tree now. So the trivial truth does not suggest that the things I think about as existing$_a$ now cannot exist$_a$ at times when they are not 'in' any mind. Equally, it does not have any tendency to suggest that the tree Hylas is thinking about now could not have existed$_a$ at this moment in time even if neither Hylas nor anybody else had been thinking about it. If it may have existed$_a$ unthought of and unperceived$_b$ ten minutes ago, then it could presumably have existed$_a$ unthought of *now*, and this even though, *ex hypothesi*, Hylas does have it in mind at this moment.

And of course there is another point here. For the fact is that the claim that I cannot think of any item as existing$_a$ without perceiving$_b$ it quite obviously does not entail that the thing I suppose to exist$_a$ must be perceived$_a$ even at the time I make the supposition. And this, Hylas might say, is the important point. I must think about what I suppose to exist$_a$, but this doesn't mean that anyone is *aware* of that item. Hylas thinks about the trees he supposes to exist$_a$ in the park, but he is not *acquainted with* those trees as he is acquainted with the rose he actually sees, or even as he might be thought to be acquainted with any image he brings to his mind. Yet the immaterialist holds that sensible objects exist only in minds, and *usually* when he makes this claim he seems to mean that they can exist only when some spirit is acquainted with them. The trivial truth that I must think about any particular thing I suppose to exist$_a$ does not suggest that any spirit is aware of that object. In *this* sense the object may be supposed to exist 'out of all minds whatsoever', and this even when it is thought about.

Why did Berkeley think the argument more forceful than it was? Well, in commenting on *Pr.* 23 Wisdom suggests that 'Berkeley has shifted his ground, and replaced his doctrine of *Esse percipi* by *Esse concepi*' (p. 9), and this, while not perhaps straightforwardly false, blurs the crucial fact that for Berkeley the distinction in this context was not all that clear. *PC* 472 gives us the clue that he thought of conceiving a particular object as coming down to bringing a mental image to mind and perceiving *that image*, the perception of an image involving *acquaintance with* an item in the mind. The same assumption is implicit in *Pr.* 23, for Berkeley says that when the reader supposes he conceives a tree or book existing unperceived *all he does* is to frame an idea or mental image to which he gives the name 'tree' or 'book', and he obviously thinks both that I am *aware of* the named item because the named item is an idea I have produced in my mind *and* that the named item cannot exist unperceived because mental images are mind-dependent. The assumption behind all this is false. It hardly needs saying that when I mention, for example, the trees in Hyde Park, I am neither mentioning nor referring to any mental image I may have produced in my mind. The trees in Hyde Park exist, if they do exist, in a strong sense, and as things that are or might be perceived *by sense*. Even for Berkeley mental images are not constituents of the real world, and they are not, and cannot be, perceived *by sense*.

Now once we see that Berkeley did think of conceiving a particular object as amounting to framing a mental image of the object and perceiving that, we are, I think, in a position to see why his argument strikes us as so outrageous. Put briefly, the point is that what the reader thinks he can conceive as existing unperceived is a book or tree, an object we can label X. Now it may be that when he conceives the tree the reader frames a mental image of a tree, which mental image we can label Y. And while we are prepared to admit that Y may be in the reader's mind when he thinks about X and that Y is mind-dependent, we see that Berkeley is suggesting more than this and that X is in his mind and mind-dependent. Indeed if he is not suggesting this his argument has little interest. At the most he will have shown that it makes no sense for me to talk of X existing if I am not aware of Y when Y is mind-dependent, which is a quite different thing from proving that X can exist only so long as someone is aware of it. Berkeley's argument fails because when we claim that a tree exists unperceived we are *not* referring to a mental image. Even allowing the dubious assumption that when I think about a tree (a sensible object) I *must* frame and perceive an idea (a mental image), we should not confuse the two objects and suppose that because the image is mind-dependent then the tree I think about is in my mind. Berkeley is wrong in supposing that I cannot think of a sensible object as existing with nobody perceiving$_b$ it (i.e. thinking about it), and this for reasons already given. But he is also wrong when he confuses the object thought about with the mental image we may frame in thinking about it, and when he supposes that what is perceived$_b$ must be an object of actual awareness.[10]

VII

Not everyone has agreed with Wisdom that the argument we have been discussing is unworthy of academic consideration, and a lot has been written on it. But the basic criticism has perhaps nowhere been better put than by Dawes Hicks when he says:

> Berkeley was clearly entitled to assert that material things cannot be *thought of* as existing, apart from a thinking mind. Just as we can see things only by turning our gaze upon them, so we can think of things only by directing our thought upon them. So much, certainly, may be affirmed without fear of contradiction. But it is quite another affair to maintain that material things cannot be thought of as existing-apart-from-a-thinking-mind. The former proposition merely indicates that this, like every other act of thinking, presupposes a thinker; the latter implies that a thinking mind is an essential condition of the existence of that which is thought about. All that Berkeley's argument appears to me to have proved, if, indeed, it needed proving, is the first of these two propositions. (pp. 117-18)

Taking the hint from Hume, Dawes Hicks illustrates his point by suggesting that just as it is nonsense to talk of a husband without a wife but not of a man without a wife, so it is nonsense to talk of a thing existing as an *object* (or as something actually cognized) without a perceiver, but not, for all that has been shown, nonsense to deny that everything is an object in this special sense.

Steinkraus's attempted defence of Berkeley in effect relies upon the fact that there is a clear distinction to be made between cases like the husband/man case on the one hand and the object/thing case on the other. First, then, we have all known and met men without wives, and thus have every justification for claiming not just that it is meaningful to talk of men who are not husbands but indeed that such creatures exist. By contrast we have none of us come across sensible things that were not being actually sensed, and thus, Steinkraus wants to say, have no evidence at all to support the claim that there are such things. Hence his claim, referred to earlier, that if, as he thinks, Berkeley's point is merely that reality without the mind is not a reasonable probability, the usual criticisms of him will be seen to miss the mark. Against Steinkraus we have of course consistently assumed, and I am sure rightly, that Berkeley's claim is a much stronger one than Steinkraus supposes, and that he really does think that the supposition of existence without the mind is inconceivable and one that involves a repugnancy. I cannot think of something existing outside the mind, for when I conceive it I find that it is in *my* mind.[11]

It is perhaps worth mentioning here an argument from Stace which is similar to that provided by Steinkraus, though Stace is not concerned to interpret Berkeley and does not mention him. What Stace says is that we would certainly be arguing fallaciously if we supposed that the fact that we had never met an unperceived object *proved* that there were no unexperienced objects. He argues, though, that we clearly have no *evidence* for maintaining that there are such objects and so should not believe in them. Thus:

> Now, lest I should be misunderstood, I will state clearly at the outset that I cannot prove that no entities exist without being experienced by minds. For all I know completely unexperienced entities may exist, but what I shall assert is that we have not the slightest reason for believing that they do exist. And from this it will follow that the realistic position that they do exist is perfectly groundless and gratuitous, and one which ought not to be believed. It will be in exactly the same position as the proposition 'there is a unicorn on the planet Mars'. I cannot prove that there is no unicorn on Mars. But since there is not the slightest reason to suppose that

there is one, it is a proposition which ought not to be believed. (pp. 146-7)

The proposition that 'some entities sometimes exist without being experienced by any finite mind' should not, then, be assented to.

Now though we are not primarily concerned with this argument, there is clearly enough in common between what Stace says and Berkeley's thinking for us to be justified in making perhaps two observations on it. And the first is that *if* the argument works it is certainly going to undermine not just the proposition that 'some entities sometimes exist without being perceived by any finite mind' but also the belief of the man who holds that all sensible entities are mind-dependent though not dependent on his own mind. Obviously if I have no evidence for the claim that unexperienced objects exist, and this because I have never come across such an object, it is also true that I have no evidence for the claim that anything has ever existed when unperceived or unexperienced *by me*. Stace seems to half realize this for on p. 148 he approves of the following from Russell:

> Belief in the existence of things outside my own biography must, from the standpoint of theoretical logic, be regarded as a prejudice, not as well-grounded theory.

In general, though, Stace represents himself as arguing for a less extreme view. Like Berkeley he suggests he is arguing against the belief that things exist outside *minds*, and fails to draw the equally justifiable conclusion that nobody is entitled to hold that anything exists when not perceived *by him*.

The second point is that it is wrong to suggest that the proposition concerning unexperienced objects is in the same position as that claim about the unicorn on Mars. The fact is, of course, that I have good positive reasons for supposing that there are no unicorns on Mars, and that even if the planet were more of a mystery than it is I should at least know how one might set about discovering whether the proposition was true or false. There may indeed be purely practical obstacles in the way of mounting an expedition now, but these obstacles will be overcome, and it may well be that my grandsons will be able to make an actual check. The case is different with the unexperienced entities. No developments in technology are going to enable my grandsons to perceive things they are not perceiving. Certainly we need to distinguish between propositions which could in principle be verified or falsified and the proposition Stace is concerned with and which he supposes we could never be in a position to confirm. In the context of the dispute between the realist and the idealist it is not, for example, reasonable to claim, with Stace, that the onus is on the realist to prove that there are unexperienced entities, *if* the only proof the idealist will accept is one that could in principle never be supplied. Ultimately Stace does rest his case against realism on the fact that nothing could count as experiencing an unexperienced thing.

The type of argument proposed by Steinkraus and Stace is best understood against the background of Perry's well-known examination of Berkeley's argument in which he charges Berkeley with improper exploitation of what he calls 'the egocentric predicament'. Perry quotes from *Pr.* 23 and observes that the argument owes any plausibility it has to the following fact:

No thinker to whom one may appeal is able to mention a thing that is not an idea, for the obvious and simple reason that *in mentioning it he makes it an idea*. No one can report on the nature of things without being on hand himself. It follows that whatever thing he reports does as a matter of fact stand in relation to him, as his idea, object of knowledge, or experience. (p. 129)

Now Perry certainly does not think that this (alleged) fact should worry us unduly, or that there is anything here which can contribute to an argument for the claim that there *are* no unexperienced entities. I think he is right here. Indeed some of the things he says could be quoted to illustrate the proper way of dealing with Berkeley's argument. Further, it does not seem that the consideration appealed to can justify even the claim that it is *improbable* that unexperienced entities exist. What I want to stress now, though, is that Perry's characterization of the egocentric predicament in the above passage is itself misleading, and this because it fails sufficiently to distinguish two 'problems' which should not be muddled. In view of what Berkeley says in *PC* 472-3 in particular, it must be crucially important to distinguish between the sense in which what we report on as an object of our present experience is an idea, and that in which what we mention is an idea. Equally, it is important not to confuse the relationship holding between a person and what he *experiences* and that holding between a person and what he *mentions*.

If what I experience when, say, I look at a tree is an *idea*, this is only obviously so in the sense (S1) that it is an object of present awareness. Again, if it is related to me it stands in the relation (R1) of being experienced or perceived. And it has been thought that there is a problem (P1) arising from the fact that nobody can be aware of an object which is not (when he experiences it) an idea in S1 standing *to him* in the relation R1. Ignoring the solipsistic tendency of his argument (and the implicit challenge to consider what should count as acceptable evidence for any claim concerning the existence of anything *he* is not experiencing), Steinkraus deals with this problem by claiming that it must be judged highly improbable that any sensible thing exists which is not an idea in S1 standing *to someone* in the relation R1. Now we usually suppose that we can *mention* things we are not actually experiencing, and Berkeley himself assumes this when he supposes we can refer to things unperceived *by us*. And Perry tells us that *'no thinker to whom one may appeal is able to mention a thing that is not an idea'*. Clearly, though, if what we mention (given we are not perceiving it) is an *idea*, it is only obviously so in the sense (S2) that it is a mentioned thing standing to the speaker in the relation (R2) of being mentioned by him. So if there is a problem here it is the not very worrying one that I cannot mention anything which is not (when I mention it) an idea in S2 standing to me in the relation R2. 'Problem' P2 can, then, only be that we cannot mention anything which is not then mentioned. In fact, of course, there is no problem here. The claim that we cannot mention things which are not then mentioned is wholly uninteresting, and acceptance of it leaves quite open the question whether mentioned things are always (when they are mentioned) ideas in S1 for someone. If Berkeley supposes differently it is only because he allows himself the untenable assumption that *I* must be aware of what I refer to.

Luce takes a quite different line on *Pr.* 23 when he claims that, 'It has not hitherto been noticed that while section 22 deals with sensible existence, section 23 deals with imagined existence' (Luce 5, p. 86). Unfortunately, just what it is that all the other commentators have missed here is obscure, and it is obscure partly because it is difficult to know what to make of this notion of *imagined* existence. Up to a point Luce's line is clear enough. The tree in my garden I take to have *sensible* or *real* existence, and if we ask what sensible or real existence is, Berkeley tells us that it is to be perceived by sense. Indeed, if Luce is right Berkeley has said what he wants to say concerning *sensible* existence by the end of *Pr.* 22, so that when in that section he repeats that we cannot *conceive* a sensible object existing unperceived he is, in effect, 'stressing the sufficiency of his former argument'. On this view the argument in sect. 23 is not intended to provide further support for the claim made in sect. 22. Rather, it introduces and deals with another kind of existence – 'imagined existence'.

Reading through the relevant pages in Luce, though, it is very difficult to make out what Luce means by *imagined* existence, and it would seem that there are two possibilities. First, it may be that an object having *imagined* existence is simply one I imagine or suppose to exist, as in *PC* 472 Berkeley imagines or supposes that the books in his study exist 'w^n no one is there to see them'. But if talking of imagined existence is meant to draw our attention to this sort of situation, and Luce suggests that it is, then it seems highly implausible to suggest that Berkeley is dealing with a new sort of existence. Surely, when I claim that I can imagine or suppose books to exist in my study when they are not perceived I imagine that they have *real* and sensible existence there. So on this interpretation it would seem that when Berkeley deals with *imagined* existence he is really dealing with the supposed *sensible* existence of those things we take to exist even though we believe nobody is at present actually perceiving them. And this being so there can be no question of his being concerned with a special *type* of existence, or of all commentators having failed to notice that this is so. Indeed there can be no question but that the argument in sect. 23 *is* intended to provide support for the claim made in the previous section. I take it to go without saying that Berkeley could not properly claim to have completed his case for holding that it is impossible to *conceive* an unperceived existent if the possibility were still left open that we might *imagine* one.

Sometimes, though, Luce does seem to mean something quite different by *imagined* existence, and the suggestion seems to be that while the things having *sensible* existence are real or sensible things (like the books in my study), the things having *imagined* existence are quite different entities and in fact *mental images*. Thus Luce thinks it relevant to stress that 'there is no imagination without an imaginer; mental imagery without a mind is nonsense'. The claim would seem to be, then, that in sect. 22 Berkeley finishes the case for saying that *sensible* existents cannot exist outside a mind, while in sect. 23 he is concerned to make the same point about mental images. We might think that the point here hardly needed arguing for.[12]

If trees exist *in a park* or books *in a study* then clearly they have sensible or real existence there. Similarly, if I imagine trees existing in a park or books existing in a study 'and no body by to perceive them', I imagine these as real or sensible existents. It follows that it would be a great mistake to appeal to the undoubted truth that mental images cannot exist unexperienced to support the claim that what I imagine or suppose to exist cannot exist unperceived. I am quite sure that Berkeley makes this mistake and tolerably sure that Luce makes it too. Thus we return to the case of the trees in the park:

> 'Surely there's nothing easier than to imagine trees, for instance, in a park, or books existing in a closet, and no body by to perceive them.' Quite so, says Berkeley, but that is not sense perception; that is imagination. Consider your instance with care. What exactly have you done? You have framed a mental picture of a tree or book, and have omitted to include an observer. I should have said, 'an observer other than yourself,' for *you* are tacitly included in the picture. *You* are observing the book or tree imagined. *You* are picturing. *You* are imagining; for there is no imagination without an imaginer; mental imagery without a mind is nonsense. (p. 88)

If I am puzzled about this passage it is partly because Luce introduces the argument by saying that it is wrong to suppose 'we could have an object of sense unperceived', but concludes only that imagined books or trees 'are imagined as ordinary books or trees . . . in actual *or possible* relation to mind' (my italics). It may indeed be that the passage is capable of a charitable interpretation. On the other hand, though, we can't help suspecting that the appeal to the fact that 'mental imagery without a mind is nonsense' is supposed to support the claim that we cannot imagine a sensible object existing with nobody aware of it, and this support it quite fails to provide. Whatever else we may want to say about the above passage we can hardly stress enough that the trees I imagine or suppose to exist in the park are *not* observed by me. The supposition that they are is a quite calamitous error.

Berkeley's argument, then, seems to fail in the sense that it does not prove what he thought it did. If he went wrong, this was primarily because he erred in his consideration of two questions which *are* difficult, the first being what it is to *conceive* a state of affairs and the second being that concerning the nature of *existence*, on which he thought he had achieved such a breakthrough. We will say something more on each of these questions.

We mentioned earlier that Mates finds Berkeley's argument in *Pr.* 23 'tricky' and unconvincing, but we must note now that he claims to remain quite unimpressed by the standard criticisms of it. And one reason why he is dissatisfied with what the critics say is that they suppose, as we have supposed, that we can indeed think of something existing unperceived, but do not themselves give any account of what it is to do this and how we do it. What the critic can do, as Mates sees it, is to give reasons for questioning the importance of mental imagery in conceiving something, and then to claim that Berkeley's argument presupposes that imaging is more central to conceiving a state of affairs than it in fact is. We might note, for example, that envisaging the world population growing to four billion (which we can do) does not depend upon our being able to form an image of four billion people (which we cannot do). But until an *adequate* account is given of what it is to conceive something, it cannot, Mates argues, be asserted baldly that it *is* possible to conceive a sensed object as existing unperceived.

Now it does seem to me that Mates is asking rather a lot from the critic here, and that the critic has done enough if he has revealed a fatal flaw in Berkeley's argument. We can say, though, that it *is* conceivable that things exist unperceived, at least in the sense that no linguistic impropriety is involved in supposing they do. I suppose that trees exist unperceived in a certain park. Now I may be wrong *in fact*, either because, unbeknown to me, someone is perceiving the trees, or because God always perceives everything there is to be perceived. But no appeal to dictionaries or to the ordinary usage of words will establish that my supposition is *nonsense*, as it would, for example, establish that it is repugnant to talk of an unmarried husband or a five-sided square. If, for all this, someone does want to claim that it is repugnant to suppose an unperceived tree, the onus is surely on him to provide some demonstration that this is so. In Berkeley's case the supposed demonstration fails, and it fails because he confuses the state of affairs envisaged with the mental image I may frame in making the supposition. It must be stressed that framing an image of books in a study cannot *be* supposing books to exist in my study (any more than it can be remembering that they existed there once[13]). We should certainly note that our ability to conceive a state of affairs cannot be tested by our ability to frame an image representing that state of affairs. But the really important point is that the state of affairs I think of (like the state of affairs remembered, feared, planned for or wished for) is necessarily distinct from any image I frame. If I fear the cockroach I believe to be under the sheets I am not fearing the mental image I may have in my mind. Rather similarly, if I *suppose* a cockroach to exist there (though I do not perceive it) my supposition concerns a cockroach, or something I do not perceive, and not any image of a cockroach which we can suppose I *do* perceive. What we mention, refer to or think about in circumstances such as this is always something *outside* our present experience.

Berkeley goes wrong in the argument we have been considering when he confuses the state of affairs imagined with the image I may frame when I imagine, and it may be of interest if we note that he is capable of making the same mistake in other contexts. The particular passage I have in mind here is the one in which he argues that while the objects of sense and mental images are alike 'in the mind', there are differences enough between them for the distinction between the real and the products of our fancy to remain secure. Thus:

> There are spiritual substances, minds, or human souls, which will or excite ideas in themselves at pleasure: but these are faint, weak, and unsteady in respect of others they perceive by sense, which being impressed upon them according to certain rules or laws of Nature, speak themselves the effects of a mind more powerful and wise than human spirits. These latter are said to have more *reality* in them than the former: by which is meant that they are more affecting, orderly, and distinct, and that they are not fictions of the mind perceiving them. And in this sense, the sun that I see by day is the real sun, and that which I imagine by night is the idea of the former. In the sense here given of *reality*, it is evident that every vegetable, star, mineral, and in general each part of the mundane system, is as much a *real being* by our principles as by any other. (*Pr.* 36)

It is not, I think, often enough remarked that as it stands this contains one remarkable howler. For quite clearly the sun that I imagine by night is *not* the idea of the sun I see by day, nor is it a fiction of the mind. I imagine by night that very sun which I see by day, and on Berkeley's reckoning this sun remains *a real being*. He is in fact identifying the images I can call to mind with the things imagined, the image framed with the object thought about, and however tempting this identification may seem it cannot be allowed to stand. Even in the case where I imagine something that does not really exist – as I might imagine the perfect woman – it is clear on reflection that the object of my thought must not be confused with any mental picture in my mind, and this if only because the picture may be fuzzy but the imagined woman is not. But in the case of the sun the point is really quite evident. The sun I imagine is hot and huge; the image I frame is not. The object is, in fact, totally distinct from the image. So far as *Pr.* 36 is concerned Berkeley's slip in missing this point may not matter too much. A substitution for six words to make it clear that the concern is with the image we frame rather than with the sun imagined would be sufficient to rectify the matter. In *Pr.* 23, though, and in the parallel passage in the *Dialogues*, the slip is material. Conceiving a tree is supposed to come down to imagining a tree, and the tree imagined is confused with an image of the tree. Because the image is in the mind, Berkeley supposes the tree we claim to be able to conceive as existing unperceived must be perceived by us.

We shall be brief in summing up on Berkeley's thinking about *existence*. Perhaps the main point to be made is that it is not surprising that Berkeley had difficulty with this concept. It *is* a tricky concept, as the long and continuing debate on the question as to whether 'exists' is a predicate shows. I suppose, though, that the starting point for Berkeley is the view, to be found in Locke's *Essay* at II vii 7, that existence is a simple idea 'suggested by every object without, and every idea within'. Berkeley criticizes this in *PC* 670 when he says:

> Strange it is that Men should be at a loss to find their Idea of Existence since that (if such there be distinct from Perception) it is brought into the mind by all the Ways of Sensation & Reflection; methinks it should be most familiar to us & we best Acquainted with it.

He asserts in fact that we have 'no such idea of Existence or annext to the Word Existence' (*PC* 671). Ultimately he believes that when I am aware of a thing my knowledge that I perceive it cannot be distinguished from my knowledge that it *is*, the two pieces of knowledge amounting to one and the same thing. But he also holds both that to conceive a thing and to conceive it as existent are identical, and that conceiving a thing involves and indeed amounts to perceiving that thing. It follows that we cannot conceive an unperceived existent, and indeed, Berkeley would say, that to suppose X existent and to suppose it perceived are equivalent.

It seems odd to say that whatever we conceive we conceive as existent, for surely when I conceive the chimera I think of it as mythological, or as something which *does not* exist. But Berkeley has his generous sense of 'exist', and in *this* sense he would take it to be obvious that we conceive an existent chimera, though we may not suppose it exists in the real world. Hume takes a similarly generous line when he says:

> The idea of existence, then, is the very same with the idea of what we conceive to be existent. To reflect on any thing simply, and to reflect on it as existent, are nothing different from each other. (*Treatise*, Bk. I Pt. II Sect. vi)

Indeed we can look later than Hume. For if we think it strange to find Berkeley suggesting that what I mention must then exist (*PC* 472) we can remind ourselves that the early Russell thought it obvious that 'to mention anything is to show that it is' (Russell 4, p. 449). And though for the early Russell the mentioned unicorn is supposed to *be* rather than to *exist*, Berkeley's suggestion that 'in one sense' chimeras exist points at some such distinction, implying and being meant to imply that there is a sense, the 'ordinary' sense, in which chimeras do *not* exist. We shall not dwell on Berkeley's belief that what we conceive we must conceive as (in some sense) existent, though we should at least point out that if we do take the common, less generous sense of 'exists', the claim made is plainly false. I think of the chair I destroyed as *having* existed, of the chair I plan to build as one that may *come to have* existence, and of the chair I planned to build but never built as something that never had and *never will have* existence. And of course it is this sense of 'exists' that needs explication if we are to account for the meaning of 'exist' 'when applied to sensible things'. The problem we will move on to, though, is that as to how Berkeley could ever have come to believe that the existent sensible object must be conceived and perceived.

Now when he considered materialism and the notion that the *real* objects lie hidden from us beyond a veil of perception, Berkeley certainly thought of his opponents as forgetting the context in which the notion of existence gets its meaning and application. The ultimate vacuity he takes to be reflected in the philosophers' conception of *matter* as the unknown and unknowable *substratum* of all qualities whatsoever. Thus:

> If we inquire into what the most accurate philosophers declare themselves to mean by *material substance*; we shall find them acknowledge, they have no other meaning annexed to those sounds, but the idea of being [i.e. existence] in general, together with the relative notion of its supporting accidents. The general idea of being appeareth to me the most abstract and incomprehensible of all other ... (*Pr.* 17)

But he holds in general that the term 'exists' is one that has meaning for us in relation to the *known* objects of sense experience, while it does not and cannot when applied to the supposed objects which we *never* perceive. We can, in short, conceive X as *existing* only where we have some conception of X, and we can have no conception of any object which, though it is supposed to exist, could never be perceived or known. And the important point here is *conceivability*, and the availability of the supposed existent for perception. We need not endorse this argument and we may not find it as clear as we might wish, but we can at least see it as having a certain plausibility.

In fact, though, Berkeley attacks the representative realist (and the believer in substratum-substance) not just for supposing we can meaningfully predicate existence of unknowable items which could never be perceived, but for supposing it can be predicated of other than mind-dependent ideas. And so the interpretive problem becomes that as to why it seemed so obvious to Berkeley, not just that the existent must be coextensive with the knowable, conceivable or perceivable, but that each existent must be an object of present awareness. It seems obvious *to us* that when we say an object such as a book *exists*, that it *really* exists, in the world of bookshops, libraries, publishers and readers, part at least of what we are claiming is that the object could be perceived by anyone, and this though it may contingently be the case that nobody is actually perceiving it. And similarly, when we suppose a book to exist (in front of us, in the library or wherever) our conception is of an object which we might perceive and read, but no more of one that *must* be perceived than it is of one that must be read. We noted in the last chapter that there is no linguistic impropriety involved in talking of an existent but unperceived table, and that any appeal to ordinary usage is bound to fail. Equally, though, and as Hylas points out, there is at least no patent absurdity involved in the conception of an unperceived but existent sensible object. Berkeley's attempt to show otherwise is that contained in the psychological approach. It fails because Berkeley rests his case upon the assumption that *I* must perceive what I suppose to exist. And this assumption is false.[14]

CHAPTER SIX

Perception

'If I compliment a girl on her appearance I do not expect her to be insulted because I have complimented her appearance and not her. To treat appearances as objects would seem to be a paradigm example of a category mistake, and, so far from its being the case that we can never perceive things but only their appearances, the truth is that if we cannot perceive things we cannot perceive their appearances either, since to perceive a thing's appearance is itself to perceive that thing.' (Don Locke, pp. 37-8)

I

In considering Berkeley's arguments for his position we have been struck by the extent to which his thinking is conditioned by acceptance of some of the more dubious views of those he thinks of as his main opponents. We noted for example that at the opening of the *Principles* he does not *argue* that in sense perception we are aware only of mind-dependent ideas, but rather insists that this is 'evident to any one who takes a survey of the objects of human knowledge'. Simplifying somewhat we can say that in sects. 1-2 Berkeley takes this 'evident' truth for granted and then, quietly assuming that the things we are aware of in perception are the real things, concludes that real things are ideas or (better) collections of ideas. Then in sect. 3 he appeals to what we ordinarily mean when we say a table, an odour, a sound, colour or figure exists, and expects us to agree that we can only mean that it is at least perceivable. But again here he relies on the representative realist's belief that only ideas are perceivable to effect a transfer to his own viewpoint which is that things like tables and their qualities must be *actually* perceived. The shared belief Berkeley does not attempt to support.

But this is not the only way in which the Lockian background is presupposed. For Berkeley also assumes that if he is to dispose of the view that there are external physical objects 'without the mind' he can rely on the account of such objects given by the materialist. And one quite crucial point here is that (because it is assumed that we are acquainted only with ideas) the external objects are supposed to be things which we are never aware of in sense experience. Sects. 7-20 contain an attack on one particular analysis of the nature of the external reality, or on a supposed realm in which there are unperceivable objects made up of unperceivable qualities inhering in a mysterious (and again unperceivable) substratum. In sect. 18 for example, Berkeley says:

> But though it were possible that solid, figured, moveable substances may exist without the mind, corresponding to the ideas we have of bodies, yet how is it possible for us to know this? Either we must know it by sense, or by reason. As for our senses, by them we have the knowledge only of our sensations, ideas, or those things that are immediately perceived by sense, call them what you will; but they do not inform us that things exist without the mind, or unperceived, like to those which are perceived. This the materialists themselves acknowledge. It remains therefore that if we have any knowledge at all of external things, it must be by reason, inferring their existence from what is immediately perceived by sense. But what reason can induce us to believe the existence of bodies without the mind, from what we perceive, since the very patrons of matter themselves do not pretend, there is any necessary connexion betwixt them and our ideas?

Note just how much is assumed to be common ground between Berkeley and his readers. It is supposedly *agreed* both that we perceive only ideas and that if there are external objects these things are never perceived. So the *issue* is whether ideas (which certainly exist) and external objects (the existence of which is in question) share the ontological stage. It is *because* perception is confined to mind-dependent ideas, and *because* the external world is supposed to lie beyond the veil of perception, that the existence of a world other than a world of ideas is in doubt.

Everything we have said so far is consistent with Hospers' judgement that idealism 'builds on the basis of the theory of representative realism', modifying this theory 'in one important respect' and this by denying that there are *unperceivable* external objects. We can also agree with Hamlyn when he says:

Berkeley's philosophy ... results in large part from an attempt to rid Locke's view of inconsistencies – in particular to dispense with notions which are inconsistent with the general empiricist doctrine that all ideas are derived from sense-experience. ... Berkeley gives us a new picture of the world in terms which might be called those of a 'purified Locke'. But the purification led him to views which have often seemed far more paradoxical than any that Locke produced. (pp. 104-5)

We could easily multiply expressions of this interpretative view. In it we have the clue to the dissatisfaction the average reader is likely to feel on meeting Berkeley's *Principles*. He will feel that of course *if* the external world were as Berkeley's materialist says it is (and in particular something hidden from us on the dark side of a veil of perception) then there would at the very least be scope for scepticism about its existence. Equally, he may concede that *if* it were made plain to him that the only objects of perceptual awareness were ideas then he would at least have to look seriously at the notion that things like tables are somehow constructed out of such entities. But of course the plain man does not believe that the external world is as Berkeley's materialist says it is, or that we are aware only of ideas. His judgement on the *Principles* may be that the arguments in it are either contemptible (and he will instance here that in *Pr.* 23) or else such that they leave his own position untouched. Essential to this position is the view that there are things such as chairs and tables which we *are* acquainted with in sense perception but which are *not* dependent upon the perceiving mind.

For this and another reason (see above pp. 65-7) it is obviously highly desirable that Berkeley should spell out the case for accepting what he has assumed to be 'evident'. And though the case is not made in the *Principles*, we find that in the *Dialogues* he does at least give the impression of starting from something like a scratch position. Regrettably Hylas is far from free of suspect philosophical notions, but he does need convincing that, for example, the colours we see are not 'on' objects existing independently of the observer. In this chapter we shall be concerned first with Philonous's claim that we perceive only the *immediate* objects of perception, and then with the arguments designed to show that these immediate objects are mind-dependent.

We can make a general point at the outset. It is true for all of us (including philosophers when they are not carefully analysing what goes on when we perceive) that we suppose that perception is often of substantial objects such as coaches, cats and cuspidors. Here is a penny. I look at it. I take it in my hand and feel it. The rose can be seen, touched and smelt. Berkeley takes another example in *NTV* 46:

> Sitting in my study I hear a coach drive along the street; I look through the casement and see it; I walk out and enter into it; thus, common speech would incline one to think I heard, saw, and touched the same thing, to wit, the coach.

Philosophers, though, are generally agreed that we need to take a closer look at what is going on in perception, and many have agreed that ordinary speech reflects an uncritical and inadequate approach to the subject.

Take the case of seeing a penny. We talk of this as if it were a simple, easily identifiable experience, but if we reflect we realize that the experience I have when I look down on the penny (which is one case of 'seeing the penny') is different from the experience I have when I look at it from an angle (a second case of 'seeing the penny'). It is also noted that I can have experiences which seem identical to the experience of seeing X when it is not straightforwardly true that I am seeing X. For example, seeing the reflection of X is clearly not seeing X, but under certain circumstances I may be tricked and without further investigation there may be nothing to tell me that I am seeing a reflection rather than the thing. And, to take one more example, there is the case where we put our hands in water to feel the temperature. At first we are likely to take an uncritical approach. I can feel the temperature with my right hand or my left, my elbow or my big toe. But the philosopher may suggest that this is certainly over-simplifying. Surely any adequate account of perceiving temperature must allow for facts such as that if, prior to immersing them in the water, one of my hands has been in my pocket and one in the cold air, what I feel with the one hand will be *different* to what I feel with the other.

It cannot be doubted that any satisfactory account of perception must allow for the complexities to which our attention is drawn by these examples. But if philosophers have agreed that it is necessary to pay close attention to these complexities, there has not been unanimity on the question as to what theory of perception we should adopt in order to accommodate the facts. Many philosophers have, though, drawn our attention to what they call *immediate* objects of perception (or *sense data*). The penny I take myself to be perceiving is, of course, hard, but if I am just looking at it and not feeling it I am not directly aware of its hardness. What I *immediately* perceive is its colour and shape. But this is still not quite right. For what I immediately perceive is the colour and shape the penny *appears to have from my standpoint*. It may be difficult to give an adequate description here, but we get near to one if we say that the immediate object when I look at the penny from an angle is an elliptical brown patch.

The notion of an immediate object of perception is often associated with other notions. Thus we have Aristotle's concept of a *special* object:

> I call special-object whatever cannot be perceived by another sense, and about which it is impossible to be deceived, e.g. sight has colour, hearing sound, and taste flavour, while touch has many varieties of object. But at any rate each judges about these, and is not deceived as to the fact that there is colour or sound, but rather as to what or where the coloured thing is or as to what or where the object which sounds is. (p. 25)

Towards the beginning of the *First Dialogue* Philonous asks Hylas:

> You will farther inform me, whether we immediately perceive by sight any thing beside light, and colours, and figures: or by hearing any thing but sounds: by the palate, any thing beside tastes: by the smell, beside odours: or by the touch, more than tangible qualities.

Berkeley holds that what I immediately perceive when employing a particular sense is *always* some object proper to and special to that sense, meaning by this that the object could not be perceived by any other sense. He also holds that we cannot be mistaken about what we immediately perceive.

Some examples may help to make the notion of an immediate object a little clearer. First, then, when I hear a bird singing in the woods, the same sound recorded on tape, and a clever imitation on a whistle, the experiences may be indistinguishable, and in each case the sound that I hear is the immediate object of perception. Again, when I see a shimmering patch on the road ahead I may in one way be in doubt about what I am seeing (a mirage?, water?) but I am certain about the shimmering patch, and this is the immediate object of perception. We can consider too the case of a shopper inspecting a piece of material. She runs her hand over it to feel the texture and holds it up to the light to see whether the colour will suit her, and here what she *feels* is the texture and what she *sees* is the colour or a coloured expanse. In general, if we take any situation in which the plain man wants to talk of perceiving a substantial object it is claimed that we can locate an immediate object which he is aware of.

Perhaps few philosophers would disagree with the claim that there is *some* point in the doctrine that there are immediate objects of perception, but there is nothing like general agreement as to how it should be formulated or what its significance is. Some would hold that it can be stated in an agreeably neutral way. In an interesting paper L. S. Carrier argues:

> ... the immediate-mediate contrast is but an instance of a general distinction of a purely grammatical nature. If this is so, then the distinction itself must be indifferent concerning the existence of sensory entities: the linguistic sawmill fashions no ontological planks, but serves here only to cut away the dead timber supporting the edifice of sense impressions. (p. 391)

And in a similar spirit Don Locke holds that philosophers subscribing to radically different theories of perception can all accept sense data.[1] The difference between them will be differences concerning the *status* of sense data. The Causal Theorist, for example, will insist that the immediate objects of perception are discrete *items* or *entities* which are to be distinguished from the semi-permanent things in the external world which may produce them in us. He will also hold that these entities are mind-dependent. On Berkeley's reading at least he must have it that the things we *immediately* perceive are all we *actually* perceive, though as he holds that the sense data give us clues as to what is going on outside us he can be said to allow for the *mediate* perception of external objects. In short, the Causal Theorist is committed to a *theory* concerning the nature of sense data and things in the outside world.

The direct realist, though, will take a different view. As Don Locke puts it:

> Sense data are what we immediately perceive. But this does not mean that sense data form some special class of objects which are perceived in some special way. Sense data are not, on a Realist interpretation,

objects at all, and to talk about sense data is to talk, in a special way, about the things, whatever they may be, that we happen to perceive. ... There is, therefore, no conflict between 'We always perceive sense data' (i.e. 'Whenever we perceive we immediately perceive') and the Realist's 'We perceive external objects'. Given Realism, to perceive an external object is, among other things, to perceive a sense datum, a sense datum which might be said to include parts or aspects of that external object. (p. 179)

For the direct realist the elliptical brown patch is not an *entity* which screens the penny from his perceptual grasp. He holds rather that in perception he is in a quite straightforward sense acquainted with the real penny, and this though he can also characterize his experience in terms of the immediate perception of an elliptical brown patch. We will spell this out rather more fully later, but for the present we will just stress two points. The first is that because the direct realist does not think of the elliptical brown patch as a *thing* he will not be tempted to think of it as interposing itself between him and a 'real' thing. And the second is that for a similar reason he will not feel he has to ask which of two items he *actually* perceives. The object he sees is the penny, though because from his standpoint it appears as an elliptical brown patch he can see some point in describing this as the immediate object of perception.

Berkeley's position is different again. In the *Dialogues* he assumes from the outset that sense data are discrete items. Further, it will turn out that he agrees with the Causal Theorist that these entities are mind-dependent. He holds, though, that if talk of substantial objects is to be meaningful it must be cashable in terms of ideas. Now he sometimes asks us to think of a substantial object as a *combination* or *collection* of ideas, sensations or qualities, but his actual position is more complicated than this suggests, for he really does hold that each sense datum is an entity and that ultimately the sensible reality is composed of 'fleeting' and 'changeable' items (*Dialogues*, iii, 258). Like the Causal Theorist he can make some sense of the notion that we perceive semi-permanent things in an external world, and indeed he is eager to do so, but while the Causal Theorist departs from the direct realist in holding that external objects are suggested to the mind by sense data rather than actually perceived, Berkeley departs from our ordinary thinking by claiming that in the last analysis the supposed semi-permanent things are not things at all. In case there is any doubt as to what Berkeley's view is here, we can consider what he has Philonous say in iii, 245-6:

> Strictly speaking, Hylas, we do not see the same object that we feel; neither is the same object perceived by the microscope, which was by the naked eye. But in case every variation was thought sufficient to constitute a new kind or individual, the endless number or confusion of names would render language impracticable. Therefore to avoid this ... men combine together several ideas, apprehended by divers senses, or by the same sense at different times, or in different circumstances, but observed however to have some connexion in Nature, either with respect to co-existence or succession; all which they refer to one name, and consider as one thing. Hence it follows that when I examine by my other senses a thing I have seen, it is not in order to understand better the same object which I had perceived by sight, the object of one sense not being perceived by the other senses. And when I look through a microscope, it is not that I may perceive more clearly what I perceived already with my bare eyes, the object perceived by the glass being quite different from the former.

It is for Philonous just a mistake for the philosopher to suppose that the name of a substantial object marks out one thing in Nature, and we are going to miss the truth of the matter if we rely 'not so much on notions as words, which were framed by the vulgar, merely for conveniency ... without any regard to speculation'.[2]

We have here another theory about sense data, and the theory involves the notion that in any given situation it is straightforwardly true that we perceive some immediate object, but not straightforwardly true that we perceive a substantial object. From this standpoint it is natural for the Berkeleian to make his point by equating what is *immediately* perceived with the entity which is actually perceived, and it seems to me that Philonous means to commit himself to just this way of thinking when he claims at the outset that sensible objects are 'those only which can be perceived immediately by sense' (i, 174). At any rate I want to look very closely at the assumption that sense data are *items*, and of course items that will be shown to be mind-dependent.

That Berkeley departs from our ordinary ways of thinking when he equates what is immediately perceived with an item (which is said to be all we actually perceive) is, I suppose, already obvious. It may be useful, though, if we look at some typical situations to illustrate the precise point of departure. We can start, then, by noting that though we normally suppose we can perceive the same thing, a coach perhaps, by different senses, we at the same time accept that employing a given sense will give us information of a particular sort. The shopper inspecting the piece of material learns about the colour by looking at it and the texture by feeling it, and in general it is trivially true that sight informs us about an object's visible qualities, feeling as to tangible qualities, and so on. Now the shopper handling the material will not object to being told that what she *feels* is the texture, and she will not object to the observation that she could not feel the material without feeling some tangible quality, but she will certainly jib when she is told she feels a texture *rather than* the material, or that it is more true to say she feels a texture than it is to say she feels the cloth. How, she may ask, could she possibly feel the texture without feeling the cloth?

The situation is complicated by the fact that philosophers who draw our attention to immediate objects of perception are not just concerned with what we would recognize as sensible *qualities*. The elliptical appearance I am said to immediately perceive when I suppose I see a penny is not, after all, a quality of anything. The facts are, we might say, that the penny is round but appears elliptical from an angle. If the philosopher wishes to make this point by saying that what I immediately perceive is an elliptical appearance, well and good. We can at least see the point of the move. But accepting the point will not incline us to suppose that we are perceiving an elliptical brown patch *rather than* the round penny, or to waver from our belief that what we are seeing is really round. Berkeley, though, would tell a quite different story. For he does want us to think of the appearance as itself a thing, so that the object I see when I look at the penny *is* elliptical rather than round. Indeed, though we customarily suppose that there is just one object – the penny – which *looks* different from different angles, Berkeley wants us to accept that really there is no such thing, but only various appearances which we allow to share a name.

One last example can help to make this point even clearer. We can suppose that two travellers are crossing a desert and that A sees a black spot on the horizon and asks B if he can see it too. And B, who knows the terrain, may agree that he does indeed see the black spot, but he goes on to say that what they are both seeing is in fact a solitary gravestone. Now clearly both A and B are nearer to giving a statement of immediate perception when they say they see a black spot than is B when he says they see a gravestone. But neither A nor B would want to assent to Berkeley's judgement that the black spot is itself a thing, or that it is really only this that they see. Given that he believes B, A is going to be quite happy to say that what he sees is *really* a gravestone, though it appears from a distance as a black spot. For him there is in a quite straightforward sense one item, a gravestone, which he would see more clearly as he neared it and which he might touch and lean against. In short, where he differs from Berkeley is in holding that the characterization of the object seen as a black spot is a characterization *of the gravestone itself*, but of the gravestone as it appears to a distant observer.

II

What we will do now is to locate two suspect features of Berkeley's account of immediate perception which may go some way towards explaining why he thinks it obvious that sensible objects are 'those only which can be perceived immediately by sense'. And the first of these is that Berkeley is aware of *two* doctrines concerning distinctions between immediate and mediate objects of perception, the first of which he is concerned to oppose and the second of which is his own, and that in the *Dialogues* he starts (in i, 174-5) by appealing to the doctrine he rejects. The exchange here deserves closer attention than it is usually given.

The passage opens with Philonous asking a question:

> Pardon me, Hylas, if I am desirous clearly to apprehend your notions, since this may much shorten our inquiry. Suffer me then to ask you this farther question. Are those things only perceived by the senses which are perceived immediately? Or may those things properly be said to be *sensible*, which are perceived mediately, or not without the intervention of others.

Hylas professes not to understand the question and Philonous proposes an analogy. When I read a book what I immediately perceive is the letters, but these may suggest to my mind 'the notions of God, virtue, truth, &c.' Now here Philonous chooses as things suggested to my mind things which are *clearly* not themselves sensible. Not any combination of letters would do to make his point. When I see the letters 'C-e-n-o-t-a-p-h' the letters are what I immediately perceive, but they suggest to my mind something which is normally taken to be itself sensible. If we are to take the analogy seriously, then, it would seem that Philonous is after a distinction between immediate objects of perception which can be perceived by sense, and mediate objects whose nature is such that they cannot be perceived at all, though their existence may be suggested to the mind by the things we do perceive. But it soon emerges that the immediate objects of perception are light, colours and figures, sounds, tastes, odours and tangible qualities, and as Hylas accepts this, together with the principle that sensible things are 'those only which can be perceived immediately by sense', it follows that Philonous has him committed to the view that substantial objects like the Cenotaph are not sensible. The harshness of this is somewhat mitigated when it is admitted in passing that *combinations* of the immediate objects can be thought of as sensible, but prior to this the suggestion would seem to be the surprising one that things like coaches, cats and cuspidors are not (strictly) sensible, but rather insensible things the existence of which is suggested to the mind by the things we immediately perceive.

Now the intriguing question here is what makes Hylas accept this strange conclusion at this early stage, and it is pretty clear that he accepts it because he is persuaded to think in terms of a distinction between what we are directly acquainted with when we perceive something and the real, external objects which he supposes are the *causes* of what we immediately perceive. Much later he makes this distinction explicit when he says:

> . . . I think there are two kinds of objects, the one perceived immediately, which are likewise called *ideas*; the other are real things or external objects perceived by the mediation of ideas, which are their images and representations. (i, 203)

And though this point is usually overlooked it is, I think, plain that this is the sort of distinction Hylas has in mind in the passage under examination. Here he says:

> . . . I tell you once for all, that by *sensible things* I mean those only which are perceived by sense, and that in truth the senses perceive

nothing which they do not perceive immediately: for they make no inferences. The deducing therefore of causes or occasions from effects and appearances, which alone are perceived by sense, entirely relates to reason.

What we have to appreciate is that for Hylas the reason why it is not straightforwardly true that we perceive chunky items in the external world is that these objects are thought of as the remote causes of what is actually given us in sensation. When I say I see the Cenotaph I am making an inference to the existence of an unperceived material thing which plays a causal role in relation to 'effects and appearances, which alone are perceived by sense'.

This, then, is one distinction between immediate and mediate objects of perception, but there is another doctrine and it is the one Berkeley is leading up to. Indeed Hylas's assertion that 'the senses . . . make no inferences' is often quoted by those who suppose the discussion here to have nothing at all to do with a three-term theory of perception. Warnock for example says:

> Nor is it difficult to see what he has in mind. Suppose that a noise breaks out, and I say 'I can hear a dog barking in the road'. In saying this, Berkeley urges, I *have* made an inference – indeed more than one. First, from the particular nature of the sounds that I hear I have inferred that they are made by a barking dog; and second, I have inferred that the barking dog is in the road. (Warnock 1, pp. 153-4)

Here again we have a distinction between an effect (the noise) and a cause (the barking dog), but the point this time is not one that depends on the Causal Theory of perception. Indeed it is one that could be aimed at anyone occupying the plain man's standpoint. Sticking for the moment to the specific situation described, and not for the moment drawing the general and disturbing moral Berkeley wants us to draw, we can allow that there is some initial plausibility in the suggestion that all Warnock is actually aware of is the noise, and that he only infers the existence of the dog which, we can suppose, he would perceive if he looked out of the window.

Now the argument Warnock draws our attention to is one Philonous does propose, but only towards the end of the *First Dialogue*. Here he rejects Hylas's claim that when we perceive ideas we mediately perceive 'invisible' external objects, but he goes on to claim that his own position leaves room for a distinction between immediate and mediate perception. Thus:

> ... we may in one acceptation be said to perceive sensible things mediately by sense: that is, when from a frequently perceived connexion, the immediate perception of ideas by one sense suggests to the mind others perhaps belonging to another sense, which are wont to be connected with them. For instance, when I hear a coach drive along the streets, immediately I perceive only the sound; but from the experience I have had that such a sound is connected with a coach, I am said to hear the coach. It is nevertheless evident, that in truth and strictness, nothing can be *heard* but *sound*: and the coach is not then properly perceived by sense, but suggested from experience. (i, 204.)

We should be clear here that though Philonous makes his point by taking hearing a coach as his example, he wants to make a quite general point about perception by any sense. In *NTV* 46 Berkeley remarks that 'common speech would incline one to think I heard, saw, and touched the same thing, to wit, the coach', but he concludes:

> It is nevertheless certain, the ideas intromitted by each sense are widely different and distinct from each other; but having been observed constantly to go together, they are spoken of as one and the same thing.

As, strictly speaking, we hear sounds (rather than coaches), so we see light, colours and figures (rather than coaches), and each sense is concerned with its own proper objects. But these immediate objects of perception are not to be regarded, as the direct realist regards them, as simply features or aspects of one thing, the coach, which my senses taken individually acquaint me with. Rather, they are themselves the basic things in the sensible world. Experience teaches me to associate certain ideas with others so that I come to *think of them as* constituting one thing, and it is when the perception of a member of the set suggests other members to the imagination that I can be said to perceive *mediately* the thing.

What we have, then, is two distinct doctrines concerning mediate and immediate perception. The first will be familiar, for it is precisely this doctrine that Berkeley is attacking in *Pr.* 18 when he attributes to the materialist the view that by our senses 'we have the knowledge only of our sensations, ideas, or those things that are immediately perceived by sense' and only infer 'that things exist without the mind, or unperceived, like to those which are perceived'. Taking this approach we accept a distinction between mediate and immediate perception and the notion that really we perceive *only* the immediate objects because we hold the substantial things to be remote and 'invisible' causal objects. The second doctrine is quite different and ultimately it must rely on what we might term a *phenomenological* approach. The proponent draws our attention to situations where we suppose we are faced with a substantial object, and then asks us to concentrate on what we are *actually* aware of when employing a given sense. We ordinarily suppose we hear a coach, but after some thought we are supposed to appreciate that really all we hear is a sound. And similarly, on reflection, we are expected to see both that whatever sense we employ we never come across a substantial object, and that in strict truth the table, chair, apple and bun are but (useful) fictions. To one who holds the first doctrine the immediate objects of perception will be essentially effects, produced by, and radically distinct from, the real things. But Berkeley, who holds the second, can make *something* of the notion that *his* immediate objects of perception are (sometimes) constituents of things like apples.

The claim that there are two quite different routes that can bring us to a recognition of immediate objects of perception is not of course falsified if historically philosophers have often failed adequately to distinguish them. Clearly phenomenological considerations have influenced those committed to the Causal Theory, and it seems quite plain that Berkeley at least is encouraged to think that a purely phenomenological approach should lead to certain conclusions precisely because he is influenced by the Causal Theorist's thinking about the status of sense data. What I suspect is that a phenomenological approach can lead to the location of immediate objects of perception, but that it leaves quite open the question as to the relationship between sense data and the substantial objects we sometimes take ourselves to be perceiving; indeed that a phenomenological approach may be compatible with the Causal Theory, with Berkeley's idealism, and with direct realism. But if a phenomenological approach will leave standing at least the *possibility* that in perceiving the immediate objects we are (in a quite straightforward sense) perceiving substantial things, we are surely right in being suspicious of the fact that at the outset Philonous encourages Hylas to presuppose the Causal Theory in order to establish the desired conclusion that sensible objects are 'those only which can be perceived immediately by sense'. It is by this means that he introduces the immediate objects of perception as discrete items, which he does want us to treat as the basic things in the world as sensed, and of course this move prepares the ground for his own account of how perception of these items is related to the supposed perception of things like coaches. Even if the sort of argument Warnock draws our attention to points in the same direction – and it is this which is questioned – it remains true that there is something very odd involved in the procedure of introducing an important doctrine by temporarily assuming an account of perception which is soon going to be shown to be fundamentally faulty.

Turning now to the second suspect feature of Berkeley's account I want to suggest that it is significant that in trying to persuade us that we perceive by sense only the immediate objects of perception he tends to give pride of place to the proper objects of *hearing*. Philosophers have become aware of the dangers involved in making generalizations about perceiving based on consideration of what goes on when we employ some chosen sense, and here it seems to be the case that Berkeley's doctrine has a certain plausibility when we consider certain modes of perceiving (hearing, smelling and perhaps tasting) that it lacks when we concentrate on others (seeing and feeling). Certainly we should not assume that if there is *some* plausibility in the notion that hearing somehow fails to acquaint us with substantial objects, then the more general notion that always perception by a given sense acquaints us only with some object proper to that sense must be similarly plausible. Consideration of what goes on when we see and feel may lead us to a different conclusion.[3]

Now consideration of things we say, or can quite easily be persuaded to say, about what we *hear* may at first seem to support Berkeley's contention. The fact is that though in common speech we are prepared to say we hear things like the clock, the bells in the tower, or the coach in the street outside, we are also prepared to say that what we hear are the sounds *made by* these things. In the situation to which Berkeley draws our attention we might normally say *either* that we hear a coach *or* that we hear the noise it makes as it runs down the street. When Berkeley says that 'in truth and strictness, nothing can be *heard* but *sound*', he can thus be represented as recommending one way of describing the situation in favour of the other, though both ways of talking seem acceptable to the plain man. And one reason why it may seem plausible to suggest that the one way of talking is *preferable*, and that *strictly* we hear sounds rather than the objects making them, is that there is a tendency to think of the sounds as distinct things. As Urmson notes, 'sounds . . . have some very general features in common with physical objects' (p. 119). One point here is that, though there may be problems about the location of sounds in space, there are circumstances in which we are definitely inclined to locate a sound in a place different from that occupied by the thing producing it. Broadly, then, to the extent that we do think of things like coaches as *producing* sounds, and of the sounds produced as *distinct items*, we are going to see something in the suggestion that *really* all we hear when we say we hear a coach is the sound it produces as it runs down the street. Fundamentally, we may say, there are two objects here – the coach and the sound – and if we have to say which we *really* hear, well, perhaps we should choose the sound.

To this extent, concentration on hearing serves Berkeley's purposes well, and it is not surprising that he likes to focus our attention on what we actually *hear*. If we look a little deeper, however, we find that from another point of view observations about hearing and what we hear quite fail to support him. The crucial point here is that, to the extent that we are inclined to think of sounds as discrete items produced by things, we will be less inclined to think of the sounds as *qualities* of things. Now Berkeley likes to represent himself as making a quite general point that covers the perception of sensible *qualities*. When the shopper looks at the colour of the material what she actually sees is a coloured patch which is supposed to be as much a discrete item as is the sound. But in answer to this we need to be quite clear that if we do not think of sounds as qualities, then observations about them and their relation to hearing are not going to persuade us that, in general, the perception of a quality comes down to the perception of a special sort of item.

In fact we can admit that hearing things like coaches and clocks always comes down to hearing the sounds they make without admitting that it is in any way *improper* to talk of hearing the things that make the sounds. More importantly though, we have to stress that when we think of an object as producing a sound (or emitting an odour) we do think of the sound (or odour) as being distinct from what produced it in a way in which the qualities of a thing (and, come to that, the *appearances* of a thing) are not. Of course any number of cases can be found where we choose to, or find it more appropriate to, talk of seeing or feeling a certain quality than of seeing or feeling the thing that *has* the quality, for example when we happen to be more interested in the colour or texture *of* a thing than in the particular thing that is coloured and textured. We can even find cases where we might want to say we perceived the quality and yet to deny that we felt or saw the thing. If, for example, a table was draped with a sheet we might want to say we could see the shape of the table but not the table. Given this, though, we clearly do regard the qualities of a thing as integral to it in a way in which the sounds it produces are not. This is certainly Broad's view. He says:

> I think it is plain that the ordinary man does not regard sounds and smells and tastes as parts of material things in the straightforward way in which he thinks of visual and tactual sensibilia as being so. We naturally think of a sound or an odour as *emanating from* a material thing rather than as being in any sense a *part* of it. At most we might be inclined to identify a sound which we hear with a certain event in a material object which we might see, e.g., the striking of a clapper on the surface of a bell. But I think that we should rather tend to regard the sound as something that permeates the air round the bell in consequence of the stroke that has taken place within the bell. (p. 126)[4]

And it is surely *because* the reader thinks of the noise made by the coach as it trundles down the street as something which is not part of its make-up that he sees *something* in the suggestion that it is just the sound he hears. If this is so he should be in no great hurry to admit that there is anything tempting about the view that the shopper who immediately perceives the texture really feels a texture rather than the textured material, or that the observer sees colour rather than, say, a coloured table. It may well be that the general features shared by sounds and physical objects are not shared by colours and tangible qualities.

III

So far we have located two suspect features of Berkeley's account, but to get to the root of the matter we must consider what there is to his suggestion that when I say I perceive a substantial object I am not simply reporting on what I perceive but rather making a judgement based on *inference*. We will have to spend some time on this, and the best plan may be to start by looking at some specific situations in order to see what he has in mind.

Suppose, then, I hear a certain sound and believe that I hear a firework exploding. Now here I may be hesitant in my judgement, recognizing that similar sounds can be made by other causes. Clearly, Berkeley would say, the judgement that I hear a firework involves *going beyond* my awareness of the sound which is the immediate object of perception. The immediate object here is, it should be noted, accessible to only one sense. It is not something that could be touched, smelt, tasted or seen. To take another example, we can suppose that in a party game I am blindfolded and challenged to identify a number of objects solely by smell. Now on a certain occasion I may judge that I am smelling a rose on the basis of a certain scent, and here, Berkeley would say, it is *really* just the smell I am aware of. This sort of smell is one I normally associate with roses, so I *infer* that this particular scent is produced by a rose. Clearly a similar game could be organized in which we were asked to identify objects by feel or taste, and here again I might be acutely conscious that I was making an inference when I judged that I was, say, feeling an orange, this inference being based on what I was immediately aware of when employing the particular sense.

It might be thought that it would be impossible to organize a similar game with respect to seeing, and in response to this Berkeley would certainly say that, even if it were true, this would suggest no more than that in general we find it much easier to make judgements about the existence of things like oranges on the basis of what we immediately perceive by sight than we do on the basis of what we feel, taste or smell. There are, he would say, special features relating to seeing which led him to devote his first major work to vision in in order to show how more is suggested to the mind by what we see, and less actually seen, than we normally suppose. In fact a party game *could* be organized in which we might have real difficulty in identifying even familiar objects by sight, though this would not be easy to set up. There is, however, no need to resort to party games in order to make the point. When I see a shimmering patch on the road ahead I may be quite conscious of *inferring* that there is water or a mirage as the case may be, while I have no doubt at all about the shimmering patch which is what I immediately perceive.

The examples given so far do help us to locate what Berkeley is after when he refers to the immediate objects of perception and draws attention to the role of inference in the judgements we ordinarily make. But to do justice to Berkeley we certainly need to stress that he is not concerned just with cases where we are conscious of making judgements in which we have less than complete confidence. It may be, for example, that a passenger in my car sees the shimmering patch, that he never even envisages the possibility of there being a mirage, and that his judgement that there is water on the road ahead is quite correct. Here my passenger will not be at all *conscious* of making an inference, but the fact remains that the immediate object, for him as for me, is a shimmering patch. His confident assertion that there is water on the road is as much a speculation as is my 'guess' in the same circumstances, and as such it is based on inference. Another example would be the following. At the present time I would claim to see a box of drawing pins on my desk. Now the judgement here is certainly immediate in the sense that I make it spontaneously and there is no conscious process of thinking things out. In another sense, though, it is not immediate. We begin to think in the way Berkeley wants us to think when we appreciate that I judge or infer that the box contains pins, and when we realise that from where I am placed I can see only three of the surfaces and infer that the object is a six-sided container.

All these examples are intended only to give some rough indication of why Berkeley thinks in the way he does. There are four points he might hope to make by drawing our attention to them. First, they can help us see that there is some point in talking of *immediate* objects of perception. My uncertainty as to whether I am seeing a mirage or water, when I am quite certain that I am seeing a shimmering patch, might be enough to persuade me of this. Second, the examples might help us see that there is at least some point in talking of *inferences* being made when we judge that we perceive substantial objects. The contestant playing the smelling-game may be quite conscious that he is not just describing what he immediately perceives when he says that he smells a rose. Third, they might help us see that our judgements concerning the perception of substantial objects are essentially *corrigible*. The earlier examples concerned cases where there was a very real possibility that any judgement we made would turn out to be mistaken, but the point is a general one. Now we should not suppose that each of these points can be accepted enthusiastically and without more ado, but it is the fourth and following point that is crucial. For Berkeley does suppose that the immediate object of perception is always some *discrete item* which is all we actually perceive.

The basic criticism here might well be that even if we were persuaded to go along with Berkeley on the first three points this need not incline us to sympathy with the fourth. Considering the party games again, we might say that these do help us to see what Berkeley has in mind when he talks of immediate perception, and we might agree that the contestant does make some sort of (corrigible) inference when he judges that he feels an orange or smells a rose. But if we go this far with Berkeley we certainly need not accept that it is never strictly true that we feel things like oranges or smell things like roses. Playing the feeling-game the contestant may quite see the point of saying that what he immediately perceives is a certain shape and texture, and so long as the blindfold is in place he may describe what he feels in a way pleasing to Berkeley; he may, that is, concentrate on the qualities felt. At the same time, though, and this is crucial, he will assume that the qualities are qualities *of* some object, and that in feeling the shape and texture he is also feeling that thing. In response to the suggestion that he cannot really be feeling a substantial object he will say that the whole idea of the game is for him to guess, judge or infer what the substantial object he is feeling *is*.

The same or a similar point might be made with respect to the shimmering patch case. Here I say that I see a shimmering patch and infer that there is water on the road ahead, but if I do say this I need not suppose that in truth and strictness I do not really see water at all. My puzzlement here concerns what the shimmering patch really is, and if it is in fact water then (whether I know it or not) water is what I see. Similarly, the traveller who sees a black spot on the horizon, and infers that it is a gravestone because he saw a gravestone last time he travelled that way, does not take it that if he is to speak strictly he should say he sees a black spot *rather than* a gravestone. He is more likely to say that really what he sees is a gravestone, though from a distance it *appears* as a black spot. I would suggest that none of the cases we have considered *need* incline us towards the view that sensible objects are 'those only which are perceived immediately by sense' or indeed to Berkeley's fourth point. If this is right we can be sympathetic to the notion of immediate perception, to the notion that judgements concerning the perception of substantial objects involve inferences, and to the notion that these judgements are always corrigible, without supposing that perception fails to acquaint us with substantial objects or that in the last analysis there are no substantial objects to be perceived. With this in mind we can go on to take a closer look at Berkeley's doctrine.

It is perhaps worth noting here that the suggestion that 'the senses . . . make no inferences' is misleading in a number of ways. First, and as Warnock says:

> It is clear that Berkeley cannot really mean to say that *the senses* make no inferences. For this would not be worth saying. *People* make inferences. To say that my senses make inferences would be as nonsensical as to say that my vocal chords make promises. But it is only worth saying that something does not make inferences, if at least it makes sense to suggest that it does. Berkeley must, then, if what he says is worth saying at all, have in mind certain inferences which *people* do not make. (Warnock 1, p. 153)

Warnock might have noted too that there is a suggestion that if the senses do not make inferences there is *something* they do, and this is to sense or perceive. And of course this will not do, for again it is people or sentient beings who sense and perceive and not their senses. Finally, there is something odd about the use of the term 'inference' in this context. The term suggests a conscious process of thinking things out, but as we noted just now the judgements Berkeley has in mind are most often spontaneous. Though we may sometimes go along with Berkeley in talking about *inferences* I think the fairest way of indicating what he is after is to see him as trying to isolate the sensory from the interpretative elements in perception; what is given from what we make of it.

We can consider a very common sort of experience here. It is well known that when we look at the photograph of a man who has been convicted of a particularly nasty murder we often cannot help seeing him as a brutal person, and we may find it difficult to understand how his victim could ever have trusted such an obviously vicious fellow. The point is, of course, that the victim did not see him as we see him, and that the way we see a man is conditioned by what we know about him. Someone else looking at the photo, but not knowing what we know, may well comment on how honest the subject looks. We have to stress here that the two people looking at the photo, one knowing the discreditable facts and the other not, do see the *same* thing. But at the same time they cannot help seeing it *differently*. It would be misleading to talk of the man who knows he is looking at the picture of a murderer as making any *inferences*, but it is clearly true that the way he sees the photo depends upon what he already knows. Now it is Berkeley's contention that in any perceptual situation the way in which we interpret the given is determined by our past experience to a very much greater extent than we normally suppose. The truth is, he would say, that when I employ a particular sense I perceive only an object proper to that sense. But as a result of past experience I cannot help associating what I actually perceive with other ideas and taking myself to be perceiving perhaps a rose or an orange or a coach.

IV

In this volume we will not be taking a detailed look at *NTV*, but we ought to pay some attention to it, and as things Berkeley says here are relevant to the matter under discussion it will be useful if we devote some space to it now, even if this involves some digression. The plan of the work is simple. In sect. 1 Berkeley says:

> My design is to shew the manner wherein we perceive by sight the distance, magnitude, and situation of objects. Also to consider the difference there is betwixt the ideas of sight and touch, and whether there be any idea common to both senses.

Distance is dealt with in sects. 2-51, magnitude in sects. 52-87, and situation in 88-120. As Berkeley says in sect. 121, by this time it has already emerged that 'there is no one self same numerical extension perceived both by sight and touch', and the question tackled in later sections is 'whether there be any one and the same sort or species of ideas equally perceivable to both senses'. We will be primarily concerned with points arising from what Berkeley says about the perception of distance.

Berkeley had a special reason for being interested in 'the manner wherein we perceive by sight the distance . . . of objects', and what this reason was is made explicit in *Pr.* 42-3. Here he envisages that an objection to his doctrine that sensible things exist only in the mind might be 'that we see things actually without or at a distance from us'. Surely it is just silly to say that the two houses I can see from my window are 'in the mind', when I can see them at a distance from me, the one farther off than the other. Berkeley has two arguments to deal with this objection. The first he states succinctly:

> In answer to this, I desire it may be considered, that in a dream we do oft perceive things as existing at a great distance off, and yet for all that, those things are acknowledged to have their existence only in the mind.

For the second argument he appeals to *NTV*:

> But for the fuller clearing of this point, it may be worth while to consider, how it is that we perceive distance and things placed at a distance by sight. For that we should in truth see external space, and bodies actually existing in it, some nearer, others farther off, seems to carry with it some opposition to what hath been said, of their existing no where without the mind. The consideration of this difficulty it was, that gave birth to my *Essay towards a new Theory of Vision*, which was published not long since. Wherein it is shewn that *distance* or outness is neither immediately of it self perceived by sight, nor yet apprehended or judged of by lines and angles, or any thing that hath a necessary connexion with it: but that it is only suggested to our thoughts, by certain visible ideas and sensations attending vision, which in their own nature have no manner of similitude or relation, either with distance, or things placed at a distance. But by a connexion taught us by experience, they come to signify and suggest them to us, after the same manner that words of any language suggest the ideas they are made to stand for. Insomuch that a man born blind, and afterwards made to see, would not, at first sight, think the things he saw, to be without his mind, or at any distance from him.

It is this second argument that will interest us now.

In the passage just quoted Berkeley claims to have demonstrated *two* negative points in his earlier work, the first being that distance is not immediately perceived by sight, and the second being that it is not 'judged of by lines and angles'. In fact, though, he did not think it necessary to spend much time at the outset on the first of these. In sect. 2 he says:

> It is, I think, agreed by all that distance, of itself and immediately, cannot be seen. For distance being a line directed end-wise to the eye, it projects only one point in the fund of the eye, which point remains invariably the same, whether the distance be longer or shorter.

As it stands this is perhaps not very clear,[5] but it may be enough for the present if we emphasize that Berkeley felt he could appeal to the received wisdom for the point that seeing things as at various distances from us involves judgement, and that so far as sight is concerned the three-dimensional ordering of things is not a datum of sense. What he did have to argue for was the second point, and this concerns the nature of the judgements we make when we take things to be at distances from us.

Here again Berkeley looks at the current wisdom, and he finds first a point he takes to be quite correct. It was supposed 'that the estimate we make of the distance of objects considerably remote is rather an act of judgment grounded on experience than of sense' (sect. 3). Where he strongly disagrees with current thinking is in what is said concerning the distance of objects less remote from us:

> But when an object is placed at so near a distance as that the interval between the eyes bears any sensible proportion to it, the opinion of speculative men is that the two optic axes . . . concurring at the object do there make an angle, by means of which, according as it is greater or lesser, the object is perceived to be nearer or farther off. (sect. 4)

As he makes clear in the Appendix added to the second edition, Berkeley's objection is not to geometrical optics as such. What he objects to is the supposition that lines and angles are relevant to the question as to how we actually judge things to be at distances from us. He is on strong ground when he points out that the lines and angles, which 'have no real existence in nature, being only an hypothesis framed by the mathematicians' (sect. 14), are not themselves perceived and cannot therefore play any role in explaining how we judge distance. In judging of the distance of near no less than remote objects we are, Berkeley claims, totally dependent on experience.

The details of Berkeley's own account need not concern us here. In summary his view is that there are certain depth cues – the sensations attending the turn of the eyes, the confused or distinct appearance of the visible object, the straining of the eyes to keep an object in focus – which we *learn* to associate with distance. It is these visual and kinaesthetic experiences which enable us to make 'sudden judgments from them concerning the distance of objects' (sect. 20). Outness is *mediately* perceived by sight, and as the immediate hearing of a certain sound suggests to me the thing which I know by experience to be the normal source of that sound, so the depth cues attending the perception of reasonably close objects suggests distance to me. Further, just as, if I had not learned as a result of experience to correlate sounds with other things, I would not be able to take myself to be hearing things like coaches, so the man born blind and suddenly made to see would not have correlated depth cues with distance and would at first see everything as if it were on top of him. Soon, of course, he will learn to interpret the depth cues *as* cues and then, like the rest of us, he will take the things he sees to be outside him and ordered in three dimensions.

We might note here that *NTV* can be seen as an important study in the psychology of vision, and that much that Berkeley says here is of value quite independently of whether it supports or fails to support the philosophical claims he wants to make. His attack on the notion that geometrical optics were relevant to explaining how we actually perceive distance was decisive, and though his own account has been subjected to criticism it has all the same been highly influential in the development of studies in this field. We, of course, are primarily interested in the philosophical implications Berkeley took his account to have, and it is here we will want to criticize.

There is one very fundamental criticism we should make at the outset, and this is that though Berkeley thought he had to argue against the notion that what we see is ordered in depth if his own view that they exist only in the mind was to remain plausible, it is strongly arguable that this was quite unnecessary. As Furlong notes:

> The train of reasoning which gave birth to the *TV* was . . . as follows. Visible objects, Berkeley wishes us to agree, are 'in the mind', i.e. they are not 'without the mind', i.e. they are at no distance from us, i.e. they are at no distance from our bodies. Hence Berkeley must show, he infers, that we do not really see

objects as being out from us. It does not take much acuity to see that the *TV* was not really necessary. The reasoning sketched above is fallacious: it slides from one meaning of the troublesome phrase, 'in the mind', to another. (Furlong 2, pp. 308-9)

One of these meanings is the one we found Luce attributing to Berkeley as 'official doctrine, explicit, decisive, and often repeated'. According to this, to say that sensible things exist only *in* a mind is just a way of saying that they can exist only *in relation* to or *when perceived by* a perceiving mind. And of course the word 'without' in the phrase 'without the mind' carries no spatial implications. It is only if the phrase is given *another* meaning, and saying that things exist only in the mind is taken to involve the claim that they are not at distances from us, that the question whether the things we see are ordered in depth will seem to be relevant. Here there will be spatial implications.[6]

Armstrong makes this point very forcibly. Assuming the 'official' interpretation of the troublesome phrase he says:

> We shall try to show, however, that whatever Berkeley's opinion on the matter, the view that the immediate objects of sight are two-dimensionally ordered *only*, and the doctrine that the objects of sense-perception do not exist without the mind, stand in the logical relation of indifference. The truth or falsity of the one has no bearing on either the truth or falsity of the other. (Armstrong 2, p. 27)

He makes two claims here. First, he notes that if it can be shown that the objects of vision are after all ordered in three dimensions this will not undermine Berkeley's view that they exist only when perceived. And, second, he claims that if we accept that what is immediately seen is indeed ordered in two dimensions only, we need not feel compelled to agree that what we see exists only when perceived since 'there seems to be no reason at all why a two-dimensional manifold should not exist independently of its perceivers as much as a three-dimensional one'. The argumentation here contributes to Armstrong's conclusion that 'the *New Theory of Vision* stands in no real relation to Berkeley's Immaterialism' (p. 32).

The point made by Furlong and Armstrong is acceptable. All we need to add here is that clearly Berkeley was not always as decided on what he meant when he said things were *in the mind* as Luce likes to suggest. We can remind ourselves of the criticism of Luce's exegesis that, though in the *Principles* Berkeley does have it that to say things exist *in the mind* is to say they exist *when perceived*, the unfortunate and ambiguous phrase had played a key role in the development of his thought, and continued to colour his thinking as he went into print. Given what Luce takes to be the official and decisive interpretation we must be at a loss to understand why Berkeley *ever* thought he had to show that visible things are not ordered in depth, and of course we will not see why he thought, when he wrote the *Principles*, that an appeal to *NTV* helped answer the 'objection' envisaged in sect. 42. As Furlong says when discussing *Pr*. 42-3 (and I would put the point more strongly), 'it is not clear . . . that he is not still to some extent ensnared by the phrase'.

I want to move on, though, to a different and from our point of view more important criticism of Berkeley, and it concerns the substantial gap between proving that distance is not immediately seen and showing that the things we see are not ordered in depth. And in this connection it is important to be clear that while sects. 2-40 might seem to support the claim that sight alone would be insufficient to inform us that the things we see are ordered in three dimensions, they do *not* seem to support the claim that the things we see are ordered in two dimensions. Indeed, one could accept just about everything Berkeley says in these sections without suspecting for a moment that visible objects are not three dimensionally ordered. We can perhaps make a stronger claim, for the supposition throughout these early sections seems to be that the things we see *are* ordered in depth.

It will be remembered that Berkeley begins by appealing to the accepted view that *because* distance is 'a line directed end-wise to the eye' it cannot be immediately perceived. But if this is the argument it does not even seem to follow that what we see is not at a distance from us. Rather, if we are to suppose a line drawn between the object and the eye we must be assuming that there *is* some distance between us and what we see. This becomes very clear given Warnock's interpretation of the section. Warnock has already drawn our attention to a situation where we see two trees and a gap between them. He goes on:

> Consider again the two trees. There is, we said, a gap between them; I see that there is a gap . . . But I cannot in the same way

> 'see the gap' between either of the two trees and myself. . . . The gap between myself and any object at which I look is a gap which, we might say, I can only look at from one end; and of course from the end it does not *look* like a gap – not like the gap that I can see between the two trees. It is this that Berkeley wishes to point out. (Warnock 1, p. 27)

Quite clearly if this is what Berkeley wants to point out (and I shall assume that it is) the claim can only be that *given* the things we see are ordered in three dimensions, sight alone will not be sufficient to discover this. It cannot be that they are *not* ordered in depth, because the hypothesis is that they are. And this suggests another point. For if on the assumption that things are ordered in depth we have to admit that sight alone cannot acquaint us with the gaps, it must follow that the claim that we do not immediately see distance is at least *compatible* with the claim that the things seen *are* at a distance. If they are *not* at a distance, this will have to be shown by an independent line of argument. Throughout the early sections Berkeley allows himself to talk as if visible objects were 'out there'. In sect. 21 for example we find him saying:

> An object placed at a certain distance from the eye, to which the breadth of the pupil bears a considerable proportion, being made to approach, is seen more confusedly: And the nearer it is brought the more confused appearance it makes. And this being found constantly to be so, there ariseth in the mind an habitual connexion between the several degrees of confusion and distance; the greater confusion still implying the lesser distance, and the lesser confusion the greater distance of the object.

The suggestion here is that there is one visible object which presents first a clear and then a confused appearance as it (the object we see) is brought *closer* to the eye. There is no hint here that visible objects are *not* at distances from us, and everything Berkeley says about depth cues has value also on the contrary assumption.

The turning point comes in sect. 41 where Berkeley introduces the man born blind and says:

> From what hath been premised it is a manifest consequence that a man born blind, being made to see, would at first have no idea of distance by sight; the sun and stars, the remotest objects as well as

the nearer, would all seem to be in his eye, or rather in his mind. The objects intromitted by sight would seem to him (as in truth they are) no other than a new set of thoughts or sensations, each whereof is as near to him as the perceptions of pain or pleasure, or the most inward passions of his soul.

Here there are two distinct claims being made. The first is a claim about what would at first *seem* to be the case to a man suddenly cured of his blindness, but the second, suggested by the five words in parentheses, is the quite different claim that what the patient might at first suppose to be the case really *is* the case.[7] The first claim might indeed seem to be a consequence of what has been said in sects. 2-40, but the second claim is a new one, and one that needs support. In the conclusion of sect. 41 Berkeley explains why the man born blind would not take the things he saw to be at a distance from him:

> For our judging objects perceived by sight to be at any distance, or without the mind, is . . . intirely the effect of experience, which one in those circumstances could not yet have attained to.

We might naturally take the implication here to be that the man recently cured of his blindness is not yet in a position to judge that the things he sees, which are in fact at various distances from him, are so ordered. We might well think that those of us who have learned to make judgements concerning the distances from us of the objects we see have also learned to make *correct* judgements. But the parenthetical clause in sect. 41 gives us the clue that Berkeley thinks that the man suddenly made to see, who takes what he sees to be 'as near to him as the perceptions of pain and pleasure', is nearer the truth than the rest of us.

The question naturally arises whether Berkeley *thought* that what he had shown in sects. 2-40 was sufficient to justify the claim that the things we see are ordered in two dimensions only. The wording of the summary provided by Luce *may* suggest that Luce takes it that he did. Thus:

> It is physically impossible for distance itself to be seen (§ 2), as an object is seen. Distance is not perceived by means of lines and angles (§§ 13-15). Another type of medium must be sought. Distance is suggested by the 'turn of the eye' and by confused

> appearance and by other contributing circumstances (§ 28). This explains the 'Barrovian case', i.e. the problem which Dr. Barrow felt so acutely that he called in question the principles of optics, and demanded a new theory of vision (§§ 29-40). From this account of distance it follows, in Berkeley's view, that not colour alone, the proper and immediate object of sight, but also extension, figure and motion, are at no distance from the mind, but as near as pain (§§ 41-4). (Luce 2, pp. 34-5)

We should not, though, pin too much on the wording here. It may be that Luce realizes, and Berkeley realized, that principles introduced for the first time in sect. 41-4 are absolutely crucial to the conclusion. At any rate it is important to appreciate that if the phenomenon Barrow drew attention to 'entirely subverts the opinion of those who will have us judge of distance by lines and angles' and confirms Berkeley's own principle (sect. 33), the principle confirmed is simply 'that the judgment we make of the distance of an object . . . is entirely the result of experience' (sect. 20). The solution to the Barrovian problem does not require, or suggest, the view that the things we see are ordered in two dimensions.

If this is right the argumentation of sects. 42-4 will be very important in bridging the gap between the claim that it would *seem* to a man cured of his blindness that the things he saw were at no distance from him and the claim that the things he sees are in fact not ordered in depth. Now the *ad hominem* argument Luce alludes to is contained in sect. 43, but for the important and supposedly decisive argument we have to look to the following section. Here Berkeley says:

> Suppose, for example, that looking at the moon I should say it were fifty or sixty semidiameters of the earth distant from me. Let us see what moon this is spoken of: It is plain it cannot be the visible moon, or anything like the visible moon, or that which I see, which is only a round, luminous plain of about thirty visible points in diameter. For in case I am carried from the place where I stand directly towards the moon, it is manifest the object varies, still as I go on; and by the time that I am advanced fifty or sixty semidiameters of the earth, I shall be so far from being near a small, round, luminous flat that I shall perceive nothing like it; this object having long since disappeared, and if I would recover it, it must be by going back to the earth from whence I set out. Again, suppose I

perceive by sight the faint and obscure idea of something which I doubt whether it be a man, or a tree, or a tower, but judge it to be at the distance of about a mile. It is plain I cannot mean that what I see is a mile off, or that it is the image or likeness of anything which is a mile off, since that every step I take towards it the appearance alters, and from being obscure, small, and faint, grows clear, large, and vigorous. And when I come to the mile's end, that which I saw first is quite lost, neither do I find any thing in the likeness of it.

The same argument with the same illustrations appears again in *Alciphron* IV 9.

In *Alciphron* the substance of *NTV* 2-44 is conveyed in little more than a thousand words of dialogue, and against this background the argument of *NTV* 44 looms large. But the argument is crucial in *NTV* too. It is *this* argument that, if it is successful, establishes that the things we see are not at distances from us, and it at the same time leads to the claim that the objects of sight and the objects of touch are numerically distinct. In this early work Berkeley allows himself the 'vulgar error' (*Pr*. 44) that tangible objects are indeed at distances from us, and he holds that we discover this by touch – by reaching out for things and travelling to them. His doctrine is that it is because experience teaches us that visible objects (which exist only in the mind) are closely correlated with the tangible objects (without the mind) of which they are the *signs* that we come to suppose (wrongly) that the things we *see* are ordered in depth. This view is outlined in sect. 50 where he says:

> In order therefore to treat accurately and unconfusedly of vision, we must bear in mind that there are two sorts of objects apprehended by the eye, the one primarily and immediately, the other secondarily and by intervention of the former. Those of the first sort neither are, nor appear to be, without the mind, or at any distance off; they may indeed grow greater or smaller, more confused, or more clear, or more faint, but they do not, cannot approach or recede from us. Whenever we say an object is at a distance, whenever we say it draws near, or goes farther off, we must always mean it of the latter sort, which properly belong to the touch, and are not so truly perceived as suggested by the eye in like manner as thoughts by the ear.

Berkeley believes it is God who so arranges things that we can think of the various visible objects as if they were appearances of *one* thing, and he tells us that ultimately what he has demonstrated in *NTV* 'affords to thinking men a new and unanswerable proof of the existence and immediate operation of God, and the constant condescending care of his providence' (*TVV* 1).[8] We will not be concerned with this 'proof' here. What we shall want to criticize is the notion that we never see the *same* visible object *looking* different from different standpoints, but only appearances which are themselves visible objects and which are as they appear.

V

At this point we can perhaps leave *NTV* and make a few points towards an evaluation of the doctrine that sensible objects are 'those only which can be perceived immediately by sense'. A brief summary of what Berkeley holds to be the case may be in order here. He holds, first, that there are immediate objects of perception – variously described as 'qualities', 'sensations' and 'appearances' – and that perception by any sense always acquaints us with some such object. The point here comes close to the innocuous point Don Locke makes by saying that 'whenever we perceive we perceive sense data'. But Berkeley holds, further, that the immediate object of perception is always a discrete item and that perception by any sense is always, and only, perception of such an item. I never see the thing I feel, for there is no thing to be seen and felt, and though we may suppose we see one object looking different as we get close to, the truth is that there is 'a continued series of visible objects succeeding each other, during the whole time of your approach' (*Dialogues*, i, 201). Now it is true that we do talk of perceiving things like coaches that are not immediately perceived, and Berkeley certainly intends to allow for such talk. One *wrong* way of allowing for it is to suppose that things like coaches are semi-permanent items which are somehow hidden away behind sense data. And another wrong way of allowing for it is, apparently, to suppose that they are semi-permanent items which I *am* acquainted with, though always by way of the immediate perception of some quality or aspect. It seems that the *right* answer (in Berkeley's view) is to recognize that the semi-permanent items are *fictions*. These are constructed *by us* out of sense data, because otherwise 'the endless number or confusion of names would render language impracticable'.

In Berkeley's mind the doctrine that sensible objects are immediately perceived is associated with another, and this is that I cannot be mistaken about the characteristics of the object I actually perceive. Hylas asks about the man who sees an oar dipped in water and takes the oar to *be* crooked because it *looks* crooked. Philonous answers:

> He is not mistaken with regard to the ideas he actually perceives; but in the inferences he makes from his present perceptions. Thus in the case of the oar, what he immediately perceives by sight is certainly crooked; and so far he is in the right. But if he thence conclude, that upon taking the oar out of the water he shall perceive the same crookedness ... he is mistaken. (iii, 238)

Similarly, if he takes the moon to be 'a plain lucid surface, about a foot in diameter', or if he takes the square tower to be round because the present perception is of roundness, he is mistaken, but his mistake does not concern that thing which he immediately perceives, 'it being a manifest contradiction to suppose he should err in respect of that'. In general, the possibility of error comes into the picture when inference is involved, and inference always takes us from what we perceive at present to what we imagine would be perceived in other circumstances.

To get the measure of everything said and assumed here would be a mammoth undertaking. So many philosophers have worked in this field, accepting some of the points, rejecting others, and arguing about the significance the points would have if accepted, that doing justice to it all would be impossible. What we will do is to restrict ourselves in the main to the perhaps unambitious task of asking whether Berkeley's arguments are such as to convince the opponent, who *starts* from the position that perception acquaints him with substantial particulars, that this position is untenable. I want to make only three points: one about *statements* of immediate perception, one about *inferences*, and one about *appearances*.

First, then, there does seem to be a legitimate question as to whether it is desirable, when examining Berkeley's views, to talk of *statements* of immediate perception. And I want to say that in a way it is undesirable, and in a way essential, that we should. To see why it is undesirable we can start by looking again at the situation where A says he sees a spot on the horizon and B says he sees a solitary gravestone. Now this sort of case can help bring home to us the extent to which our judgements are conditioned by what we already know, or by what Berkeley sometimes calls our *prænotions*, but though A may be nearer to it than B it is clear that he does not provide a 'pure' statement of immediate perception. For A does imply that there is something (substantial?) which he sees and which B might help him identify, he claims that he *sees* it, and he locates what he sees within the context of the desert he and B are walking in. It seems to be the case, though, that Berkeley wants to focus our attention on the *given* in perception in a way which involves taking us back to a stage where we have made no progress at all towards interpreting the given. Thinking things out in this way we might try to imagine ourselves faced with William James's 'blooming, buzzing confusion', and to suppose that we have not even begun to make sense of our experiences. In practice, of course, I find myself quite unable to take myself back to this stage in imagination. When in *NTV* Berkeley says that the things I see do not even *appear* to be 'without the mind, or at any distance off', there is a clear sense in which what he says is false. For even if the things I see are not really at any distance from me, it is certainly true that now I *cannot help* reading distance into the situation and seeing things *as if* they were ordered in depth. Putting myself in the shoes of the man born blind is, however, supposed to help me appreciate that I had to *learn* to see things in this way and even to distinguish seeing from other species of experiencing. But if talking about immediate experience is supposed to focus our attention on the given quite independently of what we make of it, we should perhaps be suspicious of *statements* of immediate perception. For it seems clear that statements come into the picture only when we have begun to interpret our experiences, and indeed that making something of the given is essential to their role. This point will stand, I think, even if it turns out to be the case, as Berkeley supposes, that certain statements are particularly innocuous in that the judgements involved in them are of a specially safe sort. It is perhaps significant that when Berkeley's man born blind is shown a cube and a sphere for the first time he is quite unable to describe them as they are or even as they seem to him.

In this connection it is worth noting that Berkeley did think it important to 'clear the first principles of knowledge, from the embarras and delusion of words' (*Pr. Intr.*, 25), and that in a draft his suspicion of language led him to what seems a most extravagant position. He says:

Let us conceive a solitary man, one born and bred in such a place of the world, and in such circumstances, as he shall never have had occasion to make use of universal signs for his ideas. That man shall have a constant train of particular ideas passing in his mind. Whatever he sees, hears, imagines, or any wise conceives is on all hands . . . granted to be particular. Let us withall suppose him under no necessity of labouring to secure him self from hunger and cold; but at full ease, naturally of good facultys but contemplative. Such a one I should take to be nearer the discovery of certain great and excellent truths yet unknown, than he that has had the education of the Schools, has been instructed in the ancient and modern philosophy, and by much reading and conversation has attain'd to the knowledge of those arts and sciences, that make such a noise in the learned world. (*Works* II, p. 141)

Berkeley concedes that 'the knowledge of our solitary philosopher is not like to be so very wide and extended', but he adds that 'if he is like to have less knowledge, he is withall like to have fewer mistakes than other men'. The conceit of the solitary man is not used in the published introduction, but there is an echo of it when Berkeley resolves to take the ideas he considers 'bare and naked into my view', seeing it as one advantage of this that:

. . . so long as I confine my thoughts to my own ideas divested of words, I do not see how I can easily be mistaken. The objects I consider, I clearly and adequately know. I cannot be deceived in thinking I have an idea which I have not. (sect. 22)

Warnock notes that the object here seems to be 'the mere contemplation or perception of ideas'. He also finds it necessary to point out that:

It is only when I say (or think) something *about* what I perceive that I can be mistaken; but unless I say or think something, I cannot *know* anything either. If I confine myself to the mere contemplation or perception of ideas, I avoid the possibility of saying or believing something false only because I do not take the risk of saying or believing anything at all. To abandon speech and thought in favour of 'attentive perception' indeed eliminates the risk of mistake; but it eliminates knowledge as well. (Warnock 1, pp. 79-80)

Berkeley's solitary philosopher would in one sense 'know' things – that is, he would be acquainted with the given in perception. In another sense, forbidden the use of language, safeguarded from the need to act in the world, and restricted to the passive reception of what Berkeley takes to be 'a constant train of particular ideas passing in his mind', our philosopher will *know* nothing.[9]

Now if, at one level, Berkeley's aim is to focus our attention on the given in perception quite independently of what we make of it, there is clearly another level at which it is quite impossible to avoid thinking in terms of *statements* of immediate perception, this because Berkeley does want to cast doubt on the accuracy of many of the things we are normally inclined to say, and to recommend instead a 'strict' way of talking in which we would recognize as sensible objects only what we immediately perceive, and in which we would make no inferences. One suggestion as to how we might easily formulate a statement of immediate perception in any perceptual situation is that provided by Warnock which involves what Austin calls a process of 'progressive hedging'. Thus, to use Warnock's initial example, instead of saying 'I hear a car' I might say, not 'I hear a sort of purring (engine-like) noise', nor even 'I hear what *sounds to me* like a purring noise', but 'It seems to me as if I were hearing a sort of purring noise'. The judgement here does seem peculiarly *safe*. In making it, Warnock says, 'I am making no assumptions whatever' (p. 163).

Criticizing Warnock's suggestion that material object statements are related to statements of immediate perception in much the same way as verdicts in court are related to the evidence given, Austin says:

> ... Warnock's picture of the situation gets it upside-down as well as distorted. His statements of 'immediate perception', so far from being that from which we *advance* to more ordinary statements, are actually arrived at, and are so arrived at in his own account, by *retreating from* more ordinary statements, by progressive hedging. (There's a tiger – there *seems* to be a tiger – it seems *to me* that there's a tiger – it seems to me *now* that there's a tiger – it seems to me now *as if there were* a tiger.) It seems extraordinarily perverse to represent as that on which ordinary statements are based a form of words which, *starting from* and moreover incorporating an ordinary statement, qualifies and hedges it in various ways. (pp. 141-2)

This, though, may not be the last word. Clearly the advantage of Warnock's suggested method for *formulating* statements of immediate perception is that by using it in any perceptual situation we would, with a minimum of ingenuity, be able to arrive at an assumption-free statement to replace the more adventurous statement we would normally be inclined to make. Defending Warnock, Ayer argues that he provides a useful alternative to the laborious but possible task of constructing 'a purely sensory vocabulary, which would not draw on the vocabulary which we use to refer to physical objects' (Ayer 2, p. 148).

I shall suppose that we could construct this purely sensory vocabulary and use it in what we can think of as a purely sensory language (PSL). If we do allow this, though, interesting questions arise concerning the relationship between PSL and the language (OL) which contains our more ordinary statements. To begin with we can note that as a matter of fact we, Berkeley's readers, do start from a position in which we have a language – we have something on our plates – and that the obvious way for us to arrive at PSL would be by revision of that language, or by messing about with what we have on our plates. For us, then, PSL will be parasitic on OL, even though it may be, as Berkeley would think, that PSL describes what is going on when we perceive in a more philosophically acceptable way. It may be, however, that there is nothing necessary about this relationship. After all my knowledge of French is parasitic on my knowledge of English in that *I* learned the language by being told the French equivalent for certain English words, but for many French is their first and only language. Berkeley *might* argue that though a language containing only statements of immediate perception is not a first and only language for anyone there is in principle no reason why it should not be. It is, however, doubtful whether *this* claim would be supportable. It will be remembered that so far as the man cured of his blindness is concerned 'the objects intromitted by sight would seem to him . . . no other than a new set of thoughts or sensations, each whereof is as near to him as the perceptions of pain or pleasure, or the most inward passions of his soul'. The story is, of course, meant to suggest that at first things seemed like this to those of us who have been blessed with sight from birth, and Berkeley would certainly hold that at first all the things we perceived appeared as on this level. A 'pure' statement of immediate perception would presumably describe the way things appeared to us at first, but it is clearly one thing to say that we, who now have a rich conceptual apparatus, can find ways of describing how things appeared at a stage when we were not able to discriminate as we do, and quite another to suggest that we might (even in principle) have accepted that things were as they first appeared and, without going beyond this, have evolved a language to describe them.

Here it is interesting to look at one point Ayer makes in answering Austin's criticisms of the line he took in *The Foundations of Empirical Knowledge*. Referring to ch. VI of *Sense and Sensibilia* he says:

> The only point of substance which Austin makes in this section is that I was taking it for granted that we were presented with a 'sensible manifold' which it was open to us to characterize in different ways, to organize in accordance with different conceptual schemes. And of course I did make this assumption, surely rightly. I am, however, willing to admit that even so it does not necessarily follow that there are no limits to the forms that this organization can take. It may, for example, be essential that some objects of perception be taken as public, for the reason that a language in which the rules of identity were such that no object perceived by one person could be identified with any object perceived by another would be incoherent. (Ayer 2, p. 142)

This is not the place to argue that some objects must indeed be taken as public for a language to be possible, nor to consider other factors which may limit the number of ways in which our experiences are characterizable. Determining what these factors are is, though, an important job for the philosopher. Here we will just take note of the suggestion that it may very well be that one who thought of all his experiences as being on a level with 'the most inward passions of the soul' could not have a language to describe them.

Ayer himself believes that it is possible to formulate *experiential statements* – statements which do not go beyond the 'evidence' yielded by the senses on a given occasion, each of which 'carries no implication about the status of what is seen' (p. 128). He holds, further, that 'statements about physical objects are at a theoretical level with respect to experiential statements' and that 'the truth of statements claiming the perception of physical objects is founded on the truth of experiential statements' (pp. 146-7). This last claim may look a little odd in view of the fact that we do not, whether as children learning to talk or as adults, *formulate* experiential statements (even unspoken ones) prior to making statements carrying implications about the status of what is perceived, and in this sense there is of course no question of our *advancing* from the one type of statement to the other. In fact, though, Ayer's point (and I think Warnock's too) is that experiential statements are *logically* prior to the committed statements, and this means that the latter are based on the former 'just in the sense that it is necessary for any perceptual statement to be true that some experiential statement be true, but possible for the experiential statement to be true even though the perceptual statement is false' (p. 148). Certainly Ayer has an important and challenging point to make. For he wants to claim that while our theory-imbued language depends upon *a* characterization of the sensible manifold in accordance with *a* conceptual scheme, other theory-laden languages are possible in which the sensible manifold is alternatively characterized in accordance with various conceptual schemes. And if we accept this it follows that a neutral language of experiential statements must be seen as parasitic not on OL in particular but on the existence of *some* theory-imbued language. The point is that *we* start by having the language we do, and that *we* move from this in our search for neutral statements. But having found the neutral statements we can see how other theory-laden languages would be possible which would adequately characterize the given without, presumably, involving references to physical objects. Equally, someone having one of these alternative languages might come to see the possibility of characterizing his experiences as we characterize them.

We will not have much more to say about Ayer's line here. We can note, though, that if we do go this far with Ayer we naturally find ourselves concerned with two questions. First there is the question referred to earlier concerning the factors limiting the number of alternative theory-imbued languages possible. It may indeed be that, if we suppose no great changes in the given as neutrally described, the number of viable and independent theory-imbued languages would turn out to be severely limited. The second question concerns the grounds for preferring one language to another, or a language involving references to physical objects to languages involving no such references. Thus when faced with some candidate alternative language the objection might be either that the language is not independently viable or that some other language is preferable. An interesting point here is that Ayer quite rightly stresses that Berkeley's aim is to recommend a language that will reflect his *theory* that the immediate objects of perception are discrete items which he believes he can show to be mind-dependent. It goes without saying that any language embodying this assumption would carry very definite implications about the status of what is seen or experienced, that it would *not* be a neutral language, and that the question of viability can be raised. Thus Ayer says:

> ... if a theory like Berkeley's is to be refuted, it has to be on logical or semantic grounds. Perhaps it can be shown that the notion of a sensible idea is incoherent or that in introducing persons as percipients Berkeley is tacitly bringing in material bodies in a sense which he repudiates. One step towards achieving this would be to show that the only viable criterion of personal identity was that of the physical identity of the person's body. (p. 11)

What we need to be quite clear on here, though, is that a purely sensory language *will* be neutral in respect of various theories concerning the nature and status of sensible objects. The characterization of what A perceives as *just* a black spot (and thus not a physical object) must reflect a theory about the sorts of things we are acquainted with, just as much as does the statement that really what he is perceiving is a material object which he could see close to, touch, and lean against.

It will be remembered that we have set ourselves the relatively unambitious task of considering whether Berkeley can show someone who starts by assuming that he sometimes perceives substantial objects that this starting point is unsatisfactory. And this brings us to the point about inferences. For it is Berkeley's view that our normal way of characterizing our experiences (as opposed to his alternative characterization) is suspect because it involves us in making inferences we are not really in a position to make. We can consider this claim first in relation to the situation where we might normally judge that what we hear is a coach. What we have already accepted here is that in this situation if it is true that I hear a coach (and indeed some item which we could see, feel and ride in) then it is also true that I hear a sound. And if we allow that the sound is the immediate object of perception in this case, we can surely see Berkeley's point when he tells us that the judgement concerning the coach involves an inference or inferences based on what we immediately perceive, and we can take this point even if we have our doubts about the use of the term 'inference' in this context. Now of course it is quite possible that on a particular occasion I may judge wrongly. It may be that a vehicle of some other type is making the sounds, that the sounds are made by children running down the street, or that what I hear is the sound of a coach reproduced on a tape-recorder. If I 'go beyond' what I immediately perceive I am always at risk – my inference may turn out to be the wrong one. It follows that if I really do want to run as few risks as possible I might restrict myself to the claim that I hear a rumbling sound, or even that it seems to me as if I were hearing a sort of rumbling sound. Given all this, though, it does perhaps need stressing that it is still open to me to insist that my original judgement may well have been correct. I may really have heard a coach. From the fact that I infer X on the basis of Y it does not follow that I am wrong about X.

Here we need to pay some attention to the sort of step I am taking when I 'go beyond' what I immediately perceive. Is the inference involved perhaps like the inference in the following case? Suppose a traveller sees a print in the mud and judges or infers that a zebra has passed by. In this case of course the traveller may be right or wrong, though if he is experienced the strong probability is that he will be right. But the key fact we must bring out here is that the traveller is taking what he sees as the basis for making a judgement about what he does not see. If he were foolish enough to say he saw a zebra when all he saw was the print, then what he said would be, not inaccurate, but false. Or is the inference more like the one we might take to be involved in the following case? Suppose I am in a library and I pick up a book from the shelves, open it at page one and start reading: 'This book is the record of a struggle between two temperaments, two consciences and almost two epochs. It ended, as was inevitable, in disruption....' I might infer here that I was reading an autobiography (and I would be right), but though I would be conscious that it might after all be a novel I would not have much time for the suggestion that it was *more accurate* to say I was reading a book than that I was reading a certain type of book. It may be false that I am reading an autobiography, in which case my claim is downright false, but it may be true, in which case the claim is just as true as, but more informative than, the claim that I am reading a book. Clearly the case here is very different from that involving the traveller, the print and the zebra. In the first case the traveller saw one thing (the print) and inferred the existence of something else (the zebra), but in the second I know I am reading the book and infer that the book I am reading is an autobiography. There are not two things – a book *and* an autobiography – involved here. Rather, I am reading a book and it may well be that in reading the book I am reading an autobiography.

When considering the sort of judgement I make when I say I perceive a substantial object we should not expect that any inference involved must be just like the inference made by the traveller or, alternatively, exactly like the inference I made when I judged that the book I was reading was an autobiography. It might be fair to say, though, that Berkeley would regard the inference made by the traveller as providing the better analogy, while Berkeley's opponent might think there was something to be learned from considering the other case. Thus Berkeley holds that what I immediately perceive is always a special kind of entity, so that when I say I see the moon the thing I see is *in fact* 'a round, luminous plain of about thirty visible points in diameter'. On the basis of what I perceive now the only inferences I am strictly *entitled* to make concern the discrete objects I suppose I would perceive under different circumstances. These inferences take me from object to object in a related series, rather than from one judgement concerning the object I now perceive to another judgement concerning that same object. Against this, Berkeley's opponent might well say that there is of course just *one* entity that he is acquainted with, that because it appears from a great distance as 'a plain lucid surface, about a foot in diameter' this can be said to be what he *immediately* perceives, but that his inference is that the very object which *seems* small is *in fact* a very large object 'fifty or sixty semidiameters of the earth distant from me'. As in the case of the book and the autobiography we have one thing and not two, but now one thing that can be described as luminous flat (because this is how it appears from where I am), *or* as a large globe (because this is what we take it to be). A slow trip to the moon will not discountenance either Berkeley *or his opponent*. The Berkeleian will announce that he sees 'a continued series of visible objects succeeding each other' and that at each stage he can infer what object he will see next. But the opponent will simply reaffirm that he sees one object all the time, looking at each stage as he would expect it to look from the distance.[10]

As it stands the point this suggests is unambitious. Both the Berkeleian and his opponent share the same experience, and an experience which might be neutrally described in terms of a statement of immediate perception. Both recognize that in interpreting the experience they 'go beyond' such a neutral description. But the Berkeleian interprets his experience in the light of his belief that ultimately only proper sensibles exist, while the opponent interprets the same experience in the light of his view that there are material things, that he is acquainted with these in perception, and that the so-called *immediate* objects are or may be either features, aspects or appearances of the things he actually perceives. The two make sense of their experiences by using different conceptual schemes, and Ayer would make the point by saying that they have different *theories* to account for the given. Ayer adds a warning here:

> The point to which I want to draw attention is that they are not theories in the scientific sense. They are not testable by observation. No experiment could be devised which would decide between a follower of Berkeley who thought that all that people ever perceived was ideas in their own minds and a naïve realist who thought that he directly perceived material things. For the experiment would itself have to produce a perceptual state of affairs; and then this would simply be interpreted by either party in accordance with his own view. (Ayer 2, p. 10)

As an illustration of this Ayer suggests that Dr. Johnson certainly should not have expected to *refute* Berkeley by kicking the stone and 'showing' that it had independent existence. And this may seem in a way to be a plus point for Berkeley. But there is another side to the coin, and this is the point we must be clear on. It is that the 'naïve' realist who is allowed to start from the assumption that he directly perceives material things is not refuted by the mere *assertion* that the only objects available for perception are proper sensibles (let alone percepts). So far as he is concerned Johnson's experiences can be adequately characterized in terms of his theory, and if it so happens that another characterization is *possible* this certainly does not mean that his theory must be false.

It is not intended to go far beyond this relatively unambitious point here, but there are two additional points we can make just briefly. First, it is surely significant that Berkeley regularly *locates* situations in terms of the theory-laden language we ordinarily employ.[11] He asks us, for example, to consider the case where we would normally suppose, and say, that we see a red-hot bar of iron, and as the situation, not only can be, but *is* located for us in these terms, the onus is surely on Berkeley to show that the characterization is inadequate. But he quite fails to show that this is so, for the features of the situation he supposes should discomfort us are all features we can quite happily cope with in terms of *our* theory. We can agree for example that if we are just looking at the poker we will not be directly aware of its heat and solidity, that we don't *see* the heat of the poker, and that the heat is never immediately perceived by sight. Indeed we might add that this is a case where it seems natural to talk of *inferences* being involved in that we infer that the object is hot because the tip is red and because it has been in the fire. But there is nothing here to worry the realist, unless the realist supposes — and why should he? — that if what we see is hot we should see its heat and thus have no cause to infer *that* it is hot. There is an unfortunate tendency for opponents of realism to make the work of demolition easy by foisting on to the realist principles he would never countenance.

The second point to be made here is that the language we use, and the theory that might be thought to be involved in it, is in a strong position *vis-à-vis* the theory-imbued language Berkeley recommends in that it is actually used, and thus undeniably usable as a means of interpreting our experiences. The claim here is that our conceptual scheme is viable and that its viability is proved in use. The importance of this claim should neither be overestimated nor underestimated. Don Locke gets the balance about right when he refers to Ayer's 'theory-neutral' facts and says:

> The facts *are* theory-neutral in the sense that they can be interpreted in accordance with Realism, Idealism or the Causal theory, and no appeal to the facts which does not already involve an interpretation of them in terms of a theory can prove one theory as against the others. The retort that common sense and ordinary language are irreversibly on the side of the Realist interpretation does not prove either that this is the only or that it is the correct interpretation. What it does prove, I think, is that this is the most convenient interpretation. (p. 45)

The point that emerges is that there must be a *presumption* in favour of realism. Locke develops the case for realism by showing that the reasons usually given for dissatisfaction with the theory are spurious, and he outlines problems the alternative theories will find it difficult to cope with. But ultimately he opts for realism *because* it is the theory we find ourselves implicitly accepting in all our day to day talk about the world:

> ... it is for this very reason that it is the preferable theory. Not because it must be true if we all say it but because if we all say it, and no proof that it is false is forthcoming, it is best to accept it as true, rather than adopt some unfamiliar and difficult alternative. (p. 138)

In this connection it is obviously interesting that Berkeley specifically allows that words purporting to stand for substantial particulars 'were framed by the vulgar ... for conveniency', and that a language reflecting what he takes to be the truth would be 'impracticable'. But he insists, of course, that the *convenient* characterizations involve a radical distortion of the basic facts.

Retracing our steps, then, we have to return to the question as to why Berkeley finds it just obvious that proper sensibles are the basic things. And the argument we need to look at now is the one we found in *NTV* 44. This argument occurs in *Alciphron* too, and we can look at it in the form it takes there. It will be obvious that a number of the points we have already made are relevant to an evaluation of this particular argument, which is introduced when Euphranor has outlined the case for saying that 'distance is perceived only by experience'. Note that the first conclusion drawn from this concerns what will *seem* to be the case to the man cured of his blindness. Thus:

> *Euphranor* Will it not thence follow that a man born blind, and made to see, would, upon first receiving his sight, take the things he saw not to be at any distance from him, but in his eye, or rather in his mind?

But the exchange continues:

> *Alciphron* I must own it seems so. And yet, on the other hand, I can hardly persuade myself that, if I were in such a state, I should think those objects which I now see at so great a distance to be at no distance at all.
>
> *Euphranor* It seems, then, that you now think the objects of sight are at a distance from you?

Alciphron Doubtless I do. Can any one question but yonder castle is at a great distance?

Euphranor Tell me, Alciphron, can you discern the doors, windows, and battlements of that same castle?

Alciphron I cannot. At this distance it seems only a small round tower.

Euphranor But I, who have been at it, know that it is no small round tower, but a large square building with battlements and turrets, which it seems you do not see.

Alciphron What will you infer from thence?

Euphranor I would infer that the very object which you strictly and properly perceive by sight is not that thing which is several miles distant.

Alciphron Why so?

Euphranor Because a little round object is one thing, and a great square object is another. Is it not?

Alciphron I cannot deny it.

Immediately reference is made to what we actually see when we look at the moon and the same moral is drawn. The moon is 'a vast opaque globe, with several unequal risings and valleys', and it is allowed (for the sake of the argument) that this *is* at a distance. But what I *see* is 'no bigger than a sixpence', and *this* object is at no distance at all.

Now we have to concede that this argument does not occur in this form in the *Dialogues*, and that when it is used in *NTV* and *Alciphron* the context is a discussion of the perception of distance. It is also true that the argument concentrates on what we actually perceive when employing the sense of sight. This admitted, though, we do at least have an *argument* here to support Berkeley's contention that the immediate objects of sense (or of sight at least) are discrete *things*. The trouble is that the argument is grotesque.

The basic criticism of the argument is that once again we are allowed to *locate* a situation by using language appropriate to our ordinary ways of thinking about the world, and that the ensuing discussion which is supposed to show that our starting point is unsatisfactory in fact shows no such thing. Let us follow it through. We find that Euphranor and Alciphron locate what they are going to talk about by pointing to something which they both see and which they take to be a castle, the 'great square object'. It is the spotting of 'yonder castle' that gets things going. Note the use of the word 'it' by both Alciphron and Euphranor. Alciphron says that from a distance *it* (the large building) 'seems only a small round tower', and Euphranor says that *it* (that which seems from a distance to be a small round tower) is really a large building which he has been at. There can be no doubt that at this stage both Alciphron *amd Euphranor* are assuming that there is just *one* object they are talking about, and that this *is* a large object which *seems* small from a distance. It is quite inexplicable that Euphranor supposes he can infer from the facts as thus described that really the object they see must be a small one.

It may be worth noting in passing that there is a possible ambiguity in what Euphranor says just before he makes his inference, and when he has it that the object which seems small is in fact 'a large square building with battlements and turrets, which it seems you do not see'. For it is quite true the suggestion here *could* be that there is a large building (with battlements and turrets) which Alciphron does not see. But it is equally clear that, given what has gone before, the claim *should* only be that the large building Alciphron sees has battlements and turrets which he does not see. Obviously *if* we did allow Euphranor's claim to carry the first implication then his inference might go through, but there is absolutely no reason why we should allow this and every reason why we should not. Both men have assumed that what they see is a tower with turrets, and Euphranor has gone so far as to say that he knows this to be so because he has been at *it* (i.e. the tower they see). But clearly the fact that from where they are they cannot make out various features of the object they have *agreed* they see has no tendency whatsoever to suggest that what they see lacks these features. Euphranor might just as well argue that because we cannot see the segments of an unpeeled orange then the orange we see can have no segments.[12]

Using a different illustration, Don Locke states and disposes of the basic argument here with commendable brevity:

The argument from appearance can be stated:
(1) This penny is circular.
(2) What I perceive is elliptical.
(3) Therefore what I perceive cannot be the penny and must be something else.

The argument is also, perhaps more frequently, stated in the form that since what different people perceive is different (the penny is elliptical for one, circular for another) they cannot be perceiving the same thing. In each case the argument is valid but the second premiss is obviously false – or else begs the question. For the Realist it is simply incorrect to say that what I perceive is elliptical. The truth is that it looks or appears elliptical, and no contradiction is involved in saying that something looks elliptical but is circular. (p. 109)

Locke finds it 'quite astonishing how often reputable philosophers from Berkeley to Ayer have confused "looks" with "is" in this way'. What Euphranor says to Alciphron provides a fine illustration of this confusion.

VI

When we read Berkeley we find that we are sometimes invited to think of the things we perceive by sense as *qualities*, but that on other occasions we are expected to think of them as *feelings*, or *sensations*, or *appearances*, or even as things like tables which remain as real as ever. We have seen that Philonous does not demur when Hylas refers to the immediate objects of perception as 'effects and appearances', but as the debate continues it is taken for granted that the topic is sensible *qualities*. And of course the location of light, colours, figures, sounds, tastes, odours and tangible qualities as the only things sense acquaints us with is supposed to be only a preliminary to showing that the things we perceive by sense cannot exist unperceived.[13] Pages 175-94 in the standard edition are devoted to convincing Hylas that each of these qualities is mind-dependent. The first step (pp. 175-87) is to persuade him that this is true of heat and cold, tastes, odours, sounds and light and colours. He then says:

> I frankly own, Philonous, that it is in vain to stand out any longer. Colours, sounds, tastes, in a word, all those termed *secondary qualities*, have certainly no existence without the mind. But by this acknowledgement I must not be supposed to derogate any thing from the reality of matter or external objects, seeing it is no more than several philosophers maintain, who nevertheless are the farthest imaginable from denying matter.

He has, he says, 'been a long time sensible' that philosophers did divide sensible qualities into the primary and secondary, allowing the former, but not the latter, an existence independent of the mind, but he was 'never thoroughly convinced of its truth till now'. Philonous continues (pp. 188-94) by arguing that if the so-called secondary qualities are mind-dependent then so are the so-called primary.

The arguments Berkeley uses to show that the so-called secondary qualities of objects are in the mind are basically two. The first, which is used in relation to heat and cold, tastes and odours, is that these are *feelings* or *sensations* which quite obviously cannot exist without a mind. The second, which is applied in the case of all the secondary qualities, is that perceiving these is always perceiving *appearances*, which again are clearly mind-dependent. We shall look first at the argument Philonous uses only in discussing heat and cold, tastes and odours. The argument here will not do, but it can be made to seem attractive.

It is no accident, I think, that Berkeley has Philonous start his programme of pulling sensible qualities into the mind by referring to touch, and to what we feel when we feel something to be hot. Before looking at the argument we can say something about touch and something about heat. First, we should note that it is desirable to refer here to the *sense* of touch rather than simply to touch. Objects such as chairs and tables cannot see, hear, smell or taste, but they can touch one another, and people can touch things without perceiving them while they are necessarily perceiving when they see, hear, smell or taste. For this reason touch is the odd man out. Of course if we substitute 'feel' for 'touch' here these discrepancies disappear. The table cannot feel the chair, and we cannot feel a sensible object without perceiving it.

The next thing to note is that though we can touch a physical object without feeling it, we cannot (as things stand) feel it without touching it. Touching, as Warnock observes, 'is certainly different in important respects from the other senses; and we are perhaps apt to think that touching is peculiarly "direct" and "immediate"' (Warnock 1, p. 47). It is not surprising that when Dr. Johnson wanted to refute Berkeley he attempted to do it, not by pointing to something, but by kicking it and thus coming into 'direct' contact with it. However, though we may be inclined to think of feeling something as providing the best evidence there could be that there is something *there* to be felt, it is significant that while we talk of feeling things like the heat of the fire, the shape of the orange and so on, we also talk of having feelings where these feelings are bodily sensations. One way of convincing us that what we feel is mind-dependent would be to persuade us that we feel *only* bodily sensations, for we do not need persuading that bodily sensations exist only when some sentient being is actually having them.

Now there would be no plausibility whatsoever in the suggestion that all perception, by whatever sense, comes down to the awareness of sensations which we would all recognize straight off as being subjective. Take the case of seeing. Clearly sometimes seeing is accompanied by bodily sensations, and it might indeed be argued that all seeing is accompanied by slight sensations of which we are dimly aware, such as those that result from the turn of the eyes. Given this, though, there is no doubt at all that we can distinguish the perception of light and colours from the awareness of any bodily sensations that might accompany it. The case can be made to seem quite different with touch. If I run my hand along the edge of the table I feel sensations *in* my fingers. Many thinkers have concentrated their attention on these subjective feelings and asked themselves whether there is really any more to feeling a thing than being aware of feelings which we extroject and (falsely) attribute to external things. If this line of thought seems at all attractive we can quite see why concentration on feeling at an early stage serves Berkeley's purposes well.

Feeling the heat of something is a special case and it is indeed quite usual to distinguish the temperature sense from touch proper. It is worth noting that while we cannot feel the shape or texture of an object without being in physical contact with the object, feeling the heat of an object need not involve touching it (even *with* something). I can feel the heat of the poker, for example, by putting my hand *near* it, and I feel the heat of the fire in the living-room as I sit at a safe distance from it. And this brings us to the crucial point. For just as I sit near the fire to enjoy the bodily sensations which go with being pleasantly warm, so feeling the heat of objects is in general associated in my mind with often quite pronounced bodily sensations. It is significant that those philosophers and scientists who made a distinction between primary and secondary qualities thought of tangible qualities such as texture, shape and solidity as being primary, but of heat as being secondary. In focusing attention on heat first, Philonous is choosing a tangible quality which many were already prepared to admit was not (as felt at least) *in* the object at all.

Now Philonous chooses to start by asking Hylas not about heat in general but about feeling an *intense* heat, and it may seem at first that this case suits Berkeley particularly well. For if when I feel the edge of the table I have no inclination to say that really I am aware only of feelings in me, when I touch something that is extremely hot I may well be conscious *only* of the sensations produced in me. When the red-hot poker is held against my arm there is no need for me to *note* that I have a sensation in me, for the feeling will be so intense that it may overwhelm all else, leaving me conscious only of an exquisite agony. With this sort of situation in mind Hylas rashly accepts that an intense heat *is* a great pain, and as pains can, of course, exist only in us he agrees that an intense heat can exist only in us. Thus:

> . . . because intense heat is nothing else but a particular kind of painful sensation; and pain cannot exist but in a perceiving being; it follows that no intense heat can really exist in an unperceiving corporeal substance. But this is no reason why we should deny heat in an inferior degree to exist in such a substance. (i, 177)

Of course once he has admitted that an intense heat exists only in the perceiver his plea that the same might not be true of lesser degrees of heat is bound to seem implausible and the move of a desperate man. Equally, though, Philonous's rejoinder that a more gentle degree of heat *is* a pleasant sensation, and that pleasant sensations can exist only in us, is less than convincing. Hylas certainly remains unconvinced and in the end Philonous has to offer an argument of a different sort.

In looking for some criticism of Philonous's 'proof' that an intense heat can exist only in a sentient being we can start by noting that even in the extreme case it is perhaps not as obvious as Berkeley thinks that he has analysed our experience aright. Thus Luce says:

> When the intense heat of the poker is communicated to the living hand, pain follows; but awareness of the heat of the poker and the air surrounding it, and awareness of the heated hand are different things, and awareness of the pain of the burnt hand is different again. Often there is a perceptible time interval. First one feels the contact, then the burning and then the pain. (Luce 9, p. 80)

And Don Locke takes a similar line when he says:

> The fact is that we all know and can feel the difference between heat and pain. So if we put our hand in the fire we will feel what we know to be heat, or we will feel what we know to be pain, or we

will feel distinct sensations of both at once, or, most probably, we will feel a single sensation compounded of heat and pain. Yet the fact that heat and pain might combine to form a distinct sensation, different from the individual sensations of heat and pain, does nothing to show that the two are, in the end, identical. Similarly the fact that a trumpet and a trombone might combine to form a distinct sound, different from the individual sounds of trumpet and trombone, does nothing to show that the sounds are, in the end, identical. (p. 82)

Philonous's case appears to rest on our agreeing that when we feel an intense heat we are aware only of 'one simple, or uncompounded idea'. He fails to allow for the possibility that others might judge differently.

There is obviously something in this criticism. We should not pretend, though, that Berkeley's argument has yet been demolished, and we should note that Locke's way of putting the counter-argument is unfortunate. It is important for us to appreciate that often the question as to what I feel can receive two different *types* of answer. In the first place I can refer to a material thing or quality felt, so that I might say I feel the rough surface of a wall or the sharpness of a pin. And in the second place I can refer to the sensations felt, as I might refer to the sensations I feel in my fingers as I move my hand up the wall. When the question is asked it will usually be clear from the context which type of answer is expected, but the important thing so far as we are concerned is to be clear that the answers *are* of different types. Now we would normally suppose that to say we feel heat is to give an answer of the first type (an answer in terms of the *quality* felt), and that to say we feel pain is to give an answer of the second type (an answer in terms of the *sensation* felt). And when Berkeley tells us that heat *is* a pain, and that *really* we feel only what we would normally recognize as a mind-dependent sensation, he is in effect telling us that only the one type of answer is appropriate. Given this, it would seem that if we want to resist Berkeley's attempt to make heat mind-dependent we will want to insist that an answer in terms of the quality felt *is* appropriate and that this answer is neither equivalent to, nor reducible to, an answer of the second type. The criticism of Locke's counter-argument is that this point is not brought out. For though Locke does want to make a distinction between feeling heat and feeling pain he still refers to the object in each case as a *sensation*, and even allows that heat (a quality) and pain (a sensation) can combine to form 'a single sensation compounded of heat and pain'. The analogy with the two sounds makes things worse rather than better, for the sound of a trumpet and the sound of a trombone are on a level, so that we can make sense of the notion of their combining to make a new sound (rather as colours can be combined to form a new colour). But the sensation of pain and the quality of heat are, we believe, not on a level, and if this is so the heat we feel and the pain we feel can no more combine to form a distinct sensation than they can to form a distinct quality. The fact is that though Locke is concerned to refute Berkeley's argument he has, in this passage, allowed himself to go too far along the road with his opponent.

To be fair to all concerned I think we do have to recognize that we are on tricky ground here. We are of course on Berkeley's chosen ground. We are concentrating on feeling – the sense he chooses to start with, and on heat – the quality he chooses to start with. And, moreover, Locke at least is approaching the question in the way Berkeley chooses to approach it. Anyone inclined to be totally contemptuous of Berkeley's line here might try the following simple experiment. He might put a finger on a moderately hot surface, close his eyes, and concentrate on what he *feels*. He should discount the solidity of what he feels as well as the texture and any peculiarities of structure and attend only to the heat, which is what we are interested in. At this point he is challenged to claim with confidence that he can distinguish the heat felt from the feeling in the finger.

It may be, though, that Philonous overplays his hand when he starts by considering what we feel when we feel an *intense* heat, for I would suggest that, paradoxically, the very fact that we are inclined to admit that here we may feel only pain should tend to make us suspicious of the claim that feeling any degree of heat *is* feeling a bodily sensation. Suppose, then, we found some victim on whom to make a trial and that, having blindfolded him, we put a red-hot poker on his arm. And suppose that when questioned he answered that he had felt *only* a pain. Would this prove that an intense heat was a great pain and thus only a bodily sensation? Clearly it would not. We might compare the following situation. If I put the tips of my fingers against a wall and lean forward putting my weight on them I am aware of the hardness of the wall *and* of sensations in my fingers. Here it would be grossly implausible to say that I felt *only* sensations in my fingers, for an answer in terms of the quality felt is appropriate and the sensations felt may be scarcely noticible. If I continue in this position, however, the sensations in my fingers will become more and more unpleasant so that in the end they dominate and I may be inclined to say that I am aware of nothing else. And the point we need to be clear on now is that if I do say this I will in effect be admitting that my concentration is focused *exclusively* on the pain in me and that I am no longer concerned with or conscious of any quality of the wall.

It is in a similar spirit that Luce points to the time interval there may be between awareness of the intense heat of a poker and then feeling the pain resulting from this. If we found this convincing we might well say that if and when the subject feels *only* pain then it is true that he is aware only of a bodily sensation, but at the same time false that he is aware of the heat. The point does, though, need careful handling and we can bring this out by considering the following case. Here we can suppose our hands held against a cool object which is gradually heated until the heat becomes intense. Now a natural way of describing what went on here would be to say that at each of the earlier stages we had bodily sensations such that *through these* we were able to make judgements concerning the heat of the object. At a certain stage we would begin to feel pain and would judge that what we were feeling was now very hot, and eventually we would be in such a state that we would lose our ability to discriminate between different degrees of heat and would continue screaming whether the temperature was further increased or returned to cold. It is when we consider our state at *this* stage that we might be most inclined to talk of feeling *only* pain, and of course it is at just this stage that we have lost the ability to make judgements concerning temperature. Here the only appropriate answer to the question as to what we feel may indeed be an answer in terms of the *sensation* felt. Conversely, though, we can claim that so long as we are able to make temperature discriminations through feeling then a quite different type of answer in terms of the *quality* felt will be proper.

A natural objection to Philonous's line is that he concentrates exclusively on *feeling* heat and makes no allowance for our normal assumption that heat is that quality of red-hot poker by virtue of which it can not only cause pain but, for example, be used for poker work or for mulling beer. As Hylas says, though rather late in the day:

Hold, Philonous, I fear I was out in yielding intense heat to be a pain. It should seem rather, that pain is something distinct from heat, and the consequence or effect of it.

In answer to this Philonous simply insists that when I feel heat I feel only 'one simple uniform sensation', but this, though Hylas fails to make the point, invites the response that if the only sensation we feel is indeed that of pain then we should conceive of the heat as causing that pain, just as it causes the scorching of the carpet if a hot coal falls on it. In addition, Hylas should have pointed out that if Philonous is trying to prove something about a quality of objects then he should certainly take account of the fact that we judge things to be very hot in situations where we cannot feel their heat at all. He might have added further that we can feel that an object is intensely hot without coming into close enough contact with it for it to cause us pain, avoiding close contact with the object *because* we can feel its heat. It begins to look as if Philonous is equating an intense heat with a great pain when he would be grossly oversimplifying if he identified the *sensation* we feel when we feel heat with such a pain.

Now at this stage we are ready to look at the really fundamental problem raised by Philonous's argument. For the trouble with it is that if it succeeds then heat of any intensity *ceases to be a quality of objects*. Indeed Philonous seems quite ready to admit that this is the case. At one point Hylas objects:

> But after all, can any thing be more absurd than to say, *there is no heat in the fire*?

And in his reply Philonous seems to be taking the line that however absurd the judgement may seem it is nonetheless *true*. The exchange continues:

> *Philonous* To make the point still clearer; tell me, whether in two cases exactly alike, we ought not to make the same judgment?
> *Hylas* We ought.
> *Philonous* When a pin pricks your finger, doth it not rend and divide the fibres of your flesh?
> *Hylas* It doth.
> *Philonous* And when a coal burns your finger, doth it any more?
> *Hylas* It doth not.

> *Philonous* Since therefore you neither judge the sensation itself occasioned by the pin, nor any thing like it to be in the pin; you should not, conformably to what you have now granted, judge the sensation occasioned by the fire, or anything like it, to be in the fire.

Of course if Philonous were simply arguing here that the sensation occasioned by the coal burning one's finger is no more in the fire than the sensation occasioned by the pin piercing one's finger is in the pin, we would not want to gainsay him. But this is not the argument. Philonous is defending the view that '*there is no heat in the fire*', and the way he chooses to defend it at once reflects, and is necessitated by, his earlier claim that there is no distinction to be made between the quality and a bodily sensation. In the light of what has gone before, this exchange is not surprising. What is surprising is that a Berkeleian should have allowed himself to get into this position, for we saw in an earlier chapter that Berkeley liked to think it one big plus point for his system that it avoided 'those odd paradoxes, that the *fire* is *not hot*, nor *the wall white*, etc.'. 'In ye immaterial hypothesis', he had boasted, 'the wall is white, fire hot etc' (*PC* 19).

One way of understanding how Berkeley came to deny what he wanted to affirm is to return to Berkeley's materialists and look at the line they took on heat. Galileo, for example, denies 'that heat is a real phenomenon, or property, or quality, which actually resides in the material by which we feel ourselves warmed', and he explains what happens when we come into contact with an object we think of as hot in terms of the pleasant or unpleasant sensations produced in us by the action of minute particles. Drawing an extreme conclusion, he tells us that heat 'belongs so intimately to us that when the live body is taken away, heat becomes no more than a simple name' (see Popkin 3, pp. 65-8). John Locke is always less extreme, but he is quite happy to identify heat and warmth *as they are ideas* or *as we experience them* with what bodies produce in us (II viii 16). In effect Locke wants to make *two* points, though for him they are sides of one coin. And these are, first, that heat as felt exists only in us, and, second, that it is not a real quality of the things we call hot. Obviously, from this point of view, assimilating the idea of a great heat to a feeling of pain is a trick that serves its turn. For pains, we agree, do exist only in us, and of course they cannot exist in senseless things. But Berkeley's ambitions are different. He wants to have it that heat (like all qualities) belongs intimately to us, but he also wants to insist that it should be thought of as a quality of the hot object. Clearly assimilating heat to pain will serve the first of these purposes, and for this reason the assimilation may have seemed irresistible, but it does it only at the enormous cost of making it impossible for Berkeley to maintain that heat can be properly thought of as a quality of things.

Berkeley is thus faced with a dilemma, and with a dilemma of the sort with which we are by now familiar. He needs to preserve some sort of distinction between the *qualities* of things, which he likes to say we 'perceive by sense', and bodily *sensations* such as pains, just as he wants to preserve a distinction between what we perceive by sense and mental images. Against this, he wants to deny that there is any distinction in order to show that heat is *obviously* mind-dependent. But of course if there is no distinction it is difficult to see how heat can be regarded as a quality of even a Berkeleian red-hot poker, while if there is a distinction then the mind-dependence of pain will not after all entail the mind-dependence of the quality. Another way of making the same point is to say that though Philonous is supposed to be showing that sensible *qualities* are in the mind, his argument if successful, would show that heat at least is not a quality.

There is no need to give separate attention to the arguments designed to show that sweetness (which is supposed to be 'a particular kind of pleasure'), bitterness ('some kind of uneasiness or pain'), and odours ('so many pleasing or displeasing sensations') must all be only in the mind. We can note, though, that the identifications here lack plausibility, and that if we accepted them we would seem to have no ground for thinking of these sensations as qualities even of mind-dependent objects. Beyond this we can make the general point that Luce must be oversimplifying when he says:

> A *sensation* in Berkeley's usage is not a subjective sensing, but an object sensed, an idea-thing. Such sensations constitute nature, and happen in accordance with the known laws of nature, and are independent of my will. . . . [Berkeley's sensations 'from without' are not] subjective things like aches and pains, and dreams and stirrings of sense . . . [they are] objective things like the thunder-clap heard above the storm, the starry heavens seen on a frosty night, and the goodly smell of the vine in flower. Such things are obviously external . . . (Luce 7, p. 191).

Against Luce we have to stress that, in the opening stages of the argument in the *Dialogues*, the Berkeleian goes so far as to *equate* heat and cold, tastes and odours, with sensations of pleasure and pain, and indeed argues that it is *because* the equations hold that the 'qualities' must be thought mind-dependent.[14]

Elsewhere Luce has taken Furlong firmly to task for suggesting (in a review) that Berkeley 'has taken the road away from common sense' when he claims that we perceive only our own sensations, but in fact what Furlong says can hardly be denied. Of course it would not do to suggest that when Berkeley refers to the things we perceive by sense as *sensations* he must be thinking *either* that the whole story is that they are 'subjective things like aches and pains' *or* that it is that they are idea-things which are somehow 'obviously external'. A recurrent theme of this commentary has been that he wants to have it both ways. He would like us to think of his ideas in the one way, so as to be convinced of their dependence on the mind, and he would also like us to think of them in the other way, so as to remain convinced that they are as real and objective as ever we thought they were. And the question is always whether he can have it both ways.[15] A general challenge to Berkeley (and Luce) might take the form of asking how, if the things we perceive by sense are so obviously in the mind, we can yet be justified in thinking (or even come to think) that they are obviously external, and how if they are somehow obviously external, we can be sure they exist only in the mind. Given the argumentation early on in the *Dialogues* it is difficult to see how Berkeley could answer this challenge if it were pushed in relation specifically to heat and cold, tastes and odours.

The second argument Philonous uses is applied not only in the case of heat and cold, tastes and odours, but in the case of all the so-called secondary qualities and eventually to all qualities. For it is claimed that we perceive only *appearances*, and appearances are said to exist only in the mind. We return, in fact, to the argument from the relativity of perception, and what we say here will supplement what we have said earlier and in particular in our second chapter and in section V of the present chapter. The argument is one Berkeley attributes to the materialists, though he sees the materialists as using it too selectively. The fact that the same water can feel cold to one hand and warm to the other is supposed to show that neither the felt warmth nor the felt coolness is properly attributable to an external object. But equally,

Berkeley thinks, the fact that the apparent size of an object varies as we look at it from different positions is one that should suggest that extension belongs only in the mind.

As we just mentioned in Ch. 2, the fact that Berkeley uses this argument in the *Dialogues* has been thought to pose a problem in that in *Pr.* 15 he candidly admits that it proves less than he needs. There he holds that the argument 'doth not so much prove that there is no extension or colour in an outward object, as that we do not know by sense which is the true extension or colour of the object'. Commenting on *PC* 265, where the same point is made, Luce notes that, with it, Berkeley 'has come to the end of his *cul de sac*, and can go no further' for his old method of arguing has 'failed him' (Luce 7, p. 89). The problem is that in the *Dialogues* he seems to follow the old road very enthusiastically, and that in this work (unlike the *Principles*) he fails to acknowledge that it comes to a dead-end. Though I don't think the charge can stand, Berkeley might seem to be arguing disingenuously.

One possible defence here might be that in the *Dialogues* Berkeley is not *relying* on the argument from the relativity of perception but rather again using it in a purely *ad hominem* way. This seems to be Jessop's opinion when he says:

> The . . . observations on the complication of heat, cold, tastes and smells with pleasure and pain . . . are intended as an *argumentum ad hominem*; and so also is the argument from the relativity of sense-qualities to our bodily position and condition, as is made clear in *Principles*, Sect. 15. (*Works* II, p. 192n)

Filling this out a bit, we might think that Berkeley holds that anyone who is prepared to commit himself unreservedly to the argument from the relativity of perception can be forced to conclude that extension is no more a quality of an outward object than is colour. In the *Dialogues* he does not admit that he lacks faith in the argument, but his silence on this point can be accounted for. After all, in the *Principles* Berkeley is concerned to present his arguments for immaterialism in a quite straightforward way, and if at any stage he is arguing *ad hominem* he must say so. In the *Dialogues*, however, he is presenting a discussion between a Berkeleian and his opponent, and here it might be thought quite legitimate for him to begin by drawing out the implications of his opponent's principles without stressing every reason he has for disagreeing with those principles. Allowance must be made for the dialogue form and the conventions of debate.

There may be something in this defence, but I am fairly sure that it is not enough. Fundamentally, I find it just impossible to read the relevant pages on the assumption that Berkeley is allowing Philonous to follow a line of argument in which he does not believe.[16] Indeed it seems to me that Berkeley *needs* the argument from the relativity of perception to pull the things we immediately perceive into the mind, and that the only alternative he has is to appeal to what is 'evident to any one who takes a survey of the objects of human knowledge'. But the defence we are considering is unsatisfactory for another reason. In the *Principles* Berkeley is able to point to a group of philosophers who, he says, do believe that the argument shows *certain* qualities to be mind-dependent. And here it is quite proper for him to suggest that this argument, if admitted, would prove more than they want. But the situation is quite different in the *Dialogues* in that, initially, Hylas has no use for the argument at all. It is Philonous (the Berkeleian) who convinces him he should accept it in the case of the secondary qualities and who then forces him to extend its use. Clearly it is one thing to say to an opponent that if he accepts A he should accept B, and quite another to persuade him to accept A and B. To defend Berkeley from the charge of disingenuousness we need to look elsewhere.

What we suggested earlier is that if Berkeley had come to believe that the argument from the relativity of perception was less powerful than he would like, this does not necessarily mean either that he had spotted its *real* weakness or that he thought the argument to be of no use at all. It is quite clear that he thought that the argument proved *something*, for though he acknowledges that it fails to prove that the external object lacks colour and extension, he still thinks of it as showing that 'we do not know by sense which is the true extension or colour of the object'. The wording here is suggestive. What Berkeley says is that the line of arguing 'doth not so much prove' the one thing as the other, and I cannot help seeing this as indicating that Berkeley thinks of what the argument *does* prove as at least marking a step towards what he wants to prove.

If we ask what Berkeley thought the argument *did* prove we have to say, I think, that he thought it showed that when we take ourselves to be perceiving a quality of an outward object we are in fact aware only of a mind-dependent appearance. Thus if Hylas believes we see colours, for example, 'on' objects, the argument from the relativity of perception proves him wrong. In this sense the argument is not a failure. By means of it Hylas is brought to the position Berkeley assumes at the opening of the *Principles* and into line with Berkeley *and the materialists* in holding that in sense-perception we are acquainted only with mind-dependent ideas. In the earlier work Berkeley felt he could just take this for granted. In the *Dialogues* he feels he has to persuade Hylas to share the common ground. It is from this point of view that we have to take the argument seriously, particularly as we have seen that the materialists took the *conclusion* to be evident because they were committed to holding, as Berkeley was not, that it is because external objects play a causal role in perception that it must be supposed that they themselves are not perceived.

Why did Berkeley express dissatisfaction with the argument when he wrote the *Principles*? The answer must be, not that he thought it proved nothing worth proving, but rather that it failed to make the point Berkeley wanted to make against the materialists. What it proved was that we are never aware of any quality in an external object. It did not prove that there are no external objects with qualities. The reason for this was that it left it open to the materialist to insist that there are external objects and that these objects have qualities *though we are never acquainted with them*, and in this way it had to be seen as merely making explicit what Berkeley took to be one of the most objectionable features of materialism. As he says in *Pr.* 87:

> Colour, figure, motion, extension and the like, considered only as so many *sensations* in the mind, are perfectly known, there being nothing in them which is not perceived. But if they are looked on as notes or images, referred to *things* or *archetypes* existing without the mind, then are we involved all in *scepticism*. We see only the appearances, and not the real qualities of things. What may be the extension, figure, or motion of any thing really and absolutely, or in it self, it is impossible for us to know, but only the proportion or the relation they bear to our senses. Things remaining the same, our ideas vary, and which of them, or even whether any of them at all represent the true quality really existing in the thing, it is out of our reach to determine.

That the materialist will in the end have to admit this is doubtless unfortunate for him, but it does not prove him *wrong*. So in the

Principles Berkeley needs to put all the emphasis on arguments designed to show that the notion of unperceived things and qualities is an incoherent one. When Philonous begins to debate with Hylas the situation is quite different. Indeed at the stage when the Berkeleian is concerned to demonstrate that qualities *as perceived* are mind-dependent he dismisses as irrelevant the claim that there may be unperceived qualities in external things. Hylas suggests that we should not 'conclude absolutely, that there is no heat in the fire, or sweetness in the sugar, but only that heat or sweetness, as perceived by us, are not in the fire or sugar'. And Philonous responds:

> I say it is nothing to the purpose. Our discourse proceeded altogether concerning sensible things, which you defined to be the things we *immediately perceive by our senses*. Whatever other qualities therefore you speak of, as distinct from these, I know nothing of them, neither do they at all belong to the point in dispute. (i, 180)

The irrelevant question *becomes* relevant only when Hylas has finally been convinced that all qualities *as perceived by us* are indeed mind-dependent, and it is at the earlier stage that the argument from the relativity of perception is supposed to have its role to play.[17]

In criticizing Berkeley's use of the argument we can start by noting, as we have before, that he has to *start* by using the descriptions we would ordinarily use if he is going to locate the situations he wants to talk about. The initial assumption cannot be that we perceive discrete appearances, let along percepts. We *begin* with a bowl of water, a lump of sugar, or any object we are going to examine under varying conditions, and we are asked to agree that none of these things can have incompatible qualities. No object can be warm and cool, sweet and bitter, or large and small. Now at first we may see no cause for concern in the fact that one and the same object can *appear* to have incompatible qualities. The same water can feel warm (to one hand) and cool (to the other). The same food can taste sweet (to one person) and bitter (to another). And the same object can look large (from one distance) and small (from another). Hylas gets into trouble only when he agrees that an object must have any quality it appears to have, for he is now forced to accept both that the water for example *must* be warm and cool (for it appears warm to the one hand and cool to the other) and that it *cannot be* warm and cool (for these are incompatible). The way out of this difficulty may seem obvious. Hylas should withdraw his claim that any object must have any quality it appears to have. Philonous, though, insists he should make a different move. Rather than saying, for example, that the water *is* warm but only *appears* cool (to the hand that has been in the pocket) he should recognise that the warmth and coolness are equally *appearances*, that neither can be in an external substance, and that both must be in the mind.

Now at one level the argument from the relativity of perception is very easy to deal with. Its basic flaw is revealed by Cummins for example when he says:

> . . . perceptual relativity concerning a range of qualities, *e.g.*, colours or shapes, fails to prove that no quality in that range is a property of a material thing. Consider the famous 'bent' oar. In water an oar appears bent to the eye, though one's hand finds it straight. Since the two qualities are contraries, at least one of them is not an actual property of the oar. It does not follow that neither is. (p. 205)

But let us take our own example. Suppose we take a piece of paper and look at it under a good light. It may appear white, and we will say that it *is* white. This is our starting point. Now we all know that if we look at this same paper through a red filter it will look red, and we can see the point of saying that what we perceive now is *redness*. The question is what we are to make of all this. And there seems to be nothing here to force us to Philonous's conclusion *unless* we accept some grossly implausible principle such as that which Hylas accepts. If we *don't* accept that any apparent quality must be intrinsic to the thing perceived we will see no reason to deny that what we are seeing through the filter is *in fact* white, and no reason to affirm that what we are seeing must be red appearance rather than white paper looking red. Redness, we can agree, is what is *immediately* perceived. But why should I have to regard this as a property of a percept rather than as an apparent quality of the paper when viewed under special circumstances? To see the *real* colour of the paper I only have to remove the filter. To see the *real* shape of the oar I only have to take the oar out of the water.

It is obvious that if the facts of perceptual relativity are going to give us any genuine cause for concern we are going to have to look a little deeper than we have so far looked. Now we know that Berkeley believes that the argument from the relativity of perception can show the so-called secondary qualities *and* the so-called primary qualities (as perceived by us) to be mind-dependent. So we shall choose one of each and consider first what he says about extension in i, 188-9. Here his arguments are unimpressive. There are basically two.

First, we are asked to note that an object which appears small to us may appear very large to other (minute) creatures, and this of course is true. Given this unexceptionable starting point, Berkeley expects us to conclude both that the large extension perceived by the minute animal cannot be identical with the small extension perceived by the man, and that each must be in the mind of the perceiver. But it is quite clear that we need not come to this conclusion. The fact is that things can be judged large or small only by comparing them with other things. I can, for example, judge a shirt of a certain determinate size to be *too large* if I am fitting my younger son, and at the same time as *too small* for my elder boy. Alberto may be *tall* (for an Italian) and at the same time *short* (for a basket-ball player). A mite and a man complicate things only because the mite is itself small (in comparison with a man) and so will tend to choose different objects for comparison. Thus an intelligent mite would judge a scrap of paper to be huge (in comparison with the objects with which he has most to do) while the man might judge it to be small (because he could hardly write two words on it). Indeed the short way of dealing with the argument is to say that on the hypothesis that the mite and the man do see one object of a determinate size we would *expect* them to judge differently, so the fact that they do judge differently cannot undermine the hypothesis. On top of this, we should certainly not allow ourselves to be blinded to the extent to which the two can agree in their judgements. The important thing is that each should spell out his standard of reference. They can agree, for example, that the scrap of paper both is and seems large when compared with a mite's foot. Given our system of measurement, they could agree that it both is and seems to be about one inch long.[18]

The second argument Berkeley provides here is no better. Philonous starts from the undeniable fact that 'as we approach to or recede from an object, the visible extension varies'; undeniable, that is, if we take him to be drawing attention to the fact that the object *looks* or *appears* smaller as it recedes and then larger as it approaches. The question is what we are to make of this. For there seems to be no reason why we should conclude with the idealist that there is no one object with a determinate extension when we can have it that all the time we are seeing (as we started off by supposing) one object with a fixed size which *looks* larger or smaller depending on the distance we are from it. If we are to be persuaded to think differently we shall have to be convinced not just that 'no real inherent property of any object can be changed, without some change in the thing itself', but also that the appearance of an object cannot vary without some change in the thing itself. Referring to *this* principle Warnock says:

> ... unless this fantastic assumption is made, the 'argument from illusion' cannot get started; for unless we begin by supposing that things *cannot* appear to be otherwise than they are, why should we be at all put out by the obvious fact that they can and do? (Warnock 1, p. 148)

This is in fact another case of Berkeley 'defeating' the realist by attributing to his opponent a principle he would not normally accept. We might note too that the argument might seem a winner to Berkeley on the *assumption* that we are aware only of 'effects and appearances' and *never* of outward objects. But we have to stress now, first, that we have so far been given no reason for accepting this assumption, and, second, that the argument from the relativity of perception gets going only on the *contrary* assumption. We have to start by assuming that the mite and the man see the *same* extension before we can be forced to admit that it *looks* small to the man and large to the mite. And we have to assume that we see *one* object at various distances before we can be challenged by the fact that the way it appears can vary.

It might well be thought that the argument from the relativity of perception will be quite as powerless when it is applied to the case of colours, and our earlier remarks might well suggest that this is so. Let us consider the case of the piece of white paper again. Those of us who believe it *is* white are agreed that it does not always *look* uniformly white. And it is certainly not *obvious* that the fact that the *apparent* colour of the paper varies need tempt us to doubt that we are seeing one piece of paper with a determinate and fixed colour. If those of us who believe that we see colouring 'on' objects are very well aware that the objects do not always appear to have the colouring we take them to have, the 'revelation' that this is so is hardly likely to shake us. We will not, however, drop the matter here. For when we look a little deeper we do find that the perception of colour has certain worrying features. We can look at two of Berkeley's arguments to see what these are.

First, then, (in i, 184) we find Hylas agreeing that the purple and yellow clouds that he sees do not really have these colours 'on' them, this being obvious because we know that on a closer inspection we would discover only 'a dark mist or vapour'. The colouring as seen is, then, 'only apparent'. Philonous now persuades him that the principle on which he is working is that 'those [colours] are to be thought real, which are discovered by the most near and exact survey'. But if *this* principle is adopted no object can be supposed to have the colouring we normally attribute to it, for under a microscope – which affords a more near and exact survey – the familiar colouring will always be found to vanish.

In evaluating this argument I must admit that I am not sure what conclusion Philonous is entitled to draw on the premiss that only the nearest and most exact survey could reveal to us the true colour of an object. On the assumption that there could in principle be a sort of ultimate survey, conducted with the most super of super microscopes, the conclusion would be that we would have to conduct the ultimate survey to find the true colouring of any object. Perhaps, though, Philonous would deny that there could be an ultimate survey. He might argue that however sophisticated the microscope it would be possible to envisage a yet more powerful instrument which would strip away yet one more layer of apparent colour. Hylas might, I suppose, come back by suggesting that it is at least conceivable that we should reach a stage when a certain colouring remained constant as more and more powerful microscopes were developed, so that it became at least reasonable to suppose that we had at last discovered the 'true' colouring. The question is of little interest. The fact is that Hylas should not have accepted that only the nearest and most exact survey could reveal to us the true colouring of an object.

The point is that, though in certain circumstances we may want to take a closer look to determine what qualities an object really has, we certainly do not suppose that looking closer is always the important thing, or that the closer we get to the object the better. The shopper wondering about the true colouring of a piece of material is much more likely to take it to the doorway of the shop so as to see it in a good light, and away from shadows, than she is to hold it as close to her eyes as she possibly can, or to inspect it with a microscope. Indeed, even when she has the material in a good light she will hold it *away* from her in order to make a judgement. Philonous is quite right in suggesting that the colouring we suppose an object to *have* is that which it appears to have under certain circumstances, but nobody really thinks that getting the circumstances right must involve the procedure he insists on.

I think we can argue that it only makes sense to talk of the 'real' colour of an object given that we recognize some standard conditions under which that colour can be determined. I suspect too that a colour can be judged 'only apparent' only by contrasting it with some supposedly real colour which is to be determined by viewing the object under the conditions accepted as standard. And if this is so it must be incoherent to say (as Philonous does) that *all* colours are only apparent. But Philonous's argument may leave us with one worry, and this is that there might seem to be an element of arbitrariness in choosing one set of conditions as standard. It seems plausible to suggest that we might have decided, or might now decide, to regard other conditions as standard, and given this decision what we now think of as the real colour of a piece of paper might properly be judged to be only apparent. Russell has this point in mind but draws an extreme conclusion when he says:

> When, in ordinary life, we speak of *the* colour of the table, we only mean the sort of colour which it will seem to have to a normal spectator from an ordinary point of view under usual conditions of light. But the other colours which appear under other conditions have just as good a right to be considered real; and therefore, to avoid favouritism, we are compelled to deny that, in itself, the table has any one particular colour. (Russell 5, pp. 2-3)

We shall be commenting on this in a moment.

Turning now to the second argument, we find Philonous drawing attention, not to how the apparent colouring of an object varies when viewed by us under varying circumstances, but to how other creatures may see things. We know that changes in our physiological state can result in our seeing different colours than we do normally, so we must judge it highly probable both that the 'inconceivably small animals perceived by glasses' (who will have sense organs suited to their needs) see things differently, and that 'those animals in whose eyes we discern a very different texture from that of ours . . . do not see the same colours in every object that we do'. And Philonous sums up:

> From all which, should it not seem to follow, that all colours are equally apparent, and that none of those which we perceive are really inherent in any outward object?

The first argument may seem worrying because it suggests that the colours we normally suppose to be 'on' objects depend on, and are relative to, light conditions, but this second argument may seem potentially more worrying in that it points out that the colours we see are relative to *our* senses. We should not be too hasty here. In both cases no new facts are revealed. We all know that the apparent colour of an object varies with changes in the light conditions, and it is widely (though falsely) believed that white paper looks yellow to a man with jaundice. Again, there is no doubt that the visual apparatus of various animals differs markedly from our own and that this does result in their seeing things differently. We begin to feel uneasy when we consider the *implications* of these facts, but it may be that the implica- are not what Berkeley thought.

Perhaps we can start to turn a vague uneasiness into a specific worry by concentrating on the concept of a *normal* observer as used by Russell when he suggests that the real colouring of an object is supposed to be that which it will appear to have to the *normal* observer under standard light conditions. It is worth noting that an observer who is colour-blind does accept that he is not normal in this respect, and that he is willing to acquiesce in the judgements of those who can discriminate as he cannot. Similarly, a man who has taken a drug which makes things look yellow will accept that his state is not normal, and that the real colours of the objects are those he would see if he had not taken the drug. The basic difference between the colour-blind man and the man who has taken the drug is that the latter knows from experience what it is to see normally, but they have it in common that they accept their abnormality. But it might be suggested that when we talk of normality here what we have in mind is the way in which, as it so happens, things appear to the vast majority of us. We begin to get suspicious of the concept when we appreciate that those of us who consider ourselves normally sighted only happen to be in the majority, and that it might have been the case that a different eye-structure was more common and thus considered more normal. The question that raises itself is whether we are not being a little presumptuous (and at the same time unwarrantedly anthropocentric) in treating the normal human being as if he represented some sort of ultimate in normality. We can at least envisage a race of intelligent beings who see different colours in objects from those we see. Who are we say to that the colours a normal human being sees are real, and those we can suppose a Martian would see unreal? Equally, who is he to say that the colours he sees are real and the colours we see only apparent?

In dealing with this problem we have to accept at once that if there are indeed material objects then the way in which we perceive them, and thus the way in which we describe them, will depend to a very large extent on the sort of beings we are and the sort of sensory apparatus we are supplied with. It is, for example, because we have the visual apparatus we do that we see them as having colours and, in particular, the colours we see them as having. As Don Locke says:

> . . . our conception of the external world is fundamentally and essentially *sense-relative*. That is, it is because we have the senses we do, because we perceive the world in the way that we do, that we conceive and know of the external world in the way we do. (p. 120)

If we grant this, then, we have to allow that there might be beings whose sensory apparatus was markedly different from our own and whose conception of the external world would differ from our own. Certainly we must resist the temptation of supposing that if an object really *had* the colour it seems to us to have (under standard conditions) then it would have to appear the same to any sighted creature (even under standard conditions). If I do think of myself as a normal observer I must not suppose that I represent some sort of cosmic absolute in normality. In a way this is all very obvious, but the notion that our conception of the world is sense-relative can present itself as challenging, worrying or inspiring. It is easy to make false moves here. We can be misled into supposing that because the way in which we perceive and describe the world depends on our being the sort of creature we are then the universe itself, rather than our descriptions of it, must be anthropocentric. Again, there is a tendency to think of our senses, not as informing us about the world, but as somehow hiding the true nature of things from us. We may feel the urge to step outside our skins, as it were, to discover how things *really* are. The small schoolboy may even close his eyes *very* tight then open them *very* suddenly in the hope that he may be just in time to see what the world is like when nobody is looking at it.

The scientist is, however, more genuinely inspired, and it was easy for Boyle and John Locke to see the scientists as aiming at an account of bodies as they are *in themselves*. In formulating their account they were influenced by various factors, and we can mention just some of them here. In the first place there was what is sometimes thought of as the physicist's *prejudice* in favour of the microscopic. Very briefly, scientific progress has depended in large part on the microscopic investigation of objects and on *theories* concerning their basic sub-microscopic structure. Conjoined with this there has been a tendency for the scientist to suppose that he is discovering the *true* nature of the macroscopic objects and indeed showing that they are not as we normally suppose them to be. It is tempting for him to think that because his theory requires him to describe the table as 'mostly emptiness' he must pour scorn on the common belief that it is solid, and this on the seemingly unexceptionable principle that what is solid is most certainly not mostly emptiness. And so the notion is spread abroad that the discoveries of science are in radical conflict with the 'naïve' opinions of the plain man. We ought, I think, to be suspicious of this notion, if only because of the fact that the plain man has shown himself very ready to accept what the scientist tells him about the constitution of his table, while at the same time persisting in describing it as *solid*. The plain man has not missed the point here. For the truth is that the scientific account is not in conflict with any of the beliefs about the table which lie behind our assertion that it is solid. We can still sit down at it, eat our dinner off it, and sit on it if we want, and it is because this is so that we describe the table as solid. What we now know is that when we consider a solid table *from the point of view of its atomic structure* it is indeed found to be mostly emptiness. But there is nothing problematic about the fact that we want to give different and apparently incompatible descriptions of objects when considering them from different points of view. We shall feel that our ordinary descriptions have been *falsified* only if we suppose that ultimately the only proper description of an object is a description in terms of its atomic structure.[19]

Turning to a second feature of the scientific approach we can note that in addition to formulating his own technical vocabulary, the scientist shows an unwillingness to use certain of the predicates we use in describing objects. To take one simple example, he is going to think we are being lamentably imprecise when we refer to an object as *large*. From the scientific point of view (as from that of the carpenter) the statement that the table top measures 8 feet by 4 feet has a commendable rigour which the statement that it is large quite lacks. The scientist, then, is concerned with *precision*. But again we have to be careful here, noting that though an exact description may in an obvious sense be preferable to a rough and ready, or inexact, description this does not mean that the latter need be any less true than the former. The judgement that the table top is large need not be thought any less true than the judgement that it measures 8 feet by 4 feet even if it does seem very unhelpful to the man concerned with exact measurement. If nothing else, this simple example helps us to make the point that if a certain statement about an object would not appear in a scientific description this does not mean that the statement cannot be a true one. But it can also lead us to another point which is that in giving an account of objects the scientist is going to be interested in what he *can* measure. There is undoubtedly something in the suggestion that the seventeenth century scientist 'theorized in terms of extension, mass, motion, and number . . . because they were essential to any quantitative approach to reality, the sole approach of which he was capable' (Aaron, 1, pp. 125-6). It must be added, though, that if this sort of observation helps to explain why the scientist was more interested in certain qualities than in others, it does not, as it stands, even appear to justify the claim that the qualities chosen are the only genuine qualities of objects. That the scientist 'could not discover the real colours and tastes which things have' *by measurement*, does not suggest that colours and tastes are not real qualities, unless of course we are given some reason for accepting the dictum that 'what is real is measurable'[20]

There is something else which influences the scientific approach and which we can mention just briefly, and this is that, though ultimately we must rely on our sense experience for finding out about the world, the judgements we make on the basis of our experiences are in certain fields notoriously fallible. The example of the same water feeling warm to one hand and cool to the other is a useful one here, for it is very clear that how an object which has a certain constant temperature *feels* depends to a very great extent on the condition and constitution of the percipient. The bath-water which *feels* almost unbearably hot when we first immerse ourselves in it begins to *feel* cool long before there is any real cooling of the water. And similarly, the mother who wants to give her baby a comfortable bath knows as well as the scientist that dipping her fingers in the water may be an unreliable guide. We can make a much more objective judgement if we note the effect the water has on something inanimate, and a more precise judgement if we can quantify the effect it has on, say, a column of mercury. In the end, then, the scientist does not rely on the temperature sense in making judgements concerning heat, and it might be tempting to think of him as discounting the evidence of his senses here, and in this respect at least stepping outside his skin. It may seem but a short step from here to the claim that really the scientist is not concerned with heat as something he feels, and that his precise judgements concern a quality he *cannot* feel. But this claim again involves a misrepresentation of the facts. The truth is that in his search for precision the scientist finds the temperature sense unreliable, and so has an excellent reason for relying on *another* sense and on what he can *see*. The fact that the mother could use a thermometer to make absolutely sure that the water will not cause her baby discomfort does not even seem to suggest that she is not aware of the heat of the water when she puts her hand in, and the fact that the scientist cannot make a precise judgement by feel should not be interpreted as meaning that his precise judgement concerns an essentially occult quality. Taste presents additional problems, for not only do our judgements concerning taste seem particularly subjective, but we also find that the taste of an object does not affect other objects as its heat does. It is primarily for this reason that the physicist at least has little to say about tastes.

A theory concerning the sub-microscopic structure of objects is attractive because it may explain, at least in very general terms, how one object can affect other objects in various ways and be affected by them, and included in this is the possibility of giving an account of how we perceive objects as we do. We ordinarily judge that the piece of paper is white because this is the colour we see it as having under standard light conditions. But at the same time we recognize that the appearance of the paper varies according to the light conditions and that, even under what we think of as standard conditions, it will look different to a mite. This being so we welcome an account which will explain how it is that we see the paper as white under standard conditions, why the apparent colour varies when the conditions change, and why the mite sees different colours in objects from those we see. What we are offered is an account which describes the object without reference to colour, and which takes into the reckoning the nature of the object as scientifically described, the nature of light, and the characteristics of the sensory apparatus. It is primarily the explanatory force of this sort of story that persuades us to think of the scientist as telling us about the objects as they are in themselves.

To repeat, it is the philosopher (and sometimes the scientist) who sees the scientific story as being in conflict with the beliefs of the plain man. By and large the plain man is enthusiastic in his acceptance of the findings of science and yet prepared for ordinary purposes to go on talking as he always did. But this should not surprise us. For, given that Russell is even roughly right in saying that when we attribute a colour to an object we mean that this is the colour the object appears to us to have under usual light conditions, it is clear that no scientific theory need be regarded as in conflict with the ordinary beliefs. There is something faintly absurd in Russell's suggestion that it is 'to avoid favouritism' that we should refrain from attributing any colour to the table, as becomes clear when we put the emphasis on the 'we'. *We* have every reason for taking the normal human being (rather than the mite or the Martian) as our starting point, and *we* can give good reasons for (say) not choosing to regard the light conditions at twilight as standard. The truth is, rather, that we refrain from attributing colours to objects when we have a very specific purpose in mind, and when we want an account of objects which will contribute to an explanation of how they come to look to us as they do. Rather similarly, perhaps, retailers would not stop labelling arsenic as a poison if it were discovered that Martians thrived on it, but the plain man would be interested in, and certainly not affronted by, any account of arsenic which could help explain how it is that arsenic is a poison for us and a food for others.

No doubt there is more to be said about the relationship between, say, the description of a tomato as red and the scientific description which appears in the account of how we see it as red, for there are mistakes to be avoided and the claim that neither description is false and both appropriate in context is one that leaves various questions unanswered. If our main concern was with Locke it would be appropriate to follow some of these questions up, for Locke was impressed and influenced by the scientific thinking of the day, and many of the things he says can be understood *only* in the light of his concern to see what implications a scientific view has for our more ordinary views about the world. To do justice to Locke we would have to dwell on what is known as *the argument from physics*, the argument which says that the tomato cannot *be* red because physics has 'shown' it to be colourless. We shall have one further comment to make on this argument in a moment. First, though, and this is more important, we must be clear that *Berkeley* was in no position to appeal to the findings of the physicists. Locke accepted the scientific story and could legitimately concern himself with the question as to whether and to what extent our ordinary beliefs must be modified by this acceptance. Berkeley's position is quite different. Berkeley vigorously *rejects* the pretensions of science to give a description of the world as it exists independently of our perception of it.

This point has to be made and indeed stressed, and we must bear it in mind when we consider an argument such as the following from Benson Mates which is given in support of Berkeley's claim that the data of sense can exist only when perceived:

> Everything known about perception indicates that our data are the joint product of a number of factors always including certain states of the nervous system and usually, but not always, including an external stimulus. The striking correlation between the occurrence and nature of data and the occurrence and nature of our neurological processes is evidence for the view that without these processes there would be no data. That this correlation exists is, I suppose, a contingent fact. It could have happened that what was perceived always depended simply upon the external stimulus and not upon the internal states of the perceiver, and if that had been the case we should have had far less reason for believing that the data do not exist independently. (pp. 172-3)

Of course much in this passage reads strangely in a paper entitled 'Berkeley was Right'. Throughout the paper Mates is quite happy to help himself to the view that there are external objects, and as he allows both that in *one* sense of 'see' we can be said to see these, and that they do exist independently, he seems to be committed to just that sort of representationalism which Berkeley was so concerned to *oppose*. Indeed if Berkeley was *right* on something in Mates's eyes it seems to have been at just that point at which Berkeley took himself to be at one with the materialists, and that is in holding that the immediate objects of perception are mind-dependent data which, in one important sense of the word, are all we ever see. If I read him right, Mates is really much more Lockian than Berkeleian. This may explain his use of the argument contained in the above passage, for the point we need to be clear on is that, whatever its merits or demerits, the argument is one *Berkeley* was not entitled to use. Locke could take for granted the scientific explanation of perception because he believed that neurophysiological processes played a causal role in the production of data. Not so with Berkeley. Berkeley is quite clear on the point that any physiological apparatus which we *suppose* plays a causal role in the production of ideas will itself consist of ideas and thus be incapable of playing the causal role.[21]

Having made this point about what he was *entitled* to appeal to, we must go on to admit that Berkeley was influenced by what the materialists said concerning the mental existence of secondary qualities, and that as Locke was influenced by the scientific story then this story may have had, and surely did have, an *indirect* influence on Berkeley. It is from this point of view that we cannot ignore Locke's reason for taking it to be obvious that colours as we perceive them are only in the mind. And I take it that Locke accepted this view partly because he saw the scientist as denying that objects have colours on them, and partly because he believed that we are aware only of data produced in the mind *by* external objects. We are back in fact with the unfortunate dualism between perceived ideas and outward objects. Given that the colouring is not 'on' the outward object or the object as it is in itself, the natural conclusion is that it can be only a characteristic of the idea produced in the mind *by* the object.

It seems to me that however understandable it may be that Locke should have made it, there is a false move in his thinking. Indeed we have to revert here to the criticism we made of the Causal Theory in Ch. 2. We said there that the scientist purports to account for our awareness of external objects, and that if we are impressed by his story we should not interpret him as showing that really our awareness is limited to ideas in our minds. At this stage we should remind ourselves that when the scientist talks about the perception of *colour* we must see him as explaining, not how we become aware of colour sensations or coloured appearances, but rather how we come to see the external object *as* coloured. Equally, of course, he can explain how we come to see it differently in different lights, and how a creature with unusual sensory apparatus might see it yet differently. What we need to insist on is that nothing in scientific thinking need suggest that when we see the paper as white (or as any other colour) we are perceiving anything but the paper. Indeed if it is the plausibility of scientific explanations that worries us I think we *must* say that it is implicit in the enterprise that what we see is the surface of the paper as scientifically described, which surface we see as white because the light is as it is and our sensory apparatus is what it is. In this context at any rate the ideas, sensations or appearances (conceived of as distinct items) must be thought of as the result of a *misinterpretation* of the findings of science. It is one thing to say that the colour we see a tomato as having depends (in part) on the nature of our sensory apparatus. It is quite another to say that the colour characterizes an item existing within the mind. Really the only live issue is whether, if we accept a scientific account of objects, we are bound to regard many of the things we would ordinarily say as false. And here I am strongly inclined to defend the right of sentient beings to describe objects on the basis of the way they characteristically appear to them.[22]

To sum up, then, the suggestion is that Locke supposed colours as we see them to exist only in the mind because he held (as Berkeley did not) that science gives a true account of objects as they are in themselves, *and* because he combined with this a theory of perception according to which the corporeal objects were thought of as the remote causes of those things we immediately perceive. I very much doubt whether, had he not been thinking in these terms, he would ever have thought that the argument from the relativity of perception was sufficient to prove that colours, odours, tastes and sounds (as we perceive them) are only in us. Locke was impressed by the obvious and undisputed fact that the way a thing appears depends in part on the *circumstances* in which it is perceived and on what we can characterize broadly as the *condition* of the perceiver, and he saw that the fact of the relativity of perception invited an attempt to give a scientific account of the object in terms of which we can explain variations in the way it appears. But if Locke treats the appearances as themselves perceived objects this is not (at least primarily) because of the argument from the relativity of perception. The primary reason is that he is a Causal Theorist.

Whatever we may make of Locke's thinking, though, it is quite plain that Berkeley *does* have to rely on the argument from the relativity of perception to make his point. He cannot draw support for his claim that colours are mind-dependent appearances from an appeal either to the scientific story (which he does not accept) or to the Causal Theory (which, in the form in which the materialist holds it, he takes to be incoherent). And the truth is that without this background he cannot prove either that the things we perceive are discrete items or that they exist only in the mind. To get the argument going Berkeley has to characterize situations as we would normally characterize them, and given this starting point his aim must be to show that the perceptual facts are inconsistent with the initial characterization. Unfortunately, though, the fact that the object we suppose we all perceive will, for example, look different as the circumstances change does not suggest that what we are seeing is anything other than one public object with determinate qualities. So long as we refuse to admit, for example, that any object which under special circumstances *appears* yellow must *be* yellow and that any white object must *look* white whatever the conditions, there would seem to be no reason why we should posit appearances as things, or, indeed, why we should discard our belief that, even when it looks yellow, what we see may yet be white.

CHAPTER SEVEN

The Perceiving Self

'From the principles we have laid down, it follows, human knowledge may naturally be reduced to two heads, that of *ideas*, and that of *spirits*.' (*Pr.* 86)

I

Writers on Berkeley have tended to make two mistakes in treating of his views on spirit, the first being that of supposing that because he says relatively little about spirit in the published works he must have had little to say, and the second being that of supposing that the view he did hold was essentially the same as Locke's. To those who make these mistakes it seems that little time need be spent on examining what Berkeley says about the knowing self, and that at any rate Berkeley is culpable for not having realized that his arguments against material substance had equal force against spiritual substance. The very common criticism of Berkeley that he just failed to realize, as Hume did realize, that on his principles matter and spirit should be treated as on a par, is one that very largely misses the mark, and this because too often it rests upon a false assumption about what the view actually was.

It must be admitted that Berkeley himself is to some extent to blame for the misinterpretation here. Locke had emphasized that if there are difficulties about the concept of material substance, there are equally difficulties about the concept of spiritual substance. For example in II xxiii 5 he says:

> It is plain then, that the idea of *corporeal substance* in matter is as remote from our conceptions and apprehensions, as that of *spiritual substance*, or spirit: and therefore, from our not having any notion of the substance of spirit, we can no more conclude its non-existence, than we can, for the same reason, deny the existence of body; it being as rational to affirm there is no body, because we have no clear and distinct idea of the substance of matter, as to say there is no spirit, because we have no clear and distinct idea of the substance of spirit.

Locke suggests, then, that there are the two sorts of substance and that these should be treated as on a par in that we have no clear apprehension of the nature of either, but feel bound to posit a substratum for the passions and operations of the mind just as we feel bound to posit a substratum for the qualities and powers of body. In view of this one might have expected that if Berkeley was going to exclude matter from his system, but accept spirit, he would have been acutely conscious of the need to make a special case for spirit. In fact, however, he is scathing about matter, but, in the first editions of the *Principles* and *Dialogues* at least, almost complacent in his acceptance of spirit. Spirit is introduced rather casually in *Pr.* 2, and in a way which does nothing to make it clear that he is not operating with the Lockian concept, and when he returns to it in later sections the one point he seems really concerned to emphasize is the negative one that we have and can have no idea of it. The alert reader should spot that Berkeley's view of spirit does differ from Locke's in important respects, but these differences are not spelt out in any detail and the reader is not left with the impression that Berkeley is alive to the pressing challenge implicit in Locke's claim that it is as rational – or irrational – to accept the existence of the one sort of substance as it is to accept the existence of the other.

The notion that Berkeley blithely and uncritically accepted the Lockian concept of spirit and left it to Hume to disabuse us of it is, however, quite implausible. We can hardly avoid the conclusion that there must be something wrong with it when we realize, first, that Berkeley himself anticipated the objection that there is parity of case between the two sorts of substance and indeed stated the case against including one and excluding the other very forcibly, and, second, that, though there are difficulties of interpretation here, at one stage when he was filling the notebooks he was himself prepared to talk about mind in what looks like a Humean way. Clearly he at least thought that he had an answer to the objection and that he had good reasons for modifying the view of mind taken at one stage in the *Commentaries*.

The problem is stated by Hylas in the *Dialogues*:

> You say your own soul supplies you with some sort of an idea or image of God. But at the same time you acknowledge you have, properly speaking, no idea of your own soul. You even affirm that spirits are a sort of beings altogether different from ideas. Conse-

> quently that no idea can be like a spirit. We have therefore no idea of any spirit. You admit nevertheless that there is spiritual substance, although you have no idea of it; while you deny there can be such a thing as material substance, because you have no notion or idea of it. Is this fair dealing? To act consistently, you must either admit matter or reject spirit. (iii, 232)

And again:

> Notwithstanding all you have said, to me it seems, that according to your own way of thinking, and in consequence of your own principles, it should follow that you are only a system of floating ideas, without any substance to support them. Words are not to be used without a meaning. And as there is no more meaning in spiritual substance than in material substance, the one is to be exploded as well as the other. (iii, 233)[1]

In the *Dialogues* Philonous vigorously rejects this, arguing that there is 'upon the whole no parity of case', but at one stage in the *Commentaries* Berkeley had talked as if he himself had accepted what he was to make Hylas claim. Thus in *PC* 579 he says:

> Consult, ransack y^r Understanding w^t find you there besides several perceptions or thoughts. W^t mean you by the word mind you must mean something that you perceive or y^t you do not perceive. a thing not perceived is a contradiction. to mean (also) a thing you do not perceive is a contradiction. We are in all this matter strangely abused by words.

Mind, he says in the next entry, is simply 'a congeries of Perceptions'. By the time he came to publish, though, mind was something 'very different from ideas, and which being an agent cannot be like unto, or represented by, any idea whatsoever' (*Pr.* 27).

One reason for the rather skimpy treatment of mind in the *Principles* is that the work we have was originally intended to be but the first volume in an inquiry extending to perhaps four volumes. When the *Principles* first appeared in 1710 the words 'Part 1' were printed on the title page, at the head of the text after the introduction, and then at the top of every page. Nor is there any mystery about the topics the second volume would have dealt with. Four entries in the *Commentaries* are relevant here:

> The 2 great Principles of Morality. the Being of a God & the Freedom of Man: these to be handled in the beginning of the Second Book. (508)

> The Existence of any thing imaginable is nothing different from Imagination or perception. Volition or Will wch is not imaginable regard must not be had to its' existence at least in the first Book. (792)

> Say you, at this rate all's nothing but Idea meer phantasm. I answer every thing as real as ever. I hope to call a thing Idea makes it not the less real. truly I should perhaps have stuck to ye word thing and not mention'd the Word Idea were it not for a Reason & I think a good one too wch I shall give in ye Second Book. (807)

> Extension tho it exist only in the Mind, yet is no Property of the Mind, The Mind can exist without it tho it cannot without the Mind. But in Book 2 I shall at large shew the difference there is betwixt the Soul & Body or Extended being: (878)

Of course when it came to it Berkeley was not quite so reticent about mind in Part 1 as it appears he had at one stage intended to be. He is primarily concerned with bodies or extended beings, but he could hardly defend his view that these are mind-dependent ideas without saying something at least about the minds they are dependent on. He is, though, careful not to say too much, choosing when he does deal with spirit to stress the essential difference between the active and the passive in experience. His thoughts about mind would have been developed in Part 2.

Nearly twenty years after the publication of Part I Samuel Johnson, the American philosopher, wrote to Berkeley raising some interesting questions and objections based on his reading of the *Principles*. Many of these were in fact such that one would have expected them to be dealt with in the second part, and Johnson himself remarks:

> ... I shall live with some impatience till I see the second part of your design accomplished ...

To this Berkeley replies:

> As to the Second Part of my treatise concerning the *Principles of Human Knowledge*, the fact is that I had made a considerable progress on it; but the manuscript was lost about fourteen years ago, during my travels in Italy, and I never had leisure since to do so disagreeable a thing as writing twice on the same subject.

In a second letter Johnson again expresses his desire to see the second part completed, but Berkeley makes no further mention of it in his reply.[2] In the 1734 edition the words 'Part 1' were dropped from the title page, though they remained at the head of the text and the top of each page, perhaps, as Jessop suggests, 'as a confession and reminder of the incompleteness of the work' (*Works* II, p. 5).

There are writers on Berkeley who loyally maintain that it was only the loss of a manuscript that prevented the appearance of a volume which would have presented a full account of the nature of mind and its relation to body, but it is very difficult to escape the conclusion that Berkeley would have found it far from easy to produce this volume, and that he was genuinely worried about paradoxes and serious problems arising from what he wanted to say. It is a mistake to think that Berkeley did not realize that he had to show that his arguments against Lockian material substance left room for an account of spiritual substance, for he did realize this and he thought he had a convincing answer. It is equally a mistake to suppose that at one time he had in his possession a manuscript which contained the details of a view which he could regard as in every way satisfactory. There were, as Jessop says there may have been, 'problems that he could not work out in detail to his satisfaction' (*Works* II, p. 7). It seems clear that it was the intransigence of these problems, as much as the loss of a manuscript, that accounts for his failure to publish Part 2.

As it is, the most important source for our knowledge of Berkeley's thinking about spirit is the *Commentaries*, and here we learn something just by looking at the distribution of 'S' entries – he uses this sign to stand for 'Soul or Spirit' – through the two notebooks. In the first notebook there are just fifteen of these entries – 34, 84, 96, 121, 145, 145a, 146, 149, 155, 166, 176, 176a, 194a, 230 and 357. But in the second notebook there are 121 such entries – 423, 478, 478a, 479, 490, 499, 499a, 523, 539, 548, 572, 576, 576a, 578, 582, 585, 587, 599, 609-11, 611a, 612-13, 616, 621, 626-31, 635, 643-5,

The Perceiving Self

649-54, 656-61, 661a, 663, 665, 667, 672, 672a, 673-4, 681, 684, 689, 692, 699-701, 704, 706-9, 712-4, 743-5, 752-3, 756, 776-7, 780, 785-6, 788, 791, 795-9, 806, 808, 810, 812, 814-6, 819-22, 828-9, 833, 841-2, 847-50, 854, 857, 863, 867, 870-2, 875, 879, 886-8. The first eleven 'S' entries in the second notebook are spread thinly over 37 folio pages, but with 576, the first of the 'Humean' entries, there begins an amazing concentration. 110 of the 136 'S' entries in the *Commentaries* are contained in the last 324 entries, so that over a third of the later part of the second notebook is devoted to spirit.[3]

Just looking at the distribution of 'S' entries in the *Commentaries* suggests, then, that Berkeley was at first concerned to develop his case against the independent existence of sensible objects (to be argued for in Part 1 of the *Principles*) rather than to consider the nature of the perceiving subject (to be dealt with in Part 2). We have seen that by entry 378 he had developed his attack on matter to a stage where he felt able to give a summary of arguments to be 'proposd shorter & more separate in the Treatise'. Up to this stage he had given scant attention to the mind or that which perceives ideas. This is not to say that he had given *no* thought to the question. In entry 14 for example we find him making a distinction between the *soul* and the *person* and saying:

> Eternity is onely a train of innumerable ideas. hence the immortality of ye Soul easily conceiv'd. or rather the immortality of the person, y^t of ye soul not being necessary for ought we can see.

The hesitation over terminology is typical of Berkeley's thought during the period when doctrines to be found in the published works were being developed. Similar hesitation about the use of the words 'soul' and 'person' will be found in entry 25.

If, though, the first notebook contains relatively little on the self, Berkeley did come to realize that if he was to claim that sensible things are mind-dependent he had to be able to give a coherent account of the nature of the perceiving subject and one compatible with his rejection of material substance, and so we have this problem dominating his thought in later entries. In fact the last 110 'S' entries can be seen as reflecting the rapid development of his thought towards the position he takes up in the *Principles* as published in 1710, though, as he makes quite clear, the position was one he intended to work out fully only in the second book. We have here, then, notes for a work which was never published, but they are essentially early notes.

No doubt Berkeley originally intended to publish the second part of the *Principles* at an early date, though, as has been suggested, it is difficult to believe he could have done this. At any rate we do know that the reception given to the first part was such as to decide him to delay continuing with the project, at least until he had published the *Dialogues* to clarify what he had already said. The manuscript of Part 2 was lost when he was in Italy in 1716. This was some eight years after the completion of the *Commentaries*, and doubtless the manuscript would have revealed developments in his thought. It may be that if we had to rely on the 'S' entries for our knowledge of Berkeley's view of spirit we would be in a position comparable to that we would be in if we had to rely on, say, the first 378 entries in the notebooks for our knowledge of his arguments concerning sensible objects. Luckily our position is not quite that desperate. Even if Berkeley does say less about spirit in the published works than we would like, we do have what he says in the first editions of the *Principles* and *Dialogues*, together with relevant contributions elsewhere, including those in additions to the *Principles* and *Dialogues* when these were republished in one volume in 1734 and Berkeley realised there was going to be no second part to the *Principles*.

II

As is so often the case, the move Berkeley makes in arriving at his own view of spirit is essentially simple, and we can best understand what it is if we take our cue from the very hesitant distinction he makes in *PC* 14 and 25 between the *soul* and the *person*. For what he clearly has in mind here is the distinction to be found in Locke between the substance of spirit and the intuitively known self or person. Of the person, the *I* we are conscious of in all experience, Locke says:

> As for *our own existence*, we perceive it so plainly and so certainly, that it neither needs nor is capable of any proof. For nothing can be more evident to us than our own existence. I think, I reason, I feel pleasure and pain: can any of these be more evident to me than my own existence? If I doubt of all other things, that very doubt makes me perceive my own existence, and will not suffer me to doubt of

that. For if I know I feel pain, it is evident I have as certain perception of my own existence, as of the existence of the pain I feel: or if I know I doubt, I have as certain perception of the existence of the thing doubting, as of that thought which I *call doubt* (IV ix 3)

Here we have, then, in Locke's view, something which is apprehended in experience and intuitively known. When I smell a rose or look at the sun, reason, doubt or fear, I am conscious not only of the smell of the rose, the appearance of the sun, the reasoning, doubting or fearing, but also of myself as a perceiving *thing* for which the objects I am conscious of are objects. The problem arises not when we try to justify the claim that there is that in us which thinks, for this 'neither needs nor is capable of any proof', but rather when we try to investigate the nature of the thinking thing. For Locke had had things to say about spiritual substance earlier in the *Essay* and he had claimed that it is the *unknown* substratum of reasoning, thinking, fearing and the like.

When it came to considering the relationship between the person, which is something I am aware of, on the one hand, and spiritual substance, which is something we suppose must exist though it is 'remote from our conceptions and apprehensions' on the other, what Locke had to say was, not surprisingly, less than satisfactory. In II xxvii, a chapter added in the second edition of the *Essay*, he maintains that it is *consciousness* that makes a self, that the identity of a person through time, unlike that of a spiritual substance, depends upon consciousness, and that it is *conceivable* that unbeknown to us the thinking substance could change and yet the person remain the same. In IV iii 6 he even goes so far as to admit that it is *possible* that God may have chosen to add the power of thought to *material* substance. Berkeley thought this concession 'dangerous' (*PC* 695), but we can see that he is writing in the spirit of Locke when he says it is the continuity of consciousness after death that is the important thing and not the immortality of any particular soul or spiritual substance.

I have argued elsewhere (see Tipton 1) that Berkeley's mature view involves essentially the whole-hearted rejection of Lockian spiritual substance and the development of doctrines about the person, which Berkeley takes to be the conscious thing we are aware of in all experience, the *esse* of which is just to be conscious or *percipere*. In *PC* 713-4 he helps to obscure things for us by resolving not to use the word 'person' so as to avoid criticism from the Church, and in the published works he uses 'mind', 'spirit', 'soul' or 'myself' to refer to what is basically Locke's *person*. In the simplest terms the development is from an acceptance of the distinction between the soul or spiritual substance on the one hand and the person on the other, through the rejection of the first to the acceptance of the second as a substance which supports ideas in the sense that it perceives them. This move parallels the move he makes in his analysis of the objects of sense experience. What he is prepared to accept are the things Locke agrees we are immediately aware of, ideas and the person, and what is rejected is anything mysterious and unknown lying behind these. Further, as the rejection of anything material lying behind our ideas of sense leads to the recognition of these ideas as themselves constituents of a real world, so rejection of any unknown spiritual substrate leads to the recognition of the *I* which each of us is conscious of in his experience as itself a perceiving and active substance. The simple answer to the Lockian objection, that if material substance is to be rejected then spiritual substance should be rejected too, is that this point is valid if we are thinking of spiritual substance as the unknown substratum of mental acts, but that the objection has no weight at all against Berkeleian spiritual substance which is essentially Locke's person and something which, in Locke's own words, has an existence which 'neither needs nor is capable of any proof'.

This, then, is the story in outline. Any detailed study of entries in the *Commentaries* complicates the picture somewhat. For, as we have already seen, it was only in the second notebook that Berkeley seriously turned his attention to the perceiving subject, and when he did, he had to work out his position against a background of principles, terminology and arguments which had seemed sound when his primary concern was with the sensible, but which now began to seem less obviously satisfactory. The view outlined so briefly in the published works was not arrived at easily, and when the concentration of 'S' entries referred to in the last section begins, soul and person have alike gone into the melting-pot from which a developed account of the person eventually emerges but in which the soul, or Lockian spiritual substance, is quickly lost.

What had happened was that in formulating his attack on material substance Berkeley had used principles which made it very difficult for him to give *any* account of the perceiving subject as something distinct from its ideas and operations. There were two distinct factors here. First, in his demonstration of entry 378 he had been happy to rely on the Lockian axioms that all knowledge is about ideas and all significant words stand for ideas, and, again taking his cue from Locke, he had claimed that our ideas include just those 'from without', which would be sensed ideas and mental images, and those 'from within', which he says are the operations of the mind. And the trouble with this is that if the soul and person are supposed to be distinct from the mind's passive objects and its operations, then not only can they not be known, but the words standing for them must be insignificant. Strict adherence to these axioms in effect meant that Berkeley found himself wielding a two-edged sword, one which came down heavily on external existence as it was designed to do, but one which unfortunately seemed just as capable of demolishing any account of the self as something distinct from passive ideas and mental operations. The second difficulty arose from the fact that while wanting to hold that the *esse* of the perceiving subject was *percipere* (entry 429) Berkeley also held that sense-perception was simply the passive reception of ideas. The great advantage of this was that it ruled out the concept of an act of perception, and thus provided him with an easy answer to anyone who might suggest that the act of perception is mind-dependent but deny that the same is true of the object of perception. The disadvantage was that it made it difficult to see how the mind conceived of as that which perceives, or passively receives, can be thought of as distinct from the ideas perceived. If perception is passive the perceiving mind can only be the passive receiver or container of ideas, and it seems certain that we have no awareness of any such thing in experience.

Eventually, the way out of the first of these difficulties was not hard to find, though it is essentially two-pronged. First, as to the soul or Lockian spiritual substance, Berkeley wants to say that we have no idea of it, and are not aware of it in experience, and that therefore talk of it is meaningless. This is essentially what he is saying in entry 579 – 'a thing not perceived is a contradiction. to mean (also) a thing you do not perceive is a contradiction'. But with the person the case is different. Accepting that we are aware of ourselves as conscious things Berkeley had a choice. That is he could say *either* that our ideas include not only those referred to in entry 378 but also the person which is to count as an idea because we have an intuition of it, *or* that the person is something we have an immediate awareness of in all experience but that as an object it is different enough from other objects for us to mark this difference by not calling it an idea. This is the answer he hints at in entries 522-3. First he notes down the axiom he had used as proposition 2 in his demonstration, now giving a reference to Locke to show that at this stage the axiom is not being used but rather put up for critical examination:

All knowlege onely about ideas. V. Locke B.4 c.1.

The marginal sign 'M' here suggests that Berkeley is acknowledging how useful he had found the axiom in disposing of the concept of matter. The following entry, though, has the marginal sign 'S':

It seems improper & liable to difficulties to make the Word Person stand for an Idea, or to make our selves Ideas or thinking things ideas.

Already (entry 490) he had queried whether he should after all call the operations of the mind *ideas*, and eventually, finding support in what Locke says about particles (entries 661 and 667) he decided to restrict the term to sensible and imaginable objects. He did not, though, accept the suggestion of entry 523 at once. We find him using the Lockian axiom as late as in entry 639 – an entry later marked with the reject sign.

Combined with the fact that in the published works he refers to the person as 'spirit', 'soul' and 'substance', Berkeley's claim that we have, and can have, no *idea* of it was bound to trouble his contemporary readers. As Hylas says, it seems unfair to use the fact that we have no idea of material substance as a reason for saying there is no such thing while insisting that though we have no idea of spirit it none the less exists. As we have seen, Berkeley did not want to say much about spirit in Part 1 of the *Principles*, but his allowance there, and in the *Dialogues*, that we can 'in a large sense' be said to have an *idea* of it was his way of forestalling the objection and saying that what he is talking about is something we do have experience of. His own view is that the natures of the passive objects of experience on the one hand, and the active subject which is known through its activity on the other, are 'perfectly disagreeing and unlike' (*Pr.* 139) and that this fundamental dissimilarity should be reflected in the terms we use to refer to them. The doctrine becomes that there are things we are aware of that are not (Berkeleian) ideas and that these include not just the self but also acts of the self and, by 1734, relations. Doubting, to take one case of an act of mind, is not an idea because it is not primarily an object for mind but rather something we are aware of through doing it. Spirit is not an idea because whereas the *esse* of ideas is *percipi*, spirit is known through its perception of, or operations about, ideas. And relations are said to be not ideas because they *include* an act of mind.

The well known 'Humean' entries (576-81) and later entries in a similar vein are difficult to interpret, but I considered these in my earlier article and here a more summary approach may be useful. And what I want to say is that these entries are less Humean than they look and that, while the person and the soul were alike in the melting-pot at this stage, Berkeley is tackling his problems piecemeal and is primarily concerned here with a container theory of the self. First he concentrates his attention on the understanding conceived of as the unknown substratum of ideas, then he turns to consider the will conceived of as the unknown substratum of volitions, and only later does he salvage the person, which is something he can claim we know, and are aware of, in experience. It is easy to miss this, for in entries 576-81 he talks about the *mind* and *soul* (not, note, the *person*) and only afterwards (entry 587) suggests that his conclusion may refer only to the *understanding* conceived of as that which perceives ideas, and that further attention must be given to the *will*. Eventually (entry 615) he comes up with the provisional answer that just as the understanding is not distinct from its perceptions so the will is not distinct from its volitions, but, as he tells us on the verso, this was 'alter'd hereafter'.

In his note on the 'Humean' entries Luce claims that the person 'stands in the background'. He would agree that Berkeley is indeed tackling his problems piecemeal, and that he is concerned first with the mind conceived of as 'Somthing unknown wch perceives & supports & ties together the Ideas' (entry 637). We should not suppose though that he had fully made up his mind about the person, or reached a final decision as to how (or even whether) he could incorporate it into his system. His mature doctrine still had to be developed and whereas by the time he came to publish he could say that the *esse* of the self is *percipere* and that the self is an active *thing* distinct from its perceptions, mid-way through the *Commentaries* he was not ready to say this. At this stage perception was simply the passive reception of ideas. In entry 301, for example, he had said:

> Whatsoever has any of our ideas in it must perceive, it being that very having, that passive reception of ideas that denominates the mind perceiving. that being the very essence of perception, or that wherein perception consists.

This suggests, of course, that perception is rather something that happens to the mind than something we do, and though even at this stage Berkeley did want to hold that the *esse* of the perceiving mind was *percipere*, it struck him, I think, that we are not *aware* of the self as a passive container. It is interesting to note that entry 301 was originally marked with the marginal signs 'M' and 'S' but that the 'S' is crossed out, giving us ground for supposing that here too Berkeley realized, or came to realize, that he was operating with a principle that was useful in his attack on the independent existence of sensible objects, but that it gave rise to serious difficulties when one came to consider the self.

One obvious way out of the difficulty was, of course, to make perceiving an act of mind, and this is the one Berkeley takes. He continues to think of the mind as passive in sense perception in that in a given situation we cannot choose what we shall perceive, but rather have it presented to us, but he at the same time regards it as active in that the activity of the perceiving mind is essential to awareness. Some late entries in the *Commentaries* point to this change of view. For example:

> While I exist or have any Idea I am eternally, constantly willing, my acquiescing in the present State is willing. (791)

> It seems there can be no perception, no Idea without Will, being there are no Ideas so indifferent but one had rather Have them than annihilation, or annihilation than them. (833)

> I must not Mention the Understanding as a faculty or part of the Mind, I must include Understanding & Will etc in the word Spirit by w[ch] I mean all that is active. (848)

The last entry here continues with the explicit rejection of the position taken in entries 614-5 where the understanding was taken to be not distinct from its ideas, and the will not distinct from its volitions. The mature view is that the understanding is not the mind as it passively receives ideas because understanding is 'in some sort an Action' (entry 821), and indeed that perceiving must be thought of as something we *do* in that the activity of the mind is essential to it. Locke would agree with this last point. In summarizing his view Aaron draws attention to the 'involuntary' aspect of sense perception, but adds:

> Of course, the mind must receive, it must 'take notice'. Sense-perception like other forms of perception is an act, it does not proceed mechanically. . . . If the word 'impression' is used it is important to remember that in respect of mind this term is metaphorical only. The mind is not a piece of wax to take an impression . . . [it] is an active entity possessing this power of being aware of things, although in sensation it must take what is given it and cannot at all choose . . . (Aaron 1, p. 133)

This I think fairly summarizes Berkeley's view of the matter too, and the shift enables him to regard sense perception as being one manifestation of the activity of that perceiving thing which is essentially active. In *Pr.* 27 he summarizes his own view of spiritual substance by saying:

> A spirit is one simple, undivided, active being: as it perceives ideas, it is called the *understanding*, and as it produces or otherwise operates about them, it is called the *will*.

It is, of course, only because he has come to recognize activity in perception that he can take this line.[4]

III

Berkeley holds, then, that in experience we are aware not only of what are essentially objects for mind but also of the mind's operation about ideas and of the mind itself which is the centre of consciousness and action. In replying to Hylas, Philonous is able to insist that 'I know or am conscious of my own being' and that there is no parity of case between spiritual substance and material substance because 'you neither perceive matter objectively, as you do an inactive being or idea, nor know it, as you do your self by a reflex act'. He also holds that, while no sense can be made of the notion of matter *supporting* ideas or qualities, we can make sense of the notion of spirit supporting ideas once we realize that supporting ideas comes down to perceiving them.

In the *Principles* much is made of the basic distinction between the passive objects of experience and the active being which is the self, but Berkeley's views about spirit are not spelt out in very much more detail. In *Pr.* 27, though, he does oppose his own view to the view that there are two distinct powers, the will and the understanding, and that the conception of a soul or spiritual substance is again distinct from either of these. Elsewhere the notion that the soul is uncompounded is used as evidence that it is naturally immortal.[5]

Whether or not Berkeley's view of spirit will do, many common objections to it seem to miss the mark. We have already seen how Berkeley tried to forestall the Lockian objection that matter and spirit should be treated as on a par, and in the 1734 editions of the *Principles* and *Dialogues* he tried to make his position rather clearer by coupling his denial that we have an idea of spirit with the assertion that we have a *notion* of it. As it turned out this was not a wise move. Rather than taking him at his word and seeing his point here as being that 'we understand the meaning of the word' (*Pr.* 140), and that we know the meaning of the word because we have immediate and intuitive awareness of spirit through a reflex act or inward feeling, too many commentators have supposed that for Berkeley a notion is itself a sort of *thing* distinct from whatever it is a notion *of*. Mistakenly, then, these commentators take it that Berkeley is introducing a dualism between notions on the one hand and spirit and acts on the other. If he were, he would of course be in trouble. Again, though it was not directed specifically at him, Berkeley would not have had much time for Hume's objection. He would have agreed with Hume that the metaphor which has percepts being in the mind as actors are in a theatre is ultimately an unfortunate and misleading one, but he would dispute Hume's claim that philosophers are wrong when they say 'we are every moment intimately conscious of what we call our SELF', this self being conceived of as something having 'perfect identity and simplicity'. Berkeley would, I am sure, have noted that Hume was himself dissatisfied with his alternative analysis of the mind in terms of impressions and ideas, and he would have said that Hume was looking in the wrong place when he looked for a distinct impression or perception of the mind quite apart from its doings and what are essentially its objects. Berkeley would say that there is and can be no perception of the self in any way comparable to, say, the perception of redness or of weight. What I am aware of is that the perceptions are *mine* and that *I* perceive them, that my doings are *my* doings or acts. It is this, he would say, that Hume fails to allow for, and this which makes Hume unhappy with his own account.[6]

There is, though, one objection to Berkeley's view which he would himself have taken much more seriously, though it is rarely canvassed in the literature. For it is a fact that his view of spirit at least seemed to lead him to a paradox which his readers might have judged to be just as startling as the doctrines concerning sensible existence. For if in Part 1 Berkeley had to support the claim that ideas are dependent on the mind and that all the choir of heaven and furniture of the earth exists only so long as it is perceived, so in Part 2 of the *Principles* he would have had to recognize that the mind is dependent on ideas. If the *esse* of the mind is *percipere* it must follow that we, selves, exist only for so long as we are conscious, so once again Berkeley would seem to be in radical conflict with what the man in the street believes.[7] The claim that I cease to exist when in a dreamless sleep, or that you cease to exist when stunned, looks to be just as shocking as the claim that sensible objects are mind-dependent.

Now in the case of the dependence of sensible objects on a perceiver Berkeley felt that he was able to avoid too great a clash with ordinary views by maintaining that on his doctrine any given sensible object can be supposed to exist at any time when we normally suppose it exists, and this because God perceives things when we do not. And it is in fact true that Berkeley believed he had a way of escape from the position that *selves* have only an intermittent existence. On his view we do *not* have to say that I cease to be when I do not happen to be having ideas, any more than we have to say that a table or chair ceases to be when I cease to perceive it. The difficulty here was that the doctrine which enabled him to avoid intermittency with regard to spirit was not one that could be presented as bringing him closer to ordinary views, for the doctrine was one that would seem to the plain man to be quite as shocking as the notion that we cease to be when not perceiving.

Perhaps because the line he takes is so shocking, writers on Berkeley have tended not to notice the answer he does give but to attribute to him other answers, and sometimes answers he would have made no sense of. Russell, for example, is grotesquely wrong when he suggests that, for Berkeley, my mind when inactive continues to exist as an idea in the mind of God. And he is of course wrong again when he says that God's main function for Berkeley is 'to ensure the continued existence of minds' (Russell 6, p. 222). Though he gets Berkeley's position right later in this book, Johnston is at least misleading when he says:

> In dealing with persons, he simply reaffirmed, against Locke, the Cartesian view that the mind always thinks. Even in sleep the mind is active, and thus the mind as thinking substance is permanent and self-identical. (pp. 49-50)

Berkeley certainly held that Locke was wrong in supposing that a spirit could exist without thought (*PC* 650-1), but he shows no inclination to argue that therefore the mind must be thinking even at times when we would normally suppose it was not thinking. Obviously he *could* have solved his problem by saying that a sleeping man will *always* have thoughts even if he is not always conscious of them, but there is no reason to suppose that he would not have been just as contemptuous as is Locke of this notion. Finally, I cannot see any alternative to saying that Luce is plainly wrong when he suggests that Berkeley would have welcomed yet another expansion to his principle to make the *esse* of the self not simply *percipere* but rather *percipere aut posse percipere* (Luce 6, p. 7, and 7, p. 129). It is in fact very doubtful whether Berkeley would have regarded the expanded principle as intelligible, but, whether or not anything can be said for it, it is clear that the suggested expansion receives not one shred of support from anything Berkeley says, and that it is incompatible with the answer he actually gives to the problem of intermittency.

To see what Berkeley's way of escape was, we have to understand the idiosyncratic view of *time* which he had formulated in its essentials even before he started writing entries in the *Commentaries*. From a very early stage he was totally against the view of space and time which makes these, as it were, containers in which things and events happen to occur but which could exist independently of them. The Newtonian concept of absolute time he found unintelligible, and he came to regard it as an abstract idea. But Berkeley was also unhappy about Locke's thinking. Locke, who was clearly aware of problems connected with the concept of time, finds that for each of us the notion is *based in* the succession of ideas in his mind. This, though, is only the starting point. It is because I take duration to be something *other* than the succession of ideas in my mind that I am able to conceive of time as having passed during a period, as for example when I am in a dreamless sleep, when I am not aware of any succession. Again, Locke holds that 'the constant and regular succession of *ideas* in a waking man, is, as it were, the measure and standard of all other successions' (II xiv 12), but he recognizes that our subjective judgements are notoriously fallible and that we need an agreed standard if we are to order our lives aright. This we have chosen to find in the supposedly regular movement of the sun. Yet even this is not the end of the story. For Locke says that whatever standard we adopt we must be careful to distinguish between duration itself and the measure we use to judge of its length. Thus:

> Duration, in itself, is to be considered as going on in one constant, equal, uniform course: but none of the measures of it which we make use of can be *known* to do so ... (II xiv 21)

And so it is that time for Locke becomes not something subjective but something objective, the notion of which is rooted in the succession of ideas in the mind but which is itself such that I must regard it as distinct, not only from the succession of ideas in my mind, but also from any succession in nature which men may choose as a basis for measurement. As one writer on time has observed, Locke's treatment 'in spite of its subjective aspects, rather presupposes Absolute Time than constitutes any refutation of it' (Gunn, p. 69).

Now there is scope for argument about what Berkeley's view of time actually was, but one dominant strand in his thought is certainly that time is wholly subjective. The view is, as Johnston says, that 'each man's time is private' (p. 241), and this seems to mean that *for me* time is the succession of ideas in my mind while *for you* it is the succession of ideas in your mind. This is the line we find Berkeley taking on the first folio page in the *Commentaries* where he appears to be rejecting, not only the concept of absolute time, but also the concept of a public time which would allow the time that passes for me to be identical with the time that passes for you. The view seems to be essentially similar to that which Newman's Angel explains is held in heaven:

> And time is not a common property;
> But what is long is short, and swift is slow,
> And near is distant, as received and grasped
> By this mind and by that, and every one
> Is standard of his own chronology.
> *(The Dream of Gerontius)*

In this field, according to Berkeley, what seems to the individual to be the case is in fact the case.

From Berkeley's view of time here certain rather odd consequences are supposed to follow, and we can mention just two of them now. First, then, we are all aware that in certain circumstances, for example when we are bored, time seems to pass slowly, whereas on other occasions, for example when we are engrossed in what we are doing, it seems to pass quickly. Of course we normally suppose that what seems to be the case here must be opposed to what is really the case, but the subjectivist account of time seems to rule out any appeal to what is really the case if this is conceived of as distinct from what seems to be the case. Berkeley takes it to follow that if I am bored and you are engrossed then the time for me *is* longer than the time for you. We are reminded of the lunatic logic of Joseph Heller's Dunbar in *Catch 22*, for Dunbar believed he could 'slow down time' and he 'loved shooting skeet because he hated every minute and the time passed so slowly'. Berkeley's similarly paradoxical conclusion is that because time for a fly *is* the succession of ideas in the fly's mind:

> The age of a fly for ought that we know may be as long as y^t of a man. (*PC* 48)

We need not suppose that Berkeley welcomed this sort of conclusion. We know that he remained worried about the concept of time, and he may indeed have been struck by the suspicion that, in Johnston's words, 'the very description of the succession of one man's ideas as swifter than another's implies some standard' (p. 241).

The second odd consequence, and it is one Berkeley seems to have welcomed, is very relevant to our present inquiry. For whereas Locke found it quite possible to think of time as having passed when he was in a dreamless sleep, Berkeley has to say that as time for any agent is simply the succession of ideas in his mind there can be no question of time passing when he is not conscious. In *PC* 590 he says:

> No broken Intervals of Death or Annihilation. Those intervals are nothing. Each Person's time being measured to him by his own Ideas.

One way of putting the point would be to say that because for me there can be no distinction between time and the succession of ideas in my mind it must follow that when I stop thinking time stops passing. But this would obviously be misleading. The fact is that if Berkeley is right I cannot make any sense of the notion of my *stopping* thinking, or of time as ceasing to pass when this happens. Berkeley's position here has been misinterpreted, but Jessop surely gets it exactly right when he says: 'The soul always thinks because "always" has no meaning apart from something thought' (*Works* II, p. 270).

We can now see how Berkeley arrives at the notion that the soul always thinks from two quite different angles, both of which are reflected in one key passage in the *Principles*. First he says:

> Time therefore being nothing, abstracted from the succession of ideas in our minds, it follows that the duration of any finite spirit must be estimated by the number of ideas or actions succeeding each other in that same spirit or mind. Hence it is a plain consequence that the soul always thinks . . .

Here the approach is from his view of time. But he continues:

> . . . and in truth whoever shall go about to divide in this thoughts, or abstract the *existence* of a spirit from its *cogitation*, will, I believe, find it no easy task. (*Pr.* 98)[8]

And here the approach is from a quite different angle and from the explication of the meaning of 'exist' as applied to the perceiving subject or to that conscious thing which we cannot conceive of except as being conscious. What needs to be noted is, of course, that though both arguments are supposed to lead to the conclusion that we always think, the second unsupported by the first would suggest that when an agent is supposed to be unconscious he must necessarily be supposed to have ceased to exist. It is thus only Berkeley's surely unsatisfactory view of time that enables him to escape this consequence by ruling out the possibility of there being a time when the agent is not conscious. In brief, the soul always thinks (a) because the soul is what it is, and no sense can be made of the notion of a thing whose *esse* is *percipere* existing but not perceiving, and (b) because time is what it is and, to repeat Jessop's words, ' "always" has no meaning apart from something thought'. It is because Berkeley holds (b) as well as (a) that he is able to avoid the conclusion that the soul has only an intermittent existence. His thinking about time is, though, so odd that his answer to the problem of intermittency with regard to the self, rather than allowing for even the appearance of a reconciliation with ordinary views, leads to a further affront to those views.

In concluding this section we can look at something Johnson (Berkeley's American correspondent) says, for Johnson was understandably puzzled when he considered Berkeley's views about the person and about time. In the course of his questioning he points to what is clearly a very real difficulty when he says:

> ... when I suppose the existence of a spirit while it does not actually think, it does not appear to me that I do it by supposing an abstract idea of existence, and another of absolute time. The existence of John asleep by me, without so much as a dream is not an abstract idea, nor is the time passing the while an abstract idea ...

Johnson himself hankers after a Lockian soul – something which has the power of consciousness but whose *esse* is not *percipere* – which he can suppose continues to exist when the agent is not thinking, but ignoring this for the moment he is surely right in supposing that he can conceive time passing with John not thinking, just as John when he wakes up will be able to accept that time passed while he slept. It is, though, the possibility of John or Johnson thinking of such a time without indulging in illegitimate abstraction that Berkeley seems to be committed to denying.

Berkeley's reply to Johnson on this point is interesting, not because he indicates any way out of the difficulty, but because it shows that, years after the loss of a manuscript in which he is supposed to have made 'considerable progress' on questions concerning the relation between body and mind, he still adheres to the subjectivist view of time while acknowledging that he has long been aware that it gives rise to problems:

> A succession of ideas I take to *constitute* Time, and not to be only the sensible measure thereof, as Mr. Locke and others think. But in these matters every man is to think for himself, and speak as he finds. One of my earliest inquiries was about Time, which led me into several paradoxes that I did not think fit or necessary to publish; particularly the notion that the Resurrection follows the next moment to death.

That the paradox instanced does indeed follow from the position we have attributed to Berkeley is clear, for on this view no sense can be made of the notion of a period when I shall not be thinking coming between my death, when consciousness might be supposed to cease, and my resurrection, when consciousness is resumed. But on a more general point it is surely significant that here, as in the *Principles* and some entries in the *Commentaries*, his thoughts about time, which he 'did not think fit or necessary to publish', are related to doctrines concerning the person. That his views on the person are closely related to his views on time, and that together these gave rise to serious difficulties is, then, obvious. The fact that Berkeley realised this should, I think, give pause to those who suppose that only the loss of a manuscript prevented the early publication of a second part of the *Principles*.

IV

Philosophical problems concerning the nature of time and the relation of mind to body are almost as old as philosophy itself and these topics continue to be the subject of lively debate today, so it is clearly too much to expect that in two sections of one chapter of a book on Berkeley we should correct what he says by showing what the right answers are. What we can usefully do is to take another look at his thinking on these questions to see how moves that are at the very least suspect led to perplexity rather than enlightenment. On time the natural place to start is with Augustine's well known question in the *Confessions*:

> What, then, is Time? If no one asks me, I know; if I wish to explain it to one that asketh, I know not.

Berkeley too is aware that normally we find no difficulties in *using* temporal concepts:

> Time, place, and motion, taken in particular or concrete, are what every body knows; but having passed through the hands of a metaphysician, they become too abstract and fine, to be apprehended by men of ordinary sense. Bid your servant meet you at such a *time*, in such a *place*, and he shall never stay to deliberate on the meaning of those words: in conceiving that particular time and place, or the motion by which he is to get thither, he finds not the least difficulty. (*Pr.* 97)

Where Berkeley differs from Augustine is that he does not go on to confess his own difficulties when *he* considers what time is. Instead he points the finger at the Newtonian view which, he says, leaves one 'lost and embrangled in inextricable difficulties'. There is no hint that 'several paradoxes' follow from his own rival answer, and no suggestion of a suspicion that he might have failed to find a convincing answer to Augustine's question. Certainly we never find in Berkeley ground for supposing that it ever occurred to him that the question as posed might have no answer.

When Berkeley writes about time, particularly in the *Commentaries*, we find the subjectivist and solipsistic tendency in his thinking at its strongest. The lure towards solipsism must always be strong for a philosopher who equates the objects of experience with experiences, and who at the same time holds that an experience must be the experience of some one person, for then, rather than seeing experience as informing him of a world which can be supposed to have an existence independent of his perception of it, he will be inclined to suppose that all he can ever be aware of is experiences that are essentially and exclusively *his*. Inevitably it will seem problematic as to how he can be justified in making claims about the experiences of others, let alone about things which, as it happens, are not being experienced at all. That there is a general tendency towards solipsism in Berkeley's thought is clear. We can remind ourselves here of what happens in *Pr.* 23 and how his line of argument there leads towards the conclusion, not just that sensible things cannot exist unperceived, but that I cannot suppose them to exist when not perceived *by me*. It is of course true that Berkeley's official line is decidedly *not* solipsistic.[9] In general we find that he does allow that experience informs me of a world existing quite independently of *my* perception of it, and that he is at least prepared to talk as if the ideas I have when I perceive, say, a table are public.

Essential to Berkeley's official line is the recognition of various standpoints and the allowance that in seeking for truth I can properly take into account, not just how things appear to me, but how they appear to other people and even to God. If my standpoint was the only one I was allowed to recognize I should have to say that if the *esse* of sensible things is *percipi* then if I am not actually perceiving X, X does not exist. Recognizing other standpoints, though, I can say that when X ceases to be an object of perception *for me* it can still be an object of perception *for you* and *for God* and thus exist not just for you and for God but for all of us. By an obvious extension of this thinking there would seem to be no reason why I should not suppose things exist which I have never even thought of (though God at least must perceive them), and why I should not say that things have existed, not just when I was not aware of them, but when I did not perceive at all, as for example during periods of dreamless sleep and before I was born.

When Berkeley considers what time is, though, the case is different and the standpoint of the particular individual becomes all important. At a very early stage he seems to have asked himself to what he was referring when he used the word 'time'. We can imagine him watching a pot coming to the boil and supposing that he was aware of the pot coming to the boil *and* of the passage of time. He believed he could account for his awareness of the pot coming to the boil in terms of certain sensed ideas, but when he looked for some additional idea of the time in which the events occurred he could find none. It seemed natural to say, then, that being aware of time passing was nothing distinct from awareness of a sequence of events. Firstly because at this stage Berkeley still thought of our ideas of sense as essentially private, and secondly because he realized that we could be aware of time passing as our thoughts succeeded one another in cogitation or a reverie, he came to think that *time* for any individual must be the succession of ideas in that individual's mind, and thus be something private to him.

This I think is the doctrine Berkeley needs if he is to convince himself that he always thinks. The argument would go something like this. When I refer to time, or the passage of time, I at least should be referring only to some sequence of events in my own consciousness. To talk, then, of time passing when I am not aware of some sequence of events is to say something meaningless. The trouble is that this doctrine is one Berkeley cannot consistently maintain, and that it leads to many odd consequences of which the conclusion that I always think is only one. We can look at some of the criticisms that can be made under three heads.

First we should note that the statement that the soul always thinks must mean what it says, and that it is not just periods of dreamless sleep which are ruled out. Berkeley is apparently prepared to allow that on his doctrine there can be no period between my death and resurrection because my conceiving such a period would involve my conceiving time passing with no succession of ideas in my mind.

Similarly he is prepared to accept, and indeed to welcome, the consequence that there can be no periods of unconsciousness during my life. Such periods, he says, are 'nothing'. But equally, on his doctrine it must follow that I can recognize no period before I was born, for time for me must begin and end with the succession of ideas in my mind. It will no more make sense to suppose a period before I became conscious than it does for me to suppose a period in which consciousness is interrupted. The position seems truly startling. If 'always' has no meaning for me apart from something thought by me, it follows that I have always existed, and also of course that I cannot meaningfully talk of things happening before I was created. Before complicating things further it is worth emphasizing that Berkeley nowhere comes near a view of time which might suggest to me that periods of dreamless sleep are nothing without also suggesting that I have quite literally always thought. He should have said, though he in fact did not, that 'whenever I attempt to work with the notion of time as the succession of ideas in my mind, I am lost and embrangled in inextricable difficulties'.[10]

So far we have concentrated on what an individual might say about the duration of his own soul if he thought of time as being just the succession of ideas in his own mind. The second ground for criticism arises when we take various standpoints into account. Very simply, the problem is that of explaining how time for me can be said to be only a succession of ideas in my own mind if I recognize that there are various successions of ideas in various minds. Certainly it does not now seem that whenever I refer to time I am always referring to the succession of ideas in my mind, for I may be referring to the succession in Tom's mind, or to Dick's time or Harry's time. Here, we feel, is a real muddle, and we begin to wonder what point there can be in labelling the succession of ideas in A's mind 'A's time'. The introduction of various standpoints poses another problem. We have located the argument which might persuade Berkeley that he always thinks, or me that I always think, but so far there seems to be no reason why any particular individual should suppose that everyone else always thinks. Starting again from the position that time for me is just the succession of ideas in my mind, it would seem that I can be aware of time passing when I see your inert body with none of the signs and tokens that might suggest to me that the body is presently inhabited by some active perceiving spirit. Can I not say then that I am able to think of time (my time) passing when you are not thinking, and thus when you as a spirit have ceased to exist? Perhaps too the recognition of various standpoints and various times should encourage me to think that I can make some sense of the notion of time passing and *my* not thinking. Certainly it would appear that you can conceive this, but at any rate while it seems impossible that anyone should conceive 'Tipton's time' (i.e. the succession of ideas in Tipton's mind) passing with no ideas in Tipton's mind, it does not seem so obviously impossible for me to think of, say, 'Berkeley's time' (i.e. the succession of ideas in Berkeley's mind) passing with no succession of ideas in *my* mind.

The criticisms made under this second head are less tidy than one would like. What has happened is that we are now very vague as to what can be meant by referring to the succession of ideas in A's mind as 'A's time', and it is because of this that we have become unclear as to whether and why it follows from Berkeley's views about time that A cannot think of time passing and B not thinking, or even of time passing and himself not thinking. We shall return later to the suggestion that the most Berkeley could hope to do would be to convince someone who was resolutely determined to ignore all other standpoints that *he* always thought. Beyond this it begins to look as if the statement that A's time cannot pass without A having ideas is not a truth about time as conceived by A, but simply a misleading way of expressing the truism that there cannot be a succession of ideas in A's mind without there being a succession of ideas in A's mind.

Finally there is of course the criticism that the suggestion that I am aware of time as something private to me is one that completely fails to illuminate, account for, or even allow for my day to day use of temporal concepts. In general we do treat time as if it were a common medium and something which, in Berkeley's words, 'flows uniformly, and is participated by all beings', judging of its passage not by our own chronologies but by public chronometers. I can, for example, talk of having been in a certain place at the *same* time as you, and I find no difficulty in the supposition that I have passed an hour in a dreamless sleep, or that countless ages passed before my birth. This failure to accommodate our use of temporal concepts hardly needs spelling out further, but it does raise a problem, and perhaps even an objection to, what we have said so far. The problem would be that of accounting for the fact that Berkeley often seems to presuppose some objective standard for the passage of time, and that he normally uses temporal concepts as the rest of us do. The objection would be that as this is so, his view of what time is cannot be what we have supposed. The answer to this objection is interesting.

There are two preparatory points to be made. The first is that *if* we decided that Berkeley must have thought, or have come to think, of time as in some sense a common medium, we would find it difficult to see why he thought that a proper understanding of what time is shows that the soul always thinks. Take the case where you have watched the hands of the clock move from five to six while I (who we will suppose to have slept in the interim) had a perception of them when they pointed to five and then perceived nothing until they pointed to six. What is Berkeley to say about this? Well, there are two possibilities. He can adhere to a view of time such that we have to suppose that (really) no time has passed with me not thinking, *or* he can adopt some other account of time to allow for the supposition that time did pass while I was in a dreamless sleep. On the first view it would seem that time is not a common medium and that there is no time at which I do not think, and on the second view it would seem that time is in some sense a common medium but that there are times during which I do not think. What Berkeley cannot do is to have it both ways. He cannot hold that time is a common medium *and* that therefore I always think.[11]

The second point to be noted is that the fact that Berkeley sometimes talks *as if* time were a common medium does not prove that he did not hold each man's time to be private, though it might suggest that his views were incoherent or inconsistent. Even this, though, may be too strong. As is well known, he was prepared in all sorts of contexts to *say* things that on the face of it seem inconsistent with firmly held doctrines. The best known example of this concerns causality – he is prepared to say that fire causes water to boil while believing that strictly speaking it does not – but this is not the only example. Elsewhere we find Euphranor telling Alciphron that *in a strict sense* he does not see Alciphron, persons being immaterial, and this we might describe as the 'official' position. But in less rigorous moments the Berkeleian is of course prepared to talk in other than the strict way, and as if we *did* see people. Clearly it might turn out to be the case, as I believe it is, that Berkeley was prepared to allow us to go on using temporal concepts as we normally do while believing that ultimately each man's time *is* private.

When we were discussing Berkeley's views on meaning I referred to the controversy about just how Wittgensteinian Berkeley's most Wittgensteinian remarks are, and I did not attempt to adjudicate on it. But we can now note that his scattered references to time do provide some relevant material. We have already seen that the young Berkeley believed that all significant words stood for ideas, but that he moved away from this position, coming to hold, first, that not all words stand for *ideas*, and, second, that it is not always the case that a word can have meaning for us only by *standing for* things. His 'Wittgensteinian' remarks are those in which he puts the stress on our *use* of words for other purposes. We know that in *PC* 378 it was an axiom that:

All significant words stand for Ideas

So at this stage we would expect him to ask what idea(s) the word 'time' stands for. We know that he did ask this question and we know what answer he came up with. We also know that the answer gave rise to 'several paradoxes', so that he had a good reason for looking for another answer or (better) questioning the propriety of the question. A later change in his thinking about meaning might well have resulted in his ceasing to wonder what time *was*, and to an escape from the paradoxes that had worried him earlier.

Now it is quite certain that by the time he came to write *Alciphron* Berkeley's thinking about meaning had become somewhat sophisticated as compared with the views he had held when he first began to wonder about time. Thus for example in VII 13-14 Euphranor says:

> I am inclined to think the doctrine of signs a point of great importance and general extent, which, if duly considered, would cast no small light upon things, and afford a just and genuine solution of many difficulties. Thus much, upon the whole, may be said of all signs: – that they do not always suggest ideas signified to the mind: that when they suggest ideas, they are not general abstract ideas: that they have other uses besides barely standing for and exhibiting ideas . . . that signs may imply or suggest the relations of things; which relations, habitudes or proportions, as they cannot be by us understood but by the help of signs, so being thereby expressed and confuted, they direct and enable us to act with regard to things . . .

We can admit that neither this extract nor the long passage from which it is taken is crystal clear,[12] but it might well seem that we could expect *this* Berkeley not to ask what the word 'time' stands for, and to reconsider his earlier doctrines about time in the light of his belief that words 'have other uses besides barely standing for and exhibiting ideas'.

In view of this it is obviously very interesting that in his reply to Johnson (written at about the time he was writing *Alciphron*) Berkeley reveals that he does think the doctrine of signs relevant to an understanding of our talk about time. He lists four factors which he supposes may help to account for our perplexities here, the last being:

> Not considering the true use and end of words, which as often terminate in the will as in the understanding, being employed rather to excite, influence, and direct action, than to produce clear and distinct ideas.

He does not elaborate on this, but it seems that he was aware that much of our talk using temporal concepts cannot be understood simply in terms of an account of what time *is*. To make further progress we have to focus our attention on the use of these concepts in regulating our actions in connection with the practical concerns of everyday social life. Presumably it is only by doing this that we can account for A's talk of having been in the same place at the same time as B and for the fact that it seems easy to conceive of, and be grateful for, periods of dreamless sleep.

This shift of attention from denotation to use is one that will appeal to contemporary philosophers who have stressed that we are bound to be perplexed if we ask what time *is*, and that we can only hope to escape from perplexity if we concentrate on the use we make of words. Indeed it is in just this sort of area that the writings of Wittgenstein have been influential. Thus we find Wittgenstein saying:

> This kind of mistake recurs again and again in philosophy; e.g. when we are puzzled about the nature of time, when times seems to us a *queer thing*. . . . It is not new facts about time which we want to know. All the facts that concern us lie open before us. But it is the use of the substantive 'time' which mystifies us. . . . First the question is asked 'What is time?' This question makes it appear that what we want is a definition. We mistakenly think that a definition is what will remove the trouble (as in certain states of

indigestion we feel a kind of hunger which cannot be removed by eating). The question is then answered by a wrong definition; say: 'Time is the motion of the celestial bodies'. The next step is to see that this definition is unsatisfactory. But this only means that we don't use the word 'time' synonymously with 'motion of the celestial bodies'. However in saying that the first definition is wrong, we are now tempted to think that we must replace it by a different one, the correct one. (Wittgenstein 1, pp. 6 & 27)

If we are impressed by this we are likely to be impressed too by Berkeley's suggestion that we should concentrate on 'the true use and end of words', and the way they 'direct action', if we are to escape puzzlement about time. And of course we might also be impressed by the suggestion in *Pr.* 97 that master and servant have no difficulties concerning time 'taken in particular and concrete', and that things go wrong only when the concept has 'passed through the hands of a metaphysician' and become 'too abstract and fine, to be apprehended by men of ordinary sense'. Cannot we here locate a truly Wittgensteinian insight?

Well, perhaps we can. It is not my purpose here to belittle the development that did take place in Berkeley's thinking about meaning, nor indeed to deny that Wittgenstein would have approved of the way in which it was developing. But I would certainly want to stress that, if we consider *everything* Berkeley says about time in the *Principles* and in his reply to Johnson, we find that on this issue at least he has not emancipated himself from his old thinking about meaning. One way of making the point would be to say that the 'Wittgensteinian' insight is not nearly so Wittgensteinian as it can be made to look. More generously, we could say that if there is a genuinely Wittgensteinian insight it is not yet, so far as Berkeley is concerned, the *dominant*, insight. After all, the moral of *Pr.* 97-8 is not in the end that things go wrong whenever a concept such as that of time passes through the hands of a metaphysician. It is that things go wrong when the *wrong* metaphysician (a Locke or a Newton) gets his hands on the concepts. The claim is not so much that metaphysicians have asked the wrong question, it is that they have given wrong answers. Berkeley is still prepared to tell us what time *is*, and while he castigates the Newtonian answer because it 'lays one under an absolute necessity of thinking, either that he passes away innumerable ages without a thought, or else that he is annihilated every moment of his life', he is quite unembarrassed when he puts forward the 'plain consequence' of his own answer. The case is similar with the reply to Johnson. We do have the Wittgensteinian snippet. But we also find Berkeley saying that a succession of ideas *constitutes* time and, apparently, still accepting it as a consequence that the soul always thinks. Indeed it rather looks as if Berkeley wants us to concentrate on the use of words to direct action only when we want to understand how the vulgar can speak about time as they do. When we think with the learned (or at least with Berkeley) we will still go along with Berkeley's old answer. This old answer of course depends on a most un-Wittgensteinian approach to language and meaning, and I am going to continue to treat it as Berkeley's answer.[13]

In concluding this section we can usefully return to the problem of John-asleep-by-me and look at the envisaged situation first from John's standpoint and then from Johnson's. Starting with John, then, we can easily see why, *so long as he is not prepared to take any standpoint other than his own into account*, he may be inclined to deny that there was a period during which he was not thinking. There are two relevant features of John's situation. First there is the fact that so long as he sleeps he cannot think of time passing, and this for the simple reason that necessarily a man who is not conscious cannot think of anything. This feature may have misled Berkeley. It is indeed true that in *one* sense we cannot conceive time passing when we are not thinking, but this is not the sense Berkeley needs. It is true that if John is in a dreamless sleep at time t1 he cannot (at t1) conceive time passing. But it does not of course follow from this that if John is asleep at t1 he cannot at time t2 suppose time to have passed while he slept. Second, there is the fact that when John wakes it may seem to him that no time has passed. The reason for this is that because he has been in a dreamless sleep he has not been aware of the passage of time.

Normally when we wake from sleep we wake with full knowledge that we have slept and a fairly good idea of how long we have slept for. Heavy eyes and fuddled brain are signs that we have slept, and various changes in our environment since we were last conscious enable us to estimate the duration of our sleep. In unusual cases, though, as perhaps when we have been under an anaesthetic, we may have no idea how long we have slept for, and one can imagine an extreme case where we might have no notion that we had been unconscious. Locke is certainly envisaging an *unusual* case when he says:

> ... if Adam and Eve, (when they were alone in the world,) instead of their ordinary night's sleep, had passed the whole twenty-four hours in one continued sleep, the duration of that twenty-four hours had been irrecoverably lost to them, and been for ever left out of their account of time. (II xiv 5)

The point of the story is, of course, that we are to suppose Adam and Eve find no clues in their environment to tell them they have slept, and (significantly from our point of view) that there is nobody to tell them. Their position is different from John's, for John has Johnson to tell him that he has slept.

The argument which might convince John that John always thinks seems to depend upon ruling out the possibility of his (properly) taking standpoints other than his own into account, and so long as this possibility is ruled out he will always be in a position similar to that in which Locke places Adam and Eve. The one difference will be that whereas Adam and Eve are able to conceive periods of dreamless sleep, and are *usually* able to determine when they have slept and for how long, John is not allowed at any stage to take into account either any clues he might normally think his environment gives him, or the reports of others to the effect that they have been aware of times when he slept. As we pointed out earlier, John is required here to isolate himself from others in a way in which he is not expected to isolate himself when he considers the existence of sensible objects when they are not perceived by him. He is allowed to conceive a table existing unperceived by him (for some other spirit may perceive it), but he is not supposed to be able to conceive a period of time of which he is unaware. And this creates one more problem for Berkeley, though it is not one he faces.

To return to a situation we envisaged earlier, we can suppose that John is aware of the hands of the clock pointing to five and then of the hands pointing to six, there having been no awareness of anything in the interim. Now it would seem that here John has to say *either* that as he was not aware of any events between the perceptions, then any supposed interval is 'nothing', *or* that certain events did take place, including the hands pointing to the half and quarters, when he was not conscious of anything. But if Berkeley would have him take the second alternative and is prepared to allow, as surely he must, that we cannot conceive events as occurring outside time, he will have to concede that John can after all conceive time passing with him not thinking. If, though, he would recommend the first alternative the odd consequence will be that John will have to insist that the moment at which the hands pointed to six immediately suceeded the moment when they pointed to five, so that the events he might normally suppose occurred in the interim must be as much nothing as the supposed period of unconsciousness. That Berkeley can be forced to this conclusion is hardly surprising, it being necessarily true that if I cannot conceive a time during which I was not thinking then I cannot conceive any events as having taken place at times when I was not thinking. It certainly needs emphasizing, though, that Berkeley's views on time have disturbing implications for the duration of sensible things, as well as for the duration of the perceiving thing. For example, if we were right in claiming that on Berkeley's view I will not be able to make sense of the notion of a period *before* my creation, it must follow that I cannot suppose any events to have preceded that creation. The converse is, of course, that if Berkeley *is* going to allow me to think of events as taking place either prior to my creation or at periods during my life when I am not conscious, he will have to allow that I can suppose times when I am not thinking.

Turning now to Johnson's standpoint the problem arises as to why he, to whom it seems as if time is passing while John sleeps, should ignore what seems to him to be the case, and adopt John's standpoint. This is the problem we raised earlier when we said that Berkeley might be able to convince someone prepared to ignore other standpoints that he always thought, but seems to have no principle that might convince anyone that someone else always thinks. The problem is that of seeing *why* 'the duration of any finite spirit must be estimated by the number of ideas or actions succeeding each other in *that same* spirit or mind' (my italics). If it is true that time for Johnson is the succession of ideas in Johnson's mind and that Johnson can have experiences when it seems to him that John is not thinking, it would seem that Johnson *may*, and perhaps even that he *must*, suppose time to be passing with John not thinking. Why, then, does Berkeley expect Johnson to ignore his own standpoint and accept John's?

This is not an easy question to find a plausible answer for, but perhaps the best we can do is to return to that problem as to what it means to say that time for A is the succession of ideas in A's mind. The obvious interpretation is that when A conceives, or thinks about, time he *can* only conceive a succession of ideas in his own mind, and though this notion seems highly implausible we can just about see how Berkeley might have come to take it seriously. Ultimately the view seems to depend on a mistaken notion as to what it is for a person to think of something, but if this theory were justified it would indeed follow that A was just *incapable* of thinking of time passing (i.e. of a succession of ideas) with him not thinking. The suggestion that time for A is the succession of ideas in A's mind might, though, be open to another interpretation. That is, it might now be supposed that B, say, can conceive a succession of ideas in some mind other than his own and that when he thinks of time in relation to A he *should* have in mind, not what is going on in his own mind, but what is going on in A's. Under this interpretation A's time will not be the one private succession A *can* conceive when he thinks of time, but rather the succession we *should* all have in mind when talking about time with reference to A. Clearly this is the interpretation Berkeley needs if he is to convince us that we should never suppose a time at which A is not thinking. It seems to me that he shifts from the first interpretation to the second without noticing that the second interpretation widens considerably our powers of conception, and certainly without giving any reason why B should choose to accept the succession of ideas in A's mind as the standard for judging of the duration of A. If this is so we must conclude that even if John can somehow be persuaded to discount what Johnson tells him about things going on while he slept, Johnson is quite right to wonder why *he* should deny the possibility of time passing and John not thinking when he can see John 'without so much as a dream' beside him.

V

As has already been said, questions concerning the mind and its relation to body exercise philosophers still. Here we will content ourselves with pointing out that the moves Berkeley makes are at least not obviously satisfactory. We can start by seeing what he *might* have said in answer to the problem of John-asleep-by-me had he given up his surely unworkable view of time and been persuaded to admit that Johnson is right when he supposes time to be passing as he looks at the inert form beside him. Now we can get a clue as to the line Berkeley might have taken by looking at the way in which Locke juggles with three concepts in his chapter on personal identity. The three concepts are, first, that of a *man*, the physical organism we can see, touch and shake hands with, second, that of a *person*, which is based on the immediate awareness each of us has of himself but no other as a conscious being, and, third, that of a *soul* or *spiritual substance*, which soul is not supposed to be something we can see as we can see a man, nor something we are conscious of as we are conscious of ourselves as persons, but rather something we suppose must exist as the substratum of thoughts and mental operations. It is significant that for Locke in II i 9ff it is the soul, not the person, that can exist when not thinking.

Now Locke seems to think that personal pronouns, and presumably proper names too, are systematically ambiguous in that they can refer to the person *or* to the man. Hence his answer to one objection that can be made to his account of personal identity. He holds (unlike Berkeley) that I am the same person as the person who did X if and only if I can remember having done X, and this seems odd, if only because we are all inclined to suppose that we have done things in the past which we have completely forgotten about and are quite incapable of remembering. I may have good reason for supposing that I once read *Great Expectations*, perhaps finding an entry in one of my old diaries to this effect or being told by my parents, but according to Locke's criterion it would seem that if I have completely forgotten reading it then I am not the person who read it. Locke is aware of this sort of problem, and in answering it he says:

> ... we must here take notice what the word *I* is applied to; which, in this case, is the *man* only. And the same man being presumed to be the same person, I is easily here supposed to stand also for the same person. (II xxvii 20)

It appears, then, that *I*, the man Tipton, did read *Great Expectations* years ago, though *I*, the person I am now conscious of being, am not the person who read it.

It will be quite obvious that this does not provide a satisfactory solution to Locke's problem,[14] but it seems to me that it does suggest one way in which Berkeley might very well have tried to answer Johnson's problem concerning the existence of John-asleep-by-me.

That is, he might have said that Johnson is quite right in supposing it to be evident that John continues to exist when he is not conscious given that the proper name here refers to the physical organism Johnson can see, the *esse* of which is *percipi*. Certainly *something* persists through the period when John sleeps, but it is not a Lockian soul, for there is no such thing as a Lockian soul, and it is not the person, for the *esse* of the person is *percipere*.

To develop this point a little, Berkeley might have stressed that of course we do sometimes use proper names as if they referred to perceptible beings. Thus, when we say that John is tall our assertion does concern the body we can see. But for Berkeley the John who is worried, is not a physical organism, and just as we have to infer from signs and tokens – a wrinkled brow for example – *that* John is worried, so we have to infer that there is a being, the person John, who is worried. Now since Berkeley does want to say that *strictly speaking* a proper name should refer to the thinking thing, and not to the body with which it is allied, he must insist that the real truth is that John does not exist if he is not thinking. But, as for ordinary purposes we find it convenient to use the name to refer also to the physical organism which is usually associated with the person, it can be allowed that it is as true to say that John exists when he is not thinking as it is to say that John is tall.

At this level, then, the paradox which we said would have been apparent in the second part of the *Principles* has a fairly simple solution. Berkeley can hold that the *esse* of persons (finite spirits) is *percipere*, and that consequently persons (finite spirits) exist only so long as they think, while allowing that in speaking with the vulgar we can refer to the *body* as John and say that John exists when there is no thinking going on, the body being something which at certain times, but not now, behaves in such a way that we take it to be associated with the thinking thing which, strictly speaking, *is* John. He might point out that many of the things we ordinarily say are misleading, but that they can be accepted by the philosopher as easily translatable into more philosophically respectable expressions. Thus Euphranor can *say* that he sees Alciphron, even though he holds that *really* he perceives 'only such visible signs and tokens as suggest and infer the being of that invisible thinking principle or soul' (IV 5). Similarly we can *say* that John is tall, though we should realise that *really* it is John's body, or the body normally associated with John, that is tall. Again, we can *say* that at a funeral we are burying John, though clearly we are not burying a conscious being. And, finally, Johnson can *say* that he sees John in a dreamless sleep beside him, though of course *really* what he sees is a body in repose. Strictly the person is the mind or spirit, and this, Berkeley must say, does not exist if it is not thinking.

Now it is not of course being suggested here that this proposed solution leaves Berkeley with a position we would want to accept, but it does seem fair to say that this, or something very like it, would have been the position he would have had to adopt had he not been tempted to deal with the problem of the duration of spirits in terms of his views about time. His contemporary readers would not have *liked* the doctrine that the mind ceases to be when it is not perceiving,[15] but they would have received the notion with nothing like the blank incredulity with which Johnson confronts the notion that time does not pass when John is not thinking. Further, if it can be accepted that this is the answer Berkeley *should* have given, his views on sensible objects and finite spirits being what they were, we may perhaps think that our reason for being dissatisfied with the position will centre not so much on the intermittency issue as on the suggestion that persons *are* spirits and radically distinct from their bodies. We would, in short, object to the statement that (strictly speaking) persons exist only when they are thinking for precisely the same reason as we would object to the statement that (strictly speaking) we do not see persons.

A question that needs asking here, then, is whether Locke and Berkeley are doing justice to the situation when they treat the mind and the body as separate entities and identify the person with the mind. I do, after all, talk of myself as being worried and as being tall without any consciousness of ambiguity, and I do not normally think of myself as *being* my mind. It is perhaps worth taking seriously the possibility that my normal ways of thinking and talking may be less inaccurate than Berkeley supposes, and indeed that I may not be a spirit who happens to be associated with a body, but rather a creature of flesh and blood who can be weighed and measured. Against Berkeley's surely far from obvious claim that we do not see persons, it is at least tempting to say with Flew that 'people are what you meet' and that:

> ... persons, are in fact corporeal. Person words are quite manifestly and undeniably taught and learnt and used by and for reference to a certain sort of corporeal object. We do meet people, not just the

containers in which they are kept. They do see us, and not just what we happen to inhabit.... Wherever we may end quite certainly this is where we have to begin. (Flew 4, pp. 25-6)

If nothing else, this might convince us that even if Berkeley does have some genuine point to make when he denies that we see people, at least we are not speaking loosely when we assert that we do.

The last thirteen words in the quotation from Flew must, however, be taken seriously. If he is right, as I would say he is, in insisting that we must *begin* with people as corporeal things, there is still scope for a long debate as to where our investigations should end. Clearly one of the characteristics of the corporeal objects we are prepared to call persons is that they are conscious, thinking and intelligent beings, and recognising that people are corporeal leaves open the question as to what it is to have a mind. Of course many different accounts have been given of mind, and here we can mention as examples Ryle's behaviouristic account and the currently fashionable, if controversial, view that mental states can be identified with brain states. Both these views suppose that persons are *wholly* corporeal. Berkeley, though, belongs in a long and not yet dead tradition which takes it that to have a mind is to have in one, or at least associated with one's body, not just a liver, a heart, a brain and so on, but something fundamentally different in character, an immaterial and invisible *thing*. It is this aspect of the story we must concentrate on now. We can note in passing, though, that as this thing could think, and the corporeal could not, it seemed natural to identify the individual as a thinking being with the one thing that was capable of thought. If we go on to consider the attractiveness of the notion that this thinking thing, which is so different from the corporeal, might survive the dissolution of the corporeal and continue to enjoy a conscious life, we can see how one might come to the conclusion that the bodies we see around us are but the housings or containers for the *true* persons, the persons we never see. This of course is Berkeley's position.

I do not intend here to criticize the view that *if* we are thinking beings only because we have thinking things in us then the *true* person should be identified with the thinking thing. Nor shall I attempt to demolish the claim that to have a mind is indeed to have in one (or associated with one's body) this special sort of entity. But I would suggest that it is at least worth asking ourselves why it seemed so obvious to Berkeley that the mind *is* an incorporeal thing. To understand this we need to consider not only a claim he would make about what we are conscious of when we are conscious of being persons, but also his beliefs about the nature of the corporeal. In concluding this chapter we can say something on both these points.

First, then, it needs stressing that it does not *follow* from the fact that I, Tipton, a creature of flesh and blood, am conscious of being a person, that there is in me, or associated with my body, a special thinking thing. Reminding ourselves of what Locke says in IV ix 3, we can note that if Locke, a creature of flesh and blood, is aware of pain or doubt, he will at the same time be aware of himself as a conscious being. But of course it does not *follow* from this that there must be an immaterial, thinking thing *in* Locke, or associated with that corporeal body which we might see, touch and X-ray, for all we are *forced* to conclude is that Locke, the creature of flesh and blood, has that consciousness of being a thinking creature which is part of what it is to be a person. It might indeed be put forward as an *hypothesis* that corporeal objects are capable of consciousness and self awareness only because they have incorporeal things inside them, but this is not the only hypothesis possible, and we are likely to feel driven towards it only if we find some reason for supposing that anything merely corporeal would be incapable of consciousness. Locke seems to have been at least dimly aware of this, for in the second edition of the *Essay* at II xxiii 15 he wrote:

> Every act of sensation, when duly considered, gives us an equal view of both parts of nature, the corporeal and spiritual. For whilst I know, by seeing or hearing, &c., that there is some corporeal being without me, the object of that sensation, I do more certainly know, that there is some spiritual being within me that sees and hears. This, I must be convinced, cannot be the action of bare insensible matter; nor ever could be, without an immaterial thinking being.

In short, it does not follow just from the fact that Locke thinks that there is a thinking thing in him. Locke sees that the desired conclusion requires not only the premiss that Locke thinks, but also the premiss that if Locke were purely corporeal he could not think. If there is a weakness in his case it is that he provides us with no *reason* for supposing that the purely corporeal cannot think, and of course this weakness is underlined in IV iii 6 when he has to admit that we 'possibly shall never be able to know whether any mere material being thinks or no'. Thought requires a thinker. It does not *obviously* require an incorporeal thinker.[16]

There is a temptation to suppose that we *cannot* be simply corporeal objects for the reason that corporeal objects have only a certain range of qualities (such as being coloured and extended) and not attributes such as being worried, being capable of doubt, and having awareness of self. These non-physical properties, it might be suggested, *must* be attributed to something incorporeal. Locke is trying this move when he suggests that matter 'is evidently in its own nature void of sense and thought' (IV iii 6). But the trouble with this sort of point is that it begs the question. What is at issue is whether corporeal things as such are capable of consciousness, and clearly we are not justified in assuming that all corporeal objects have only the limited range of qualities until we can show that we are not corporeal only. If we are corporeal only then of course some things that are merely corporeal *are* capable of consciousness, for we are conscious beings. Another temptation is to say that being aware of self is clearly not being aware of any sensible component of one's body, and that therefore it must be a matter of being aware of some rather special, non-sensible thing associated with one's body. Again, though, this temptation must not be given in to too easily. When Locke talks of self-awareness as *perceiving* he may already be choosing a description which pushes him towards, if it does not depend on, the supposition that there is a special item we perceive. It is interesting, then, that Berkeley, though he is quite definite that only immaterial things are conscious, does realise that awareness of self is a totally different sort of awareness from that involved in experience of other objects and that he refuses to say that we *perceive* the self. To get the balance of interpretation right we might say that Berkeley would hold that awareness of self is that consciousness we, *whatever sort of being we may be*, have that we are conscious beings. His certainty that we are *spiritual* things seems to rest in the end on his belief that corporeal things are incapable of consciousness.

Turning to the second point, then, we find that it is indeed because Berkeley thinks he can show that corporeal things cannot be agents that he supposes agency *must* reside in the incorporeal. This is made quite clear in the following passage from the *Dialogues* where Philonous says:

> How often must I repeat, that I know or am conscious of my own being; and that I my self am not my ideas, but somewhat else, a thinking active principle that perceives, knows, wills, and operates about ideas. I know that I, one and the same self, perceive both colours and sounds: that a colour cannot perceive a sound, nor a sound a colour: that I am therefore one individual principle, distinct from colour and sound; and, for the same reason, from all other sensible things and inert ideas. (iii, 233-4)

In Berkeley's view not only tables and chairs and other objects which we normally regard as being distinct from ourselves are made up of ideas, for our bodies too are sensible objects and thus made up of inert ideas which by their nature are incapable of consciousness or of doing anything. Ideas are passive and agents active, and this means that agents cannot be corporeal.

So it is that in examining Berkeley's views on the self we are brought back to his views on the sensible, his claim that the perceiving subject is distinct from the body depending ultimately on his claim that all sensible objects are (or are made up of) units of experience which have no existence except as presentations to consciousness. There is in fact no contradiction is suggesting that things we can sense can themselves sense, but so long as Berkeley can defend the view that the things we experience in sensation are *just experiences,* the claim that the self is radically distinct from the sensible is going to seem as obvious as the truism that experiences cannot experience. It follows of course that getting the measure of Berkeley's case for the spiritual nature of the perceiving subject involves challenging his views concerning the nature of what we perceive. For if persons are at least partly corporeal, and being corporeal is not just being a presentation in sensory awareness, the possibility will at least remain open that minds are not *things* to be sharply distinguished from bodies, but that as persons we are bodies endowed with certain powers and attributes that we categorize as mental.

CHAPTER EIGHT

God

'Berkeley's system, whatever may be the right textbook label to apply to it, was plainly a piece of religious apologetics, the outline of a constructive natural theology, of a theistic metaphysic. From the *Principles* onwards he was fashioning a reasoned case for the existence of God, of a certain kind of God with a certain kind of relation to the world.' (Jessop 1, p. 98)

I

We are often urged by those most sympathetic to Berkeley to take his work as a whole, and in particular to appreciate the dialectical presentation of his views in the *Principles* and *Dialogues* and elsewhere. And though those who make this plea sometimes seem to be asking us to eschew careful analysis of particular arguments in favour of taking a loftier view and somehow feeling our way into sympathy with the totality of his thought, they are right if they mean just to remind us that an adequate understanding of Berkeley's position can be arrived at only if we take into account not only some few things that he said, but also his overall purpose in writing at all. Luce says:

> Some expositors have declared that God is an afterthought in the Berkeleian philosophy, a buttress for a tottering metaphysic, a *deus ex machina* dragged in to save a collapsing theory of perception, originally conceived in terms of human psychology. (Luce 5, p. 68)

And Luce is right in criticizing this view, for in writing at all Berkeley was impelled by a desire to bring men to a sense of the immanence of the Deity. Though in the *Principles* and *Dialogues* the case for the claim that sensible objects are mind-dependent is completed before God's existence is supposedly proved, we can hardly do justice to Berkeley's analysis of the perceived world in terms of ideas unless we appreciate that the point of the whole exercise is to show that any view of the world is bound to be inadequate or incomplete unless God is seen, not only as creator of the natural world, but as vitally concerned in all that happens in that world. In the quotation which heads this chapter Jessop provides a useful corrective to the sort of interpretation Luce attacks. Indeed Berkeley believed that he had begun to fashion his reasoned case before the *Principles*, for, as we have seen, he holds that his *NTV* 'affords to thinking men a new and unanswerable proof of the existence and immediate operation of God'.

As A. D. Ritchie stresses in his book on Berkeley, Berkeley wrote in opposition to the Great Machine theory of the universe. He was opposed not just to outright atheism but to any view of the world which pushed God to the background of thought rather than bringing him to the forefront. In *Alciphron* he says:

> Some philosophers, being convinced of the wisdom and power of the Creator, from the make and contrivance of organized bodies and orderly system of the world, did nevertheless imagine that he left this system with all its parts and contents well adjusted and put in motion, as an artist leaves a clock, to go thenceforward of itself for a certain period.

And he contrasts this with his own proof of:

> ... not a Creator merely, but a provident Governor, actually and intimately present, and attentive to all our interests and motions, who watches over our conduct, and takes care of our minutest actions and designs throughout the whole course of our lives, informing, admonishing, and directing incessantly, in a most evident and sensible manner. (IV 14)

He wrote against atheism certainly, but whether his reader was an atheist, or adhered to the view attributed to 'some philosophers', or accepted, at least in his more pious moments, that God was in some vaguely defined sense sustainer of the natural world and concerned in all that occurred, Berkeley wrote to provide him with a real sense of God's presence, and to bring home to him the existence of a Deity 'in whom *we live, and move, and have our being*'. He would have had no time at all for Hardy's conceit in the poem 'God-Forgotten' that God the Creator might have forgotten the world of men, and he would have rejected it not just because he held as a Christian that God was omniscient and that his care for man is boundless, but because he held that the notion of things continuing to exist and function without God's immediate providence was one that made no sense.

This said, there might be two criticisms of our treatment of what Berkeley says about God. And the first of these would be that we devote too little space to it and that what Berkeley considered to be of major importance we treat as if it were of minor importance. On this I want to say little. Implicit in the decision not to devote much space to Berkeley's views on God there is of course a judgement as to what is most challenging and important in his philosophy. But this can be regarded as the subjective judgement of a particular commentator. It so happens that Berkeley's main preoccupations are not ours, and that we regard his views on the nature of the sensible object as more worth discussing than his views on the nature and attributes of God. To give one example of a problem which concerned Berkeley greatly but which we shall not examine, there is the question whether God is, say, wise in the same sense that a man may be wise or whether he is wise in some other sense. And there are questions arising more directly from what Berkeley says in the *Principles* and *Dialogues* – for example the question concerning the nature of Divine perception – which we will only touch on. Again, it has been suggested, and rightly I think, that Berkeley's proof, or proofs, of the existence of God never look like showing that there is just *one* superior spirit operating in nature. Commenting on what we shall call (following Bennett) *the passivity argument*, Thomson says:

> It is worth pointing out that the causal argument is formally fallacious. Given that every one of my ideas of sense that is not caused by me is caused by some powerful spirit, it does not follow, as Berkeley wished to say, that some one powerful spirit causes all those ideas of sense. The way is thus left open for a kind of animism (one spirit for each physical object) and for views intermediate between this and theism. (p. 429n)

If there is a gap between showing that there is spiritual agency behind everything that happens in nature and establishing monotheism, we shall not dwell on it. Our concern will be with the claim that the facts of sense experience *do* point to spiritual agency.

The second possible criticism must, though, be rebutted more firmly. It might be claimed that at one crucial point we have failed to recognize that Berkeley's position must be seen in its totality if we are to do justice to it, and this is when we have supported our claim that there is a chasm between Berkeley's views and the views of the man in the street by emphasizing that Berkeley believes that sensible things exist only when they are actually perceived while the plain man holds that it makes perfectly good sense to talk of them as existing when they are not perceived. Against this the critic may want to argue that in practice, and when it comes to cases, there is very little difference between Berkeley's view and the view of the man in the street.

Thus, to take an extreme case, we can suppose that we enclose a plot of land in my garden with a brick wall and a high electrified fence, and take what other precautions you will to ensure that nobody can see what is going on within. Well, it might be claimed, there will be no difference of opinion between the Berkeleian and the plain man as to whether weeds exist behind the wall, for both will agree that they do. Indeed it might be said that Berkeley is not disputing what the plain man says about the weeds, but rather explaining why what the plain man says is true. If our plain man happens to be a theist he may well please Berkeley by affirming that when he says weeds exist in the garden, even though unperceived, he really means that they are not perceived by any *human* observer, and not that they exist unperceived by an all-knowing God. And Berkeley will tell *him* that it is because the weeds are perceived by this God that they do indeed exist. But even if our plain man happens to be an atheist he will still be saying something *true* when he says that weeds exist behind the wall. The trouble with *him* is that he is further than the theist from appreciating *why* what he says is true. On this view there will never be any dispute between Berkeley and the plain man over, say, the books in the vacated study or the cigarettes in the closed case, because Berkeley is quite determined to allow for their existence. The criticism of our position will be that we have tried to create the impression that there *is* a fundamental disagreement, and that we have done this by leaving God out of the picture at the very point at which Berkeley would insist he must be brought in.

The truth behind this criticism I take to be that when Berkeley is conducting his analysis of the nature of the sensible world, God is always waiting in the wings to save the day for common sense. When, for example, Berkeley says of sensible objects in *Pr.* 6 that when they are not perceived by any finite spirit 'they must either have no existence at all, or else subsist in the mind of some eternal spirit' we guess that the second possibility is going to be the one for Berkeley, and that he is not going to depart from common sense by saying that the table left in the empty room has no existence at all. Of course he will have to convince his readers that there *is* a spirit who perceives things when we do not, but given even that there may be such a spirit he can claim, as he does in *Pr.* 48, that the objection that he is committed to intermittency 'will not be found reasonably charged on the principles we have premised'. But acknowledging that Berkeley looks to God as omnipresent perceiver does not mean that we have to accept the criticism.

The key fact as I see it is that it is Berkeley's view that we are blinded to the immanence of God if we disassociate *esse* from *percipi* as the plain man does, and thus suppose that it at least makes sense to talk of things existing independently of any perceiving mind. It appears, then, that the arguments purporting to show that it makes no sense to talk of things existing unperceived must be judged as they stand and found adequate or wanting prior to, and without reference to, the claim that God exists as omnipresent perceiver. Luce says that one particular entry in the *Commentaries* 'contains a valid proof of the existence of God starting from the nature of the world as Berkeley saw it when he published the *Principles*' (Luce 7, p. 190), and whether we decide that the argument Luce refers to works or not we must at least agree that the proof depends upon supposed truths about the nature of the world which Berkeley has to convince us of *before* he can lead us to the desired conclusion. It follows from this that we needed to evaluate these supposed truths about the sensible world *before* seeing whether a proof of God's existence follows from them, and it was when we were doing this that we found a major clash between Berkeley's thinking and our ordinary thinking. The clash is summed up when we say that the plain man does not believe, as Berkeley does, that it is nonsense to talk of an unperceived object.

It is only if we take a superficial view that the chasm might seem to disappear at a higher level, because even if it is the case that there will be no disagreement between Berkeley and the plain man over the existence of the weeds, books and cigarettes (when not perceived by us) it *remains* true that for Berkeley, but not for the plain man, it would be nonsense to suppose them existing were it not for God's perception of them. Even the man in the pew is not really all that close to Berkeley, for though he may be persuaded that as a matter of fact God does perceive all, he would not agree that an analysis of the nature of the sensed objects shows these to be mind-dependent. The atheist may be wrong when he says there is no God to perceive the tree in the deserted quad, but his mistake in the eyes of the most pious of plain men has nothing to do with the refusal to conflate *esse* with *percipi*. Berkeley himself sees that there is this gap. At one point he has Philonous say:

> Men commonly believe that all things are known or perceived by God, because they believe the being of a God, whereas I on the other side, immediately and necessarily conclude the being of a God, because all sensible things must be perceived by him. (ii, 212)

We shall be commenting on this passage later, for there is some dispute as to how it should be interpreted. For the moment, the *only* point I want to make is that Berkeley does at least recognize that the general belief is that if God exists he must perceive all things, while he himself would hold that things could not exist were it not for the fact that a God perceived them. This makes a very real difference between the plain man's standpoint and Berkeley's standpoint, and it is this sort of difference we have wanted to stress throughout.

II

Berkeley's basic objection to the Great Machine theory was that it involved the view that the behaviour of things in the natural world could be accounted for in purely mechanistic terms. Ultimately it seemed that changes took place in accordance with causal laws which the scientist investigated or discovered, and if recourse was had to God to account for the creation of the system, or if men believed with part of their minds that somehow God's acquiescence was essential to its continued functioning, the theory itself did not demand or encourage any such view. Against the Great Machine theory Berkeley insists that there is no efficient causality manifested in nature, and thus no possibility of genuine explanations being found by investigating nature. For genuine explanations we have to look *outside* the system of nature and appreciate that only the will of a spirit can cause. To understand Berkeley's proof of the existence of God we have, then, to understand his thinking about causality.

The suggestion that there is no efficient causality manifested in nature seems odd, for the plain man finds it obvious that fire causes the paper to burn and that arsenic in quantity brings about the death of the consumer, and he takes it that we have adequate experiential backing for claiming that these relations hold. But Berkeley was not being at all original in maintaining that the situation is by no means as simple as might be supposed. Aaron quotes a useful passage from Géraud de Cordemoy's *Discernement du Corps et de l'Âme*:

> When we say, for example, that the body B has caused the body C to move from its place, if we examine carefully what we know with certainty here, all we see is that B moves, that it meets C which was at rest, and that after this meeting the first ceases to move and the second commences to move. But to say we know that B gives movement to C, is in truth, mere assumption. (Aaron 1, p. 184)

At the time Berkeley wrote, the view that experience never reveals any power in objects to originate changes had become a commonplace in philosophy. Berkeley himself holds that the supposed causes in nature should be regarded simply as *signs* of the supposed effects or *things signified*. As we have seen he allows that we can talk *as if* there were causal relations in nature and *say* that, for example, fire causes paper to burn – 'in such things we ought to *think with the learned, and speak with the vulgar*' – but he insists that to attain truth we must realize that the supposed causes are not genuine causes.

Once again it is instructive here to see Berkeley's view in relation to Locke's view, and the key chapter in the *Essay* is II xxi. Basically Locke accepted that all we observe in nature is conjunctions of events or regular sequences, but he also saw that when we say A-type events cause B-type events we are saying more than that in our experience A-type events have always been followed by B-type events, and we are saying more too than that this conjunction will continue to hold. What we are saying, in Locke's view, is that certain objects have the *power* to bring about changes in certain situations, so that, for example, the fire being held against the paper *brings about* the burning of the paper or *makes* the paper burn. But Locke had some difficulty with the notion of power, never doubting that bodies do have powers, but not finding it easy to explain how experience provides us with the idea. A not very clear passage right at the beginning of II xxi reads:

> The mind being every day informed, by the senses, of the alteration of those simple ideas it observes in things without; and taking notice how one comes to an end, and ceases to be, and another begins to

exist which was not before ... and concluding from what it has so constantly observed to have been, that the like changes will for the future be made in the same things, by like agents, and by the like ways, – considers in one thing the possibility of having any of its simple ideas changed, and in another the possibility of making that change; and so comes by that idea which we call *power*.

Here Locke does seem to be taking the view that we are never directly *aware* of power as a characteristic of objects in the natural world, though clearly he also holds that the observation of regular sequences does *somehow* furnish us with the idea. For Locke, of course, there was a dichotomy between the object with its qualities on the one hand and the ideas we have when perceiving the object on the other, and it is not I think distorting his position to say that he certainly believed that power was not manifested in the ideas given in sensation, but that it *was* attributable to the objects themselves. Against this Berkeley holds that objects are simply collections of ideas with nothing occult in them, and that the bodies Locke holds we *can* attribute powers to simply do not exist.

Locke believed, however, that we do have some sort of direct insight into the nature of power, but that this comes not through observing what goes on in the natural world but by reflecting on the activity of our own minds. Thus in sect. 4 he says:

> ... bodies, by our senses, do not afford us so clear and distinct an idea of active power, as we have from reflection on the operations of our minds. ... The idea of the *beginning* of motion we have only from reflection on what passes in ourselves; where we find by experience, that, barely by willing it, barely by a thought of the mind, we can move the parts of our bodies, which were before at rest.

The section is headed 'The clearest Idea of active Power had from Spirit'. Berkeley, by the time he came to publish the *Principles*, accepted that though we do not observe power in nature we do have experience of agency through reflection. And it seemed to him to follow that when we talk of a spirit causing, really causing, something to happen, what we say is 'grounded on experience'. If, however, we say in all metaphysical seriousness that objects in nature enter into causal relationships, what we say has no grounding in experience, so that 'we only amuse our selves with words' (*Pr.* 28).

It will be obvious that for Berkeley our knowledge of our own causal activity is absolutely essential as a basis for our reasoning to the causal activity of other spirits in general and God in particular, so it is at least interesting to consider the question whether introspection does really furnish us with any notion of power, or whether here too all we are really aware of is sequences and the fact that certain volitions are accompanied by the desired events. It might be argued that I learn, for example, that the volition that my little finger should bend is followed by the bending of the finger and therefore conclude that I have the power to bend the finger, and that in a similar way I learn that my volition that my foot should bend at the instep is not followed by the desired event and therefore conclude that I do not have the power to bend my foot at the instep. The situation, it might be said, parallels that in which I learn that a lighted match will set fire to paper but not to steel, and in neither case is there any intuition of power over and above observation of sequence.[1]

The claim that we have no intuition of power through reflection on what goes on when we will something to happen was of course made by Hume, and we find Hume holding in the Appendix to the *Treatise* that philosophers who suggest that it is because we are aware of power in our volitions that we can meaningfully attribute it to material substance are wrong in the very basis of their argument. Clearly a similar point might be made against Berkeley. *If* Hume is right about there being no intuition of power gained through reflection then he deprives Berkeley of an experiential basis for the notion, and thus makes it impossible for him to allow that we can meaningfully attribute power even to God.

Because of this it is interesting to discover that at an early stage in the development of his thought Berkeley does seem to have taken seriously the view that our volitions *occasion* rather than cause the willed events, and that the fulfilment of our acts of will is always dependent upon God's causal activity. Thus in *PC* 107, an entry which is marked with the obelus and which also has the marginal sign 'G' for 'God', he says:

> Strange impotence of men. Man without God. Wretcheder than a stone or tree, he having onely the power to be miserable by his unperformed wills, these having no power at all

It is, I think, impossible to tell *how* seriously Berkeley took this notion. The entry reports Malebranche's position, according to which human volitions are only occasions which God takes as cues to provide us with the appropriate ideas. Malebranche had claimed that in ascribing causal power to human wills and to matter, philosophers were making both into 'divinities'. We can guess that it was this aspect of the story that appealed to Berkeley. He may well have been attracted to a doctrine which made us *wholly* dependent upon God and which gave him a total prerogative of causal power.[2] Entry 461 is again significant. This reads:

> The simple idea call'd Power seems obscure or rather none at all. but onely the relation 'twixt cause & Effect. W^n I ask whether A can move B. if A be an intelligent thing. I mean no more than whether the volition of A that B move be attended with the motion of B, if A be senseless whether the impulse of A against B be follow'd by ye motion of B.

Here, then, early in the *Commentaries*, the simple idea of power is discarded in favour of the relation between cause and effect, and this relation is analysed in terms of sequence, with the volitions of human agents apparently enjoying no special status as revealing efficient causal power.

Whether Berkeley was ever fully committed to this position is perhaps questionable. The jottings in the notebooks were meant for his eyes only, and in many cases the tone suggests whole-hearted acceptance of some notion whereas probably he is just experimenting with some idea which he is quite prepared to reject if it is found wanting. In this particular case he may well have been aware of difficulties even as he penned the entry, and clearly if it involves the view that the relation between human volitions and events is essentially similar to that between the supposed causes and effects in nature the position was one he could not long adhere to. There is a dilemma here. If things in nature are not genuine agents, and agency is to be sought for in the divine will, then we must have some experiential basis for the notion of agency derived, presumably, from reflection on the power of our volitions. And this means that Berkeley must not treat the relation between our volitions and events as on a level with the supposed causal relationships to be found in nature. The alternative is that Berkeley should say that genuine agency *is* manifested in nature, agency always being analysable in terms of sequence. But the consequence of this would be that Berkeley would have to analyse the relationship between divine volitions and events in terms of sequence, and that he would not be able to point to the *absence* of efficient causal power in nature to persuade us that to explain the sequences there we must look to spirit. Ultimately it is by persuading us that the impulse of A against B does not (strictly) cause the motion of B that Berkeley hopes to persuade us to look elsewhere for agency. I would guess that in entry 461 he does not mean that there are *efficient* causes in nature, but that he also holds (in the spirit of entry 107) that our volitions are not efficient causes either.

In view of Berkeley's awareness of the challenge from Malebranche that neither sensation *nor reflection* provides us with a basis for the notion of agency, one would have welcomed from him a fresh start and a fresh look at the concepts involved when we say that fire makes paper burn, arsenic brings about the death of the consumer, and volitions bring about desired states of affairs. Unfortunately, entries in the Commentaries provide no evidence of careful rethinking, though Berkeley does reject Malebranche's position and instead insists that reflection, and reflection alone, can provide us with a notion of agency. The key entry here is 499 in which Berkeley offers what seems to be intended as a new definition of 'cause'. Thus:

> What means Cause as distinguish'd from Occasion? nothing but a Being wch wills w^n the Effect follows the volition.

The definition is very useful given Berkeley's purposes, and indeed suspiciously useful. The first consequence is that if the definition is accepted it will certainly be nonsense to say that sensible things cause – really cause – things to happen, unless, that is, we are also prepared to say that sensible things have wills. And a second consequence is that, given that I am aware that the movement of my arm follows a locatable volition, it will be undeniable that I am causally responsible for the arm's movement, and that my volitions cause. This is the point Berkeley makes in entry 548 where we find him confidently rejecting the position of entry 107:

> We move our Legs our selves. 'tis we that will their movement. Herein I differ from Malbranch.

But there is a third and, from Berkeley's point of view, most desirable consequence of accepting the definition. For *if* the definition is allowed and if at the same time we accept, as we may be strongly inclined to do, that every event in nature must have a cause, it will *follow* that we must suppose a *spiritual* cause of those events we would normally account for in terms of the action of material things.

I suspect indeed that it was the desire to provide a grounding in our experience on which mediate knowledge of God's power could be based that more than anything explains Berkeley's apparently abrupt rejection of the occasionalist account of the relation between human volitions and events. But be that as it may, he was certainly aware of the great advantage of defining 'cause' as he does in entry 499. For the entry continues:

> Those things that happen from without we are not the Cause of therefore there is some other Cause of them i.e. there is a being that wills these perceptions in us.

This is the first brief statement of what was to become his main proof of the existence of God. Entry 499 is the one Luce refers to as containing 'a valid proof of the existence of God starting from the nature of the world as Berkeley saw it when he published the *Principles*'.

There are difficulties with the definition of entry 499, and one obvious difficulty is that we certainly do not want to say that every time a volition is followed by the desired event the volition was the cause of the event. Those who back horses sometimes will their choices to win, but most people do not take the exercise very seriously and only the most gullible really believe that if the horse wins the backer's willing played any causal role. Similarly, if I now will the door to open, and it opens, I may not be seriously tempted, even if there is no other immediately obvious cause, to suppose that I brought about the event. And the trouble is that if we look a little more deeply into the question as to when and why I am inclined to attribute power to my volitions it is all too easy to slip into a regular sequence view. It seems at least plausible to suppose that I learn by experience that my volitions are efficacious in certain contexts but not in others, and we might suppose that the way in which I learn this parallels the way in which I learn by experience that certain supposed causes in nature are connected with certain supposed effects. It might be claimed, then, that in both cases all we actually observe is regular sequence. Probably if my willing that doors should open was invariably followed by the opening of the doors I would conclude that I was blessed with the power to open doors by a mere act of will, though the conclusion would not be based on some special intuition of power over and above observation of what followed what. And yet Berkeley does seem to need some intuitive awareness in particular cases of the power of the will to bring about events if he is to say that acts of will quite obviously bring things about while quite obviously things in nature do not. There is reason to suppose that he realized that this intuition can be made to appear as elusive as Locke found the intuition of power in the natural world to be.

Leaving this problem aside, there is a further difficulty for Berkeley to face, and this arises when we consider the sorts of context in which it might be supposed that I am causally responsible for events. We can spend a little time on this question. Now it can certainly be argued that passive observers would have no concept of causal relationship, and that it is only because I am aware of myself as an agent or as a being capable of doing things, bringing things about, or making things happen, that I am able to conceive of things other than myself as agents. But if I am aware of myself as an agent it seems that I am aware not only of my power over 'thoughts', as when I will the occurrence of mental images, but also of my power over things. I can, for example, bend my little finger, throw a stone, lift a weight, or smash a glass. If I ask (a) what made the mental image occur, it seems quite natural to say that the cause was my volition, and clearly we do want to say that I have (some) power over mental events. And if I ask (b) what caused my arm to move, it again seems natural to do what Berkeley does and attribute the event to my will, though here we might want to add some sort of scientific account in terms of human physiology. But if I ask (c) what caused the stone to fly through the air, part of my answer will again be that *I* caused it (by the movement of my arm). My answer to (b) illustrates that I take it that I can bring about at least some changes in the sensible world (my arm being a sensible thing), and my answer to (c) shows that I take it that by the motion of my arm, an event in the sensible world, I can bring about other changes in the natural world.

That there is a problem here for Berkeley should be obvious, for it would seem arbitrary to assert that I can obtain the notion of bringing things about from observing the power I have over my thoughts, but not from observing the power I have over my arm or, through my arm, on a stone. But, if he does allow that, when I will my arm to move thereby bringing about some other change in the natural world, my arm is doing something or causing something to happen, it would seem that he must allow that sensible things can cause. Suppose for example I will my little finger to move and score the heel of my hand. Certainly this is something I take it I have the power to do, and there is an event following a volition here so it would seem that Berkeley should regard the volition as playing a causal role. But what is clearly also true is that I cannot score my hand by a mere act of will, so that if I really am causally responsible for the event it is only because I am a being with a fingernail, which nail plays a crucial part in bringing about the effect. It would seem, then, that I can meaningfully attribute the scoring of my hand to the movement of my fingernail following my volition, and if this is proper there would seem to be no reason why I should not attribute the scoring to the nail if on another occasion this happens without my willing it. Further, if I take it that when I will the event, but also when I do not, the nail of my finger, a sensible thing, can bring about the scoring of my hand, there seems to be no reason why I should not accept that other sensible objects, an iron nail or a knife, can cause or bring about a similar effect. In general, if it is the case, as it seems to be, that I obtain the notion of agency in various contexts including some where my body is involved in initiating changes when I will them, this would seem to provide an adequate grounding for the notion that sensible things other than my body can effect changes.

One answer to this would be for Berkeley to turn occasionalist at the crucial point and deny that, strictly speaking, I can bring about changes in the sensible world or at least that by moving parts of my body I can bring about other changes. But the trouble with this is that it seems implausible to assert that the notion of bringing things about originates solely in reflection on the power I have over thoughts, and to deny that it can be obtained by observing the power I have over things, and it seems equally implausible to assert that it can be obtained by moving my arm but not by lifting a brick. In addition to this, Berkeley certainly should have been aware that the denial that certain events, which we normally take ourselves to have brought about, are in fact brought about by us, could be dangerous. For it then becomes incumbent upon him to make a special case for claiming that *sometimes* we are right and that certain events, in particular in the field of mental imagery, are indeed caused by us. If for example my volition *occasions*, rather than *causes* the movement of my arm (though it seems quite obvious to me that *I* move it), it cannot just be assumed that I have got the story right when I say that *I* bring ideas to mind in imagination.

All the same, though, it is doubtful whether Berkeley was really entitled to take the line that there is a causal connection between willing and, say, the movement of the arm, and this because of his view of what the arm *is*. For as a sensible thing the arm for him is not a chunky item that can be moved about, but rather a collection of passive ideas imprinted on the senses in accordance with *God's* volitions. David Berman has suggested to me that I might make this point by saying that efficient causality in the realm of sensations seems to fall into *creation*, so that for Berkeley to say that he moves *any* sensible thing would seem to amount to a claim that he can create ideas of sense. Berman adds: 'A common sense thing can be moved, but what sense can be given to moving "an" idea? For one thing my pen in two positions "is" two ideas. Real power over sensations or ideas amounts to the creation of ideas – which for Berkeley is done only by God.' It seems to me that this sums up Berkeley's position admirably, and if it does we should perhaps think of *God* as 'moving our arms' (i.e. presenting appropriate ideas) when we will in a certain sort of way. Whether the story would at the end of the day make sense is another matter. It may still be the story Berkeley *has* to tell if he is to stick to his claim that sensible things are ideas.

There is not much point in searching the texts to find what Berkeley *really* believes here, for certain considerations made him want to recognize that human agents can directly interfere in the world of sensible objects while others made it difficult for him to be happy with the notion. In *PC* 548 he is categorical that we do at least move our limbs ourselves and he takes the same line in, for example, *Pr.* 147 and *Siris* 291. One interesting statement is in the *Dialogues*, and it comes in answer to Hylas's charge that 'in making God the immediate author of all the motions in Nature, you make him the author of murder, sacrilege, adultery, and the like heinous sins' (iii, 236). One point Philonous makes here is that even if God is *causally* responsible for the physical actions this does not make him *morally* responsible for the sins, because the sin is not in what the body does 'but in the internal deviation of the will from the laws of reason and religion'. That is, the objection can be answered on the assumption that God is the immediate cause of *everything* that happens in the sensible world.

Philonous also claims that the materialist cannot point the finger here because ultimately he is faced with a similar problem. But he does not rest content with these points. He goes on:

> Lastly, I have no where said that God is the only agent who produces all the motions in bodies. It is true, I have denied there are any other agents beside spirits: but this is very consistent with allowing to thinking rational beings, in the production of motions, the use of limited powers, ultimately indeed derived from God, but immediately under the direction of their own wills, which is sufficient to entitle them to all the guilt of their actions.

This notion of derivative causal power is also reflected in *De Motu* 25:

> Besides corporeal things there is the other class, *viz*. thinking things, and that there is in them the power of moving bodies we have learned by personal experience, since our mind at will can stir and stay the movements of our limbs, whatever be the ultimate explanation of the fact. This is certain that bodies are moved at the will of the mind, and accordingly the mind can be called, correctly enough, a principle of motion, a particular and subordinate principle indeed, and one which itself depends on the first and universal principle.

If we *are* to comb the text we can point too to *Siris* 257 where we find the unhappy suggestion that what we do out of habit, rather than through a conscious act of will, *may* (like the bodily movement of a bee or spider) be more properly attributable to God as cause than to the power of a finite being. More significant than all this, though, may be the fact that, when Berkeley wants to convince us that we can meaningfully attribute power to spirits so as to get the passivity argument under way, what he chooses to point to is, not that power which he sometimes likes to think we have over our limbs, but rather that power by which we can bring ideas to mind in imagination.

If there is a problem for Berkeley here, and it would seem that there must be, the point is clearly connected with the one we were making at the end of the last chapter. It is crucial but it can be put quite simply. The fact is that one line of thought which would lead him to suppose that we are causally responsible for much less than we ordinarily think (and in particular only for our thoughts) is identical with the one that makes it seem obvious to him that a person *is* a spirit and thus something radically distinct from the body. It is because my head, arms, legs and torso are thought of as being composed of experiences of mine, or as passive presentations to consciousness, that it is supposed that strictly speaking I should not think of them as parts of the real me. And it is because these ideas, just as much as those which make up the table, are thought of in this way that it becomes difficult to see how I can be supposed *really* to move my arm any more than I can be supposed *really* to move the table. The self in this conception is a sort of bodiless cyclops, and as such it must be incapable of activity within the sensible world.[3]

Against this, and creating the tension, there is the fact that Berkeley cannot, and does not, consistently conceive of himself as a bodiless cyclops, and in his book on Berkeley, in which he deliberately stresses what he sees as the achievements of *NTV* rather than the paradoxes of the *Principles*, A. D. Ritchie sees it as a special merit that here at least he broke away from this conception. Thus:

> Berkeley's approach to his problems leads us definitely away from the usual assumption that experience is passive recipience and nothing else, to the conclusion that there is also something more, namely, learning by mutual encounter; and the more we actively explore the more and more effectively and instructively we encounter. A bodiless cyclops, such as many philosophers suppose themselves to be, never encounters, cannot explore and nothing for him can be either real or unreal, true or false. It is not likely that Berkeley himself fully realized what he was doing. There are passages in *Princ.*, which a bodiless cyclops might write if he were able, as he might most of Hume, J. S. Mill and Russell. (p. 8)

In a similar spirit we might note N. Bohr's admonition:

> ... it must never be forgotten that we ourselves are both actors and spectators in the drama of existence. (p. 318)[4]

If Ritchie is right Berkeley realized this, or at least half realized it when he wrote *NTV*.

The insight here is of fundamental importance, and it would be nice to attribute it to Berkeley. My feeling is, though, that throughout his book Ritchie overstates the case for seeing in Berkeley anything like a decisive break with the notion that we are essentially observers of the sensible reality. This may be a matter of emphasis, but it is surely *important* to emphasize that when it comes to what he likes to think of as the most accurate analysis of our experience of the sensible, Berkeley puts all the stress on persons as the *perceivers* of ideas. There is no question here of our having to hunt around to find odd passages in the *Principles* where Berkeley slips up and talks of himself as if he were bodiless, for the view is reflected in his most careful statements about what he is and what the sensible world is. *He*, of course, is 'one simple, undivided, active being' and as such he is 'entirely distinct' from all ideas or sensible objects, including those ideas which he would like us to think of as making up his body. Berkeley concedes that as he is a spirit it follows that he cannot be seen or encountered, and it goes without saying that *this* Berkeley cannot lift a brick or throw a stone. It is true that when we read *NTV* in particular we are encouraged to think of persons as embodied agents who can reach out and touch things, and walk to and feel things, but ultimately Berkeley is going to hold, as he tells us in *Pr.* 44, that this picture distorts the real truth. We have to shift our attention now to his beliefs about sensible objects. And when we do this we see that (strictly) there can be no question of our walking from A to B and feeling an object which was there to be felt, for the truth is supposed to be that there *is* nothing at a distance and that visual ideas are really only signs of what tangible ideas God is prepared 'to imprint upon us'. In the last analysis I cannot learn about things by bumping into them, lifting them, or trying to push them around, and this not just because a bodiless cyclops *cannot* manipulate objects, but because there *are* no manipulable objects.[5]

It is interesting that in criticizing Hume (who he takes it *was* very definitely committed to conceiving of himself as a bodiless cyclops) Ritchie introduces a Crusoe-figure who will perforce *have* to actively explore his environment if he is to stay alive. We are asked to agree that 'empirical investigation is itself a physical process; it requires the actual handling of bodies' (p. 90) and that:

> ... we can discover what bodies are doing and what is being done to them, directly by handling these bodies, indirectly by handling other bodies, and both because our own behaviour is causal in the secondary sense. Just looking gets us nowhere ... There is a great deal here that should worry visualist philosophers, but nothing to worry Berkeley. (p. 92)

What *makes* this interesting is, of course, the fact that when Berkeley wants to envisage a mortal who might naturally come at the truth of things *he* introduces a Crusoe-figure, but one who, far from being forced to explore his environment, is 'contemplative' and at the same time 'under no necessity of labouring to secure himself from hunger and cold: but at full ease'. We miss the point of this stipulation if we suppose that Berkeley wants his solitary man to be 'at full ease' just so as to maximize the time available for contemplation, for it is quite clear that Berkeley wants to debar his Crusoe from just that physical exploration that Ritchie says would be essential if he were to understand his environment. Basically, Berkeley's Crusoe *will* just look, and Berkeley holds that *this* man will both perceive and *realize* that he perceives only 'a constant train of particular ideas passing in his mind'. Surely it is significant that this truth – *Berkeley's truth* – is to be appreciated by the man who does not use his body in exploring the world.

It would seem, then, that the bodiless cyclops notion is dominant in Berkeley's thinking, though it would serve our purposes here to be given the weaker claim (which Ritchie concedes) that at least *sometimes* Berkeley does think of himself as bodiless. We can certainly recognize that on other occasions he does talk as if we were corporeal agents, and even that he *sometimes* seems to see that it is because we are physical things and can encounter other physical things that we can understand the world as we do. For what we should stress is that *when* he conceives of himself as just a perceiving spirit Berkeley is bound to be puzzled as to how we can properly be said to move our limbs, and this because a limb will be only a collection of passive ideas imprinted on the senses from without. Passive ideas cannot *do* anything and nothing can be done *to* them. They cannot boil water, and they cannot be moved. An *embodied* Berkeley should, though, see things differently. For if we have limbs and really do move them it cannot be supposed that the limbs move within a sensible world which is otherwise composed of passive presentations to consciousness. The man who can move his arms within a world where sensible things *can* be moved will surely be able to discover that we, to the extent that we are corporeal, can act on other corporeal things and bring about changes in our environment *by* moving our bodies. To a bodiless cyclops it may well seem incomprehensible both that he should move a sensible object and that one sensible object should act on another, for if Berkeley is right he will take himself to be aware only of that 'constant train of particular ideas passing in his mind'. But the other side of the coin is that a partly or wholly corporeal agent who discovers things about the world as he acts in it will be one who supposes that he has good reason for taking it that the corporeal *can* act.

III

What Bennett has called Berkeley's *passivity argument* for God's existence is really a variant on an argument used by Locke to show that though we are immediately aware only of *ideas* in sense experience, these do justify us in supposing that there are real bodies causing us to perceive them. Locke says:

> ... sometimes I find that *I cannot avoid the having those ideas produced in my mind.* For though, when my eyes are shut, or windows fast, I can at pleasure recal to my mind the ideas of light, or the sun, which former sensations had lodged in my memory; so I can at pleasure lay by *that* idea, and take into my view that of the smell of a rose, or taste of sugar. But, if I turn my eyes at noon towards the sun, I cannot avoid the ideas which the light or sun then produces in me. So that there is a manifest difference between the ideas laid up in my memory ... and those which force themselves upon me, and I cannot avoid having. And therefore it must needs be some exterior cause, and the brisk acting of some objects without me, whose efficacy I cannot resist, that produces those ideas in my mind, whether I will or no. (IV xi 5)

Much of this argument Berkeley accepts. He accepts that there is an important distinction to be made between those ideas the finite spirit produces in itself and those we cannot avoid having, and he agrees with Locke that there must be some cause of the involuntary ideas. He disagrees with Locke, though, in that he maintains the cause *cannot* be 'objects without me' and *must* be the volition of some other spirit.

We can look first at the area of agreement between Locke and Berkeley. And here there is the distinction between voluntary and involuntary ideas. Berkeley says:

> I find I can excite ideas in my mind at pleasure, and vary and shift the scene as oft as I think fit. It is no more than willing, and straightway this or that idea arises in my fancy: and by the same power it is

obliterated, and makes way for another. ... But whatever power I may have over my own thoughts, I find the ideas actually perceived by sense have not a like dependence on my will. When in broad day-light I open my eyes, it is not in my power to choose whether I shall see or no, or to determine what particular objects shall present themselves to my view; and so likewise as to the hearing and other senses, the ideas imprinted on them are not creatures of my will. (*Pr.* 28-9)

This basically repeats what Locke says. And similarly there is the assumption that there must be some cause of *all* the ideas I perceive. As Berkeley has it:

We perceive a continual succession of ideas, some are anew excited, others are changed or totally disappear. There is therefore some cause of these ideas whereon they depend, and which produces and changes them. (*Pr.* 26)

The open question is the one concerning the cause of those ideas I do not produce myself, and the break with Locke comes only when Berkeley concludes that ideas not dependent on my will must be presented by some other spirit.

The starting point for the argument is, then, a distinction between certain ideas I have where I am immediately aware of agency, as when I choose to call to mind the taste of sugar, and other ideas, such as those I have when I look out of my window, the cause of which is certainly not my volition. If I ask you to imagine a blue camel you can probably frame an appropriate image, but if I ask you to look out of the window and *see* a blue camel your ability to comply will depend upon whether there is a blue camel for you to see. In a sense of course, I can choose what I shall see. In the zoo I can go to the monkey-house or to the elephant-house, and if I decide on the latter I have chosen to see elephants. In another and more fundamental sense, however, I cannot choose what I see, for what I see is dependent on what there is for me to see in the direction in which I look. The truth behind this observation can be expressed by saying that we *can* choose where to look, but that when we look we cannot choose what we shall see. It is to this characteristic of sense perception that Locke wished to draw attention when he said that 'in bare naked perception, the mind is, for the most part, only passive; and what it perceives, it cannot avoid perceiving'. Of course for Locke and Berkeley the story has to be told in terms of ideas. The ideas I have when I look at the elephant are 'not creatures of my will'. The images I frame when I think about an elephant are.

Now we can agree that there is some sort of distinction to be made here, and this even though the case when I straightforwardly choose to frame a mental image is far from typical of all imagining and though, as Berkeley saw, the distinction between ideas clearly dependent on our volition, and those clearly independent of it, did not exactly correspond to the distinction he wanted to make between ideas contributing to the make-up of 'real' things and other ideas. There are cases of imagining where the connection with the will is much looser than is the case where I deliberately call a mental image to mind, there are dream images and these seem to be independent of my volition, and there are the ideas I have when hallucinated which are not produced by any effort of my will but which could not plausibly be regarded as contributing to the world of nature. There is a lot that could be said here, but the really interesting questions from our point of view are those concerning the move Berkeley makes from the distinction to the conclusion. We want to ask, first, why he believes there must be some cause of ideas not dependent on my will, and, second, why he believes this cause must be sought in spiritual agency.

In fact there does not seem to be much one can say in answer to the first of these questions except that Berkeley found the quest for agency irresistible and that, as the quotation from *Pr.* 26 suggests, he took it for granted that all ideas must be produced rather than just occur. In this he was at one with Locke. Locke does indeed try to prove at one point that nothing can exist which is not produced by something (IV x 3), but the supposed demonstration assumes what is to be proved, so it seems that Locke did just take it for granted that all events must be caused. Luce's contribution here is muddled. He begins by quoting from *PC* 831:

Every idea has a cause, i.e. is produced by a Will.

And he goes on:

This is not, as in ordinary Christian apologetic, a deduction from Divine attributes, but is a matter of observed fact from which the being of God is correctly inferred. 'When in broad daylight I open my eyes, it is not in my power to choose whether I shall see or no' (Pr. § 29). Ideas of sense 'are not creatures of my will. There is therefore some other will or spirit that produces them'. So the real ideas that are the real world are God's ideas discovered to us and becoming *pro tanto* our ideas. (Luce 2, pp. 90-1)

The suggestion here is that it is 'a matter of observed fact' that every idea has a cause and that every idea is produced by a will. But this can hardly be right. What *may* be a matter of observed fact is that objects perceived by sense are not creatures of my will, but if we are to get from this to the conclusion that the ideas we do not produce are produced by some other spirit we have to assume, or find some argument for, the claim that every idea has a cause, and of course for the claim that the only causes are spiritual causes. It may be that Berkeley does not have any *reason* for supposing that there must be a cause of sensed ideas, and if this is so the only question we can usefully ask is why he supposes that, *given* there must be some cause, this cause must lie in spiritual agency.[6]

Now sometimes Berkeley seems to be justifying this claim by a process of elimination. Talking of ideas in general (i.e. not just sensed ideas) he says in *Pr.* 26:

That this cause cannot be any quality or idea or combination of ideas, is clear from the preceding section. [Berkeley claims that 'the very being of an idea implies passiveness and inertness in it'.] It must therefore be a substance; but it has been shewn that there is no corporeal or material substance: it remains therefore that the cause of ideas is an incorporeal active substance or spirit.

That is, spirit must be the cause because that is the only thing left that might cause. Continuing this line of thought, Berkeley can claim that in some cases – cases where we deliberately call ideas to mind – we are aware of the will of a spirit causally operative in the production of ideas. In this way the conclusion that spiritual agency *must* cause all ideas is confirmed by the fact that we know through experience that it *can* produce ideas. We might note here that though he has shown to his own satisfaction that there is no corporeal substance to cause anything, Berkeley was further encouraged by the fact that those who claimed that the cause of sensed ideas was material substance had to admit that they could give no account of *how* things in the external world produce ideas in the mind. In *Pr.* 19 he says:

... though we give the materialists their external bodies, they by their own confession are never the nearer knowing how our ideas are

L*

produced: since they own themselves unable to comprehend in what manner body can act upon spirit, or how it is possible it should imprint any idea in the mind.

The *reductio ad absurdum* of the materialist's view was, in Berkeley's opinion, the claim made by the occasionalists that outward objects can play no causal role here. In brief, the view was that external objects do not, and cannot, produce ideas in us, but that *God* causes us to have ideas on the occasion of the presence of bodies.

Basically, though, focusing attention on the process of elimination makes us lose sight of what I take to be the move Berkeley really wants to make. What we are supposed to appreciate, I think, is that *given* there must be a cause of ideas of sense, consideration of the meaning of 'cause' should convince us that the cause must be the volition of a spirit. As we noted earlier, given the assumption that there must be a cause, the conclusion he wants follows from the definition of the word in *PC* 499. Berkeley did believe that as no efficient causal power was manifested in the world of sensible objects we could not have obtained the notion by observing that world. This being the case the word must get its meaning from reflection and, if we ignore here the possibility that we move our legs ourselves, from the observation of the power each of us finds he has to create ideas in imagination. We might argue that colour predicates get their meaning within the context of descriptions of sensible objects and that to refer to the mind as red, blue, or coloured at all, must be meaningless and a mere playing with words. And similarly, Berkeley would argue, the word 'cause' can get a meaning only within the context of descriptions of mental activity, and this because it is only here that we are aware of agency. The fact is that when we refer to sensible objects or external things as causes 'we only amuse our selves with words'. For Berkeley, it is nonsense to talk of causal power where there is no volition, and this being so we must suppose that if our ideas of sense are caused they must be caused by the will of a spirit.

IV

This, then, is Berkeley's argument for the claim that spiritual agency must lie behind anything we perceive by sense and be responsible for all changes within the sensible world. The considerations which lead him to suppose that we should recognize here the benevolent God of

Christian monotheism are of less interest. Very briefly, the view is this. Certain ideas (we are told) suggest to us the existence of finite spirits, but even these should direct our attention to God for it is *he* who is causally responsible for producing those very ideas which suggest to me that there are other finite spirits about. Indeed, Berkeley wants to claim that we can be *more* certain of the existence of God than of the existence of other persons, and this because it is God who 'maintains that intercourse between spirits, whereby they are able to perceive the existence of each other' (*Pr.* 147). Beyond this, the way in which the vast majority of our ideas of sense are presented to us betokens a *wise* and *benevolent* being, and, the more we appreciate what this agent has to do, the more our awareness of his presence and his greatness will grow. In *NTV* 147, for example, Berkeley tells us that 'the proper objects of vision constitute an universal language' not just of 'nature' (first edition) but of 'the Author of nature' (subsequent editions). We are to see the scientist as discovering *regularities* in nature, and instead of regarding the world we know through sense experience as a self-subsistent machine, functioning in accordance with laws internal to the system, we must note its dependence upon the will of God and have regard to 'the divine traces of wisdom and goodness that shine throughout the economy of Nature' (*Pr.* 154).

Now the passivity argument is certainly Berkeley's *main* argument for the existence of God. But he does have another argument, and this occurs in the *Dialogues*. Philonous says:

> When I deny sensible things an existence out of the mind, I do not mean my mind in particular, but all minds. Now it is plain they have an existence exterior to my mind, since I find them by experience to be independent of it. There is therefore some other mind wherein they exist, during the intervals between the times of my perceiving them: as likewise they did before my birth, and would do after my supposed annihilation. (ii, 230-1)

Bennett sets the argument out as follows:

(a) No collection of ideas can exist when not perceived by some spirit;
(b) Objects are collections of ideas;
(c) Objects sometimes exist when not perceived by any human spirit; therefore
(d) There is a non-human spirit which sometimes perceives objects. (p. 169)

We must now say something about this, *the continuity argument*.

By way of preface it is necessary to point out that Bennett examines the argument in the context of a polemic against what he takes to be the 'standard' account of Berkeley's attitude to the continuity question, and as Ch. VII finds him at his most disputatious with 'adversaries' located and named, future commentators are bound to be nervous in this field. They will have either to find some defence of the 'standard' account, to accept Bennett's position, or to show that they can give an alternative account which avoids the mistakes of the 'standard' story. Obviously everything hangs here on what the standard account is or is supposed to be. As Bennett describes it the account is in effect a package involving a number of features all of which seem to him to be equally objectionable. It seems to me that some of the features are objectionable, while others can be allowed to stand. In order to establish his own position that the 'standard' account must be rejected *in toto* Bennett has thoroughly combed the texts. I have done the same and reached a different position.[7]

We can start by looking at an important point on which I agree with Bennett, and this is that we should be *surprised* that Berkeley uses the continuity argument. Certainly *we* should be surprised for we have assumed that Berkeley's God 'waits in the wings' to save the day for common sense on the continuity question, and that Berkeley needs to *prove* his existence as omnipresent perceiver in order to show that Berkeleian sensible objects do continue to exist when unperceived by us. If this is indeed Berkeley's position, it is certainly not legitimate for him to appeal to the supposed fact of the continued existence of sensible objects to prove the existence of God. Aschenbrenner has this point in mind when he says of the continuity argument:

> His actual use of it is circular. He has no reason to believe that remote sensibles exist except on the supposition that God perceives them, but he has no reason, leaving other arguments aside, nor any need to believe that God or any other perceiver is there present except that there exist remote sensibles which must be perceived by someone. The existence of these is begged from the start. (p. 57)

In brief, if there is a continuity *problem* for Berkeley, and if he is going to answer it by appealing to God's perception of things not perceived by us, he is just not entitled to use the continuity *argument* to prove God's existence.

But Berkeley *does* use the continuity argument. It is there in the passage quoted from the *Dialogues*. And Bennett performs a service by explaining how Berkeley might have slipped into using it on this one occasion.[8] I agree with Bennett, though, that while we need not worry too much about a slip on one occasion, it would be disturbing if we found Berkeley regularly assuming continuity in this context. As Bennett says:

> Idealism is consistent with the thesis that objects exist when no human perceives them, but it clamours for the latter to be justified. My point about 'depend' explains Berkeley's attempt to justify the thesis in one short passage, but it cannot explain his adopting it as a permanent intellectual possession. What *can* explain this? (p. 171)

Part of Bennett's answer, and I am inclined to accept this, is that we need not worry too much about the continuity argument, and this because, contrary to what has often been supposed, *Berkeley does not use it on many occasions*. It is, in short, 'a momentary aberration'.[9]

It is not necessary to spend a lot of time in showing that this is so, for Bennett has done the work. But to illustrate how a commentator can assume that he finds the continuity argument in a passage where it is at least not obviously present we can look at what Luce says about *Pr.* 6. Here, it will be remembered, Berkeley claims of sensible objects that 'so long as they are not actually perceived by me, or do not exist in my mind or that of any other created spirit, they must either have no existence at all, or else subsist in the mind of some eternal spirit'. We might think that the structure of this claim is clear. On the basis of what Berkeley has said in sects. 1-5 we are supposed to conclude of things not perceived by us that there are two possibilities: either (a) they do not exist at all, or (b) they are perceived by an eternal spirit. It is at least a very natural interpretation, then, to suppose that Berkeley would hope to *show* that there is an eternal spirit who perceives things when we do not, and thus that it is (a) which has to be rejected. As Bennett says:

> These are not the words of one who would add: 'Objects do exist when not perceived by creatures, so there must indeed be an eternal spirit which perceives them.' The natural continuation is rather: 'Unless we can show independently that there is an eternal spirit, we do not know that objects exist when not perceived by creatures'. (p. 172)

Luce, though, assumes a quite different interpretation. Thus:

> In Section 6, for instance, of the *Principles* he declares it to be a 'near and obvious' truth that all the choir of heaven and furniture of the earth, viz. all those bodies which compose the mighty frame of the world subsist in the mind of some eternal spirit. (Luce 7, p. 184)

And in the index to the *Works* we find *Pr.* 6 listed as containing a *proof* of God's existence. In criticizing this we can say, first, that this is not the only possible interpretation of *Pr.* 6, second (and this is a stronger claim) that it is not the most natural interpretation, and third, that it is incumbent on any commentator to point out that if Berkeley is indeed arguing in the way supposed then his procedure is fundamentally faulty. *Pr.* 1-5 contain an argument for the *Esse-percipi* principle and it is this principle that creates a continuity *problem* for Berkeley. It would seem obvious that, if Berkeley is claiming that the plain man is straightforwardly wrong when he takes it that sensible objects can exist outside a mind, then he can hardly just *assume* that the plain man has got it right when he supposes that things continue to exist when we do not perceive them.

So far every time I have mentioned Bennett here it has been to agree with him, and now I must make it clear at what point I begin to disagree. On p. 172 he quotes Warnock as saying:

> Berkeley ... knows that any plain man would insist that the furniture in an unoccupied room actually does exist, not merely that it would exist if the room were occupied; and he himself thinks that it would be merely absurd to question this.

And on p. 172 Bennett is quite explicit that it is *this view* he has in mind when he refers to the 'standard' view. Indeed he says quite categorically that this *is* the standard view. So let us be quite clear on what it is supposed to be. It is that Berkeley thinks it quite proper to take object-continuity for granted in order to prove that God exists, and this because nobody (least of all Berkeley) would be so foolish as to take seriously the notion that objects may not continue to exist when we do not perceive them. For ease of reference we can think of think of this as *the Warnock view*, though we should not suppose either that the notion is peculiar to Warnock or that he would want to be thought of as an enthusiastic champion of it.

The quotation from Warnock comes right at the end of sect. 37 of

Bennett's book, and Bennett proceeds to 'test it'. But already he has made an unfortunate move. Earlier we noted that *part* of his answer to the question as to how Berkeley could have come to adopt the continuity *argument* as an important weapon in his arsenal was that he did no such thing, but this is only part of the answer. Bennett asks himself what can explain Berkeley's adopting the continuity argument 'as a permanent intellectual possession' and he answers:

> Nothing; for there is no such fact to be explained. Berkeley does not regularly assume that objects exist when no human perceives them; he is not much interested in whether they do; and the continuity argument, which assumes that they do, is absent from the *Principles* and occurs in the *Dialogues* only in the two-sentence passage which I have quoted. That passage is right out of line with everything else Berkeley says about the continuity of objects, and should be dismissed as a momentary aberration.

There are *two* claims we need to distinguish here. First there is the claim that Berkeley does not regularly make the illegitimate assumption that of course things exist when not perceived by us, so as to prove that that there must be an omnipresent perceiver. And, second, there is the quite different claim that Berkeley 'is not much interested' in whether objects have a continued existence or not. Bennett holds that Berkeley does not *care* about continuity, and that he is in fact indifferent to the *issue*. This second claim broadens the range of the attack. After all, if we held that Berkeley did want to *allow* for continuity, and to make some show of aligning himself with the vulgar on the issue, but was not enamoured with the continuity argument, we should still have reason, and just as much reason as Bennett, to be disturbed by the suggestion that he just *assumes* object-continuity in order to prove the existence of God. We would still feel that he needs an *independent* proof of God's existence. One can deny that Berkeley was fully committed to the continuity *argument* while holding that he did want to find room in his system for object-continuity, so Bennett is coming into conflict with a range of opponents when he opens his attack on the 'standard' account with a section entitled 'Berkeley's indifference to continuity'.

I would certainly want to hold that there is no reason why we should not take it that Berkeley cared about continuity without at the same time believing that he was committed to the continuity *argument*. But

I would go further and suggest that evidence that he cared about continuity, far from supporting it, would actually tend to undermine the Warnock view. To make this clear we should look at two distinct positions Berkeley *might* have held. First, he *might* have held that it is demonstrable that sensible objects can exist only for so long as they are perceived, and that as it is just obvious that they exist when unperceived by us then it must be the case that there is another spirit who perceives them when we do not. On this view, object-continuity would indeed have been a premiss for Berkeley, but at the same time he would not have thought that it was incumbent on him to justify his belief in continuity. Given that this was his position we should not expect to find him agonizing over object-continuity, wondering whether he could allow for it in his system, or taking discontinuity seriously as an option, for central to this interpretation is the notion that he would have thought it 'merely absurd' to call continuity into question. But there is another possible position and I think it is nearer to the one Berkeley actually held. Certainly he *might* have realized that given that *esse* is *percipi*, object-continuity can no longer be taken for granted. He might, that is, have seen that what he says in *Pr.* 1-5 leaves open the possibility that, contrary to what we ordinarily think, things unperceived by creatures 'have no existence at all'. Now if we take it that Berkeley was prepared to treat discontinuity as a live option, and if we also assume that he found this option unpalatable, then we have located a *problem* for him and one that will make him concerned about object-continuity. But of course just as an enthusiastic acceptance of the continuity *argument* should go hand in hand with a blithe unconcern with continuity as a *problem*, so evidence that he was concerned with the problem would suggest that he was not prepared just to take object-continuity for granted.[10]

Bennett, however, continues to treat the two notions – 'that Berkeley cares about object-continuity and that he accepts it as a premiss in a considered argument for God's existence' – as if they went naturally in tandem and as if the only alternative view worth taking seriously was his own view that Berkeley was at once indifferent to continuity and not committed to the continuity argument. This is of course a possible view, but so is the view that Berkeley cared about continuity in that he wanted to find room for it in his system, but that he was at the same time far from enthusiastic about the *argument*. This being so it is obviously highly desirable to be quite clear on just which of the elements now combined in the 'standard' account any particular argument of Bennett's undermines. At the beginning of sect. 40 Bennett lists a number of objections to the 'standard' account, quoting Berkeley and saying: 'Let my adversaries answer any one of mine I'll yield – if I don't answer every one of theirs I'll yield.' We will look at these objections, asking ourselves just what interpretation they would be objections to.

The four objections share the same form. In each case we are asked to agree that had Berkeley been enthusiastic about the continuity argument we should have expected him to have done X. It is claimed that he did not do X. And we are asked to conclude that it is therefore highly unlikely that he was enthusiastic about the argument. Running the first three objections together we can say that if Berkeley had liked the argument he would surely have used it in the *Principles*, he would have used it more than once in his writings, and he would have given it prominence when he did use it. The fact that the argument is not used in the *Principles*, that it occurs once (or at most twice) in the *Dialogues* and nowhere else, and that when it does occur it 'slides by without the slightest fanfare', all this must obviously suggest that he did not like the argument. And so it does. But clearly these objections are objections only to what we have called the Warnock view. There is nothing here to worry anyone who wants to say that Berkeley *did* care about continuity in the sense that he wanted to hold that a Berkeleian could, and perhaps should, allow for object-continuity. To repeat, it is at least *possible* that Berkeley realized that his demonstration that *esse* is *percipi* raised a question about continuity, that he wanted to be able to say he was at one with the vulgar on this issue, but that he realized that he was not in a position to take object-continuity for granted. If he did take this view it would explain his not using the continuity argument except in one aberrant passage, and it would explain this just as much as would Bennett's claim that he didn't care about continuity anyway. Clearly failure to use the argument would not in itself indicate lack of concern with the issue.

The fourth objection has the same form as the first three, and I quote it only because it makes the basic point in a particularly interesting way. Bennett says:

> If Berkeley did assume that objects sometimes exist when not perceived by humans, this must be because he wanted to 'side in all

things with the Mob'; and so he must have assumed, with the 'vulgar' or 'the Mob', that the closing of eyes etc. will *never* annihilate an ordinary object – which is what the standard account always takes him to assume. So the continuity argument concludes that God perceives objects when we do not, while the passivity argument concludes that he perceives them when we do. The two are exactly complementary: without overlapping, they enable God's perceptions to cover the whole territory. Thus, Berkeley is supposed to have a perfectly economical two-part 'proof' of God's omniscience, or at least of his perceptual omnipresence; and the two parts of it correspond to the two functions which Berkeley allows to any spirit, namely perception (continuity) and will (passivity). Yet he is silent on this beautiful pattern in natural theology credited to him by the standard account. Why?[11]

We can concede here that again Bennett has located something Berkeley might have been expected to do had he been proud of the continuity argument, and that Berkeley's silence on the point contributes to the case against supposing that he *was* proud of the argument. But we must emphasize that his silence on the point need not be taken as suggesting that he was indifferent to continuity. The silence is quite compatible with the view that Berkeley saw idealism as *consistent* with an acceptance of object-continuity, that he saw that 'it clamours for the latter to be justified', *and* that he wanted to provide a justification. It is true of the four objections, then, that each of them undermines the claim that Berkeley was happy to use object-continuity as a premiss in a valued proof of God's existence, but that none of them touches what is supposed to be the other element in the 'standard' account or the claim that 'Berkeley cared about object-continuity'.

The object of the exercise to date has been merely to disentangle the question whether Berkeley liked the continuity *argument* from the question whether or not he was indifferent to the continuity *issue*. These questions seem to me to be insufficiently distinguished in Bennett's chapter. For example, though his four objections to the 'standard' account apply directly only to one element in it, he goes on straight away to tackle a point made in support of the other element, the point being that: 'It is *prima facie* hardly likely that Berkeley should be concerned about the reality of sensible things, but indifferent to their continuity.' But my main concern has not been to attack Bennett. Rather I have wanted to make it clear that not all the arguments designed to show that Warnock is wrong in supposing that Berkeley 'thinks it would be merely absurd' to question the continuity of objects will have force against anyone who claims that Berkeley positively wanted to make a case for continuity. It is just pressing this point home to say that the commentator who wants to hold that Berkeley felt a need to *justify* claims about object-continuity will definitely *welcome* attempts to show that he does not usually take object-continuity for granted. It must be stressed, however, that nothing we have said so far supports the notion that Berkeley *did* want to allow for object-continuity. To get any further forward we have to look at the texts.

V

Here it must be admitted that Bennett has been thorough in his search for relevant passages, that he has shown that there is relatively little on continuity, and that what there is is not always easy to interpret. If there is an issue between Bennett and myself, it must be as to what we are to make of what material there is. And the first point I would want to stress is that the *Commentaries* provide very clear evidence that during the period in which he prepared for publication Berkeley was certainly *not* indifferent to the continuity question. An early entry reads:

> Bodies etc do exist even w^n not perceiv'd they being powers in the active Being. (52)

And a fairly late entry reads:

> Not to mention the Combinations of Powers but to say the things the effects themselves to really exist even w^n not actually perceiv'd but still with relation to perception. (802)

In entry 312 he lists '4 Principles whereby to answer objections' and the first of these is: 'Bodies do really exist tho not perceiv'd by us.' And in entry 408 he resolves:

> I must be very particular in explaining w^t is meant by things existing in Houses, chambers, fields, caves etc w^n not perceiv'd as well as w^n

perceiv'd. & shew how the Vulgar notion agrees with mine when we narrowly inspect into the meaning & definition of the word Existence wch is no simple idea distinct from perceiving & being perceiv'd.

The existence of these, and other entries, makes it difficult to understand Bennett's claim that Berkeley attached no real importance to the continuity issue even during this period. It is clear that Berkeley thought he had a continuity *problem*, that he intended to deal with it in the *Principles*, and that he hoped to show that on this issue he was not at variance with the vulgar. The entries also show what form he saw his problem as taking. There is no suggestion that he can take object-continuity for granted and use it as a premiss in a neat proof of the existence of God. Equally, there is no suggestion that object-continuity being an undoubted fact it may be that there is something wrong with the *Esse=percipi* principle. No, the clear suggestion is that he *sees* that his immaterialism raises a question concerning continuity and that he has either to jettison continuity or to find some way of allowing for it. It seems that Berkeley wants to allow for it.

Of course it is one thing to say that at this early stage Berkeley recognized a continuity *problem*, and quite another to give an account of *how* he intended to allow for continuity .The question as to how he intended to reconcile immaterialism with object-continuity at any given stage is one that has to be asked *after* we have determined whether he wanted to effect a reconciliation. It is worth emphasising this, for though near the beginning of sect. 41 in his book Bennett suggests that he will be taking Furlong up on his view that the *Commentaries* provide evidence that prior to publication Berkeley did attach real importance to the continuity issue, it emerges that he is much more interested in criticizing Furlong's views on the way in which Berkeley's thoughts on the question developed during the period. So again we have two issues that need disentangling. It will be obvious that if Bennett disagrees with Furlong as to *how* Berkeley intended to allow for object-continuity at any given stage he is tacitly recognizing that Berkeley *was* concerned to allow for continuity at that stage, and thus that (at that stage) Berkeley was *not* indifferent to continuity. I shall take it that Berkeley did attach importance to the continuity issue during the period prior to publication and concentrate now on the question as to what he intended to say about it.

Furlong's view of the matter is stated very concisely in the following passage:

> We might put the process of thought this way. First, commonsense and *esse est percipi* are believed to clash; since *esse est percipi* is intuitively true, commonsense must go (*P.C.* 194, 293a: there is an echo of this assertion in *Principles* § 45). Then it is seen that commonsense can be rescued (*P.C.* 801, 802, *Principles* § 48). Finally it is claimed that commonsense can be used as a premiss. We have in turn the relations of exclusion, compatability and entailment. (Furlong 3, p. 405)

The final position is of course supposed to be that which Berkeley had reached by the time he came to write the *Dialogues*. So far as the period during which he filled the notebooks is concerned, then, Furlong's claim is that Berkeley moved from (1) the belief that immaterialism is inconsistent with continuity to (2) the claim that the Berkeleian can have immaterialism *and* object-continuity, given that God perceives things when we do not. Significantly, Bennett does not deny that stages (1) and (2) both occurred. What he denies is that there is 'evidence that (2) shows up in the *Commentaries* – if we take (2) as involving the belief that idealism is compatible with continuity because *God might perceive things when we do not*'.

Bennett proceeds by noting what he claims to be each and every entry which is directly relevant to the continuity question, observing that Furlong's exegesis reflects interpretations given by Luce in notes in the diplomatic edition, and that these are sometimes questionable. There is no doubt that anyone reading sect. 41 of Bennett's book will become aware of traps and pitfalls awaiting the hasty expositor. It is only fair to point out, then, that Bennett pays due tribute to Luce for providing 'the first satisfactory text of the *Commentaries*' and for accompanying the text 'with editorial notes . . . many of which are helpful in the highest degree'. It is in a similar spirit that I would like to acknowledge a debt to Luce in this area. I hold, though, that if Luce is sometimes guilty of over-confidence in giving disputable interpretations, then so too is Bennett.

I do not want to dispute Bennett's claim that (2) – the notion that immaterialism and continuity are compatible 'because God may perceive things when we do not' – does not show up (at least clearly) in the *Commentaries*. I do want to suggest, however, that Bennett's picture of what *is* going on in the Commentaries is at least not obviously correct. But we can start by making a point with which Bennett would agree. And this is that though Furlong may be right in saying that at one stage Berkeley believed immaterialism to be incompatible with continuity, this stage in fact followed one in which he did think he could have both. Thus in the very first relevant entry he tells us that bodies 'do exist even w^n not perceiv'd'. This is in entry 52, and it will be useful if we quote this very important entry again here. Berkeley says:

> Bodies etc do exist even w^n not perceiv'd they being powers in the active Being.

I shall want to say something more about this entry in a moment, but first we must stress that this entry, and one more recto entry (185) in which Berkeley weakens a little and allows existence but not 'actual' existence to things we do not perceive, both *precede* entry 194 which, as Bennett says, provides 'the only direct evidence of Berkeley's having asked "Given that objects are ideas, can an object exist when none of us perceive it?" and answered flatly "No" '. We must be clear, then, that Berkeley does not *start* by assuming that his immaterialism and object-continuity are inconsistent.

Now I think we should take entry 52 seriously and not allow ourselves to forget that at the stage where we have the first evidence as to what Berkeley's thinking on the continuity problem was we find that he takes it that *theological considerations are centrally relevant to the solution*. Bodies do continue to exist when not perceived and they exist not just as powers, but as powers *in the active Being*. Quite clearly the position here has an important point of contact with the position he takes in *Pr*. 6, for on both occasions he holds that if bodies exist when unperceived by us then they exist *in God's mind*. The differences between the two statements, which should not be allowed to obscure the point of contact, are that in the notebook entry Berkeley tells us that the objects *do* continue to exist and this as *powers* in God's mind, while in *Pr*. 6 he implies only that they *may* continue to exist and that if they do it must be as *ideas* in God's mind. We might note that at the time when he penned entry 52 Berkeley was inclined to take the notion of powers as things *in the active being* very seriously indeed. In entry 41 he says:

> Nothing corresponds to our primary ideas wthout but powers, hence a direct & brief demonstration of an active powerfull being distinct from us on whom we depend. etc.

No doubt here we are in the area of the passivity argument. Entry 52 is of course just one entry, and we should never pin too much on one solitary entry, but the point made about Berkeley seeing God as playing a crucial role in allowing for the continuous existence of bodies *is* an important one and it should not be passed over lightly. Unfortunately, the only note Bennett takes of entry 52 is to list it as one of 'a group of more or less phenomenalistic entries' (52, 98, 185, 185a, 282, 293, 293a), the others of which do not mention God or the active Being. It is significant that entry 52 is the only entry in the group which Bennett does *not* quote at least in part.

There are indeed entries that do look decidedly phenomenalistic, and these include for example entry 98 in which Berkeley says:

> The Trees are in the Park, that is, whether I will or no whether I imagine any thing about them or no, let me but go thither & open my Eyes by day & I shall not avoid seeing them.

185a is another entry in which Berkeley certainly seems to be taking a phenomenalist stance, and 293a is particularly interesting in that here Berkeley interprets the notion that unperceived perceivables are powers in a totally phenomenalistic way. He says:

> Bodies taken for Powers do exist w^n not perceiv'd but this existence is not actual. w^n I say a power exists no more is meant than that if in ye light I open my eyes & look that way I shall see it i.e ye body &c.

It may be significant that these three entries are verso entries (they may have been written after, and even some considerable time after, the entries facing them) and that only entry 293a is marked with the reject sign.

After quoting entry 98 Bennett says:

> According to this, an object's existing now may consist in the fact that if I acted thus and so I should have such and such perceptions; which implies, of course, that an object can exist now even if no spirit whatsoever perceives it.

But it implies too, on the face of it at least, that objects can exist even if there is no superior spirit who wills that if we were suitably placed we should perceive them. Again on the face of it, this treatment of the continuity question makes God quite irrelevant. The problem can be solved quite satisfactorily without any reference to the Deity.

The position is, then, that we have three entries (98, 185a and 293a) which can be cited as evidence that at one stage Berkeley was prepared to solve the continuity problem without reference to God. Whether they provide conclusive evidence is another matter. We also have one entry (52) in which it appears that God does have an important role to play, though the role is that of a container of powers corresponding to our ideas, and not that of an omnipresent perceiver. So included in the group of entries which Bennett describes as 'more or less phenomenalistic' we have one (293a) in which the notion of a power *is* interpreted phenomenalistically and one (52) in which powers are thought of as being things in God. We also have two entries (98 and 185a) which invite a phenomenalist interpretation but which do *not* mention powers. We are left with 185, 292 and 293.

Now 282 and 293 have it in common with 52 and 293a that they refer to powers, and it is clear that if Berkeley is thinking of powers in purely phenomenalistic terms these must belong with 98, 185a and 293a, while if he is thinking theologically they should be grouped with 52. Bennett is quoting 282 but thinking also of 293 (and presumably 52 as well) when he says that whenever Berkeley gives a solution to the continuity problem in terms of powers he is in effect giving the *same* solution as the one found in the more obviously phenomenalistic entries. Thus:

> Essentially the same view is sometimes expressed like this: 'Bodies etc do exist whether we think of 'em or no, they being taken in a twofold sense. Collections of thoughts & collections of powers to cause those thoughts. . . .' This is the conditionalizing approach in a different guise. To say that a body is a collection of 'powers to cause thoughts' is to imply that a body's existing now may consist in the truth of certain conditionals about what people would perceive if they did certain things.

But this is too hasty. If we interpret 282 and 293 in the light of the verso entry 293a we *will* want to say this, but it is certainly not clear that we should not interpret them rather in the light of 52. The continuation of 282, following on the portion Bennett quotes, makes it quite clear that here at least Berkeley is thinking of powers as being in God, and thus of what goes on in God's mind as being relevant to a solution of the continuity problem. As 293 is close to 298 in which Berkeley certainly thinks of powers as being in God, the same is almost certainly true of this entry too.

Instead of seeing Bennett's seven entries as constituting one group of fairly clearly phenomenalistic entries, I would want to locate *two* groups, one containing the recto entries 52, 282 and 293 in which Berkeley suggests that theological considerations are relevant to solving the continuity question, the other containing the verso entries 98, 185a and 293a in which he *can* be seen as giving a straightforward conditionalizing account. In the remaining entry – 185 – Berkeley claims to have a solution to the continuity problem but does not say what it is. As the claim here is that the existence of colours in the dark is 'not an absolute actual existence' there is obviously a case for linking it with 293a and thus with the verso entries, but though I would not myself want to do this I don't think we should be dogmatic either way. We do at any rate have to be aware that in all these entries Berkeley is consciously experimenting and rather feeling his way to a solution to the continuity problem than putting forward confident conclusions. Four of the seven entries reflect Berkeley's hesitation over whether to say that unperceived bodies *really* exist. In 185 and 293 they are said to exist but it is denied that their existence is *actual*. In 185a it is stressed that they *really* exist. And in 282 Berkeley wrote that they 'really exist' and then went on to cross out the 'really'.

I could dwell in this area for some time longer and consider how the two groups of entries are related, but the account would be tedious and it would involve a fair amount of (reasoned) speculation. For the moment at any rate I will satisfy myself with the weak claim that in the early days Berkeley was at least sometimes prepared to think God relevant to a solution to the continuity problem, and that when he talks of powers he is at least sometimes thinking of these as powers *in God*. Even this weak claim is well worth making, for the fact is that one could read the whole of the section in which Bennett is supposed to be taking account of every relevant entry in the *Commentaries* without finding one clue that it ever even crossed Berkeley's mind that God might have a role to play in allowing for object-continuity.

Now the remaining entries in the *Commentaries* which are relevant to the continuity question are less helpful than we would like. The only entries which are directly, clearly and indisputably relevant are 312 and 408, in which Berkeley claims to be able to allow for continuity but without saying how he is going to do it, 472 and 473, in which he tries a new and quite obviously unsatisfactory approach, and 802, which is a very tricky entry indeed. It is perhaps worth emphasizing that 312 and 408 are significant in that they do provide very clear evidence that Berkeley was still interested in the continuity of objects and determined to make a case for it in print, but we should not pretend that these entries give us any real clue as to what the case was to be. I have nothing more to say about these entries or about 472-3, entries which we looked at in an earlier chapter.

The remaining entry is 802, and I think we should dwell on this one a little for it is the *last* relevant entry and it should provide us with a clue as to what Berkeley's thinking was at the time when the notebooks were almost completed. We have to approach it with some caution, though, for we will find that it is a very puzzling entry and that there is probably not enough in it to enable us to decide with complete certainty exactly what Berkeley is after. The entry reads:

> Not to mention the Combinations of Powers but to say the things the effects themselves to really exist even w^n not actually perceiv'd but still with relation to perception.

The one certainty here is that Berkeley at this stage is still not *indifferent* to object-continuity and that he still intends to allow for it in print. We should agree on this even if we disagree amongst ourselves on *how* he intended to allow for it. Clearly *one* possibility is that he intends to *discard* the powers theory and to deal with the continuity problem by saying that objects continue to exist when not perceived by us because they are still perceived by God. This is what Luce and Furlong take Berkeley to have in mind. But, as Bennett points out, the wording of the entry does not give anything like solid support to the interpretation:

> This reading of 802 implies that Berkeley has failed, in four distinct ways in one sentence, to say what he meant. (1) It takes Berkeley to have written 'not to *mention* . . .' when he meant something much stronger. Yet when he says 'I must not mention . . .' in entry 441 he means just that. (2) It construes Berkeley's 'when not . . . perceived' to mean 'when not . . . perceived by humans', although the difference between 'perceived' and 'perceived by humans' is supposed to be the whole point of the entry. (3) It makes Berkeley's use of 'actually' idle, unless he is supposed to assume that

human perceptions are actual while divine ones are not. (4) It takes Berkeley to have said 'but still with relation to perception' when he meant 'but still perceived by Someone', which is no wordier and is much clearer and more direct.

Bennett is on strong ground here. In face of all this we would certainly need *independent* evidence for believing that Berkeley at this stage held the view that Luce and Furlong assume he held if we were to be convinced that Berkeley was hinting at it (however clumsily) in 802. It does not follow, however, that Bennett's own interpretation is going to be correct.

In trying to make sense of the entry I find myself puzzling over *two* questions. For if Berkeley is deciding not to *mention* rather than to reject the notion that combinations of powers are relevant to a solution to the continuity problem, one wants to know exactly how he thought them to be relevant. And if, as it appears, he wants to offer in print a solution which makes no reference to combinations of powers, one wants to know just what this solution was, and how, and to what extent it differs from the first solution. It may be that we will get some sort of clue as to the way in which Berkeley's mind was working here if we look back to entry 282, an entry in which he says:

> Bodies etc do exist whether we think of 'em or no, they being taken in a twofold sense. Collections of thoughts & collections of powers to cause those thoughts. these later exist, tho perhaps a parte dei it may be one simple perfect power.

The entry is marked with the obelus. Here Berkeley distinguishes between bodies as (collections of) powers, and bodies as (collections of) thoughts or ideas which are the *effects* of the powers. The clear suggestion is that bodies *as powers* exist 'whether we think of 'em or no' while there is at least some doubt as to whether this is true when they are thought of as collections of ideas. It seems certain that we were right in associating this entry with entry 52 and in not seeing it as phenomenalistic. But if we return now to entry 802 and interpret it in the light of entry 282, it seems natural to assume that here Berkeley is resolving not to *mention* his view that objects have a continued existence as powers in God, but instead to give an *alternative* account and to say that bodies continue to exist even as effects or ideas. I am prepared to concede that this alternative account may have been a phenomenalistic one and that it is reflected in the recto entries 98 and 185a.

Now I part company with Bennett here because Bennett is just not in a position to see Berkeley as considering two *different* accounts, one of which he will not mention and a second which he will use, for the fact is that he has already assured as that the solution in terms of powers *is* 'the conditionalizing approach in a different guise'. So far as Bennett is concerned, then, there is nothing else Berkeley *can* be doing other than deciding not to express his phenomenalistic solution to the continuity problem in a certain sort of way, or 'reminding himself . . . not to use the technical term "combinations of powers" even though it is one vehicle of the phenomenalist approach which he is contemplating'. It would be going too far to say that we can *prove* that Bennett's interpretation is wrong. We do know, however, that though Bennett never points this out, Berkeley *had* thought of powers *in God's mind* as providing an answer to the continuity problem, so it must be recognized as a very real possibility that it was this answer that he later decided not to mention. Bennett does have one good card to play in support of his interpretation, and he plays it when he says that his account 'assumes that Berkeley knew that his use of "combinations of powers" was equivalent to a phenomenalist use of conditionals; but we know that he did know this'. The card is a good one, but it may not be quite as good as Bennett thinks. Entry 293a is the *only* entry in which Berkeley takes the line Bennett attributes to him, and though we should not ignore it (any more than Bennett should ignore the fact that Berkeley sometimes thought of powers as being in God), we must be clear that it *is* only one entry, that he may have been just experimenting, and that the entry (like many of those we have been considering, but not 802) is marked with the obelus. The one rejected entry certainly isn't enough to *establish* that *when he penned entry 802* Berkeley knew or supposed 'that his use of "combinations of powers" was equivalent to a phenomenalist use of conditionals'.

There are considerations which count against Bennett. For example, he admits that his interpretation 'assumes that he [Berkeley] had difficulties with the expression "combinations of powers" which were not just difficulties with the underlying phenomenalism', and again asserts that 'we know that he had'. But the only evidence cited here is that contained in entries 84 and 282, and these entries tell *against* Bennett because we can make sense of them only if we take it that

Berkeley is thinking of powers as being *in God*. The question Berkeley raises in both of them is whether there are really power*s* in God or whether it may not be more true to have it that there is *one* power only 'one simple perfect power'. Indeed what these entries suggest is that Berkeley wanted to solve the continuity problem by having powers *in God* with a continuous existence, and effects *in us* with an intermittent existence, and that if he hesitated it was because the solution seemed to conflict with his thoughts about the nature of God. In short the difficulties are difficulties only because Berkeley does *not* think of his use of 'combinations of powers' as being equivalent to a phenomenalist use of conditionals. It is unfortunate that Bennett does not *quote* either entry 84 or the end of 282, so that this point is lost.

Again, to support his view that 'the technical term "combinations of powers" . . . is one vehicle of the phenomenalist approach which he [Berkeley] is contemplating' Bennett cites (but does not quote from) papers by Mabbott and Grave. And the point here is that the papers cited do not support Bennett. Mabbott does take the powers theory very seriously indeed, but he always supposes and stresses that the powers for Berkeley are powers *in God*. He says, for example:

> . . . the trees in the park are permanently represented only by a 'resolve' of the will of God such that as occasion arises a spatial visual pattern (my idea of the trees) appears regularly in my mind. The physical world is thus really a complicated 'good resolution' of God's. (pp. 368-9)

This is *not* phenomenalism if phenomenalism is the view that 'a body's existing now may consist in the truth of certain conditionals about what people would perceive if they did certain things'. Bennett might be able to make a case for calling it *theistic* phenomenalism, but if we accepted the label we would want to put some stress on the adjective, and to make it quite clear that for a theistic phenomenalist God plays an absolutely crucial role in the story. So Mabbott would support me rather than Bennett on the interpretation of entry 802. And so would Grave. Grave sees Berkeley as being prepared to take a phenomenalist line in print and as deciding, not against using a certain terminology to express his phenomenalism, but 'against revealing an opinion which he has not rejected' (p. 303). The answer Berkeley is going to keep quiet on involves an appeal to the content of God's mind, and if Grave is right it would bring us to what Berkeley sometimes calls the Divine *archetypes*.

There are other considerations which convince me that in entry 802 Berkeley is deciding to shelve, or keep quiet about, an answer to the continuity problem in terms of what is going on in God's mind. But here I will restrict myself to one further point, this arising from a consideration of what he says in the preceding entry. Entry 801 reads:

> I differ from the Cartesians in that I make extension, Colour etc to exist really in Bodies & independent of Our mind. All y^s carefully & lucidly to be set forth.

Bennett seems to me to have succeeded in showing (against Furlong) that this entry is *not* specifically about continuity. The entry is certainly concerned with primary and secondary qualities, for it is marked 'P', and Bennett says that it 'could be saying that Berkeley allows to "colour" the same sort of mind-independence that he allows to "extension"'. I accept this. But what justification is Berkeley intending to give for his claim that the colours, for example, we perceive by sense, 'exist really in Bodies & independent of Our Mind'? Is he thinking of them as being independent of our mind in that they are *contained in* another mind, or as being independent of our mind in that they are *produced in us by* another mind? I do not know, and perhaps Berkeley is not sure either. But what I would suggest is that Berkeley has now been prompted to think again about *God's* mind and that he has been reminded of his notion that 'Nothing corresponds to our primary ideas wthout but powers', these powers being, as entry 41 makes clear, powers *in God*. I think that this started a train of thought which led him to resolve in the very next entry not to *mention* the powers theory in dealing with continuity. It is certainly significant that in this entry he refers to ideas as 'effects'. If we ask ourselves what the effects are supposed to be the effects *of*, the only plausible answer is that they are supposed to be the effects of God's volitions, or of the exercise of powers conceived of as powers in God's mind.

Of course what I have said so far leaves a number of questions unanswered. We want to know for example exactly *why* Berkeley resolves not to mention the powers theory, *why* at this stage he prefers to give what may have been a phenomenalist solution, and *how* he thinks the two are related. On the first of these questions I am inclined to say that the answer is that he was aware of difficulties with the powers theory, one of these being that he found it difficult to reconcile the theory with his conception of the will as 'one Act' (entry 788), and with notions concerning the Deity. It may be, though, that a complete answer to this question would bring us to the area covered by the second, for it is possible that it occurred to him that a phenomenalist solution would be more acceptable to his readers simply because it allowed him to give a continued existence to, for example, colours *as we see them*, while the powers theory allowed only for the continued existence of colours as unperceived *powers*. Finally, and in answer to the third question, I suspect that a phenomenalist solution was tolerable to Berkeley only because he believed he could back the conditionals up with a story as to *how it is* that if we were suitably placed we would perceive the items referred to. Bracken refers to Berkeley's 'attempt to find an ontological sub-structure for perceiv*able* items' (Bracken 1, p. 51), and I would sugggest that even in the *Commentaries* he was able to look kindly on phenomenalism only because he felt he had a suitable sub-structure up his sleeve. He really did believe that nothing could exist apart from a mind, and the existence of those things we *might* perceive had ultimately to be allowed for, if not by an appeal to God's perceptions, then at least by a story concerning what he wills.

VI

Consideration of the relevant entries in the *Commentaries* must convince us that during the period leading up to publication Berkeley *did* care about continuity. He *did* want to be able to say that objects exist when we are not perceiving them, and he *did* intend to make a case for this in print. The entries reveal some hesitation over what the case was to be, but I hold that Bennett distorts Berkeley's position by ignoring the fact that at least some entries show that he thought *God* relevant to a solution to the continuity problem. As I see the position, it is that in the last relevant entry Berkeley resolves to keep quiet on *a* solution, this solution being essentially the one he gives in the very first relevant entry. If the tree exists when no creature perceives it, it exists as a 'resolution' in the mind of God. I suggested earlier that there is one important point of contact between what Berkeley says in *PC* 52 and what he says in *Pr.* 6. If I am right there will again be a point of contact between what he hints at in *PC* 802 and what he says in print. Summing up on Berkeley's pronouncements we can say:

(1) In *PC* 52 (cf 282 and 293) he suggests that object-continuity *should* be allowed for by a story about what goes on in God's mind.
(2) In *PC* 802 he suggests that object-continuity *could* be allowed for in this way, but that he will give another account.
(3) In *Pr.* 6 he has it that *if* there is object-continuity this can only be because of what goes on in God's mind.

There are of course differences between the three positions, and it is significant that in *Pr.* 6 it is what God *perceives* rather than what he *wills* that is important. But the point of contact (entirely missed by Bennett) is that at each stage theological considerations are considered relevant to at least a possible story about object-continuity.[12]

Now when we turn to the *Principles,* the problem is that Berkeley says *so little* about continuity, and that the few rather casual remarks he does make never amount to a fulfilling of his promise to be 'very particular in explaining w^t is meant by things existing . . . w^n not perceiv'd'. The position is not that a conditionalizing account looms large at the expense of any other account, but rather that there is no real attempt to give any account at all. Bennett admits that 'Berkeley does sometimes remark that the continuity of objects can be maintained only with help from an appropriate theology' (p. 178), but he claims that, search as we will, we look in vain for any sign that Berkeley thought it important to make the case out. In *Pr.* 6 for example he says of sensible things not perceived by us that they 'either have no existence at all, or else subsist in the mind of some eternal spirit', but he does *not* say that he will show there *is* an eternal spirit and thus allow us to reject the first of these possibilities. Similarly, sects. 45-8 are supposed to be dealing with the continuity issue, but the very lame conclusion is only that we should not conclude of sensible objects that 'they have no existence except only while they are perceived by us' because 'there may [note, *may*] be some other spirit that perceives them, though we do not'. He may have the same point in mind in sect. 90 when he says that 'when I shut my eyes, the things I saw may still exist, but it must be in another mind'. There were thus three occasions when Berkeley might have been expected to say that he believes in object-continuity *and* has the appropriate theology, and on each occasion he does not make the point. It needs stressing that what Bennett calls 'the relaxed and unargumentative remarks' Berkeley makes seem to have the effect of ruling out a phenomenalist solution, but we must agree that they do not provide us with a categorical assurance that objects *do* exist when unperceived by us and that there *is* an eternal spirit who has them in mind.

Of course taken on its own what Berkeley says (or rather, does not say) in sect. 6 need not be regarded as at all worrying. It is interesting that though this passage is the first Bennett quotes and examines under the heading 'Berkeley's indifference to continuity', he in fact concentrates on his other main target and disputes only the suggestion that here Berkeley is *assuming* object-continuity in order to prove God's existence. As I have said, I agree with Bennett on this and accept that what the section suggests is that, 'Unless we can show independently that there is an eternal spirit, we do not know that objects exist when not perceived by creatures'. This we might naturally read as giving the reader a very broad hint as to what Berkeley is going to say *when* he has proved there is an eternal spirit. And the puzzle arises only because, when he *has* made the case for God's existence, he does not go on to say that of course *now* he can and will assert object-continuity. Instead four rather unsatisfactory sections lead up to the observation that:

> Wherever bodies are said to have no existence without the mind, I would not be understood to mean this or that particular mind, but all minds whatsoever. It does not therefore follow from the foregoing principles, that bodies are annihilated and created every moment, or exist not at all during the intervals between our perception of them.

We might hold that again Berkeley is giving us a broad hint as to what the immaterialist *should* say on the continuity issue, but the problem remains as to why he *satisfies* himself with hints. He has his omnipresent spirit (via the passivity argument). He even has an omnipresent spirit who perceives ideas. Why then does he not come straight out with it and *say* that objects do exist when not perceived by us, and this because the omnipresent spirit *does* perceive them?[13]

Bennett believes that Berkeley fails to press the point home because he does not really want us to take the hints at all seriously. He thinks Berkeley saw the continuity issue as a tedious irrelevance, that 'he is not much interested' in it, and that really he does not care *what* we say. But I want to suggest that Berkeley is reticent because he is not wholly happy with the solution which he hints at and would like to be able to expand on. The conjecture here is not unduly fanciful. Certainly there is plenty of evidence that Berkeley tends to tread very gently when he is less than sure of his ground. We need only remind ourselves here of those thoughts about time which led him into 'several paradoxes that I did not think fit or necessary to publish', and we should note too that he tends to be especially cautious when his views might seem to conflict with accepted theological beliefs. If we could show that there were problems arising from the line we have supposed he wanted to take on continuity, and in particular if we could show that his solution was difficult to reconcile with his theological beliefs, then we might reasonably conclude that he wants the hint of *Pr.* 48 to be taken very seriously, but is reluctant to develop the point because (as in the case of his thinking about spirit) there are 'certain problems that he could not work out in detail to his satisfaction'. That he was aware of such problems cannot be seriously doubted.

In the first place we can note that the solution we have supposed Berkeley would *like* to press demands that we accept the existence of ideas in the mind of God. Now problems are bound to arise for Berkeley when he considers the relationship between our ideas and God's ideas, and it is certain that he should have been worried about these, and only less certain that he *was* worried. His American friend, Samuel Johnson, was most unhappy about the implications here:

> The divine idea, therefore, of a tree I suppose (or a tree in the divine mind), must be the original or archetype of ours, and ours a copy or image of His . . . of which there may be several, in several created minds, like so many several pictures of the same original to which they are all to be referred.

Others since Johnson have seen Berkeley as in danger of committing himself to a dualism between human and Divine ideas, and to a dualism which is going to have at least some of the unsatisfactory features of the rejected dualism between ideas and matter. Stack, for example, observes that 'many of the arguments which Berkeley has directed against the representational theory of perception could be, with equal validity, turned against his own position' (p. 71), and Acton notes that 'Berkeley's claim to have reinstated the direct, unmediated perception of common sense . . . cannot be substantiated' (p. 301)

Johnson's two letters bring the problems here into sharp focus, and Berkeley's replies betray a definite lack of confidence in the area. Again, there is something very puzzling about the supposed *nature* of the divine ideas, and of divine perception too. In *Siris* Berkeley tells us:

> There is no sense nor sensory, nor anything like a sense or sensory, in God. Sense implies an impression from some other being, and denotes a dependence in the soul which hath it. Sense is a passion; and passions imply imperfection. God knoweth all things as pure mind or intellect; but nothing by sense, nor in nor through a sensory. (sect. 289)

And in the *Dialogues* we are told that 'God knows or understands all things' and 'hath ideas' but that he 'perceives nothing by sense as we do'. In particular, he knows pain, or has the idea, without ever having a sensation of pain or feeling discomforted (iii, 240-1).

Mabbott recognizes that Berkeley had good reason to be unhappy about the Divine ideas and he stresses (as does Grave) that he is always very guarded in his references to them. He also makes a much stronger claim (and this is *too* strong) when he says that 'there is good reason to doubt whether he believed in them at all' (p. 370).[14] But what is particularly significant about Mabbott's analysis is that he holds that really what Berkeley believed in was not Divine ideas but *powers* in God's mind corresponding to our ideas. What makes this suggestion interesting is the fact that *if* we accepted it then we would not have to be surprised by Berkeley's reticence on the continuity issue in the published works, and this because the reticence would have been signalled *well in advance* with his decision not to mention the combinations of powers. We would want to say, I suppose, that Berkeley had come to believe that he could do himself justice on the continuity issue *only* with help from an appropriate theology, but saw that doing himself justice would involve committing himself to a solution which he had decided *not* to reveal *because* he was aware of difficulties with the theology. Now I deny that by the time Berkeley came to publish he did still hold to the powers theory, but all the same there may well be something in this point for us. For if it is a feature of the answer which Berkeley resolves to be reticent on in *PC* 802 that it involves an appeal to what is going on in God's mind, and if only some of the considerations that led him to determine to keep quiet about powers in

God's mind when talking about continuity were such that they would apply also to a solution in terms of *ideas* in God's mind, we could again take it that his reticence had been signalled. Indeed we might take it that his reticence had been signalled twice. In entry 185 (an entry in which Berkeley refers to a truth about continuity without telling us what it is) the suggestion is that, rather than just telling his readers the truth pure and simple, he will allow it to 'glide into their souls insensibly'. It may well be that hints found in the *Principles* are meant to help in this sort of process.

I want to close this discussion by looking at one particular problem Berkeley faced in proposing *any* answer to the continuity problem in terms of what goes on in God's mind. The fact is that Berkeley was, as Bennett admits, 'cramped by a specifically theological belief', this being that 'God knew all things from eternity' (*Dialogues*, iii, 253). As Bennett points out, this creates the following problem:

> If the idea-content of God's mind is the same at any time as at any other, then God's present perceptions cannot secure the present existence of the book-case on which I have just turned my back; or, rather, God's present perceptions can secure this only if they also secure the present existence of the book-case which I destroyed three years ago, and of the one which will someday be made for my grandson out of planks cut from a tree which has not yet been planted. (p. 177)

I think, though, that we should be at some pains to get the emphasis right here. For it seems to be the case that Berkeley did see this as a very real problem, but that, as he saw it, the problem was that, though God's perceptions *do* 'secure the present existence of the book-case on which I have just turned my back', one difficulty remains. This is the difficulty Bennett points to. Just because everything God perceives is perceived eternally, it would seem to follow that we cannot appeal to God's perception of the book-case to allow for its present existence without allowing for its eternal existence. Bennett wants to have it that Berkeley's awareness of this problem debarred him from using God's ideas in any serious attempt to deal with the continuity problem. But the evidence suggests that Berkeley did not see the position in that way. His problem is that, though God's ideas are centrally relevant to allowing for the existence of those things we want to say exist (though they are not perceived by us), something else has to be said to allow for the *non*-existence of those things we want to say do not. Paradoxically, the continuity problem has become a *dis*continuity problem.

The only time Berkeley faces up to this problem in print is in the *Third Dialogue* (pp. 250-6) where he answers the challenge to say *what* God created when he created the sensible world. In particular:

> Do you not make the existence of sensible things consist in their being in a mind? And were not all things eternally in the mind of God? Did they not therefore exist from all eternity, according to you? And how could that which was eternal, be created in time? Can any thing be clearer or better connected than this?

Bennett finds it significant that Berkeley manifests a concern for object-continuity only when confronted by the Genesis story, but I would suggest that he felt he *had* to be more forthcoming than usual in this context simply because one of the first queries put to him after the publication of the *Principles* had concerned the Creation. The challenge, from Lady Percival, had been to explain 'if there be nothing but spirit and ideas, what you make of that part of the six days' creation which preceded man' (*Works* IX, p. 10). We will return to the passage in the *Dialogues* in a moment, but first we can look at what Berkeley says in replying to Lady Percival (*Works* VIII, pp. 37-8), and consider whether the reply backs up Bennett's claim that 'when he is in a frame of mind to take existence-when-not-perceived-by-humans *seriously*, namely a Biblical frame of mind, Berkeley is also reluctant to allow "ideas in the mind of God" as even a possible solution'. We should perhaps make it clear that Bennett does not refer either to Lady Percival's query or to Berkeley's answer.

Now Berkeley begins his reply to Lady Percival by saying:

> ... I do not deny the existence of any of those sensible things which Moses says were created by God. They existed from all eternity in the Divine intellect, and then became perceptible (*i.e.* were created) in the same manner and order as is described in Genesis. For I take creation to belong to things only as they respect finite spirits, there being nothing new to God.

And of course it is of interest here that the very first point he wants to make is that sensible things did exist before there were men to perceive them, and this because there *was* (not 'may have been') an eternal spirit who had them in mind. Bennett's statement that Berkeley is 'reluctant to allow "ideas in the mind of God" as even a possible solution' is at best misleading, for it suggests, and is clearly meant to suggest, that he thought the divine ideas *irrelevant* to the solution. But the fact is that when Berkeley wants to establish the existence of things not perceived by (human) creatures, the very *first* thing he does is to point to the Divine ideas. As he sees the position there is no problem about allowing for the existence of the things Moses says existed. We only have to look to the content of God's mind. It is quite clear that the reason he would give for claiming that the story can't be *left* here is that appealing to God's perception of sensible objects cannot account for their *coming into* existence (any more than it can explain the non-existence of the book-case Bennett destroyed). There is a difficulty *here* simply because the content of God's mind must be supposed to be unchanging. So Berkeley completes his answer to Lady Percival by suggesting that in an absolute sense nothing is ever created (or, presumably, destroyed), and that what we think of as creation 'consists in God's willing that those things should be perceptible to other spirits, which before were known only to Himself'. The passage ends with Berkeley claiming that he could give Lady Percival a much fuller answer 'if I had the opportunity of discoursing with her'.

With the best will in the world I just do not see how we can do justice to Berkeley's thinking on how things can be supposed to have existed during the six-day period prior to man's creation without giving prominence to the Divine ideas. Looking at the passage in the *Dialogues*, Bennett has it that the Divine ideas are seen not to provide a solution and he notes that the solutions Berkeley suggests are, first, that the things Moses says existed were ideas in the minds of angels (or *created* spirits other than men), and, second, that they existed in the sense that had human spirits been suitably placed (which of course they were not) they would have had the appropriate ideas. This second solution Bennett sees as resulting from 'an essentially phenomenalist line of thought'. But if phenomenalism is 'Berkeley without God', Berkeley is, for better or worse, Berkeley *with* God, and in the *Dialogues*, as in his reply to Lady Percival, what goes on in God's mind remains central to the story. Thus Philonous says:

> All objects are eternally known by God, or which is the same thing, have an eternal existence in his mind: but when things before imperceptible to creatures, are by a decree of God, made perceptible

to them; then are they said to begin a relative existence, with respect to created minds.

The Creation is again said to have been 'entirely in respect of finite spirits', things coming into 'relative' or 'hypothetical' existence, or existence-for-us, when God decrees that what he has always perceived should become perceptible to finite creatures. Whether the decree at the Creation was that things should be for the first time *actually* perceived by creatures (and if not by men then by angels), or that these should become available to humans (even though they had not yet been created), the fact clearly is that what is given relative existence is supposed to be something which exists because God has decided to reveal to creatures that of which he was always aware. Following up the line of thought according to which it is availability to (rather than actual perception by) creatures that is essential, we can say that, for Berkeley, X has relative existence given that God perceives X and decrees that were creatures suitably placed they would perceive X. He would apparently be prepared to accept that the book-case Bennett destroyed three years ago *does exist* (because perceived by God), but he would want to accommodate Bennett by saying that it lacks relative existence, and this because God does not decree that we should ever again perceive it.[15]

Had Berkeley been fully satisfied with this answer to the challenge originally put to him by Lady Percival we should again be faced with a problem, for we would have to explain why it was that, though he had a way of allowing for object-continuity with which he at least was pleased, he kept so quiet about it, particularly in the *Principles* where he satisfies himself with hints. It is significant, then, that in the *Dialogues* he acknowledges a residual difficulty with which he is unable to deal. It is this difficulty that gives substance to our claim that his 'specifically theological belief' was such as to give rise to an objection to *any* attempt to solve the continuity problem by a story about what goes on in God's mind. The reason why he cannot solve the continuity problem *just* by appealing to God's present perception of what we are not perceiving is, he thinks, that this move leaves a *dis*continuity problem. And it leaves a discontinuity problem because any idea God perceives now will be an idea he has always perceived. Unfortunately, though, attempting to solve *this* problem by appealing to God's resolution that things should become perceptible to creatures leads very quickly to the same sort of problem, given that the content of God's mind is supposed to be unchanging *in every respect*. Thus Hylas says:

> Well, but as to this decree of God's, for making things perceptible: what say you, Philonous, is it not plain, God did either execute that decree from all eternity, or at some certain time began to will what he had not actually willed before, but only designed to will. If the former, then there could be no Creation or beginning of existence in finite things. If the latter, then we must acknowledge something new to befall the Deity; which implies a sort of change: and all change argues imperfection.

Philonous, of course, is not silenced. He insists both that the problem here is not *just* a problem for the immaterialist, and that we must not expect 'that any man . . . should have exactly just notions of the Deity, his attributes, and ways of operation'. His line becomes that as finite creatures *we* can only think of events as occurring in time so that *the best we can do* is to think of God as making available to us what he has always known. It remains clear, however, that Berkeley did think of the problem posed by Philonous here as being a *genuine* problem, and thus that his thinking about object-continuity led him into an area in which we know he was always nervous.

I take it that entries in the *Commentaries* suggest that Berkeley was *not* indifferent to the continuity issue prior to publication, that he *did* want to allow for continuity, and that even then he believed that ultimately 'the continuity of objects can be maintained only with help from an appropriate theology'. If he says less in print than we might have expected, I would hold that this was because he was reluctant to go into detail on the theology. It is significant, though, that even the published works contain quite enough to have convinced most commentators that he thinks we *should* look for the appropriate theology. And I would suggest that in this respect at least most writers on Berkeley have got Berkeley right.

Notes

CHAPTER ONE

1. On Berkeley's American sojourn see Luce 8, chs. VII-IX. Popkin 2 is good on Berkeley's considerable influence on philosophy in America. I will mention too a book called *George Berkeley in Newport* which is by Alice Brayton and which was published in Boston in 1954. We are told that 'Dean Berkeley . . . is a legendary personage in Newport and has been for two centuries'. The volume contains much of interest, but unfortunately there is a culpable lack of documentation throughout and one does not know how much reliance one should put on particular claims. Alice Brayton is particularly harsh when writing about Mrs. Berkeley. She says, for example: 'The Dean had grown very fond of his wife during their stormy honeymoon. It was well he had her beside him; she had, as he wrote, turned out better than he had expected. He continued to like her all his life.' We can locate the source for this, and what Berkeley *says* (*Works* VIII, p. 204) gives a quite different impression: 'Among my delays and disappointments, I thank God I have two domestic comforts that are very agreeable, my wife and my little son; both which exceed my expectations, and fully answer all my wishes.' I don't know what to make of the story that Anne Berkeley looked down on the local people in Newport, and was unpopular with them because of this.

2. For an account of how Berkeley first heard about tar-water, arguments against the usual assumption that he discovered it in America, and a judgement as to how reasonable and responsible it was for him to take up the cause, see Tipton 2. It may be of interest to point out here that the title Berkeley chose for his last major work was an ingenious one. There was some speculation about it at the time, and a correspondent to the *Gentleman's Magazine* for January 1745 came up with the suggestion that the title came from the Ethiopic name for the Nile: "The rich soil of Ægypt being of a blackish colour, and mixing with the water of the river when it is overflown by it, imparts a blackishness to it . . . And hence I imagine the bishop chose to amuse his readers with this name for his infusion, as the tar, when mixed with the water,

communicates something of its hue to it.' The editor apparently thought this explanation extravagant, and he suggests the obvious answer which is that the title comes from the Greek word for a chain. In fact the correspondent and the editor shared the truth between them. Berkeley *was* concerned with the virtue of tar-water which he saw as 'flowing like the Nile from a secret and occult source', but he was also influenced by the fact that the word is the word for a chain: *Siris* is a chain of reflections and it at the same time reveals his commitment to the notion that there is a Chain of Being (see *Works* V, p. 185).

3. Cf. Anne Berkeley's tribute: 'He was also pure in heart and speech; no wit could season any kind of dirt to him, not even Swift's.... he struck a light at twelve to rise and study and pray, for he was very pious; and his studies were no barren speculations, for he loved God and man, silenced and confuted atheists, disguised as mathematicians and fine gentlemen.... Humility, tenderness, patience, generosity, charity to men's souls and bodies, was the sole end of all his projects, and the business of his life' (quoted Luce 8, pp. 181-2).

4. For a tribute to Berkeley's style see the paper by Dobrée and the appendix to that paper by Donald Davie. There is a study of Berkeley's use of language in *Siris* in particular in Davie's own paper, 'Berkeley's Style in *Siris*'.

5. Though I don't really want to characterize Dr. Johnson as a smaller man it may be of interest if I quote from a little known letter to which Berman has recently drawn attention. In it George Berkeley Jr., the Bishop's second son, tells of how he silenced Johnson's criticism of the Bermuda Project. 'Johnson brought upon the carpet the subject of my father's plan for erecting *St Paul's College* on the island of *Bermuda*; and lamented, in his grandiloquos style, that so pious and beneficent a design had not been concerted with more prudence. "For (said he) had not a corrupt administration defeated the bishop's design, it must in a short time have defeated itself. The *fellows of St Paul's College* would soon have degenerated into *farmers* or *merchants*; the love of money would have proved too strong for the love of learning." Young as I was, and prepossessed with the highest veneration for Johnson, to whom I had just been introduced for the first time, I instantly threw behind me every consideration, which regarded not truth and my father's fair fame, and asked my antagonist, Whether he had ever read Bishop Berkeley's proposal for founding that American university? and whether he was accurately acquainted with the extent, produce, and situation of Bermuda? To the *former* part of my question he replied in the negative; to the latter he answered nothing. On this I admonished him to be in future less ready to censure venerable characters, or to impute his own *nescience*

to others as *imprudence*; for that had he read the pamphlet published thrice on this subject, he must have seen the bishop's consummate wisdom guarding against every inconvenience which commerce or agriculture might occasion. Farmers the *fellows* could hardly have become, as their estates were all of them to be purchased on the continent of *North America*, at the distance of a week's voyage; and the island of Bermuda, blessed as it may be with a fine climate, is so begirt with rocks, and its harbours so ill calculated for shipping, that it could never be the seat of such commerce as to call the minds of tutors from the nobler pursuits. Johnson was surprised and silenced; and on my leaving the room, being asked why he so rudely attacked my father's scheme? he replied, *I thought the young man might be vain, as well he may, of such a father; and so I resolved to keep him humble by discussing the plan in that manner.*'

6. Referring to the writings of certain free-thinkers, the author of one piece in the *Guardian* said 'they have only raised our longing to see their posthumous works'. I think it is a mistake to suppose, with Furlong 4, that this is something Berkeley would never have written, and if there is venom behind the remark this would not incline me to think that he was not the author. As Luce points out in a note in his introduction to Berkeley's *Guardian* essays in *Works* VII (but not in the first edition): 'The words in question are a strong argument *for* Berkeley's authorship of all No. 39, and not *against*. Of his twelve essays in the *Guardian* practically every one ends with something of the sort. Some of his Parthian shots at the free-thinkers are full of *odium theologicum*, and say much harder things about them than anything in No. 39.'

7. The two faces of idealism are quite clearly reflected in two very different definitions given by C. H. Whiteley. On one occasion he says that idealism is 'the doctrine that reality consists entirely of minds or spirits and their experiences' (p. x), but on another it becomes 'the philosophy which denies that Matter, as conceived by the physicists and the materialist philosophers, is an independent reality, or indeed a reality at all' (p. 60). There is a similar ambivalence in the term 'immaterialism'. Recognizing that this term originated (with Berkeley) in 1713, the definition in the *Shorter Oxford Dictionary* brings out very well the positive and negative aspects. Immaterialism is, 'The doctrine that matter does not exist in itself as a substance or cause, but that all things have existence only as the ideas or perceptions of a mind.'

CHAPTER TWO

1. The review, which appeared in 1713, is reprinted as Appendix C in Bracken's *The Early Reception of Berkeley's Immaterialism*. Bracken's

book provides an excellent survey of discussions of Berkeley's philosophy in the period 1710-33. The period chosen culminates with the appearance of Andrew Baxter's *An Enquiry into the Nature of the Human Soul*.

2. The episode is reported by Boswell. In a similar spirit we find Dr. Johnson referring in the *Idler* (No. 10) to 'the follower of Berkley (*sic*), who, while he sits writing at his table, declares that he has neither table, paper, nor fingers'.

3. This judgement is not intended to be as harsh as was Andrew Baxter's evaluation of Berkeley's attack on scepticism: 'This is, I think, as if one should advance, that the best way for a woman to silence those, who may attack her reputation, is to turn a common prostitute. [Berkeley] puts us into a way of denying all things, that we may get rid of the absurdity of those who deny some things.' (See Bracken 2, p. 10.)

4. Justifying this, Russell says: 'Causal continuity makes the matter perfectly evident: light-waves travel from the brain that is being observed to the eye of the physiologist, at which they only arrive after an interval of time, which is finite though short. The physiologist sees what he is observing only after the light-waves have reached his eye; therefore the event which constitutes his seeing comes at the end of a series of events which travel from the observed brain into the brain of the physiologist. We cannot, without a preposterous kind of discontinuity, suppose that the physiologist's percept, which comes at the end of this series, is anywhere else but in the physiologist's head.' There are at least two confusions here. In the first place, Russell starts by taking the line that the physiologist *observes* the subject's brain but *sees* something in his own brain. But at one point he says that the physiologist 'sees what he is observing'. If we take this seriously we must conclude that the physiologist either observes only his own percept or (after all) sees the subject's brain. In the second place, it is certainly wrong to talk of events as objects which can *travel*. Note how the event coming at the end of the causal process is conceived of (a) as something which has travelled to the observer's brain, (b) as the *seeing of* something (presumably a percept), and (c) as something (a percept) seen. Russell concedes that the conclusion which he takes to be forced upon us by a consideration of the implications of the scientific story is one which goes against what we find it 'natural to suppose'. 'It is extraordinarily difficult to divest ourselves of the belief that the physical world is the world we perceive by sight and touch; even if, in our philosophic moments, we are aware that this is an error, we nevertheless fall into it again as soon as we are off our guard.'

5. A classic statement of this sort of thinking can be found in the long quotation from Karl Pearson given by Hospers in pp. 385-7. Pearson

likens our position to that of a telephone operator whom we are to suppose '*never to have been outside the telephone exchange, never to have seen a customer or any one like a customer – in short, never, except through the telephone wire, to have come in contact with the outside universe*'. Pressing the analogy Pearson says: 'Very much in the position of such a telephone clerk is the conscious ego of each one of us seated at the brain terminals of the sensory nerves. Not a step nearer than those terminals can the ego get to the "outer world", and what in and for themselves are the subscribers to its nerve exchange it has no means of ascertaining.' Pearson was writing towards the end of the last century. More recently another analogy has been popular. Rather as the television viewer sees pictures which represent the goings on in the studio, so, it is suggested, the perceiver is directly aware of sense-data which are causally linked to what goes on in the physical world.

6. Thus in answering Russell (n 4 above) we will want to agree that the *event* which constitutes our seeing is the culmination of a process, but we will want to insist that *what* we see is the object we observe: i.e. the object 'out there'. Berkeley, on the other hand, is going to accept that we see only a percept in our own mind. He will have it, though, that there is no distinct object to be observed, and that chairs and the like are *collections* of percepts.

7. Cf. here *Don* Locke (pp. 116-18): 'Science has shown that various causal processes are responsible for, are the causal conditions of, our perception. The mistake has been to think that these causal processes involved in perception are responsible for, are the causal conditions of, what we perceive. The theory is that stimulation of the retina, etc., produces a visual percept in our minds, but quite obviously what these processes produce is not what we see but the perception itself. The end result of these causal processes is perception – what we perceive is the thing, whatever it is, that comes at the beginning, the thing that reflects the lightwaves onto our retina. . . . In short, so far from resting on the physical and physiological facts the causal theory seems to me to rest on a gross, and implausible, misrepresentation of those facts . . .'

8. See for example Aaron 1, pp. 101-5.

9. Berkeley may well have this particular passage in mind when he challenges the materialist by saying: 'It is your opinion, the ideas we perceive by our senses are not real things, but images, or copies of them. Our knowledge therefore is no farther real, than as our ideas are the true representations of those originals. But as these supposed originals are in themselves unknown, it is impossible to know how far our ideas resemble them; or whether they resemble them at all. We cannot therefore be sure we have any real knowledge' (*Dialogues*, iii, 246).

10. Woozley takes a similar line in the introduction to his edition of the *Essay*. The traditional interpretation, he says, 'has Locke not merely holding that to see a table is identical with having an idea in the presence of and caused by the table, but also that seeing a table is identical with *seeing* an idea of the table; and this indeed is to attribute to Locke a category mistake of which there is no evidence whatever that he was guilty' (p. 28). The issue here is a very live one amongst Locke scholars at present. For a defence of the traditional interpretation against Yolton and Woozley see Matthews. Matthews concludes that critics from Berkeley onwards 'did, after all, live in the same intellectual atmosphere as Locke, and took the same things for granted. It is more likely, therefore, that they would interpret him correctly than that his perhaps over-subtle modern defenders should do so' (p. 21). He acknowledges, though, that 'any criticisms which might be made of his (alleged) representationalism do not seriously affect the value of his philosophy as a whole' (p. 16).

11. We should perhaps make it clear that for Locke the real world of external objects contrasts not with a familiar world containing (for example) a familiar table, but rather with the realm of mind-dependent ideas. There is for Locke but one table, the table on the dark side of the veil of perception, and then there are ideas which represent various features of the table. It will turn out that Berkeley does think of ideas as fit to constitute familiar objects such as tables, but of course he denies that there is any 'real' table existing without the mind.

12. Cf. T. H. Huxley, writing towards the end of the last century: 'If the universe contained only blind and deaf beings, it is impossible for us to imagine but that darkness and silence should reign everywhere' (p. 253).

13. Cf. Galileo: '. . . whenever I conceive any material or corporeal substance, I immediately feel the need to think of it as bounded, and as having this or that shape; as being large or small in relation to other things, and in some specific place at any given time; as being in motion or at rest; as touching or not touching some other body; and as being one in number, or few, or many. From these conditions I cannot separate such a substance by any stretch of my imagination. But that it must be white or red, bitter or sweet, noisy or silent, and of sweet or foul odour, my mind does not feel compelled to bring in as necessary accompaniments' (see Popkin 3, p. 65). It is interesting that in this particular passage Galileo goes on at once to conclude that *because* the mind does not feel compelled to attribute certain qualities to objects we should not attribute these to them. Obviously he is moving too fast here.

14. Berkeley opposes this sort of analysis when he says: 'As to what philosophers say of subject and mode, that seems very groundless and unintel-

ligible. For instance, in this proposition, a die is hard, extended and square, they will have it that the word *die* denotes a subject or substance, distinct from the hardness, extension and figure, which are predicated of it, and in which they exist. This I cannot comprehend: to me a die seems to be nothing distinct from those things which are termed its modes or accidents. And to say a die is hard, extended and square, is not to attribute those qualities to a subject distinct from and supporting them, but only an explication of the meaning of the word *die*' (*Pr.* 49).

15. The substratum doctrine is quite obviously independent of the veil of perception doctrine and the primary/secondary qualities doctrine to the extent that I might suppose I had to posit a substratum for qualities even if I believed that I was, in a quite straightforward sense, *aware of* the qualities of things (and this without the mediation of ideas), and even if I believed that the qualities Locke calls secondary were (as we perceive them) really in objects. If Berkeley was not as clear on this as he should have been, some of his commentators have been very confused. Luce, for example, says: 'I, therefore, venture to beg the novice who wishes to master the authentic teaching of the historic Berkeley, to keep on reminding himself that the *matter* at issue, *i.e.* the material substance which Berkeley denied (*a*) is not sensible body or sensible parts of body . . . but (*b*) is a "something we know not what", a guess-substance, a conjecture of the ancient Greeks, a something vaguely supposed to serve as invisible, intangible, non-spiritual support of all that we actually see and touch' (Luce 5, p. 24). Here, then, matter *is* Locke's substratum of qualities. Later, though, the veil of perception doctrine and the primary/secondary qualities doctrine are brought into the picture when Luce tell us that for the 'matterist' certain of our ideas *resemble* matter. Thus: 'Do we see and touch pictures of matter? Are the objects we immediately perceive by sense, or any privileged class of them, resemblances, copies, or representations of that elusive "something we know not what". The matterist says, Yes; Berkeley says, No. The matterist who is careful of his terms admits that, strictly, we do not perceive matter; but he affirms that we perceive something like it. Pressed on the point, and asked if there is anything like colour in matter, he usually takes refuge in the famous distinction between primary and secondary qualities' (pp. 78-9). But this is a muddle. Locke does *not* believe that our ideas of primary qualities are like the something-we-know-not-what which is essentially a support of qualities: he believes they resemble the original qualities. Clearly it is no objection to Locke (as Luce supposes it is) to say that it is absurd to suppose a sensed idea resembles the substratum. Berkeley's objection here is at least relevant, though not directly to the substratum

doctrine. He takes it to be absurd to suppose that a sensed idea can resemble a quality which (because it lies behind the veil of perception) is insensible.

16. We should note that when Locke talks of 'the minute particles of bodies, and the real constitution on which their sensible qualities depend' as being *insensible*, the reason is not that he wants to bring out the implications of the veil of perception doctrine. The minute particles are insensible simply because they are so minute. Given this it makes sense for Locke to suggest that if our senses were acute enough we should be able to discern the internal constitution of body (see II xxiii 11). In criticizing Locke here (*Pr.* 77-8 and 136, cf. *PC* 601 and 724) Berkeley has the veil of perception doctrine right at the forefront of *his* mind. The 'real constitution' of things is insensible because only ideas are sensible. Even if we had an extra sense or the most acute senses imaginable we would be enabled only to perceive fresh ideas.

17. It hardly needs saying that if it does justice to the plain man's view to say that a substance is simply the joint instantiation of qualities, the plain man does not believe that these qualities are mind-dependent ideas. Thus in taking away the mysterious substratum and asserting that objects are collections of ideas in the mind Berkeley may indeed be taking away something the layman never saw the need for, but he is at the same time making an assertion that conflicts radically with our ordinary thinking.

18. Allaire argues that it is *very much* more than this. After quoting from *Pr.* 91 he says: 'This passage marks Berkeley's arrival at idealism. Qualities need a support, a substance in which to exist. But the only substances available are minds. Hence, qualities must be supported by minds, they must be in minds' (p. 235). Thus for Allaire Berkeley is totally *dominated* by the conviction that qualities require a substratum, and it is because he thinks he can prove that there is no *material* substratum that he takes it to be obvious that qualities are ideas supported by minds. Allaire continues: 'Berkeley's steps to idealism are firm and definite. Only minds (in reflection) and sensible objects (in sense) exist, for they are the only *kinds* immediately known. Moreover, sensible objects are merely collections of qualities, and qualities need a substantial support. Since minds are the only substances, sensible objects must be *supported by* minds, they must be *in* minds, they must be *perceived by* minds their *esse est percipi*.' Allaire's claim that these steps are 'firm and definite' must, though, be seen in the light of his avowal that: 'I am, of course, not claiming that Berkeley himself unfolded idealism as described above; nor am I claiming that he was aware that it could be so unfolded. The *Principles* is clearly not developed in strict conformity to that pattern.' The view is, ultimately,

that 'the pattern has an extraordinary hold on him'. There is no reason why we should disagree with this last claim. We should be clear, however, that if Berkeley did think that given there is no material substratum then qualities must be ideas in the mind, he was also very willing to argue the other way round and to say that as qualities are ideas in the mind then it is absurd to suppose a material substratum.

19. We should note here that the French reviewer we met earlier in fact saw Berkeley not as a Lockian but as 'Malbranchiste de bonne foi'. There were special reasons why the reviewer, a Jesuit, should want to make Berkeley 'a "leftwing" Malebranchist', and on this see Bracken 2, p. 16ff.

20. The term 'Pyrrhonism' derives from Pyrrho of Elis (*c.* 300 B.C.). Popkin's paper 'Berkeley and Pyrrhonism' provides a very full treatment of the influence of Bayle on Berkeley. It is made clear that 'Berkeley set out to refute scepticism because of "la crise pyrrhonienne" that Bayle had just brought to light' and that Berkeley's 'new theory of reality' in which the real world *is* the world of appearances was designed to meet the challenge explicit in Bayle. We can make one additional point about Bayle. We saw earlier that he may have been responsible for suggesting to Berkeley that 'those arguments, which are thought manifestly to prove that colours and tastes exist only in the mind . . . may with equal force, be brought to prove the same thing of extension, figure, and motion'. But it may have been Bayle too who suggested to Berkeley that the 'new' philosophers *did* rely on the argument from the relativity of perception. On this see Cummins, pp. 204-5. Cummins quite rightly puts the emphasis on the scientific mathematization of nature, and he holds that Bayle (and Berkeley) were 'historically inaccurate in claiming that the reality of secondary qualities was denied because of perceptual relativity'.

CHAPTER THREE

1. This tendency to eschew argument has often struck commentators. Thus C. R. Morris for example says: 'Of all philosophers Berkeley was perhaps by nature the most confident. . . . He expounded his system boldly and shortly, offering in the first place very few arguments in support of it except that of its obviousness' (p. 65).

2. In a letter written shortly after the publication of the *Principles* Berkeley is referring to his own theory when he says that 'whatever doctrine contradicts vulgar and settled opinion had need been introduced with great caution into the world' (*Works* VIII, p. 36). A revealing passage is that in *Pr.* 56 where he sets himself to account for the *universal* belief in external existence and sees the philosophers and the mob as *alike* committed to contradictory notions. Here the philosophers are given

credit for having 'in some degree corrected the mistake of the vulgar' in that they have seen that the things we immediately perceive are mind-dependent. Commenting on this section and on what he takes to be Berkeley's general attitude to the mob, C. J. Sullivan says: 'The vulgar and the philosophers differ regarding the status of what they perceive, the vulgar taking those things to be real which the philosophers take to be images, but they agree in supposing that real things, whether perceptions or the causes of perceptions, can and do exist independently without the mind, they agree in supposing there is a real material world. This is their common error, according to Berkeley, an absurdity as great in the one case as in the other, for it is the same absurdity in both, the absurdity of supposing that anything perceived, or anything like anything perceived, can exist unperceived. Had Berkeley been more forthright, more like a prophet of old than an eighteenth-century gentleman, he might have said to both the philosophers and the vulgar, "A plague on both your houses. To be is either to perceive or to be perceived"' (pp. 25-6).

3. It may be worth looking at the reason Hosper's idealist gives for supposing realism to involve a contradiction. 'Chairs and tables are what we *perceive*; and if you use physical-object words in the way realism does, you will get "Physical objects (unobservables) are observed", which is self-contradictory' (p. 393). But note that of course on *this* argument only those realists (the *representative* realists) who say that physical objects are *never* observed contradict themselves. A second argument which comes later is in fact quite different: 'To speak of physical objects existing unexperienced is just as self-contradictory as to speak of experiences existing unexperienced; and physical objects, remember, are complexes of experiences; therefore it is *logically* impossible for them to exist unexperienced. When we assert that physical objects do not exist unperceived we are uttering a tautology; and if we deny it we are uttering a self-contradiction' (pp. 403-4). Now this second argument does concern the plain man as much as the representative realist, but it requires the premiss that 'physical objects ... are complexes of experiences'. So far as this argument is concerned, the position is not that either representative realism or the plain man's thinking is *inherently* contradictory, but that both are inconsistent with idealism and must be false if it is true. We might add here that the representative realist could fairly claim that the *first* argument does not really show him to be guilty of *self*-contradiction. Of course it would be contradictory to assert that physical objects (unobservables) are observed, but he does not assert this. What he does is to contradict the plain man and Berkeley, who take it that the things we perceive by sense are the real things.

4. Berkeley's diagram would thus be:

I claim that the plain man's diagram should be:

Comparison of the three diagrams brings out the following points. First, Berkeley agrees with the plain man but conflicts with the materialists in holding a two-term theory of perception. Second, Berkeley diverges from the mob, and conflicts with the philosophers, in holding that real things are mind-dependent ideas.

5. In brief, Berkeley's answer is that *given* we are aware only of mind-dependent ideas then we can have no grounds for supposing external objects to exist, that the notion of a material substratum of external qualities is empty, and that nothing can be like an idea but an idea. Armstrong (1, pp. 17-18) sees this last point as 'probably valid' and as leading to 'a *reductio ad absurdum* of the Representative theory'. The same point is critically examined by Givner in his paper (see especially pp. 653-6).

6. Johnston is drawing attention to this move when he says: 'It is . . . clear, Berkeley avers, that Locke has gone wrong *somewhere*; and he argues that Locke's error lies in the postulation of something which does not really exist at all. This non-existent thing is Locke's external material world. What Berkeley does, then, is simply to accept Locke's view that the relation of the mind and its ideas is immediate, and to deny that there is anything over and above the mind and its ideas. In other words, Berkeley reaches his view of the immediacy of perception by this drastic Procrustean method of "simplifying" Locke's theory' (pp. 151-2).

7. The doctrine that we perceive only ideas leads to other oddities. In a review of the *Dialogues* which appeared in 1713 the reviewer listed nine 'conséquences du sentiment de M. B.' These included (in Luce's translation):

   (1) In approaching an object, at every step I take, it is another object I see.
   (2) When I look at an object through a microscope, I do not see the same object as I perceive without the instrument.
   (3) The object I feel is not the same as that I see.
   (8) I cannot speak to any one without the intervention of an infinite spirit to arouse in the mind of him to whom I speak, the ideas I wish to excite there.
   (9) God is obliged to make these characters I write visible to all who shall cast their eyes on this paper.

   The review is reproduced as Appendix B in Bracken 2, and Bracken is surely right in saying: 'These conclusions indicate how far Berkeley has moved from common sense...' (p. 49). What is interesting is that Luce disagrees, saying: 'These *conséquences*, drawn by the French reviewer, only indicate how far he was from understanding Berkeley, and they furnish no evidence, so far as I can see, of Berkeley's alleged departure from common sense.' (8) and (9) he lists as 'derisive misrepresentations of Berkeley's teaching about God and about ideas'. I maintain that they are completely fair. See *Pr.* 147. (1), (2) and (3) he recognizes to be 'true to fact' (i.e. properly attributable to Berkeley), but he claims, most surprisingly, that they are 'common sense statements'. We all accept, for example, that an object looks different as we approach it, and thus that the 'perceivings' are different. But this, of course, will not do. We all do accept that the object *looks* different as we approach, but we have no doubt that we are seeing the same *item* at each stage. Berkeley commits himself to the view that at each stage we perceive different items, and it is here that he comes into radical conflict with our ordinary thinking. For Luce's contribution to the discussion, see Luce 1.

8. In *Dialogues*, iii, 247 Berkeley does allow Hylas to raise the objection: 'But the same idea which is in my mind, cannot be in yours, or in any other mind. Doth it not therefore follow from your principles, that no two can see the same thing? And is not this highly absurd?' Philonous's reply – that 'all the dispute is about a word' – is usually judged to be highly unsatisfactory. See for example Braybrooke's paper, Johnson (pp. 154-6), Grave (pp. 300-1) and Marc-Wogau 1 (pp. 349-50).

9. I agree with Bracken that 'the price of a consistent interpretation of Berkeley's Immaterialism is either the recognition that (unfortunately

for *his* consistency) Berkeley himself takes ideas of sense both ways, or, a restriction of one's interpretation to passages where but one view dominates' (Bracken 1, p. 42). I also agree with his comment that: 'Luce and Jessop cannot hold, as they now do, that there is one Berkeleian philosophy, that it is Common-Sensical and/or Realistic, and that by ideas of sense Berkeley is to be understood as meaning sensa' (p. 41).

10. We have already found Grover Maxwell supporting a Causal Theory and saying that 'all of the external world, including even our own bodies is unobserved and unobservable'. In the same paper he says of allegedly publicly observable objects that 'insofar as they are observable, they are mentalistic and *not* public – insofar as they are public, they are *not* observable' (p. 159). There will be any number of similar dilemmas. For Maxwell if an object is such that I could wash, wear, or eat off it it will not be observable, while if it is observable it will not be washable, wearable or edible. Berkeley saw Locke as committed to just this sort of thinking, and he thought it absurd. He has his own problem though. He reaches his position by denying that there are objects in addition to Lockian-ideas, and I think he does need his ideas to be 'mentalistic' (i.e. not public and not such that we can do things *in*, *on*, or *with* them) if he is to regard them as obviously mind-dependent. If we do start to think of them as public or as things we can do things in, on or with, then we find that it ceases to be obvious that they are mind-dependent. Of course to get to the conclusion that physical objects are public, manipulable *and* observable we need to break away from the notion that the things we perceive are in the mind, and to criticize the Causal Theory at a point other than the one Berkeley chooses.

11. For more on this point see Ch. 6, pp. 203-5 and note 6.

CHAPTER FOUR

1. I don't think that there can really be any doubt about this. Berkeley does on occasion say (as for example in *Pr.* 133) that *if* immaterialism had been proposed 'only as an *hypothesis*' we should still have had excellent grounds for accepting it, but the truth as he sees it is that he has *demonstrated* the falsity of materialism and the truth of idealism. Indeed so sure is he that the notion of external existence involves a repugnancy that in *Pr.* 22 he goes so far as to say: 'And as for all that *compages* of external bodies which you contend for, I shall grant you its existence, though you cannot either give me any reason why you believe it exists, or assign any use to it when it is supposed to exist. I say, the bare possibility of your opinion's being true, shall pass for an argument that it is so.' A man who

thought external existence 'a logical possibility' could hardly issue *this* challenge.

2. Certainly we should not suppose that *in general* Berkeley was prepared to take what we ordinarily *say* as a good guide to what is *true*. One of his dominant concerns is to show how our language misleads us and how our ordinary ways of talking reflect erroneous beliefs. In *Pr*. 52, for example, he warns that 'language is suited to the received opinions, which are not always the truest'. And in *TVV* 35 he warns that 'language being accommodated to the prænotions of men and use of life, it is difficult to express therein the precise truth of things, which is so distant from their use, and so contrary to our prænotions'.

3. Don Locke has asserted quite categorically that it is 'an obvious error' to suppose that 'X is perceived' entails 'X exists'. Commenting on the later introduction of 'two types or kinds of existence' Margolis says: 'The irony of course, is precisely that, on this explication, Locke cannot maintain his denial of the entailment: he means to support it but to hold that it is subject to an equivocation' (p. 405). Margolis's paper provides a useful critique of what Locke says in pp. 16-20.

4. Luce makes a similar mistake when he considers the *esse* of 'percipient, willing, active beings'. The *esse* of the perceiving subject is, Berkeley tells us, *percipere*, and this means that it must be nonsense to talk of an agent existing when not actually perceiving. Now if this strikes us as odd it will not be because we believe that we can perceive but not exist, but rather because we believe we can exist when not perceiving. But we find that Luce attempts to support Berkeley by ignoring our main worry and stressing the point that is not in dispute. What is it for us to exist? 'Berkeley answers that the existence of the percipient is *percipere*, and that when we say the percipient *exists*, we mean that he perceives. It is hard to see what else it could mean. To say "I perceive the table, and I exist" would be just as ridiculous as to say, "I perceive the table and it exists" ' (Luce 7, pp. 122-3). It is quite true, as Luce goes on to say, that he could not perceive the table unless he existed. Our feeling is, though, that his *esse* is not *percipere* because he can be supposed to exist when not conscious.

5. Here I mean to suggest only that Berkeley has not given us any reason to suppose that *on any given occasion* we can know (i.e. have intuitive certainty) that we are perceiving something real and not dreaming or suffering an hallucination. I am not sure, though, that he really has any answer to the challenge that he may *always* be dreaming. In trying to convince the materialist that we need not believe in external and unperceivable bodies he says: '. . . it is granted on all hands (and what happens in dreams, phrensies, and the like, puts it beyond dispute) that it is possible we might be affected with all the ideas we have now, though no

bodies existed without, resembling them. Hence it is evident the supposition of external bodies is not necessary for the producing our ideas: since it is granted they are produced sometimes, and might possibly be produced always in the same order we see them in at present, without their concurrence' (*Pr.* 18). But this is a dangerous argument for Berkeley to use. Presumably it must be conceivable that *he* might be affected with all the ideas *he* has now even if he was alone in the world with his ideas, with no God concurring in their production. Certainly he is mistaken if he supposes that his rejection of a dualism between ideas and things makes him wholly invulnerable to sceptical attacks.

6. In supporting the view that for Berkeley *esse* is *percipi* (and not *percipi aut posse percipi*) Marc-Wogau draws attention to *Pr.* 78 where Berkeley says: 'Qualities, as hath been shewn, are nothing else but *sensations* or *ideas*, which exist only in a *mind* perceiving them; and this is true not only of the ideas we are acquainted with at present, but likewise of all possible ideas whatsoever.' Marc-Wogau concludes: 'The existence of a possible idea thus seems to mean that it is actually perceived by a mind. When I am out of my study, the table in the study is, according to Berkeley, always actually perceived, at least by God. If it exists, it is actually perceived. The counterfactual that I should perceive it, if I were in my study, may be true, but it is irrelevant to the question of the existence of the table' (Marc-Wogau 2, p. 325).

7. This does not affect the argument, but we should perhaps point out that the notion of a hot snowball is not contradictory.

8. Again we find that for Berkeley 'idea' is hardly a 'term of precision'. Note that the premiss Berkeley takes the appeal to ordinary usage in *Pr.* 3 to *establish* is identical to the premiss which Philonous thinks necessary to *supplement* the appeal to our ordinary thinking in the *Dialogues*. The appeal in *Pr.* 3 is supposed to establish that 'ideas imprinted on the sense ... cannot exist otherwise than in a mind perceiving them'. But Philonous takes it that the appeal he makes requires supplementation by arguments for the claim that the ideas we perceive are mind-dependent.

9. I am sure that Warnock is right in holding that Berkeley never seriously considered the possibility that where the representative realist had gone wrong was not just in supposing that external objects were unobservable but in taking it that we perceive only ideas. Warnock says: 'It surely will not do to assume at the very beginning, as Berkeley does, that this extraordinary doctrine can simply be stated as "evident" ... No doubt Berkeley felt that the principle that we perceive only "ideas" stood in no need of argument partly for the reason that, on this point at least, he and Locke were in agreement; but may it not be just *because* they were

in agreement on this that they appear to force upon us a choice between two alternative doctrines, with *neither* of which we are really inclined to agree? In philosophy it is always good policy, when two theorists appear to offer a choice between two positions neither of which is acceptable, to consider whether, underlying the divergences between them, there may not be some dubious principles which they have in common. In this case, we do not have to agree with either Locke or Berkeley *unless* we accept, as they both did, the initial supposition that in perception we are aware *only* of "our own ideas". But neither—I must here state dogmatically—actually produces any arguments sufficient to establish so strange a view' (Warnock 2, p. 32).

CHAPTER FIVE

1. Locke adheres to what O'Connor calls 'the translation theory of meaning'. O'Connor sums the theory up thus: 'When we are talking or reading or listening to a lecture there are two simultaneous and parallel mental processes going on in our heads. When we are talking ourselves, for example, we are thinking and at the same time translating our thoughts into language which our listeners will understand. Our listeners, on the other hand, are decoding or translating our language into their own thoughts. The whole procedure, in fact, is very like what happens at an international conference where the speeches have to be interpreted before they are universally intelligible' (p. 125). We thus have what Bennett calls 'a synchronous-act theory of meaning'. For criticism of the translation theory of meaning see O'Connor pp. 124-32 and Bennett pp. 1-11.

2. It would appear that when I use the word 'John' meaningfully I do this by having an image of him in my mind. But how can having the image = thinking of John? Suppose I have never *seen* John or had him described to me and have no idea what he looks like. Or suppose I do know what he looks like and that he looks *exactly* like his twin. Must I make the picture corresponding to 'John' subtly different from the one corresponding to 'Bill'? Finally, if I can have a mental picture of a man when I talk of John *and* when I am just day-dreaming about nobody in particular, what is it about the first case that allows the image to give significance to the word? Not just that I bring the image to mind when uttering the sound, for I could parrot the sound when day-dreaming. No, when I have the image I must at the same time be thinking about John in particular. But now we are back where we started. For having the image was supposed to *be* thinking about John. We should be clear that the main grounds for dissatisfaction with Locke's account of meaning become

apparent before the 'queer' images corresponding to general words come on the scene.

3. Bennett allows that Berkeley had 'reservations about the core of Locke's theory of meaning', but stresses the incompleteness of his rejection of it, holding that Flew drastically overstates the case when he supposes that we find in *Alciphron* a 'revolutionary and historically premature insight'. See Bennett pp. 52-8. There is a reply in Flew 1. The dispute here really concerns the supposed *development* in Berkeley's thinking about meaning long after the publication of the *Principles*, and I shall have one relevant point to make on this in Ch. 7. I don't think anyone would want to claim that those doctrines in the *Principles* which are related to claims about meaning (and to criticism of Locke's theory) are such as to reflect Wittgensteinian insights.

4. This probably looks more exciting than it is. Presumably Berkeley has appreciated (but failed to be sufficiently worried by) the fact that introspection does not normally reveal mental items corresponding to the words we use. Patently we *can* use a word meaningfully without having an appropriate idea in the mind. The clear suggestion is, though, that with at least many words we must be *able* to bring an appropriate idea to the mind if we are talking meaningfully. Indeed Berkeley thinks that we should cultivate the habit of actually having the ideas rather more often than we usually bother to do. The introduction to the *Principles* closes with the words: 'Whoever therefore designs to read the following sheets, I entreat him to make my words the occasion of his own thinking, and endeavour to attain the same train of thoughts in reading, that I had in writing them. By this means it will be easy for him to discover the truth or falsity of what I say. He will be out of all danger of being deceived by my words, and I do not see how he can be led into an error by considering his own naked, undisguised ideas.' If Berkeley is right none of these ideas will be *abstract*, though many will have a representative function (representing all particulars of a sort) and thus be *general*.

5. As we shall see, Berkeley thinks that philosophers have again indulged in illegitimate abstraction when they have talked of substance as a *support* of qualities. The fact is that if we think of an object and then try to think away all its qualities we are left with *nothing*, or with the empty concept of bare being.

6. It appears that when I use a determinate image I may be thinking not about it but about all figures which have it in common with the image that they instantiate triangularity. Berkeley does not explain how I manage to do this trick.

7. I must confess that I cannot make much of Ayer's suggestion (in the introduction to *British Empirical Philosophers*) that 'when Berkeley ... declares that the existence of sensible qualities consist of their being perceived, he must not be understood to be putting forward a factual thesis. What he is doing to is lay down a convention' (p. 16). Certainly Berkeley's claim is not straightforwardly *factual*. He thinks of himself as making a conceptual point. But the claim is not supposed to follow from a *choice* to use the word 'existence' in a certain way. Anyone saying that sensible things can exist unperceived is not just operating with a different convention. He is saying something unintelligible.

8. In a most interesting paper Denis Grey claims that the argument here is distinct from and incompatible with anything to be found in sects. 4-6. 'In section 6 the thought of an unperceived object is "unintelligible" and involves "a manifest contradiction"; now, it is not only possible and easy, but it turns into *the reason why* the mind "is deluded to think it can conceive bodies existing without the mind", that is *any* mind: it forgets *it* is thinking of them' (p. 339). The argument of sect. 23 'requires that the impossibility [of sect. 6] be possible' (p. 340). And again: 'Berkeley himself is muddled. He has slipped into the mistake ... [of] supposing that it *does* make sense to talk of our imagining or thinking of an unperceived object; he has *forgotten* that it is "perfectly unintelligible and involving all the absurdity of an abstraction". This is why the two passages of the *Principles* are contradictory ... '(p. 342). I am not happy with this. In the first place I want to say that Berkeley has to regard his claim in sect. 6 concerning the inconceivability of an unperceived object as being compatible with a recognition that we *suppose* we can conceive the inconceivable. (How else could he account for the 'opinion strangely prevailing amongst men'?) And in the second place it seems to me that though he may seem to suggest otherwise at the opening of sect. 23 he does not *really* allow that we can think of or imagine an unperceived object. His suggestion that 'there is no difficulty in it' has to be seen in the light of his insistence in the same section both that the supposed conception involves 'a manifest repugnancy' and that the mind is 'deluded' when it supposes it can conceive the inconceivable.

9. Bernard Williams has just this difficulty in mind when he refers to the 'extraordinary feature of his [Berkeley's] argument, that Hylas is not supposed to conclude from his thought-experiment, as one might suppose, that he cannot conceive an object unperceived by himself; he is supposed to conclude that he cannot conceive an object unperceived by any mind' (p. 117). Cf. Armstrong: '... it is clear that there must be something wrong with the argument because, if it were valid, it would establish the truth of patent absurdities. For I can use the same method of argument

to prove that the existence of anything, past, present or future that is unthought of *by me* is inconceivable' (Armstrong 1, p. 10).

10. In an earlier note we suggested (in criticizing Locke) that attaching significance to an utterance of the sound 'John' cannot *be* framing a mental picture of John, because if we did frame the image we would still have to think of it as being an image of John himself. Now we see that thinking of a tree which we suppose to exist in the sensible world cannot *be* framing an image of a tree and thinking about that, for we would still have to think of the image as being the image of an existent tree. The point should be clear anyway, but it becomes unmistakeably clear if we concentrate on the case where we think of some particular *known* tree – say an old oak on which we once carved our initials. For if I think of my image as an image of that tree I must be thinking not (just) of the image but of that tree. And what we want to know is whether the tree I think of (not the image) can exist unperceived. We might note in passing that Berkeley *should* be worried by cases similar to those we looked at when commenting on Locke on proper names. Suppose for example that I want to think about one tree and then another which I suppose to be *exactly* like it. Must I incorporate some subtle difference into the second image? And what about the case where I am thinking about Chartres Cathedral and just *can't* visualize it or remember what it looks like?

11. As well as being correct, our interpretation is surely the *standard* interpretation. Cf. Armstrong: 'Berkeley does not maintain simply that we can never *know* whether such things as trees exist unperceived. Nor does he maintain even that trees do not, *as a matter of fact*, exist unperceived. He maintains the far more radical thesis that physical objects *cannot* exist unperceived. The notion of the existence of unperceived objects, he holds, *involves a contradiction*' (Armstrong 1, p. 7). The point can be made by saying that Berkeley is most decidedly a *strong* rather than a *weak* idealist. A strong idealist holds that 'to speak of a physical object existing unobserved is not a hypothesis for which we unfortunately lack confirmation; it is not a hypothesis at all; its very assertion is a *self-contradiction*' (Hospers, p. 403).

12. Cf. the opening of *Pr.* 3: 'That neither our thoughts, nor passions, nor ideas formed by the imagination, exist without the mind, is what every body will allow.' There is no question of anyone being deluded about *this*.

13. At one stage Locke held that: 'Memory is always the picture of something, the idea whereof has existed before in our thoughts, as near the life as we can draw it: but imagination is a picture drawn in our minds without reference to a pattern.' See Aaron 1, pp. 138-9. This seems unhelpful

for two reasons. First because the account doesn't even look like covering all cases of remembering – remembering dates, remembering that I did so and so at such and such a time, etc. But second because even if we agreed that having a more or less true to life picture played a role in some cases of remembering we would certainly have to say that having the picture cannot be *enough*. In II x 2 Locke concedes that memory consists in the power the mind has 'to revive perceptions which it has once had, with this additional perception annexed to them, that *it has had them before*'. Obviously this 'additional perception' must be crucial. But doesn't *perceiving* that we have had an idea before look awfully like *remembering that* we have had it before? And it is remembering that Locke is supposed to be analysing.

14. Of course Berkeley would add that it must be nonsense to talk of sensible objects as existing unperceived because sensible objects are *ideas* and it is *agreed* that ideas are mind-dependent. This move, though, takes us away from the meaning of 'exist'. We still have to find some justification for the claim that sensible objects *are* mind-dependent ideas. We should perhaps note that in the *Dialogues* Hylas quickly becomes enthusiastic about the notion that thinking of X comes down to framing an image. Thus: 'As I was thinking of a tree in a solitary place, where no one was present to see it, methought that was to conceive a tree as existing unperceived or unthought of, not considering that I myself conceived it all the while. But now I plainly see, that all I can do is to frame ideas in my own mind. I may indeed conceive in my own thoughts the idea of a tree, or a house, or a mountain, but that is all. And this is far from proving, that I can conceive them *existing out of the minds of all spirits*.' The confusion between the image framed and the object thought about is quite apparent here.

CHAPTER SIX

1. Thus: '. . . "sense datum" is a theory-neutral term, and to insist that whenever we perceive we perceive sense data, is not to commit oneself to any particular theory of perception. In particular it is not to say that whenever we perceive we perceive percepts [i.e. mind-dependent entities]. The question at issue between the different theories of perception is, in part, the question of whether sense data are percepts, or whether to talk about sense data is to talk, in a special way, about the various external objects which we happen to perceive' (p. 39).

2. Berkeley's suggestion that we should think of things like apples, stones, trees and books as *collections* of sense data may seem to come close to the ordinary view if we think of sense data as we normally think of *qualities*.

Berkeley does sometimes encourage us to think of them in this way. It is when 'a certain colour, taste, smell, figure and consistence' are 'observed to go together' that we can account them one thing – an apple. Reading Berkeley in this spirit we may see his essential point as being that things like apples are no more than the sum of their qualities – there is no mysterious substratum. If he departs from our ordinary thinking it will only be when he tells us that qualities are mind-dependent. But this reading will not do, for Berkeley does not normally think of sense data as *we* think of qualities. When I take it that I am looking at a round penny from various angles, he will tell me that ultimately it is just false to suggest that there is one object with one fixed shape that I see at each stage. Sense data are essentially *appearances*, and when Berkeley thinks of them as qualities he is thinking of apparent qualities or the qualities manifested in the appearances. If a penny is a 'bundle' of sense data, then, it is a bundle of appearances – including the round appearance, the elliptical appearance, etc.

3. What Berkeley says in *NTV* 47 suggests that he was aware of a problem here: '... a man is easily convinced that bodies and external things are not properly the object of hearing; but only sounds, by the mediation whereof the idea of this or that body or distance is suggested to his thoughts. But then one is with more difficulty brought to discern the difference there is betwixt the ideas of sight and touch: Though it be certain a man no more sees and feels the same thing than he hears and feels the same thing.' Note too that at a stage when Hylas still wants to insist that we see colours *on* bodies he needs no convincing that sounds 'inhere not in the sonorous bodies' (i, 181).

4. Not everything here is *wholly* satisfactory. Surely we feel *no* inclination to identify effect with cause – the sound produced by the bell with the striking of a clapper on the surface of the bell.

5. The statement is difficult to interpret largely because it is not clear how much of what was accepted by writers on optics Berkeley was prepared to go along with *for the sake of the argument*. Armstrong, who examines the statement at length, takes it that Berkeley unwisely commits himself to the view that what we immediately perceive by sight is an image on the retina (see Armstrong 2, p. 9ff). It is, I suppose, because of this that Armstrong assumes, as I do not, that Berkeley is suggesting at the outset that what we see is two dimensionally ordered. The question whether, why and when Berkeley commits himself to the view that we see retinal images is often discussed in connection with his treatment of 'situation' in sects. 88-120. The problem he faces here is that, given we see the retinal image, it might seem that what we see should appear inverted. Now this problem arises only if it is assumed that we see the retinal image,

and as Berkeley seems to have appreciated that this is *not* what we see (*PC* 268 and 274), and in effect dissolves the problem in *TVV* 50 by pointing this out, it has naturally puzzled commentators that he does not disabuse his readers of the notion when examining the problem in *NTV*. Armstrong argues that he could not do this because he was 'hoist with his own petard', having played along in sect. 2 with the notion that *'the immediate object of sight is the fund of the eye'* (p. 52). A full discussion of this issue is contained in Furlong 2. Here we can just emphasize that Berkeley certainly *could* have proposed the argument of sect. 2 without supposing that we see the fund of the eye *and* without thinking that it was sufficient to show that the things we see are not *in fact* ordered in depth. As Furlong says: 'Berkeley had, admittedly, accepted that distance is a "line directed endwise to the eye" and had inferred from this that since the same point, say R, in the retina corresponds to any point whatever in the line, say P, we have no way, using the one eye, of telling how far away P is. But this inference provides no ground for supposing that it is R, the point on the retina, that we see; all we can say is that we see a point P, where the position of that point is left indeterminate, so far as sight is concerned' (p. 311).

6. White's discussion of the issues involved here is excellent. He says: 'We can assert that nothing is "without" (*sine*) and yet not have to prove that nothing is "without" (*extra*). Objects may exist at a distance and yet not exist unperceived (p. 61). Though he locates 'one passage in which it could be argued . . . that Berkeley himself saw this' he makes it quite clear that in general Berkeley was confused on the issue and never really came to terms with the ambiguity of the phrase 'in the mind': 'Long after the Principles were published Berkeley welcomed the support of the Chesselden case (*TVV* 71) where the blind man "thought all objects whatever touched his eyes". Berkeley did "hold that there is no external world and that he sees everything . . . right up against his eyes", though Dr. Luce is correct in thinking that an immaterialist *need* not do so' (p. 65). Commenting on a suggestion made by Luce that in the *Principles* (as distinct from *NTV*) Berkeley recognizes that mind-dependent sensible objects are ordered in depth because *external*, White notes that as used by Berkeley the term 'external' is itself ambiguous. In *Pr.* 90, which Luce cites, things are allowed to be external in two senses: first, 'in that they are not generated from within, by the mind it self, but imprinted by a spirit distinct from that which perceives them', and, second, in that they may exist in some mind other than my own. Clearly the fact that things can be said to be external in one of these senses does not mean that as perceived by me they must be three-dimensionally ordered.

7. The man born blind appears again in sects. 79 (when Berkeley is discussing magnitude), 92ff (in the discussion concerning situation), and 132ff (when the case is made for the dissimilarity of the objects of sight and touch). In sects. 132ff Berkeley draws attention to a problem posed by William Molyneux and published by Locke in the second edition of the *Essay* at II ix 8: 'Suppose a man *born* blind, and now adult, and taught by his *touch* to distinguish between a cube and a sphere . . . so as to tell, when he felt one and the other, which is the cube, which the sphere. Suppose then the cube and sphere placed on a table, and the blind man be made to see: *quære*, whether *by his sight, before he touched them*, he could now distinguish and tell which is the globe, which the cube?' Locke and Molyneux thought he would not be able to tell, for 'though he has obtained the experience of how a globe, how a cube affects his touch, yet he has not yet obtained the experience, that what affects his touch so or so, must affect his sight so or so'. As Berkeley sees the position, if Locke is right, and if what we see and what we touch are numerically distinct, it follows that felt extension and seen extension are not characteristics of the same sort. So again the man born blind, who appreciates how different what he sees is from anything he has felt, is held to be nearer the truth than the rest of us. The point about *numerical* distinctness has supposedly been established earlier. In sect. 49 Berkeley says: '. . . if we take a close and accurate view of things, it must be acknowledged that we never see and feel one and the same object. That which is seen is one thing, and that which is felt is another. If the visible figure and extension be not the same with the tangible figure and extension, we are not to infer that one and the same thing has divers extensions. The true consequence is that the objects of sight and touch are two distinct things.'

8. It is perhaps worth pointing out that the first edition always refers to 'nature' rather than to 'the Author of Nature'. Indeed the first edition of *NTV* gives no clue that Berkeley is aiming at bringing men to an appreciation of the immanence of God. That this was his aim is made clear in a letter written in March 1710. See *Works* VIII, p. 31.

9. For an examination of Berkeley's conceit concerning the solitary man and his reasons for not using it in the published introduction see Aaron 2, p. 46ff. In part the conceit is what Luce says it is in his note on *PC* 566 – 'an attempt to reach the pure data of experience', though in this entry Berkeley does ask us to appreciate 'how after long experience he [the solitary man] would know wthout words'. Apparently one great and excellent truth he may be near to is that *esse* is *percipi*. At least: 'A good Proof that Existence is nothing without or distinct from Perception may be Drawn from Considering a Man put into the World without company'

(*PC* 588). From our point of view what needs stressing is that Berkeley does not use the conceit *just* to draw our attention to the given independently of what we make of it. He supposes that the solitary man will naturally and unhesitatingly put what Berkeley takes to be the correct *interpretation* on the given. Indeed Berkeley clearly sees him as a primitive idealist.

10. It is sometimes suggested that the language in which the realist describes his experiences must at the very least be seen as deplorably loose. After all, even if there is a substantial particular corresponding to the name 'moon', the realist will have to admit that at any one time he can see only one surface of the thing. If he wants to be strictly accurate he should never say he sees *the moon*. The argument depends on the assumption that we can properly be said to *see* something only if we are able to take in each aspect and characteristic of the thing in one grand perceptual gulp. The correct response to this is provided by Carrier: 'Surely, we are not required to see all the surfaces of an object at once in order to see it. One can see a dog without inspecting every part of it, just as one can kick the poor brute without covering it with bruises. The sentence "Xantippe kicked a dog", once true, does not lose its truth value because it is later established that Xantippe only kicked the hind end of a dog. Similarly, the sentence "Xantippe saw a dog", once true, remains true even if it is later determined that her view of the animal was from far away and from a very sharp angle' (p. 402).

11. Equally of course he has to rely on our conceptual scheme to *develop* his doctrines. Note for example how he is happy to talk of an oar being put into and taken out of water (*our* way of thinking of the situation) even when bringing out the implications of *his* view that there is no one item seen at each stage. Our conceptual scheme seems to provide a framework *within which* we can make some sort of sense of what Berkeley is saying. We find an interesting example of this when we consider his claim in *NTV* that though visible objects are not at distances from us they nevertheless suggest distance. For in *NTV* he allows us to suppose both that *tangible* things are at distances from us and that we discover this by touch. What is suggested to the mind is, then, *perceived*, though not by sight. Now though in *Pr.* 44 Berkeley tells us that he does not *need* this prop, the assertion there that really *nothing* is at any distance from us is bound to raise enormous problems for him. If *nothing* I perceive either is or seems to be at a distance, how do I come by the notion of distance, and just *what* is suggested to the mind by, say, the fuzziness of the visible object? Clearly Berkeley must try to convince us that tactual (including kinaesthetic) sensations are enough to explain all that needs explaining, but it is noteworthy that even in *Pr.* 44 he helps himself

to the notion of our exciting motion in our own bodies. It is of course highly questionable whether we can make sense of *this* notion without supposing that our bodies have their place in a world in which things are ordered in depth.

12. This criticism shows that Euphranor's argument is insufficient to fault the initial characterization of the experience of seeing a distant tower. It does not show that there is anything wrong with the way in which Euphranor would prefer to characterize the experience. But Euphranor (or Berkeley) can now be put on the defensive. If the 'small round tower' (the visible object) is at no distance from Euphranor, what was he doing when he *pointed* to it so as to draw it to Alciphron's attention? Can we make sense of the notion of pointing without supposing the hand moving away from the pointer and towards some distant object? Well, perhaps a tangible (and invisible) hand pointed to a tangible (and invisible) tower. But this will not do, for we know that Berkeley in fact believes that *nothing* is at a distance. It is very difficult to see how the debate could get going if the Berkeleian believed his own doctrines.

13. We need to remind ourselves again that Berkeley does not think of qualities in quite the same way as we normally think of qualities. If he did his suggestion that a penny, say, is a *collection* of qualities would not be implausible. A penny can have only one shape, and we would include roundness in the 'bundle'. In fact, though, Berkeley talks of qualities as being *immediately* perceived, and of judgements concerning them as being *incorrigible*, and this will not do for the qualities of objects as we normally conceive them. Note that I can be mistaken about the 'real' shape of something when I look at it from an unfamiliar angle. No, the *quality* I perceive when I look at a penny from an angle is, for Berkeley, the quality of being elliptical.

14. This point holds good even if it is true (as Luce elsewhere insists) that later in the *Dialogues* Berkeley explicitly 'distinguishes pain and pleasure from sensible qualities' (Luce 9, p. 80). Luce draws attention to i, 191, where Philonous talks of pain and pleasure as being 'annexed to' the secondary qualities, and to i, 204, which, very questionably, he sees as justifying the claim that for Berkeley: 'We do not perceive the pain precisely as we perceive the heat. We perceive the heat immediately; we perceive the resulting pain mediately....' Now of course if it really were the case that Berkeley came to regard the heat and the pain as distinct objects, there would be no problem in seeing how he could regard heat as a *quality* and pain as a *bodily sensation*. But as soon as he distinguishes the quality from the sensation he must sacrifice the argument we have been considering, and it becomes open to Hylas to insist that though the sensation clearly is mind-dependent

this does not reflect upon the quality. Berkeley, the idealist, *needs* the identification.

15. Cf. the quotation from Bracken given in n. 9 to Ch. 3, above. And White too: 'It is said (e.g., Luce and Jessop) that the word "idea" for Berkeley meant "object of sense". He himself used it synonymously with "object of perception", "perception", and "sensation"; and explicitly refused to allow the usual distinctions between them (D. 194-7). He uses "sensation" as ambiguously as "idea". Naturally this gives rise to some very queer logic. It is meaningful, in the ordinary use, to talk of perceiving objects but not of perceiving sensations (Ryle, *Concept of Mind*, Ch. vii); we can "have" or "feel" sensations of various kinds but we do not in this sense have or feel objects of perception. . . . Of course it is quite permissible to introduce a new meaning for "perceive sensation". All I am saying is that since Berkeley also uses "perceive" as it is ordinarily used in "perceive objects", and also uses "sensation" as it is ordinarily used in "have sensations" (e.g., painful, pleasant, muscular, in the eye, etc.) his terminology is misleading, and, whenever there is a combination of these meanings, his logic is confused' (pp. 58-9).

16. We are not concerned now with Philonous's 'observations on the complication of heat, cold, tastes and smells with pleasure and pain', but can we *really* see him as arguing *ad hominem* here? Poor Hylas has to be *pressured* into accepting the relevant identifications, and he tries so hard to resist.

17. In i, 205-6 Philonous does eventually face up to the suggestion that 'our ideas do not exist without the mind; but that they are copies, images, or representations of certain originals that do'. In reply he says: 'How then is it possible, that things perpetually fleeting and variable as our ideas, should be copies or images of any thing fixed and constant? Or in other words, since all sensible qualities, as size, figure, colour, &c. that is, our ideas are continually changing upon every alteration in the distance, medium, or instruments of sensation; how can any determinate material objects be properly represented or painted forth by several distinct things, each of which is so different from and unlike the rest? Or if you say it resembles some one only of our ideas, how shall be we able to distinguish the true copy from all the false ones?' He presses the point home by claiming that a colour, for example, as we perceive it, cannot be *like* an invisible quality, and that, in general, we cannot conceive of a sensible thing *representing* an insensible thing.

18. We might remember here that when Galileo says that he cannot conceive a body without supposing it to have some determinate size he says that he feels bound to think of it 'as being large or small *in relation to other things*' (my italics).

19. A vigorous defence of our description of objects as solid is to be found in the following from Wittgenstein: 'We have been told by popular scientists that the floor on which we stand is not solid, as it appears to common sense, as it has been discovered that the wood consists of particles filling space so thinly that it can almost be called empty. This is liable to perplex us, for in a way of course we know that the floor is solid, or that, if it isn't solid, this may be due to the wood being rotten but not to its being composed of electrons. To say, on this latter ground, that the floor is not solid is to misuse language. For even if the particles were as big as grains of sand, and as close together as these are in a sandheap, the floor would not be solid if it were composed of them in the sense in which a sandheap is composed of grains. Our perplexity was based on a misunderstanding; the picture of the thinly filled space had been wrongly *applied*. For this picture of the structure of matter was meant to explain the very phenomenon of solidity' (Wittgenstein 1, p. 45).

20. Similarly, of course, if we allow that shape, say, is essential to the very concept of body but that colour is not, it certainly does not *follow*, as we found Galileo suggesting, that there are any objects which are not in themselves coloured. But of course he, Boyle and Locke were onto *something*. The materialists realized that in giving an account of bodies as they are in themselves they *had* to attribute certain qualities even to corpuscles. And they saw that they could describe objects as colourless in themselves and then explain how (through the action of light) we see them as coloured. It is just unfortunate that they mishandled the point by suggesting that when we suppose we see colour 'on' an object we are *really* acquainted only with an item produced in our minds *by* the object.

21. When Hylas suggests that the perception of ideas can be explained in terms of 'various impressions or traces ... made in the brain', Philonous replies: 'The brain ... you speak of, being a sensible thing, exists only in the mind. Now, I would fain know whether you think it reasonable to suppose, that one idea or thing existing in the mind, occasions all other ideas. And if you think so, pray how do you account for the origin of that primary idea or brain itself?' (ii, 209).

22. The notion that our senses are somehow deceiving us rather than informing us even when we see the tomato as red or the table as smooth is really a very odd one. Consider Russell on the texture of the table: 'With the naked eye one can see the grain, but otherwise the table looks smooth and even. If we looked at it through a microscope, we should see roughnesses and hills and valleys, and all sorts of differences that are imperceptible to the naked eye. Which of these is the 'real' table? We are naturally tempted to say that what we see through the microscope is more real, but that in turn would be changed by a still more powerful microscope.

If, then, we cannot trust what we see with the naked eye, why should we trust what we see through a microscope? Thus, again, the confidence in our senses with which we began deserts us' (Russell 5, p. 3). One is tempted to ask just how my senses deceived me when I looked at the table with a naked eye. They informed me that the table would be satisfactory for table-tennis. Did they then deceive me as to its microscopic structure or as to what description a mite would think appropriate? No, because I do not *expect* unaided sight to inform me as to an object's microscopic structure – let alone as to its corpuscular or atomic structure. We can agree, however, that the microscope reveals that a very small creature would neither see nor describe the surface of the table as flat.

CHAPTER SEVEN

1. These quotations are taken from a long passage added for the third edition. The exchanges here supplement what is contained in a passage common to all editions in which Hylas poses the basic problem by raising the question as to how talk of God's mind can be meaningful: 'Since therefore you have no idea of the mind of God, how can you conceive it possible, that things should exist in his mind? Or, if you can conceive the mind of God without having an idea of it, why may not I be allowed to conceive the existence of matter, notwithstanding that I have no idea of it?' (iii, 231). In his reply Philonous claims that I have *immediate* knowledge of my own mind and thus 'though not an inactive idea, yet in my self some sort of active thinking image of the Deity'.

2. The two letters from Johnson together with Berkeley's replies will be found in *Works* II, pp. 271-94. Describing him as 'the father of American philosophy', Jessop introduces Johnson's letters by saying that they 'contain the earliest known criticism of any length and weight of Berkeley's theory'. It is unfortunate that the replies were 'wrote in a hurry', the first just after Berkeley had recovered from a debilitating illness. They do not show Berkeley at his best.

3. Studying the entries actually marked with the 'S' gives us only a rough guide. A number of relevant entries are marked '+' – i.e. with the sign Berkeley uses to indicate that he is no longer satisfied with what he has said on a given point. There are twenty-two of these in the first notebook. Of the fifteen 'S' entries in the first notebook three are not concerned with spirit at all, and the three verso entries may have been written after the completion of that notebook. A detailed study does not, though, change the basic picture. It is only in the second notebook that Berkeley concentrates his attention on problems concerning the mind and our knowledge of it.

4. Doney takes a contrary view and argues that for Berkeley perception was always *simply* the passive reception of ideas. He supports this claim by quoting from *PC* 286 (an early entry which is marked with the obelus), *Pr.* 28 (which does not in fact support him) and *Dialogues*, i, 194-7. The passage from the *Dialogues* is certainly tricky, for here Philonous does insist that 'you are in the very perception of light and colours altogether passive'. I don't think we should underestimate the difficulty here. We can note though that Berkeley certainly did continue to regard perception as passive in *one* sense because he was impressed by the involuntary aspect, but that even in the *Dialogues* he does not deny that we are active whenever we perceive. Luce has insisted that for Berkeley 'there is activity *in* seeing, not only *after* it' (Luce 5, p. 50). I would suggest, too, that Johnston does justice to Berkeley's perhaps ambivalent thinking on the question when he says: 'Presentational experience as such is not, it is true, active; but, inasmuch as it *is* the experience of a spirit, it is accompanied by or pervaded with volitional activity' (p. 201).

5. For example in *Pr.* 141: 'Nothing can be plainer, than that the motions, changes, decays, and dissolutions which we hourly see befall natural bodies (and which is what we mean by the *course of Nature*) cannot possibly affect an active, simple, uncompounded substance: such a being therefore is indissoluble by the force of Nature, that is to say, *the soul of man is naturally immortal.*'

6. For Hume on personal identity see Bk. I Pt. IV Sect. vi of the *Treatise* together with the Appendix to the *Treatise*. What I have said so far in this chapter is based on the case I made in my paper 'Berkeley's view of spirit'. There I concluded: 'Enough has now been said for us to see that it is a gross oversimplification to suppose that Berkeley simply accepted Locke's account of spiritual substance. It is not intended here to defend Berkeley's own concept. There are fundamental objections to it that we can now see; there are objections to points of detail that perhaps he should have seen, and there are objections, or difficulties rather, that he certainly did see. He saw and fully accepted, for example, that the existence of spirit could not be abstracted from its cogitation or thought, and thus that it was impossible to conceive of spirit as existing but not perceiving. That this consequence became connected in his mind with difficulties he experienced with the concept of time is another story' (pp. 70-1). In the remainder of this chapter I tell the story about Berkeley's difficulties with the concept of time and the relevance of these to his thinking about the person.

7. Johnson saw this quite clearly. In the second of the letters referred to earlier (n2) he asked Berkeley: '. . . is there not such a thing as sleeping without dreaming, or being in a *deliquium* without a thought? If there

be, and yet at the same time the *esse* of a spirit be nothing else but its actual thinking, the soul must be dead during those intervals; and if ceasing or intermitting to think be the ceasing to be, or death of the soul, it is many times and easily put to death.'

8. Perhaps not unwisely Berkeley decided not to labour this point in Part 1. In a draft, though, he had expanded on it a little, saying: 'Sure I am that shou'd any one tell me there is a time wherein a spirit actually exists without perceiving, or an idea without being perceiv'd, or that there is a 3rd sort of being which exists tho it neither wills not perceives nor is perceived, his words would have no other effect on my mind than if he talk'd in an unknown language. Tis indeed an easie matter for a man to say the mind exists without thinking, but to conceive a meaning that may correspond to those sounds, or to frame a notion of a spirit's existence abstracted from its thinking, this seems to me impossible, and I suspect that even they who are the stiffest abetters of that tenent might abate somewhat of their firmness wou'd they but lay aside the words and calmly attending to their own thoughts examine what they meant by them' (*Works* II, p. 85). Had Berkeley published Part 2 this passage might have found a home there.

9. I will take this opportunity of complaining about a certain type of 'defence' of Berkeley. Those who assert that the tendency of Berkeley's thinking is towards solipsism are sometimes criticised for (in effect) not knowing the text and not realizing that he holds we have inferential knowledge of the existence of other finite selves and good reasons for supposing that these selves have experiences like our own. The criticism misses the point. There are many cases where we can say that Berkeley's premisses commit him to P where Berkeley not only denies P but also argues for some proposition inconsistent with P. Thus Bennett says for example: 'Berkeley is in fact deeply committed to saying: "I am alone in the universe with God. There are sensible things, but these are a sub-class of my mental states and God's, there are perhaps mental states which God has and I do not, and many of my mental states must be God's also; but there cannot be any reason for supposing that the universe contains any spirits, or mental substances, other than the two of us"' (p. 221). My purpose here is not to defend this highly defensible view, nor to raise the question as to whether we should allow Berkeley even God. What I want to stress is that we will not refute it by pointing out that there are no passages where Berkeley admits the point and many passages where he either assumes or argues for the contrary. Writers sympathetic to Berkeley seem particularly prone to the unhelpful line of defence that his basic premisses can't lead to certain odd or worrying consequences if he says that they don't.

10. It might be thought that Berkeley could solve his puzzlement about time by allowing that as well as successions of ideas in finite minds there is one continuous succession in God's mind, this succession in some sense setting the standard. In his reply to Johnson Berkeley denies that there is any succession of ideas in God's mind. But of course if he had found a solution along these lines acceptable he would have had to deny that periods of dreamless sleep are nothing.
11. In his note on *PC* 9 Luce argues that we need not see Berkeley as being committed to a solipsist or subjectivist view of time and that he may well have regarded time as 'a public continuum'. I am not convinced by the argument, which seems to rest largely on the fact that in *Pr.* 97 Berkeley allows the master and servant to meet at an *agreed* time. What I would want to emphasize, though, is that if we suppose that he did regard time as a public continuum we will find it impossible to see why he thought it followed from his view of time that the soul always thinks.
12. This is one case where the dots signalling omissions in the quotation should not be taken as suggesting that what is omitted can be regarded as unimportant or irrelevant to the point at issue. The long passage is examined by Bennett (pp. 54-5), and in Flew 1.
13. There is one fundamental difference between Berkeley's attitude to what we ordinarily say about causal relationships between objects and his attitude to what we ordinarily say about time. This is that though Berkeley believes that *strictly* the fire does not cause the water to boil he can give an account of how God has so ordered things that we can talk as if it did. The underlying relationship is said to be that holding between sign and thing signified. On time, though, it is not at all clear that he can explain how, if *strictly* each man's time is private, we are *able* to talk as if time were a public continuum.
14. As Berkeley saw (*Alciphron* VII 8), we are left with the objection that if I can now remember being the person who did A but not being the person who did B, while the person who did A could then remember being the person who did B, then I must both be and not be the person who did B. Berkeley saw that Locke's criterion would not do, and in *Alciphron* he makes use of this fact to suggest that people shouldn't be dismissive of the concept of the Holy Trinity just because it involves difficulties. 'To me it seems evident that if none but those who had nicely examined, and could themselves explain, the principle of individuation in man, or untie the knots and answer the objections which may be raised even about human personal identity, would require of us to explain the divine mysteries, we should not be often called upon for a clear and distinct idea of *person* in relation to the Trinity, nor would the difficulties on that head be often objected to our faith.' Flew describes this as 'a

very typical piece of Berkeleian intellectual judo' (Flew 3, p. 173). His paper contains a useful examination of Locke's views on personal identity.

15. Of course Berkeley would not have *liked* the doctrine either, for he would have lost his proof of the soul's immortality. As Johnson said, 'if ceasing or intermitting to think be the ceasing to be, or death of the soul, it is many times and easily put to death' and if this is so 'I don't see upon what we can build any natural argument for the soul's immortality'.

16. Descartes was certainly aware of the gap between establishing his existence and establishing that he was 'a substance whose whole essence or nature consists entirely in thinking, and which, for its existence, has no need of place, and is not dependent on any material thing' (*Discourse on Method*, Part IV). His basic argument seems to be that as a person can feign that he has no body but not that he does not exist, he cannot *be*, and must in fact be *distinct from*, the body. For a full examination of Descartes' position here see Ch. 4 of Kenny's *Descartes*, noting that this chapter is entitled '*Sum res cogitans*' and that it follows a separate chapter entitled '*Cogito ergo sum*'.

CHAPTER EIGHT

1. The notion that volitions are introspectible happening or events, or internal 'prods' which precede the desired consequences, is highly suspect. I shall not, though, examine it here. For criticism of what Bennett has called 'the volition-and-upshot account of deliberate (intentional, voluntary) action' see Bennett pp. 206-9 and Melden's paper.

2. As noted, Locke did hold that we must look to reflection for the clearest idea of active power. He concedes, though, that we are as much in the dark when we consider *how* our volitions can bring about bodily movements as we are when we consider how bodies can bring about changes in other bodies or give rise to sensations in us. Ultimately 'the original rules and communication of motion' must be ascribed to 'the arbitrary will and good pleasure of the Wise Architect'. See IV iii 28-9.

3. It is not *just* the idealist who conceives of himself as a bodiless cyclops. In Ch. 2 we found Karl Pearson talking about 'the conscious ego of each one of us' as being 'seated at the brain terminals of the sensory nerves' and studying the 'messages' transmitted from outside. Here 'the conscious ego' is being thought of as a perceiver perceiving sensations, and *its* problems – for example, how can it know there is an external world? – are supposed to be *our* problems. Locke, of course, often talks in this way. For much of the time the flesh and blood perceiver of corporeal things seems to have got lost, and instead we have ourselves as *minds* perceiving *ideas*. This picture gives rise to obvious problems in

the philosophy of perception. But it poses problems about *action* too. If we think of ourselves as corporeal we find we can answer questions as to how we do things – bowl a cricket ball, cut out a paper pattern, model clay, and so on. You bowl a ball by moving your arm in such and such a way. If, though, we think of ourselves as agents *in* the body we encounter all sorts of difficulties when we ask how we (as incorporeal things) can do so simple a trick as moving the arm. We should be quite clear that Berkeley's identification of the self with the soul or ego is quite explicit. In *Pr.* 139 for example he insists that 'that which I denote by the term I, is the same with what is meant by *soul* or *spiritual substance*'.

4. Cf. Don Locke: 'It is undeniable that philosophers have often distorted the facts by overemphasizing the contemplative aspects (thinking, reasoning, perceiving) of the human mind and underestimating the fact that man is an active agent. Indeed it is well nigh impossible to exaggerate the importance of our movements and actions in our coming to know and conceive of the world in the way that we do' (pp. 230-1). Locke, though, would positively deny that Berkeley appreciated this.

5. Don Locke seems to be quite right when he sees this as a central feature of idealism. Thus: 'According to the Idealist what we describe as our motion can be nothing more than a change among entities which exist only in our consciousness. In so far as we want to say that we move among things, that they move around us, that we bump into them and they into us, that we notice changes in their appearance due to our or their movement, so far we are forced to reject an Idealist theory. This is another point at which the Idealist parts company with common sense, and, I think, it counts more against the Idealist than his denial of the real, non-sense-dependent existence of what we perceive' (pp. 235-6).

6. I am treating the question whether there must be a cause of sensed ideas and the question concerning the nature of the cause as separate questions, assuming that we would want an affirmative answer to the first of them before even raising the second. Bennett, though, performs a useful service by drawing attention to *Pr.* 146 where Berkeley argues straight off that it is 'repugnant' to suppose an idea without a spiritual cause. Thus: 'But though there be some things which convince us, human agents are concerned in producing them; yet it is evident to every one, that those things which are called the works of Nature . . . are not produced by, or dependent on the wills of men. There is therefore some other spirit that causes them, since it is repugnant that they should subsist by themselves.' Bennett (who is not sure how much weight Berkeley placed on the argument) suggests that it rests on an ambiguity in the expression 'dependent on'. Berkeley believed he had shown that (a) all ideas are dependent on a mind in the sense (S1) that they must be *owned* or *had*

by a mind. But he also saw that (b) some ideas are not dependent on any human mind in the sense (S2) that they are not *caused by* any human mind. From (a) and (b) it does not follow, as Berkeley apparently thought it did, that (c) ideas not dependent (S2) on any human mind must be dependent (S2) on some other mind. The argument commits the fallacy of equivocation. On this see Bennett, pp. 166-7.

7. We should perhaps make it clear at the outset that there is certainly *no* standard account if this means an account that has won anything like universal acceptance. For example, I have seen it suggested (though not in a specialist work) that the continuity argument was Berkeley's *only* argument for the existence of God. And at the other extreme Thomson has to apologize for having suggested (when his paper first appeared) that Berkeley uses *only* the passivity argument. The authors Bennett mentions in criticizing the 'standard' account are Luce, Warnock and Furlong.

8. The suggestion is that Berkeley is again misled by the ambiguity in the phrase 'dependent on'. This time: 'Berkeley takes the premiss that some ideas are independent of (not caused by) my mind, muddles himself into treating it as the premiss that some ideas are independent of (not owned by) my mind, and so infers that some mind has ideas when I do not. How else could we explain his saying that "I find by experience" that some ideas are "exterior" to my mind in a sense which implies their existing "during the intervals between the times of my perceiving them" ' (pp. 170-1).

9. I should myself be embarrassed to find Berkeley regularly using the continuity argument. I must admit, though, that Bennett has not convinced me that it does not show up *twice* in the *Dialogues*, for I think Berkeley does have it in mind in what Bennett calls 'the "false imaginary glare" passage', this being found in ii, 210-3. A snippet from it is quoted above on p. 302. Bennett examines this passage in sect. 39 of his book and holds that here Berkeley is *not* concerned with the existence of things when not perceived by us. We should be clear, though, that in introducing the sensible objects he is going to talk about in this passage Berkeley deliberately includes things which we are not perceiving, and in particular 'innumerable worlds revolving round the central fires' which 'feeble narrow sense cannot descry'. He tells us that 'neither sense nor imagination are big enough to comprehend the boundless extent with all its glittering furniture'. Philonous seems to have *all* the choir of heaven and furniture of the earth in mind when he says of sensible objects that 'seeing they depend not on my thought, and have an existence distinct from being perceived by me, *there must be some other mind wherein they exist*'. Bennett concedes that his opponents may be able to 'capture' this passage, and I am afraid they may.

10. Ayer is one writer who has no doubt that Berkeley wanted to find some way of incorporating object-continuity into his system, but who does not have him assuming continuity in order to prove God's existence. In his introduction to *British Empirical Philosophers* we find him taking it that Berkeley proves God's existence by means of the passivity argument and then uses this God to allow for continuity.

11. The argument here is very neat. But we should perhaps make it clear that Berkeley *thought* that the passivity argument proved (or was but a short step from proving) rather more than Bennett suggests. It took him to a superior spirit who now perceives anything any creature perceives by sense, but it also took him to a God who *orders* our perceptions, who speaks to us in a language, and in whom 'we live and move and have our being'. One can quite see how Berkeley could think that *this* God (whose existence is proved by the passivity argument) could be appealed to in order to allow for continuity. For if the Deity is now prepared to imprint certain ideas on my mind whenever I am suitably placed, and if the Deity must *now* perceive whatever he is prepared to imprint, then it is clear that the Deity now perceives those things I might perceive. There is a short cut to this position. For Berkeley would hold that if God perceives now what I perceive now then he must continue to perceive it when I cease to perceive it, and this because the content of God's mind is unchanging. Unfortunately, though, and as we shall see, the principle appealed to here is one that raises a very real problem for Berkeley.

12. It would help my case if we could show Berkeley moving from the notion that things exist in God's mind as *powers* to the notion that they exist there as *ideas*. And we can do this. In *PC* 812 he says: 'The propertys of all things are in God i.e. there is in the Deity Understanding as well as Will. He is no Blind agent & in truth a blind Agent is a contradiction' (cf. *Dialogues*, iii, 239, where Philonous insists that 'a thing which hath no ideas in itself cannot impart them to me'). I am not suggesting that Berkeley is specifically addressing himself to the continuity question in *PC* 812. But what I would suggest is that when he saw, or thought he saw, that the redness I now perceive must exist in God's mind now (and not just as a power) it would also seem to him that those ideas which God wills I should perceive, if I were suitably placed, must exist in God's mind now (and not just as powers). This shift from Divine powers to Divine ideas may well have seemed attractive to Berkeley. As Mabbott says, 'it is much less alarming and revolutionary to think of the trees in the park existing when nobody perceives them, because they, with all their friendly, familiar qualities, are perceived by God, than to think of them as represented in God's mind by powers or volitions quite unlike them in character' (p. 374).

13. Berkeley's reticence on the continuity question is particularly apparent in the *Principles*, and it may well be that he hoped to be able to say more in Part 2. Certainly he is more forthcoming in the *Dialogues*, and what he says here really leaves us in no doubt that he wanted to commit himself to the view that the things we might perceive *do* exist in the mind of God. There is the 'false imaginary glare' passage and the passage where the continuity argument is proposed. Again, in claiming that it is not odd to say that sensible things are ideas, Philonous assures Hylas that 'the proposition . . . in effect amounts to no more than this, to wit, that there are only things perceiving, and things perceived; or that every unthinking being is necessarily, and from the very nature of its existence, perceived by some mind; if not by any finite created mind, yet certainly by the infinite mind of God, in whom *we live, and move, and have our being*' (iii, 236). Bennett misses this passage. Finally, there is the long passage on the Creation in iii, 250-6, and we shall be looking at this in a moment. In general, what Berkeley says in the *Dialogues* reflects a deeper commitment to object-continuity (and to a certain way of allowing for it) than Bennett recognizes. But for all this, we can concede that in print he says less on continuity than we might have expected.

14. Cf. Stack: 'As a matter of fact, there is strong evidence that Berkeley would deny that God 'perceives' IDEAS or anything at all. Though to be sure, Berkeley often seems to suggest that God perceives what is not perceived by a finite perceiver or finite perceivers, his considered opinion seems to be that God WILLS the sense-data we experience and knows – or contains in His understanding – all things' (p. 73). But Stack's position is not as close to Mabbott's as this may suggest. Mabbott holds that Berkeley did not believe in the Divine ideas. Stack holds that Berkeley quite certainly did believe in them, and his doubt is as to whether he really believed that God *perceived* them. Stack is very much alive to the difficulties Berkeley would have got into had he attempted to expand on the nature of the Divine archetypes and on the relationship between these and the perceived phenomena.

15. We can now see more clearly why Berkeley was at one stage tempted to suggest a phenomenalist solution in print. He held that X exists (for us) if and only if (a) God has it in mind, and (b) God wills that, were we suitably placed, we should perceive it. But clearly, given God's omnipotence, it follows from the fact that God wills that I should perceive X were I suitably placed, that, were I suitably placed, I should perceive X. Because he is reluctant to dwell on the theology, Berkeley is tempted (in *PC* 802) to put all the stress on the conditional. But he *has* to reverse this decision, for he cannot follow it through without appearing to go against his central claim that *esse* is straightforwardly *percipi*. From his

Note to p. 349

point of view any suggestion that a sensible thing can be properly said to exist when it might be, but is not, perceived would be disastrous. It goes without saying that Berkeley would have been nearer to a genuine reconciliation with the mob had he decided that *esse* was *percipi aut posse percipi*. A genuine reconciliation is ruled out so long as he insists that *esse* is *percipi*.

Bibliography

As stated in the Preface, references to Berkeley's writings in the text are to the nine volume edition edited by A. A. Luce and T. E. Jessop: *The Works of George Berkeley* (Edinburgh, 1948-57). References to Luce's notes on entries in Berkeley's *Philosophical Commentaries* are not to *Works* I but to the diplomatic edition published Edinburgh, 1944. The texts of the *Principles* and *Dialogues* are included in Armstrong 1 and Warnock 2, and I have provided a concordance (p. ix, above) to enable the reader who uses either of these to trace references to the *Dialogues*.

AARON, R. I. (1) *John Locke*, 3rd ed. (Oxford, 1971).
—— (2) *The Theory of Universals*, 2nd ed. (Oxford, 1967).
ACTON, H. B. 'George Berkeley', in P. Edwards (ed.) *The Encyclopaedia of Philosophy* (New York, 1967).
ALLAIRE, E. B. 'Berkeley's idealism', *Theoria*, **29** (1963).
ARDLEY, G. W. R. *Berkeley's Renovation of Philosophy* (The Hague, 1968).
ARISTOTLE *De Anima. Books II and III*, trans. D. W. Hamlyn (Oxford, 1968).
ARMSTRONG, D. M. (1) ed. *Berkeley's Philosophical Writings* (New York, 1965).
—— (2) *Berkeley's Theory of Vision* (Melbourne, 1960).
—— (3) ed. (with C. B. Martin) *Locke and Berkeley* (London, 1968).
ASCHENBRENNER, K. (1) 'Bishop Berkeley on existence in the mind', in Aschenbrenner 2.
—— (2) ed. (with B. Mates and S. C. Pepper) *George Berkeley* (Berkeley, 1957).
AUSTIN, J. L. *Sense and Sensibilia* (Oxford, 1962).
AYER, A. J. (1) ed. (with R. Winch) *British Empirical Philosophers* (London, 1952).
—— (2) *Metaphysics and Common Sense* (London, 1969).
BENNETT, J. F. *Locke, Berkeley, Hume: Central Themes* (Oxford, 1971).
BERMAN, D. 'Some new Bermuda Berkeleiana', *Hermathena*, no. 110 (1970).
BOHR, N. 'On the notions of causality and complementarity', *Dialectica*, **2** (1948).
BOYLE, R. *The Origin of Forms and Qualities* (Oxford, 1666).

BRACKEN, H. M. (1) 'Berkeley's realisms', *Philosophical Quarterly*, **8** (1958).
—— (2) *The Early Reception of Berkeley's Immaterialism* (The Hague, 1959).
BRAYBROOKE, D. 'Berkeley on the numerical identity of ideas', *Philosophical Review*, **64** (1955).
BRAYTON, A. *George Berkeley in Newport* (Newport, 1954).
BROAD, C. D. 'Berkeley's argument about material substance', *Proc. of the British Academy*, **28** (1942).
CARRIER, L. S. 'Immediate and mediate perception,' *J. of Philosophy*, **66** (1969).
CRAIG, E. J. 'Berkeley's attack on abstract ideas', *Philosophical Review*, **77** (1968).
CUMMINS, P. D. 'Perceptual relativity and ideas in the mind', *Philosophy and Phenomenological Research*, **24** (1963).
DAVIE, D. A. 'Berkeley's style in *Siris*', *Cambridge J.*, **4** (1951).
DESCARTES, R. *Descartes' Philosophical Writings*, trans. N. Kemp Smith (London, 1952).
DOBRÉE, B. 'Berkeley as a man of letters', *Hermathena*, no. 82 (1953).
DONEY, W. 'Two questions about Berkeley', *Philosophical Review*, **61** (1952).
EDDINGTON, A. S. *The Nature of the Physical World* (Cambridge, 1928).
FLEW, A. G. N. (1) 'Did Berkeley become a precursor of Wittgenstein?' (forthcoming).
—— (2) *An Introduction to Western Philosophy* (London, 1971).
—— (3) 'Locke and the problem of personal identity' [orig. *Philosophy*, 1951], in Armstrong 3.
—— (4) 'Some objections to Cartesian views of man', in J. R. Smythies (ed.) *Brian and Mind* (London, 1965).
FRASER, A. C. ed. *The Works of George Berkeley* – in 4 vols. (Oxford, 1901). [For Fraser's edition of Locke's *Essay*, see under Locke].
FURLONG, E. J. (1) 'An ambiguity in Berkeley's Principles', *Philosophical Quarterly*, **14** (1964).
—— (2) 'Berkeley and the "knot about inverted images"', *Australasian J. of Philosophy*, **41** (1963).
—— (3) 'Berkeley and the tree in the quad' [orig. *Philosophy*, 1966], in Armstrong 3.
—— (4) 'How much of Steele's *Guardian* No. 39 did Berkeley write?', *Hermathena*, no. 89 (1957).
GIVNER, D. A. 'Berkeley's ambiguity', *Dialogue*, **8** (1970).
GRAVE, S. A. 'The mind and its ideas: some problems in the interpretation of Berkeley' [orig. *Australasian J. of Philosophy*, 1964], in Armstrong 3.
GREY, D. 'The solipsism of Bishop Berkeley', *Philosophical Quarterly*, **2** (1952).
GUNN, J. A. *The Problem of Time* (London, 1929).

HAMLYN, D. W. *Sensation and Perception* (London, 1961).
HEDENIUS, I. *Sensationalism and Theology in Berkeley's Philosophy* (Uppsala, 1936).
HICKS, G. D. *Berkeley* (London, 1932).
HIRST, R. J. ed. *Perception and the External World* (New York, 1965).
HOSPERS, J. *An Introduction to Philosophical Analysis* (London, 1956).
HUME, D. *A Treatise of Human Nature*, ed. L. A. Selby Bigge (Oxford, 1888).
HUXLEY, T. H. *Hume: with helps to the study of Berkeley* (London, 1894).
JESSOP, T. E. (1) 'Berkeley as religious apologist', in Steinkraus 2.
—— (2) ed. *Berkeley: Philosophical Writings* (Edinburgh, 1952).
JOHNSTON, G. A. *The Development of Berkeley's Philosophy* (London, 1923).
KENNY, A. *Descartes* (New York, 1968).
LOCKE, D. *Perception and our Knowledge of the External World* (London, 1967).
LOCKE, J. *An Essay Concerning Human Understanding*, ed. A. C. Fraser (Oxford, 1894).
LUCE, A. A. (1) 'Berkeleian studies in America and France', *Hermathena* no. 94 (1960).
—— (2) *Berkeley and Malebranche* (Oxford, 1934).
—— (3) 'Berkeley's doctrine of the perceivable', *Hermathena*, no. 69 (1942).
—— (4) 'Berkeley's existence in the mind' [orig. *Mind*, 1941], in Armstrong 3.
—— (5) *Berkeley's Immaterialism* (Edinburgh, 1945).
—— (6) 'Berkeley's new principle completed', in Steinkraus 2.
—— (7) *The Dialectic of Immaterialism* (London, 1963).
—— (8) *The Life of George Berkeley Bishop of Cloyne* (Edinburgh, 1949).
—— (9) 'Sensible ideas and sensations', *Hermathena*, no. 150 (1967).
MABBOTT, J. D. 'The place of God in Berkeley's philosophy' [orig. *J. of Philosophical Studies*, 1931], in Armstrong 3.
MALEBRANCHE, N. *De la Recherche de la Vérité*, trans. T. Taylor (London, 1694).
MARC-WOGAU, K. (1) 'The argument from illusion and Berkeley's idealism' [orig. *Theoria*, 1958], in Armstrong 3.
—— (2) 'Berkeley's sensationalism and the *esse est percipi*-principle' [orig. *Theoria*, 1957], in Armstrong 3.
MARGOLIS, J. 'Existential import and perceptual judgments', *J. of Philosophy* **66** (1969).
MATES, B. 'Berkeley was right', in Aschenbrenner 2.
MATTHEWS, H. E. 'Locke, Malebranche and the representative theory', *The Locke Newsletter*, no. 2 (1971).
MAXWELL, G. 'Scientific methodology and the causal theory of perception', in I. Lakatos and A. Musgrave (eds.) *Problems in the Philosophy of Science* (Amsterdam, 1968).

MELDEN, A. I. 'Willing', *Philosophical Review*, **69** (1960).
MORRIS, C. R. *Locke, Berkeley, Hume* (Oxford, 1931).
O'CONNOR, D. J. *John Locke*, Dover edn. (New York, 1967).
OLSCAMP, P. J. *The Moral Philosophy of George Berkeley* (The Hague, 1970).
PERRY, R. B. *Present Philosophical Tendencies* (New York, 1912).
PITCHER, G. 'Minds and ideas in Berkeley', *American Philosophical Quarterly*, **6** (1969).
POPKIN, R. H. (1) 'Berkeley and Pyrrhonism', *Review of Metaphysics*, **5** (1951).
—— (2) 'Berkeley's influence on American philosophy', *Hermathena*, no. 82 (1953).
—— (3) ed. *The Philosophy of the 16th and 17th Centuries* (New York, 1966).
RITCHIE, A. D. *George Berkeley: a reappraisal* (Manchester, 1967).
RUSSELL, B. A. W. (1) *The Autobiography of Bertrand Russell*, vol. II (London, 1968).
—— (2) *Mysticism and Logic* (London, 1918).
—— (3) *An Outline of Philosophy* (London, 1927).
—— (4) *The Principles of Mathematics*, 2nd. ed. (London, 1937).
—— (5) *The Problems of Philosophy*, Opus edn. (Oxford, 1959).
—— (6) *Wisdom of the West* (London, 1959).
RYLE, G. (1) *Dilemmas* (Cambridge, 1954).
—— (2) 'The theory of meaning', in C. A. Mace (ed.) *British Philosophy in the Mid-Century* (London, 1957).
STACE, W. T. 'The refutation of realism', *Mind*, **43** (1934).
STACK, G. J. *Berkeley's Analysis of Perception* (The Hague, 1970).
STEBBING, L. S. *Philosophy and the Physicists* (London, 1937).
STEINKRAUS, W. E. (1) 'Berkeley and his modern critics', in Steinkraus 2.
—— (2) ed. *New Studies in Berkeley's Philosophy* (New York, 1966).
SULLIVAN, C. J. 'Berkeley's attack on matter', in Aschenbrenner 2.
THOMSON, J. F. 'G. J. Warnock's *Berkeley*' [orig. *Mind*, 1956], in Armstrong 3.
TIPTON, I. C. (1) 'Berkeley's view of spirit', in Steinkraus 2.
—— (2) 'Two questions on Bishop Berkeley's panacea', *J. of the History of Ideas*, **30** (1969).
URMSON, J. O. 'The objects of the five senses', *Proc. of the British Academy*, **54** (1968).
WARNOCK, G. J. (1) *Berkeley*, Peregrine edn. (London, 1969).
—— (2) ed. *The Principles of Human Knowledge/Three Dialogues between Hylas and Philonous* (London, 1962).
WHITE, A. R. 'The ambiguity of Berkeley's "Without the Mind"', *Hermathena*, no. 83 (1954).
WHITELY, C. H. *An Introduction to Metaphysics* (London, 1950).
WILLIAMS, B. 'Imagination and the self', *Proc. of the British Academy*, **52** (1966).

WISDOM, J. O. *The Unconscious Origin of Berkeley's Philosophy* (London, 1953).
WITTGENSTEIN, L. (1) *The Blue and Brown Books*, 2nd ed. (Oxford, 1964).
—— (2) *The Philosophical Investigations*, 2nd ed. (Oxford, 1958).
WOOZLEY, A. D. ed. *John Locke: An Essay Concerning Human Understanding* (London, 1964).
YOLTON, J. W. *Locke and the Compass of Human Understanding* (Cambridge, 1970).

Index of Persons

Names occurring in the notes are not usually indexed if the person
is referred to at the corresponding point in the text.

Aaron, R. I. 143, 146, 149, 152, 249, 269, 303, 355, 369, 373
Acton, H. B. 344
Addison, J. 6
Allaire, E. B. 358-9
Ardley, G. W. R. 98-9, 116, 129
Aristotle, 41, 155, 183
Armstrong, D. M. 204, 361, 368-9, 371-2
Aschenbrenner, K. 322
Atterbury, F. 1, 5
Augustine, St. 134, 277-8
Austin, J. L. 80, 131, 214, 216
Ayer, A. J. 215-18, 221, 222, 226, 368, 385

Barrow, I, 208
Baxter, A. 354
Bayle, P. 38-9, 48, 52
Bennett, J. F. 22, 41, 138-9, 144-5, 156, 299, 316, 321-49, 366, 367, 380, 381, 382, 383
Berkeley, Anne, 3, 5, 351, 352
Berkeley George (son), 4, 352-3
Berkeley, G. M. 9
Berkeley, Thomas, 8-9
Berman, D. 311, 352
Bohr, N. 313
Boyle, R. 30-1, 33-4, 37, 50, 248, 377
Bracken, H. M. 112, 341, 353-4, 359, 362-3, 376, 382

Braybrooke, D. 362
Brayton, A. 351
Broad, C. D. 195
Butler, J. 1

Carrier, L. S. 184, 374
Copleston, F. C. 151
Cordemoy, G. de, 303
Craig, E. J. 151
Cummins, P. D. 241, 359

Davie, D. A. 352
Descartes, R. 28, 49-51, 52, 272, 382
Dobrée, B. 9-10, 352
Doney, W. 379

Eccles, J. C. 20
Eddington, A. S. 27-8, 29, 34-5
Ensley, F. C. 97

Fardella, M. A. 48, 52
Flew, A. G. N. 20, 70, 140, 292-3, 367, 381-2
Fraser, A. C. 9, 25, 45, 75, 78, 143, 152
Furlong, E. J. 77-9, 203-5, 236, 330-1, 332, 336-7, 340, 353, 372, 384

Galileo, G. 29-30, 31, 234, 356, 376, 377

Garth, S. 6
Givner, D. A. 61, 127-8, 361
Grave, S. A. 87-8, 339-40, 345
Grey, D. 368
Gunn, J. A. 273

Halley, E. 6
Hamlyn, D. W. 180-1
Hardy, T. 298
Hedenius, I. 76, 78
Heller, J. 274
Hicks, G. D. 166-7
Hirst, R. J. 37-8
Hospers, J. 23, 62-4, 67, 180, 354, 369
Hume, D. 166, 176, 256, 257, 267, 270-1, 305, 313, 314
Huxley, T. H. 356

James, W. 212
Jessop, T. E. 2, 82-3, 237, 260, 275, 297, 298, 363, 376, 378
Johnson, S. (America), 259-60, 276, 284, 285-92, 344-5, 378, 379-80, 381, 382
Johnson, S. (England), 16, 221, 227, 352-3, 354
Johnston, G. A. 75-8, 272, 273, 274, 361, 362, 379

Kenny, A. 382

Law, W. 1
Locke, D. 66, 105-8, 179, 184-5, 210, 222-3, 225-6, 229-31, 247, 355, 383
Locke, J. 1, 18-50, 51, 60-1, 68-71, 74, 76-7, 78, 79, 80-1, 85-9, 90-1, 129, 132-53, 155, 175, 179, 181, 234, 248, 252-5, 256-7, 262-6, 269, 272-3, 274, 276, 285, 287, 290-1, 292, 294-5, 303-4, 309, 316-18, 369-70, 373, 377, 382
Luce, A. A. 1, 2, 3, 4, 5, 9, 16-17, 50, 55, 57, 62, 69, 71-2, 74-7, 82-6, 88, 92, 93-4, 101-2, 108-9, 110-11, 114-22, 125, 170-2, 204-5, 207-8, 229, 232, 235-6, 237, 267, 272, 297-8, 301, 308, 318-19, 323-4, 331, 336-7, 351, 353, 357, 362, 363, 372, 373, 379, 381, 384

Mabbott, J. D. 339, 345, 385
Malebranche, N. 22, 38, 39, 50-2, 97, 306-7
Mandeville, B. 9-10
Marc-Wogau, K. 84, 89-90, 161-2, 362, 365
Margolis, J. 364
Mates, B. 96, 98-9, 160, 173, 252-3
Matthews, H. E. 356
Maxwell, G. 21-2, 363
Melden, A. I. 382
Mill, J. S. 313
Molyneux, W. 373
Moore, G. E. 18
Morris, C. R. 359

Newman, J. H. 273
Newton, I. 28, 33, 155, 272, 278, 285-6

O'Connor, D. J. 41, 366
Olscamp, P. J. 2

Pascal, B. 2
Pearson, K. 354-5, 382
Percival, J. 3, 5, 15
Percival, Lady, 347-8, 349
Perry, R. B. 169-70
Pitcher, G. 91-3
Plato, 134, 138-9, 155
Pope, A. 5

Index of Persons

Popkin, R. H. 351, 359
Pyrrho (and Pyrrhonism), 39, 48, 52, 359

Reid, T. 25
Ritchie, A. D. 2, 298, 313-15
Russell, B. A. W. 15, 21, 29, 88, 168, 176, 245, 246, 251, 271-2, 313, 355, 377-8
Ryle, G. 28, 134, 293, 376

Shaftesbury, 9
Stace, W. T. 167-9
Stack, G. J. 344, 386
Stebbing, L. S. 27-8
Steinkraus, W. E. 97, 167, 169, 170
Stillingfleet, E. 45, 47
Stock, J. 9
Sullivan, C. J. 17, 360
Swift, J. 10, 16, 352

Thomson, J. F. 160, 299, 384
Tipton, I. C. 263, 267, 351, 379

Urmson, J. O. 194

Warnock, G. J. 10, 11, 16, 43, 137-40, 143-5, 160, 190, 193, 199, 205-6, 213-15, 217, 227, 243, 324, 326, 327, 329, 365-6, 384
White, A. R. 372, 376
Whitely, C. H. 353
Williams, B. 368
Wisdom, J. O. 160, 165, 166
Wittgenstein, L. 133-4, 140-1, 148-9, 283-6, 377
Woozley, A. D. 356

Yolton, J. W. 25, 36, 44

Zeno, 38, 39

Index of Subjects

This index is confined to certain main topics. Notes are indexed only if a topic is raised which is not dealt with in the corresponding section of the text.

Abstraction, 132-58
Appearances as objects, ch. 6 *passim*
Argument from the relativity of perception, 36-41, 223-6 (cf. 208-209), 236-55, 359

Causal theory of perception, 19-26, 35, 66-7, 184-5, 189-93, 253-5, 363
Causation (agency), 302-21
Colours, 243ff (*see also* primary and secondary qualities)
Common sense (Berkeley's affronting of), 10-11, ch. 2 *passim*
Conceptual schemes, 216ff
Corpuscular hypothesis, 28ff, 36, 44, cf. 248ff

Distance, 95, 200-10, 374-5
Duplicate worlds, 26-8

Existence—
of sensible things, ch. 4, 157-78
of the mind, 122, ch. 7 *passim*, 364
of the *posse percipi*, 100-2, 114-28 (*see also* intermittency and sensible objects)
two senses of the term, 106-8, 162-5
Existence 'in the mind', 83-4, 93-5, 203-5

Extension, 242-3 (*see also* primary and secondary qualities)

God, 6-7, 86, 119-20, 210, ch. 8

Heat, 91, 227-36, 249-50
Heterogeneity of the objects of sight and touch, 83, 154, 209, 373

Ideas—
as sensations produced in us, 20-1, 31-2, 46, 60, 85ff (cf. 235-6), 95
as qualities, 32, 45-7, 88ff (cf. 235-6), 95
as real things, 53-4, 79ff
the possibility that they resemble real things, 25, 32-3, 70-1, 376
as discrete items, 46, 185ff
in the mind of God, 86, 88, 344-50, 385
Imagination (imaging and picturing), 143-5, 156-7, 159-78 *passim*, 316-20, 366-7
Immediate perception (and inference in perception), 183-226
Immortality, 270, 382
Incorrigibility of perception, 109-12, 183, 211

Index of Subjects

Intermittency—
  and sensible objects, 118-20, 162-3, 299-302, 321-50
  and spirits, 271-92

Man as corporeal, 290-6, 312-16

Operations of the mind, 71-9, 266-7

Perception—
  as involving activity, 265, 267-9
  necessarily of the existent, 104-12
  two senses of the term, 104-8, 111-12, 163-6
Plain man's standpoint (as one of two standpoints opposed to Berkeley's), 61-7, 70-1, 82-3, 129, 181
Primary and secondary qualities, 29-41, 155-7, 226ff
Privacy of ideas, 86-8

Scepticism, 16, 19, 22, 25, 38-9, 47-54, 110-14

'Sensible' objects, 60-1, 84-5, 122
Signification of words, 131-41, 153-5, 283-6
Solidity 34-5, (cf. 27), 248
Solipsism, 88, 168-70 (cf. 161), 278, 380
Sounds, 193-5
Spirit and mind, 46-7, 71-5, ch. 7, 312-16
Strong *v* weak idealism, 97, 167ff
Substratum substance, 41-7, 176-7, 256ff

Time, 272-89
'The vulgar' (ambivalence of Berkeley's attitude to), 17-18, 56, 59

For Product Safety Concerns and Information please contact our EU
representative GPSR@taylorandfrancis.com
Taylor & Francis Verlag GmbH, Kaufingerstraße 24, 80331 München, Germany

www.ingramcontent.com/pod-product-compliance
Lightning Source LLC
Chambersburg PA
CBHW071237300426
44116CB00008B/1074